Revealed Grace

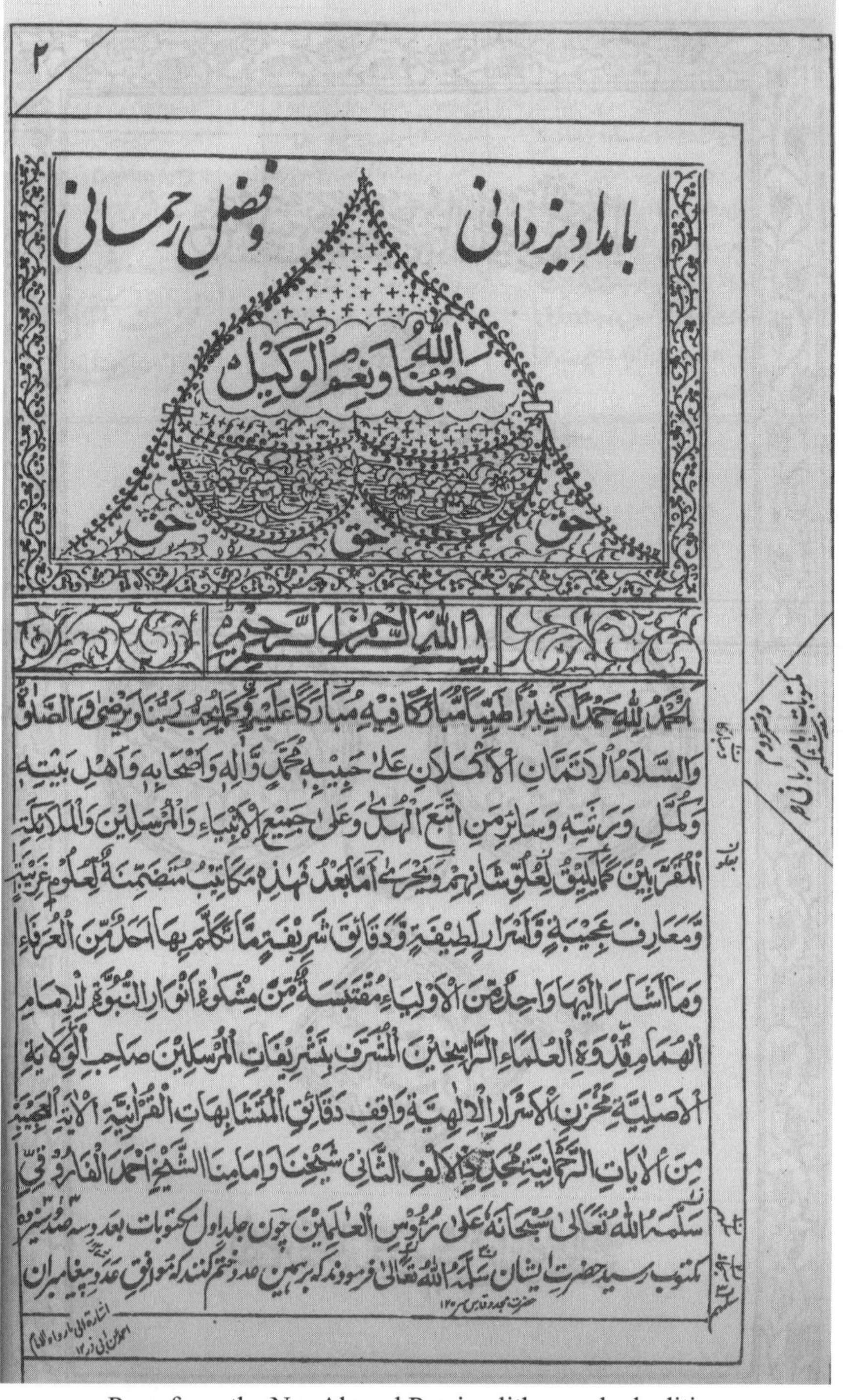

۲

بامداد یزدانی و فضل رحمانی

حسبنا الله ونعم الوکیل

حق حق حق

بسم الله الرحمن الرحیم

الحمد لله حمدا کثیرا طیبا مبارکا فیه مبارکا علیه کما یحب ربنا ویرضی والصلوة
والسلام الاتمان الاکملان علی حبیبه محمد وآله واصحابه واهل بیته
وکمل ورثته وسائر من اتبع الهدی وعلی جمیع الانبیاء والمرسلین والملائکة
المقربین کما یلیق بعلو شانهم ویحری اما بعد فهذه مکاتیب متضمنة لعلوم غریبة
ومعارف عجیبة واسرار لطیفة ودقائق شریفة ما تکلم بها احد من العرفاء
وما اشار الیها واحد من الاولیاء مقتبسة من مشکوة انوار النبوة للامام
الهمام قدوة العلماء الراسخین المشرف بتشریفات المرسلین صاحب الولایة
الاصلیة مخزن الاسرار الالهیة واقف دقائق المتشابهات القرآنیة الآیة العظیمة
من الآیات الرحمانیة مجدد الالف الثانی شیخنا وامامنا الشیخ احمد الفاروقی
سلمه الله تعالی سبحانه علی رؤوس العالمین چون جلد اول مکتوبات بعدد سه صد و سیزده
مکتوب رسید حضرت ایشان سلمه الله تعالی فرمودند که برهمین عدد ختم کنند که موافق عدد پیغامبران

Page from the Nur Ahmad Persian lithographed edition
by master calligrapher Ghulam Muhammad Amritsari

Revealed Grace
The Juristic Sufism of Ahmad Sirhindi (1564-1624)

by

Arthur F. Buehler

FONS VITAE

First published in English in 2011 by
Fons Vitae
49 Mockingbird Valley Drive
Louisville, KY 40207
http://www.fonsvitae.com
Email: fonsvitaeky@aol.com

Library of Congress Control Number: 2011939595
ISBN 9781891785894

Special thanks and appreciation to the Naqshbandiya Foundation for Islamic Education (NFIE) for their invaluable support (http://www.nfie.com), a non-profit organization established in memory of Sayyid Jama'at 'Ali Shah Naqshbandī (r) d. 1951, and Shaykh Muḥammad Ma'sum Naqshbandī (r) d. 2007.

Cover photograph:Tomb of Shaykh Ahmad Sirhindi
in Sirhind, India (photo credit Necdet Tosun)

Printed in Canada

بسم الله الرحمن الرحيم

This book is dedicated to my parents,
who rightfully wondered why it took so long

Table of Contents

Translator's Preface: Disclaimers and Confessions

Translations should have labels like processed foods have labels listing all the ingredients. These labels, if done correctly, would disclose the gap (sometimes enormous) between the original and the translation. One must never forget that translators are traitors (*traductor traittore*). I suggest you *mind the gap* and consider the issues raised here.

Before starting a partial translation of Shaykh Ahmad Sirhindi's *Collected Letters*,[1] I perused the entire 1,263 pages of the three volumes to make an index of the technical vocabulary. This expanded to seven more indexes and ended up being published in book form.[2] It was this book I had in hand to present to Shaykh Mahmud Effendi in the Ismail Ağa Mosque of Istanbul one Ramadan evening in 2004. After being introduced by his long-time student, Naim Abdulwali, the shaykh greeted me warmly from his wheelchair. At some point in our conversation I explained my translation project of Sirhindi's *Collected Letters*. There was an uneasy shift in mood but he remained silent. Then I remarked how I had been working with Shaykh Ma'sum Naqshbandi on the translation because of my difficulties in understanding the text. The mood shifted back again with an approving smile.

Right here is the middle of the gap. In spite of my knowing how to read the subject areas required in Arabic, Persian, and Urdu (which now included Sirhindi's technical vocabulary), and many years reading Naqshbandi texts, how was I going to bridge the gap between Sirhindi's level of consciousness, a result of decades of contemplative practice, and mine? Sirhindi communicated, as all good teachers do, on the level of those writing to him. Some of those simpler letters, usually on shariat,[3] did not involve this kind of gap. But I had chosen, in addition, to translate very long letters written to his most advanced students. Imagine a tone-deaf person who fluently reads all kinds of European sheet music attempting to translate

---

1. See Ahmad Sirhindi, *Maktubat-i Imam-i Rabbani*, ed., Nur Ahmad, 3 vols. (Karachi: Educational Press, 1972). From now on the abbreviated notation will be *Collected Letters,* volume number. letter number. page number.

2. See Arthur F. Buehler, *Fiharis-i tahlili –yi hashtgana-yi maktubat-i Ahmad Sirhindi* (Lahore: Iqbal Academy, 2000).

3. The Persianate shariat is used instead of the more common (and English) shariah as an attempt to keep reminding the reader that Sirhindi has a very expanded meaning of shariat.

a transcript of Mozart's *experience* of music. This is not a gap; it is a canyon. Later I will take you to this grand canyon, but for now, how did a such a "tone-deaf" person like me end up embarking on this project?

It is like this. Over a period of five years, American scholars of sufism and Naqshbandis in many different places had suggested that I start translating Sirhindi's *Collected Letters*. I continually refused, stating my lack of qualifications. Eventually the power of suggestion reached a tipping point and I said to myself that if I were able to work with Pir-i Piran Sahib in Peshawar, and if I were to get funding to do the aforementioned indexes, I would embark on a limited translating project. In 1999, I was graciously awarded a U.S. Department of Education Fulbright grant to study in Peshawar, and The Naqshbandi Foundation for Islamic Education funded the indexes.[4] After getting the index project up and running, I selected 26 letters (about 13% of the corpus) that would best provide a foundation to understand the Mujaddidi form of juristic sufism. The plan was to translate the letters with the help of dictionaries and the soon-to-be-compiled indexes, and ask Pir-i Piran Sahib's help if I got into a bind. I expected to have a rough translation done in a few months. It did not take more than a few weeks to see that this was nothing short of delusional. It turned out that what I was trying to read and understand was some of the most difficult Persian prose ever written in sufi literature.[5] Muhammad Sadiq, an Indian historian of the mid-seventeenth century, wrote in his short note on Sirhindi, "His books and letters contain many curiosities and strange things which [even] the intellects of the wise people are unable to comprehend."[6] So part of the gap is "intrinsic" and does not have to do with cultural distance and time. Simon Digby, an accomplished Indo-Persian translator and scholar of sufism in South Asia, says, "Bulk and opacity of style discourage a close reading of Sirhindi's own *Maktubat* or letters. One suspects that they are more reverenced than read."[7] By the time I discovered this it was too late to turn back.

---

4. For greater detail see the English introduction in Buehler, *Fiharis-i tahlili*.

5. Najib Mayil Harawi, one of the most prolific editors of Persian manuscript texts, informed me the following year (June, 2000) that Sirhindi's *Collected Letters* is the most difficult Persian prose in sufism. Medieval Indo-Persian sufi texts dealing with intricate details of religious experience are just as hard to read, e.g., Adam Banuri's books.

6. Translated in Yohanan Friedmann, *Shaykh Ahmad Sirhindi: An Outline of His Thought and a Study of His Image in the Eyes of Posterity* (Montreal: McGill Queen's University Press, 1971), 102.

7. See Simon Digby's review of *Shaykh Ahmad Sirhindi: An Outline of His Thought and a Study of His Image in the Eyes of Posterity* by Yohanan Friedmann in *Bulletin of the School of Oriental and African Studies* 38/1 (1975), 177-179.

Pir-i Piran Sahib was the ideal person to assist me. His name means that he is a shaykh of shaykhs, that is, he is the sufi shaykh of people who are now shaykhs.[8] In addition, he had over forty years experience reading and using the Naqshbandi sufi technical manual, *Collected Letters*. The unfolding of this translation project was ironic in a way. Eight years before, never intending to work with him on a translation, I had given him a recently republished quarto-sized copy of *Collected Letters* because his older, smaller copy was falling apart from constant use.

So I showed up on Pir-i Piran Sahib's doorstep. To my relief, he informed me in our first session that there were some of Shaykh Sirhindi's letters that he could not understand at all. With all too many people presuming non-existent knowledge, this kind of honesty was a breath of fresh air. On the other hand, I was woefully unprepared for the task. In retrospect, I was like an elementary science student who is just knowledgeable enough with the technical vocabulary to ask a question to a university professor, but not knowledgeable enough to understand the answer. He did spend a lot of time, to use a metaphor, describing what it was like to hear music. By his explaining the larger context of what I was reading, namely how Sirhindi's experiences verified corresponding realities in the unseen world, there was some progress in my understanding. After leaving Pakistan, I had the great fortune of bringing all the hard questions to the late Shaykh Ma'sum Naqshbandi (d. 2007). It was only toward the end of the translation process after four years of translating (in 2008), that it felt more like translation and less like deciphering. At some point I realized that one becomes qualified only through the actual translating process itself.

DEGREES OF *TRADUCTOR TRAITTORE*

Let's start with the small stuff. First, stop for a moment and just take a quick look at the page you are reading. You see black printed letters on a white page. This is quite different than the actual text of *Collected Letters* in its critical edition by Nur Ahmad.[9] Its quarto-size pages are a lithographic

---

8. Pir-i Piran Sahib does have a given birth name but I do not know what it is. It is not my intention to hide his identity. In *Sufi Heirs* I purposely did not mention the Naqshbandi shaykh in the Northwest Frontier Province by given name (who is also Pir-i Piran Sahib's shaykh) because of the considerable danger and illegality (foreigners are not allowed in that area) involved in getting to his sufi lodge. In 21st-century scholarship, the standard is transparency. Hiding one's sources, like some do under the so-called *al-khirqa al-akbariyya*, is to follow the example of Carlos Castaneda.

9. J.G.J. ter Haar says, "Nur Ahmad's edition is little short of an edition we would call critical." See his "The collected letters of Shaykh Ahmad Sirhindi" in *Manuscripts of the Middle East* 3 (1988), 42.

mosaic of various forms of *hand* writing by Ghulam Muhammad Amritsari, the gifted calligrapher of this edition. The main Persian text is written in a beautiful curvilinear *nast'aliq* script occasionally punctuated by a more square, *naskh* Arabic script when Sirhindi decided to write in Arabic. Decorating the space between the twenty lines of Persian text on the page are interlinear notes translating the Arabic or Persian words that may have been difficult for an educated nineteenth- or early twentieth-century Indian reader to understand. This mosaic is framed very often by notes to the text which circle around, usually beginning in the upper corner where the page is bound, and curving around to the bottom corner adjacent to the binding. There is no punctuation or paragraph separation in medieval Persian texts. So all punctuation and paragraph markers have been added in the translation. This may seem minor but it all adds up, as you will see.

The translation is altered in other ways. If there is a series of this-es and thats where one cannot distinguish one from another in the text and the whole point is to discern between the two, I replace the "this" and "that" with what is referred to. I kept in most of the spiritual politeness formulae in their entirety so the reader can get a flavor of another set of priorities. But, as I was deleting about a third of them so that the English text would not become overly burdened, I realized that I was brutally accommodating medieval Indo-Persian to modern English. *Traductor traittore*. These are not simple politeness formulae but occasions reminding the reader to pause and remember God and the other God-centered people who came before. I followed modern English usage as much as possible because the readers live in the twenty-first century and rightfully expect to be reading modern English. At the same time, I tried to retain the flavor and nuances of the original. This is a no-win situation. To the extent that one is not a traitor to one language, the translator is a traitor to the other. As a parting comment of this section, please remember that it is the epitome of impoliteness to refer to "Shaykh Ahmad Sirhindi, God bless his inner heart" as simply "Sirhindi," which I do often in the book. In conventional modern English usage there is no concept of spiritual rank—everyone is equal.

The Language Barrier

Now we move on to the next level of traitordom. *Collected Letters* is mostly written in Persian, but it is not just any Persian, it is *medieval Indo*-Persian. The Arabic is either from the Qur'an, the hadith, common sayings, poetry, or Sirhindi's own writing and is straightforward if one has the training to read those kinds of texts. But the Persian is another story. First, Indo-Persian is a dead language now and it has been for over a century. The British deposed it from its linguistic pedestal as lingua franca of the Mughal Empire (1526-1857) in 1857. The level of Persian comprehension had dropped so far almost three hundred years after Sirhindi that Nur Ahmad had to add numerous interlinear notations on each page to explain many Persian words (but maybe they were arcane even in the seventeenth century). Every so often Nur Ahmad could find the word in the only medieval Indo-Persian dictionary available, the *Language Aid* (*Ghiyath al-lughat*) compiled in 1826.[10] Understanding *Collected Letters* is not a dictionary problem. It only took me two or three times looking up a word in Dehkhuda's *Dictionary* (*Lughatnamah*), the Persian equivalent of the unabridged Oxford English Dictionary, to realize that. The *Language Aid* never had the meanings either, because if it did, Nur Ahmad had already put these in a footnote.

Figuring out what Sirhindi means when he uses words is beyond the lexical function of dictionaries. It is a necessary precondition to know the dictionary meanings of a word but it is not a sufficient condition if one is translating *Collected Letters*. A word has a dictionary meaning(s) in a certain context of everyday consensus reality, but these letters weave in and out of everyday consensus reality. Nor do we have the actual question to which Sirhindi is responding.[11] After Sirhindi passed away, a shaykh who had the requisite experience to know the connections and allusions of a given passage read the letter to others, adding his own experience. One cannot underestimate the oral underpinnings of *Collected Letters*. When I asked Shaykh Ma'sum what I thought was a straightforward, distinct question, more often than not, he would discuss it for over an hour just to draw out the basics. It was humbling to say the least.

In *Collected Letters*, Sirhindi takes a topic and then explores different aspects of it. It may seem like he goes off on tangents. Sometimes he does. But usually he is looking at the same topic from various perspectives. If one already has a synoptic view and comprehensive understanding of the topic, then one sees the entire forest and does not get lost by focusing on one tree after another. With this larger context in mind, it is easier to deal with the meaning of each strand of thought. Otherwise, the reader goes from one apparently unrelated sentence to another and nothing makes any sense. Adding to the confusion, the reader often wonders what the Qur'anic and poetic allusions are all about.[12] It is a translator's nightmare.

---

10. Nur Ahmad may very well have used the Nawal Kishur edition, Ghiyath al-Din Muhammad Rampuri, *Ghiyath al-lughat*, ed., Siraj al-Din 'Ali Khan Arzu (Kanpur: Nawal Kishur, 1878).

11. There were letters that had a larger context than just one person and were distributed and may not have been addressing specific questions.

12. In terms of Qur'anic passages, it seems as if these came spontaneously to Sirhindi as he was writing (his sufi side) and sometimes they support what he is trying to say (his jurist side). At other times, for them to fit the discussion, the Qur'anic passages need to be taken in the context of Sirhindi's discussion rather

What appears as textual disorder and lack of coherence is Sirhindi's way of communicating his experience.[13] Most of these experiences go beyond the narrow confines of conventional consensus reality. A "straight line" mode of expression using rational step-by-step arguments is the style of theologians and jurists. It is also what modern English readers expect in nonfiction prose writing. For Sirhindi to communicate in a way that "makes sense" in the rational, linear way modern English readers are accustomed to would be to distort what he is trying to communicate. In addition, much of the technical vocabulary does not correspond to consensus-reality dictionary meanings or even to prior sufi usage of the same terms.[14] Sirhindi does not intentionally make things difficult. These letters are *not* some kind of puzzle to figure out for one's spiritual development. Sirhindi mapped out a very intricate, replicable, and effective set of contemplative practices for that purpose. The intent of Sirhindi's writings is, metaphorically, to hear music and eventually play music. The experience of listening to and playing music simply do not translate well on paper.

The Time Barrier: Beyond Language

Translation difficulties go far deeper than linguistics. Let's dive into the middle of the gap. How can a translator having been culturally programmed with a modern worldview meaningfully read a text written by someone who perceives the world with a radically different set of presuppositions? One of the most intractable difficulties for translators and their readers is divergent outlooks on reality that separate pre-modern worlds from our own.[15] Sirhindi is seeking to point to the realities (*haqa'iq*) behind appearances. Language and other forms point to that vast formless unseen realm, ultimately God in Abrahamic religious terminology. For one who has experienced that realm, accounts like Sirhindi's or Ibn al-'Arabi's make sense just

---

than the Qur'anic context. I have translated the Qur'anic passages according to the Qur'anic context and have made a note where this translation does not quite fit what Sirhindi is trying to convey.

13. It is very tempting to say that Sirhindi is just a poor writer but I encounter similar kinds of difficulties when reading Gesudaraz's or Adam Banuri's writing. Maybe they are all poor writers. Here I am revealing a modern penchant for linear, logical prose.

14. Sirhindi uses Ibn al-'Arabi's categories and vocabulary, usually with the same general meaning, like the majority of sufis after the thirteenth century. When the categories correspond I have greatly benefited from William Chittick's precise terminology in English.

15. This issue is touched upon briefly by Hamid Algar in the introduction to his translation of Najmuddin Razi's *Mirsad al-'Ibad*, entitled, *The path of God's bondsmen from origin to return* (Delmar, NY, Caravan Books, 1982), 21-22.

like koans make sense to Zen roshis.

Sirhindi's *Collected Letters* are a practical manual for a science of Reality, with a carefully articulated methodology. It is a paradigm based upon a shared set of Islamic assumptions involving the primacy of Qur'an and Hadith and the Maturidi creedal tenets along with a contemplative methodology that can be confirmed by the Naqshbandi community. Time and time again Sirhindi emphasizes experiential verification through contemplative witnessing, and the primacy of reliable human verifiers to discern Truth. This is the same structure of inquiry (commonly called science) that I learned as university chemistry student involving the classroom, laboratory experiments, and grading by the professorial verifiers. Just like people fudge in chemistry lab, there are those who fudge, intentionally or not, in their interpretation of their contemplative experiences. Most of the letters in Sirhindi's *Collected Letters*, in one place or another, have Sirhindi monitoring those who think they have arrived at God and finds them wanting. We are near the middle of the gap here.

Those of us who have grown up being educated and acculturated in a cultural matrix of scientific-materialist assumptions have a worldview that makes it extremely difficult to *really* acknowledge this vast formless realm that Sirhindi has experienced (more than as simply an interesting intellectual idea). This cultural programming runs very deep. C. Roderick Wilson has investigated the inability of even the most seriously religious people in the West to transcend secular assumptions and understandings. He concludes that there is "a general reluctance in our society, even among those of a religious persuasion, to accord significance to a sacred world view."[16] In contrast, Sirhindi lived, breathed, and experienced a *God-centered* world. This is an Absolute-Truth world that includes many relative truths. Moderns acculturated in the scientific-materialist worldview live in a world of multiple relative truths. They acknowledge science of the outer world of form but not that of the inner realms beyond form. What is taken for "real" in modern everyday consensus reality would be for Sirhindi the equivalent of sitting in the darkness of Plato's cave with one's hands over one's eyes. In Sirhindi's terms, the only knowledge worthy of the name is that which can lead one to the presence of God, which is as real as one can get.

It shatters our modern sensibilities (mine at least) when Sirhindi says not to study any of the subjects that we teach in a modern university. Why not? It is because they will not help us either on the Day of Judgment or in

16. See C. Roderick Wilson, "Seeing They See Not," in David E. Young and Jean-Guy Goulet, eds., *Being Changed: The Anthropology of Extraordinary Experience* (New York: Broadview Press, 1994), 204.

the next world.[17] Modern newspapers, the daily reinforcement of everyday consensus reality, would call such a person a religious fanatic. Naqshbandis across the world have looked up to Sirhindi over the centuries as a special man of God, a beacon of guidance. There is an incommensurability here and a translator of any worth is expected to bridge that gap. If there is to be real translation from one language to another, there needs to be a commensurability between the two worldviews of the readers of both languages such that the words in both languages point to the same meaning. 'Allama Muhammad Iqbal (d. 1938) once said that *Collected Letters* could not be translated into English because there were no words in English to convey the concepts.[18] Except for one word, *shari'at*, which for Sirhindi is a multivalent realm onto itself, each of Sirhindi's words has an English equivalent in this translation. But as we have seen above, language is a living entity, inseparable from the speaker's cultural assumptions. The words are there but have the concepts been communicated accurately? Is the reader ready to assimilate them?

It is also a function of a person's level of consciousness, that is, *who* uses the language makes a big difference. If I say "*Ana al-haqq*" (I am the Truth/God) it has an entirely different meaning from Mansur al-Hallaj (mart. 309/922) uttering the same words. In one case (me), there is the I-ness of the ego-self and in the other case there really is no "I" except as a linguistic placemarker.[19] Mind the gap. This imposes a lot on any reader, the translator included. Unless one has sufficient prior preparation, it is difficult to understand that Sirhindi is not just speaking about one more theoretical construct, but reality as it is. Indeed, it is reality as he has experienced it. He spent his adult life seeking to experience divine realities, discerning what was real and what was illusion. Much of what Sirhindi is discussing in these translated letters concerns a formless, ineffable realm that is beyond space-time. In the postmodern academy we are aware of ethnocentrism, the narrowness of cultural experience, but we are hardly aware of our pervasive *cognocentrism*, the narrowness of our conscious experience.

---

17. Cf. *Collected Letters*, 1.73.55: "Any knowledge not applicable to the hereafter is also an aspect of the world. If learning astronomy, logic, engineering, mathematics, and other useless knowledge were worthwhile, then philosophers would be saved in the next world."

18. See Muhammad Ihsan Sirhindi, *Rawdat al-Qayyumiyya*, translated by Iqbal Ahmad Faruqi, 4 vols. (Lahore: Maktaba-yi Nabawiyya, 1989), 1:45.

19. Carl Ernst has noted Ibn al-'Arabi's insight that words do not have any independent meaning and are a function of the "state" of the person saying them. My point is that words are also a function of the *station* of the person saying them. See Carl Ernst, "The Man Without Attributes: Ibn 'Arabi's Interpretation of Abu Yazid al-Bistami," *Journal of the Muhyiddin Ibn 'Arabi Society* 13 (1993), 14-15.

Pause for a moment and ask yourself how prepared you are for this kind of discussion. What books on sufism in English can prepare one for this discussion? Hardly any. It is rare for modern scholars of sufism to go beyond linguistic analysis, history, socio-political context, influences and borrowings and everything else *except* what it is all about for the sufis themselves. This is embarrassing. If Sirhindi has anything to say, it is that reality is a lot more than what we think it is. But then anyone sharing his pre-modern worldview could say this. Sirhindi, however, is not just anyone. For Sirhindi, these issues were life and death issues such that human beings have an innate responsibility to wake up, and if they don't they will be held to account. Call it karma or the Day of Judgment or Newton's third law. "As above so below." People in the contemporary world have too often forgotten that there is an "above." There must have been people who had lapses like this in Sirhindi's time because in two consecutive letters he says, "For a worm hidden under a rock, the sky is the bottom of the rock."[20] Is he speaking to us?

Other Books on Sirhindi and Use of Previous Translations

The more one can understand the context of the writer, the better. Although few books in any language can prepare one for the depth mentioned above, there are books written on Sirhindi. The first academic study in English is Yohanan Friedmann's *Shaykh Ahmad Sirhindi: An Outline of His Thought and a Study of His Image in the Eyes of Posterity*, which has stood the test of time extremely well.[21] As the title suggests, the focus is on what others thought of Sirhindi. Friedmann only used about a third of the available sources, so it is a subject waiting for an upgrade. In chronological sequence, Abdul Haq Ansari's *Sufism and Shari'ah: A Study of Shaykh Ahmad Sirhindi's Effort to Reform Sufism* was the first to translate parts of Sirhindi's letters into English. As a pioneering work it deserves praise. It is a simplified translation because his use of English vocabulary does not match the preciseness of Sirhindi's writing.[22] J.G.J. ter Haar's *Follower and Heir of the Prophet: Shaykh Ahmad Sirhindi (1564-1624) as Mystic* organizes the

---

20. See *Collected Letters*, 2.54 and 2.55 in this book.

21. See Friedmann, *Shaykh Ahmad Sirhindi*.

22. See Muhammad Abdul Haq Ansari, *Sufism and Shari'ah: A Study of Shaykh Ahmad Sirhindi's Effort to Reform Sufism* (Leicester, UK: The Islamic Foundation, 1986). Examples of this tendency include his discussion of *walayat* on the bottom of ibid., 63 that do not specify which *walayat* (there are at least six levels just in the letters in this book). His black and white discussion of "abolishing or not abolishing dualism" (the former designating the path of the *wali* and the latter portraying that of the prophet) fails to recognize that the prophetic path involves both unity and dualism, ibid., 64.

corpus of Ahmad Sirhindi's letters thematically.[23] He has done an admirable job in correcting the errors in Friedmann's book.[24] Stretching the discussion to work done in Latin scripts, the latest scholarly treatment of Ahmad Sirhindi is *Imam-i Rabbani Ahmed Sirhindi: Hayatı, Eserleri, Tasavvufi Görüşleri* by Necdet Tosun.[25] In addition to its fresh analytical perspectives, his study benefits from the many printed and manuscript sources that heretofore have not been utilized. I will discuss translations of *Collected Letters* into other languages in the Introduction.[26]

Translations usually get better over time because scholars have the benefits of previous translations. I tried to make maximum use of other translations. After translating each letter from the Persian (and sometimes Arabic), I checked my translation with Zawwar Husayn's Urdu translation. Among the available translations, Urdu is the closest language to Persian, and there is the least loss of the Persian nuances. Occasionally there are even added

---

23. See J.G.J. ter Haar, *Follower and Heir of the Prophet: Shaykh Ahmad Sirhindi (1564-1624) as Mystic* (Leiden: Het Oosters Instituut, 1992).

24. There is also Alberto Ventura's *Profezia e santita secondo Shaykh Ahmad Sirhindi* (Cagliari: Instituto di Studi Africani e Orientali, 1990), and Demetrio Giordani's Italian translation of *Mabda' wa-ma'ad, L'inizio e il ritorno* (Milan: Mimesis, 2003). Understanding Sirhindi involves an intimate acquaintance with his cosmological and methodological universe. In terms of background materials, my *Sufi Heirs of the Prophet: The Indian Naqshbandiyya and the Rise of the Mediating Shaykh* (Columbia, SC: University of South Carolina Press, 1998) is recommended for understanding the contemplative practices pioneered by Sirhindi. This is particularly critical when there is also *mis*information in the scholarly literature concerning Mujaddidi contemplative practices. A chapter (pp.,183-208) in Pnina Werbner's, *Pilgrims of Love: The Anthropology of a Global Sufi Cult* [sic] (London: Hurst & Company, 2003) that could have served to update the information in *Sufi Heirs* instead functions to confuse the reader. The apparently well-meaning author of this chapter (unnamed) thought that he could rely simply on English and Urdu sources, which resulted in hierarchically confused diagrams and a seriously flawed text. I do appreciate that one of his footnoted corrections has made Figure 2 in this book one step more accurate.

25. See Necdet Tosun, *Imâm-i Rabbânî Ahmed Sirhindî: Hayatı, Eserleri, Tasavvufî Görüşleri* (Istanbul: Insan Yayınları, 2005).

26. To round out the English-language material, Sirhindi's letters dealing with shariat have been very approximately translated in *Endless Bliss*. Husayn Hilmi Işık, *Endless Bliss*, 5 vols., an English translation of *Se'âdet-i Ebediyye*, by M. Sıdık Gümüş (Istanbul: Hakikat Kitabevi, 1998). The "translations" are interrupted by paragraphs, and sometimes pages, of bracketed polemical commentary. There is an incomprehensible translation of the first volume of *Collected Letters* using English words by Muhammad Wajihuddin, *Epistles*, 2 vols. (Lahore: Pakistan International Printers, 2000).

clarifications. When there were difficulties and the Urdu translation conveniently transposed them (easy to do when the two languages are so closely related), or I disagreed with the Urdu translation, I went to the Arabic translation that was translated from a pre-Nur Ahmad Persian text. Murad Remzi al-Manzalawi's Arabic translation of *Collected Letters*, much more in use in the Islamic world than the Indo-Persian original, is an authoritative "co-eval" translation.[27] The Arabic is much easier to read because it is a simplification of the original Indo-Persian (even though the transposition situation still exists). The last resort was to ask Shaykh Ma'sum.

What is in and what is not in this translation

What you have here is the first scholarly translation of complete letters from Sirhindi's *Collected Letters* into English. What that means is that in all the other translations a large percentage of the words in *Collected Letters* are simply transposed as-is into the translation because the same words are common across Islamic languages. This is impossible to do in English. I had always wondered why translators of Ibn al-'Arabi and Sirhindi always have used ellipsis (. . .). Now I know why. It takes about four times as long to translate *all* of a letter. I wanted the reader to have the benefit of reading the entire letter like the recipient had read it. That is what is *in* the translation.

What is *not* in the translation are such words as: brotherhood, mystic, mysticism, saint, sainthood, sufi order, gnostic, and gnosis. When I had to use precise terminology in translating, I became much more aware of the slippery use of these words, which are very rarely clarified in sufi studies.[28]

---

27. A co-eval translation is one, according to Eugen Eoyang, that is "*a possible rival*" to the original. (italicized in the original) Cited in Bruce Lawrence, "Problems of Translating Sufi Texts from Indo-Persian to American English," in Mohamed Taher, ed., *Sufism: Evolution and Practice* (Delhi: Anmol Publications, 1997), 209.

28. Scott Kugle provides an excellent example of justifying the use of saint and sainthood in his study based on hagiographical sources (which is a completely different context than contemplative practice). In addition, he explains what he means by mystic, mysticism, and other terms. See his *Rebel between Spirit and Law: Ahmad Zarruq, Sainthood, and Authority in Islam* (Bloomington, IN: Indiana University Press, 1996). Gnostic and gnosis, as markers of *dualism*, are discussed in the Introduction. As for "sufi orders" we have another case of an Orientalist holdover. At some point, most western scholars finally stopped calling sufi lodges "monasteries" but they have kept the usage of "sufi orders." There are orders of monks and nuns in Christianity and Buddhism with very clear and often common rules and contemplative practices. In sufi practice, celibacy is rare and there is very little "order" in sufi practices. Multiple Naqshbandi-Mujaddidi groups stemming

The word "spiritual" and its synonym "divine" have been used as seldom as possible and mean something that is beyond physical, emotional or mental, although it can include any or all of those dimensions. I try to avoid the word "spiritual" because there are at least three levels of "spirit" between the physical and the Absolute in the Mujaddidi cosmological universe. Sirhindi uses a precise terminology and a corresponding nuanced terminology is required to render his conceptual universe accurately into English.

For an example of precision in translating, we can take the example of *walayat*. It has been translated as: intimacy with God, closeness to God, sanctity (too vague but concise), and sainthood (misleading at best). In the letters in this book, there are seven degrees of intimacy with God (*darajat-i walayat*) including the generic version: *walayat*, *walayat-i sughra*, *walayat-i kubra*, *walayat-i asli*, *walayat-i sadiq*, *walayat-i 'ulya*, and *walayat-i Muhammadi*. If one seeks to understand the nuances, and what these precise technical expressions mean, the clearest way of explaining it in English is either intimacy or closeness to God because that is the principle that differentiates these seven levels.

Another related example is the usage of "saints" (too often the translation for *wali*). Sufis (de facto *wali*s) in Indo-Pakistan do not fit in the box of Catholic saints, like Mother Theresa, who comes to many people's mind in the West when they think of a "saint." Just like Khidr in the Qur'anic narrative 18:60-82 (where an apparently innocent young boy is killed), so-called "saints" can be involved in severe behavior. It is no coincidence that it is customary to say, "Forgive me" (*Mu'af karo*) to beggars in the Subcontinent. If they happen to be "saints" (irony intended), then they are believed to be capable of serious wrath if you do not give them anything.[29] Appropriate linguistic register and choice of vocabulary is a function of the cultural context.

Last but not least in the translation department, what you have in your hands is qualitatively a better English translation of *Collected Letters* than any of its partial predecessors. But that is not saying much. First, it is only

---

from the same sub-lineages exist in one city, like Istanbul or Delhi, with minimal overlap (read dis-order) in contemplative practices. There is ample evidence for women's involvement in the Mujaddidiyya, so "brotherhood" is another yet anachronism that can be dropped in the twenty-first century. This vocabulary situation is symptomatic of deeper endemic problems in sufi studies, but that another issue. See Arthur F. Buehler, "Researching Sufism in the 21st Century: Expanding the Context," in Clinton Bennett, ed., *Continuum Companion to Islam* (New York, Continuum Publishing, 2012), forthcoming.

29. See "Stories of Saintly Wrath," in Riazul Islam, *Sufism in South Asia: Impact on Fourteenth Century Muslim Society* (Karachi: Oxford University Press, 2002), 41-48.

13% of the corpus, and second, it does not come close to the gold standard of translation (see below). It is my wish that this translation attempt will challenge someone with a more complete intellectual and experiential background to do a complete English translation of Shaykh Sirhindi's *Collected Letters* as it should be done.

Kudos for Translators

My first rudimentary textual translating attempts started when learning Iranian Persian under Wheeler Thackson Jr.'s careful tutelage. A gifted linguist and translator, he cautioned us not to read anything into the text. If one reads about Bruce Lawrence's reticence to publish *Morals of the Heart* over a period of many years until he could faithfully translate the poetry,[30] one is inspired by a meticulous translator. William C. Chittick, the doyen of Ibn al-'Arabi studies, has provided, through his painstaking translation efforts, the infrastructure of conceptual understanding and English vocabulary for further translation in sufi studies. May all translators follow in these scholars' footsteps. The pinnacle of translating is to have the translation rival the original. To my knowledge, there is only one authoritative English translation of a post-rational text integral to contemplative practice that has already begun to replace the original. It is Victor Hori's *Zen Sand: The Book of Capping Phrases for Kōan Practice*. A product of twenty-seven years effort, along with the collaboration and many careful edits by experts in various aspects of Zen training and learning, it is the gold standard of translation.[31]

Acknowledgments

Before applying for the aforementioned U.S. Department of Education Grant that I received for 1999-2000, Pir-i Piran Sahib agreed to work with me on translating the letters. Working with Pir-i Piran Sahib got everything started, along with the institutional support of the Iqbal Academy in Lahore, Pakistan, headed by the erudite Muhammad Suheyl Umar. The encouragement of Suheyl and the patience of Ahmad Javad, one of the Academy's leading research associates, provided the long-term mentoring that

30. Bruce B. Lawrence, *Nizam ad-din Awliya: Morals for the Heart* (Mahwah, NY: Paulist Press, 1992). The translator's preface of his book shines light on the many difficulties of interpreting *that* kind of sufi text.

31. See Victor Sōgen Hori, *Zen Sand: The Book of Capping Phrases for Kōan Practice* (Honolulu: University of Hawaii Press, 2003). As Sōgen Sensei explains, the title of the book is from the capping phrase: "Gold—but to sell it you mix it with sand. An honest person would not cheat a customer in that way, but in Zen things are different. Awakening is pure gold, 'undefiled by language,'. . . and to be translated to others 'it has to be mixed with the sand of language.'" Ibid., ix.

propelled me into this project. In 2002, Louisiana State University granted me an academic leave of absence that allowed me to accept a short-term Senior fellowship by the American Institute of Iranian Studies to gather Persian sources. When the translation process gathered momentum, I was very fortunate to have almost yearly research support from the Faculty of Humanities and Social Sciences of Victoria University, Wellington, New Zealand, from 2004 to 2009. In this way, I was able to visit libraries and consult with the late Shaykh Ma'sum Naqshbandi in Phoenix, Arizona. I remember deeply in my heart the time I was privileged to spend with Shaykh Ma'sum. During those visits, the combined warm hospitality of the head of the Naqshbandi Foundation for Islamic Education (NFIE), Dr. Ahmed Mirza, and Shaykh Ma'sum's son, Dr. Ja'far Naqshbandi, made these sessions with Shaykh Ma'sum possible. Dr. Mirza has supplied me with books only physically available in Pakistan while Dr. Ja'far masterfully translated his father's tri-lingual conversations. Dr. Ja'far, along with Dr. Shahryar Zamani, worked as a team to correct the Persian poetry in these translations. All mistranslations are my responsibility, especially since I differed a couple of times with their versions.

Without Dr. Hamid Algar's comprehensive and detailed scholarship the Naqshbandis would be even more hidden than they already are. He has provided a scholarly infrastructure for Naqshbandi studies worldwide. Dr. Necdet Tosun, a professor (docent) at Marmara University in Istanbul, a gifted translator and noted researcher on the Naqshbandiyya, has assisted me more often than the footnotes indicate. Here in New Zealand, our program director, Dr. Paul Morris, has been a support for this project. Two of my undergraduate students, Aidan MacLeod and Duncan McNaughton to whom I read out each of the translated letters and answered any questions they had, volunteered to help me on the last stages of the book. Two other students, Shamim Homayun and Dylan Clark, intermittently joined them. Shamim, an accomplished artist and poet, has drawn the figures of Nasruddin on the Naqshbandi path (Figure 3) and Alexandre Augusto Sawczuk da Silva, conversant and agile with computer drawing programs, has put Figures 1, 2, and 4 in this book into computer format. In the middle of 2009, the Leave Committee for the Faculty of Humanities and Social Sciences of Victoria University granted me some of my earned research leave to finish this book. This has allowed me to create the necessary focused environment to polish and finish this book, for which I am appreciative. Throughout the last year of writing, I have been blessed with the support of my wife Josemi, who never expected that she would be sharing her first year of marriage with this project, much less compiling a bibliography in strange languages.

Introduction

Contextualizing the long 16th century in India

The time period from the beginning of the Mughal Empire in 932/1526 to Shaykh Ahmad Sirhindi's death in 1034/1624 can be called the long sixteenth century.[1] This is the century in which the first Islamic millennium came to a close. Since Sirhindi was given the title "Renewer of the Second Millennium," I give both Islamic and Common Era dates to show proximity to the millennial date of 1000/1591. During this century there were three major powers in the eastern Islamic world which comprised a very loosely organized economic unit: 1) the Shi'i Safavid empire ranging from the Shi'i area of Iraq in the west, much of present-day Iran, and extending to what is today eastern Afghanistan, 2) the Sunni Mughal empire from Qandahar in the west to Assam in the east, and Kashmir and Badakhshan in the north to the Deccan in the south, and 3) the Shaybani Uzbek empire of Central Asia, which extended from the Caspian Sea in the west northward across the Kazan steppe, east to Turfan in Xinjiang, and south to Badakhshan in present-day Afghanistan. The Iranian Safavids establishing Shi'ism as the official religion in 906/1501 created difficulties, but generally the Safavids, Mughals, and Uzbeks cooperated to keep the trade routes open. In the late sixteenth century, there were large construction projects linking this expanse with roads and caravanserais, which greatly eliminated the danger of bandits. Everyone benefited from more trade at less expensive prices using mutually convertible silver currency (khanis in Central Asia, rupees in India, and tumans in Iran).

Muslims of these diverse lands already had been connected culturally for a couple of centuries. By the fourteenth century, Persian was the lingua franca of the literate Islamic world from Konya in Anatolia (present-day Turkey) to Kashgar (in the present-day province of Xinjiang China) in the East. Perso-Islamic culture integrated this large area known as the Persianate world. Even before modern Persian surfaced in the eleventh century with the *Book of Kings* (*Shahnamah*) of Firdawsi, six learned hadith scholars of Persianate background had already compiled the canonical Sunni hadith collections in Arabic three centuries before. The role of Persian culture in the development and spread of Islam is equivalent to that of Greek civilization for Christianity. Non-Persians found the superior Persian cul-

1. The empire was called the "Mughal" empire because native Indians called invaders coming from Inner Asia "Mongols." The term "Mughals" ended up being used for the Turkic Timurids who ended up ruling India.

ture irresistible. The vast majority of the scientific, literary, and religious achievements in the Islamic world for half a millennium came from this Persianate world. Persian was the language travelers and traders needed to learn, from Marco Polo to the founders of the East Indian Company. So avidly did the Mughals embrace this culture that the literary output of Persian literature during the Mughal empire (1526-1857) vastly exceeded that of Iran.[2] Especially during the sixteenth century, there was an extreme "brain drain" from both Iran and Central Asia as talented Persian speakers migrated to a wealthy and tolerant India. This is why Shaykh Sirhindi wrote his letters in Persian.

Persianate culture with a Central Asian flavor came along with the successive waves of Muslim conquerors streaming into India. Almost four centuries before Shaykh Ahmad Sirhindi was born, India was ruled by a series of five Islamic dynasties known as the Delhi Sultanates (from the Ghuri dynasty in 588/1193 to the Lodi dynasty ending in 932/1526) headed by Afghans and Turkic soldiers from Central Asia. The common thread was a Sunni Islam with the political dominance of the Turkic and Afghan elite. Over time, South Asia became a safe haven for Muslims as the Mongols ravaged lands to the west. Unfortunately, Delhi was not spared from the Mongol hoards when Timur (Timur the Lame or Tamerlane) came and sacked Delhi in 791/1389. Seriously weakened, the Delhi Sultanate, now ruled by Afghans, limped along until Babur, a Chaghatai Turk from Ferghana (in present-day Tajikistan), invaded India. Babur defeated Sultan Ibrahim Lodi at Panipat in 932/1526, but his intention was not to stay in India. He desired to regroup his forces in India, bide his time, and then reconquer his homeland in Central Asia. He passed away and his descendants stayed to create the wealthiest empire in the pre-modern world. But this was not to happen immediately. His son Humayun had to face the resistance of the ousted Afghans. Sher Shah Suri was able to defeat Humayun in 946/1540 at the battle of Chausa. Humayun converted to Shi'ism, took refuge with and received support from the Safavid ruler Shah Isma'il, and re-established his rule in northern India in 962/1555 (to become a Sunni again). The next year, eight years before Ahmad Sirhindi was born, Akbar started his long reign (963/1556-1014/1605) at the age of thirteen when his father Humayun died after falling down the staircase in his library.

Akbar, the Mughal emperor for most of Sirhindi's life, was born in Sindh from an Iranian mother. He is the first "Indian" Mughal ruler. Akbar had a much larger vision than his predecessors. He created a meritocracy that rewarded tolerance and innovation and did not let religion or birth interfere with the larger enterprise of governing an expanding empire. Thus,

2. See Richard C. Foltz, *Mughal India and Central Asia* (Karachi: Oxford University Press, 1998), 2.

fiscal reforms and laws did not discriminate between Hindus, native Indian Muslims (the *ajlaf*), and the privileged foreign-born Muslim nobility (the *ashraf*).[3] The *ashraf* did not appreciate Akbar's policies because they lost their monopoly on lucrative landownership entitlements and government posts. By worldly standards, Akbar was the emperor of the age. Mughal India became the richest area in the world during his reign with an estimated population in 1014/1605 of 110 million people and a vibrant diversified economy.[4]

Akbar's expansion of the Mughal Empire caused discontent from Central Asian and many other *ashrafi* Muslims who wanted special privileges. When Akbar was eighteen years of age he began to centralize imperial power. The Timurid Mirzas and the Uzbek clans were the first to be reined in (followed by the Turkmen Qaqshals and Afghan Atka Khail). They resisted the loss of autonomy and privileges which Timurid-Mughal custom entitled them. Among many other things, there were to be no more Tarkhans. Under Timur, a Tarkhan had free access to the palace and criminal immunity for himself and his children for up to nine offenses. Akbar could not consolidate an empire under these conditions, so he appointed native Indian Muslims and Hindu Rajputs to elite government positions. They were beholden to Akbar personally. From 962/1555 to 988/1580, the number of Central Asians (Turanis) in the Mughal elite was cut in half.[5] Akbar crushed the resulting bloody revolts between 970/1564 and 975/1568, and the rebellious Mirzas and Uzbeks retreated to nearby Kabul at the court of Akbar's half-brother and foe, Mirza Hakim, who wished to position himself as the model Central Asian Timurid political leader.

The plot thickens when we realize that Mirza Hakim's closest advisor was Khwaja Hasan Naqshbandi, a descendant of the founder-figure of the Naqshbandi sufi lineage, Baha'uddin Naqshband (d. 791/1389), married to Fakhr al-Nisa, Mirza Hakim's sister. After the 1560s, the Kingdom of Kabul became a major center of Naqshbandi and Hanafi Sunni Islam.[6] In addi-

---

3. For a more detailed discussion of the *ashraf* and the *ajlaf*, see Arthur F. Buehler, "Trends of Ashrafization in India," in Kazuo Morimoto, ed., *The Living Links to the Prophet:* Sayyid*s and* Sharif*s in Muslim Societies* (London: Routledge, 2012), forthcoming.

4. See André Wink, *Akbar* (Oxford: Oneworld, 2009), 77.

5. See Munis D. Faruqui, "The Forgotten Prince: Mirza Hakim and the Formation of the Mughal Empire in India," *Journal of the Economic and Social History of the Orient* 48/4 (2005), 500.

6. See Ibid., 497. For information detailing the immense Naqshbandi holdings in and around Kabul, see Stephen F. Dale and Alam Payind, "The Ahrari Waqf in Kabul in the Year 1546 and the Mughal Naqshbandiyyah," *Journal of the American Oriental Society* 119/2 (April-June 1999), 218-233.

tion, Mirza Hakim had quite good relations with ‘Abdullah Khan Shaybani, leader of the Uzbeks. They both had a shared loyalty to the Naqshbandis. Akbar saw a threat from the Naqshbandis centered in Kabul who supported his archenemy, Mirza Hakim. Kabul served as a convenient place for the Naqshbandis to move into India after Mirza Hakim died in 993/1585. And move in they did. Baqibillah, Ahmad Sirhindi's Naqshbandi shaykh, was born in Kabul and then moved on to India via Samarqand in 1007-08/1599.[7] In the literature of the time, both the names of Ahmad Sirhindi and his father ‘Abdulahad are often appended with the *nisbat* of “Kabuli,” to designate their *ashrafi* non-Indian putative place of origin.

Much to his credit, Akbar did not appear to discriminate against Naqshbandis. Khwaja Khawand Mahmud was in Babur's court and his son, Khwaja Mu‘in, served Akbar. Akbar appointed the great-grandson of the famous Central Asian Naqshbandi ‘Ubaydullah Ahrar (d. 895/1490), Khwaja Yahya, to lead the Mughal's official pilgrimage caravan to Mecca in 986/1578. Faydi, Akbar's poet laureate and brother of Abu'l-Fadl ‘Allami, communicated regularly with Naqshbandi sufi shaykh Baha'uddin Hasan Nithari Bukhari (d. 973/1566). There were many other Naqshbandis in the Mughal elite, but Akbar kept his own personal life aloof from them, and there is no evidence that they influenced any Mughal policies.[8] Naqshbandis were part of the Mughal landscape. Shah Kalimullah Chishti (d. 1142/1729) of Delhi remarks, “These Turanians [Central Asians], all and every one of them, are connected with the Naqshbandi order and they do not attach value to any other *silsilah*.”[9]

Akbar could easily ignore the Naqshbandis because he was not subject to the same political dynamics faced by Muslim Central Asian rulers. For almost a century, no ruler in Transoxiana could come to power without Naqshbandi support. They would be out of favor very quickly because Naqshbandi sufi shaykhs were the intermediaries between the general population and the rulers. This is the legacy of Khwaja Ahrar and

---

7. The Naqshbandiyya could not have dominated Mughal leadership, but as *ashrafi* sufi shaykhs and intermediaries between God and humans, they also functioned as intermediaries between their disciples looking for employment and government officials. For the relationship of the Naqshbandiyya of Central Asia and Mughal India, see Arthur F. Buehler, “The Naqshbandiyya in Timurid India: The Central Asian Legacy,” *Journal of Islamic Studies* 7/2 (1996), 208-228; and Muzaffar Alam, “The Mughals, the Sufi Shaikhs, and the Formation of the Akbari Dispensation,” *Modern Asian Studies* 43/1 (2009), 135-174.

8. See Irfan M. Habib, “The Political Role of Shaykh Ahmad Sirhindi and Shah Waliullah,” in *Essays in Indian Art, Religion and Society*, edited by Krishna Mohan Shrimali (New Delhi: Munshiram Manoharlal, 1987), 219-235.

9. Cited in Foltz, *Mughal India*, 103.

the Juybari Naqshbandi shaykhs in Bukhara during the century after his death. 'Ubaydullah Ahrar is often mentioned in Ahmad Sirhindi's letters (33 times). While Ahrar was alive, he was the largest landholder in Transoxiana and the political patron of Timurid rulers and the Transoxiana elite. Ahrar had a clear visionary message that he was "divinely ordained to protect the Muslims from the evil of oppressors."[10] On a practical political level, he strongly encouraging rulers to implement the shariat. For example, in 865/1460 Ahrar persuaded the Timurid ruler Abu Sa'id to abolish the *tamgha* tax (of the Mongols) in Bukhara and Samarqand, and to promise to abolish all other non-shar'i taxes throughout his kingdom.[11] In general, Ahrar took Islamic law to the political realm and demanded abolition of Turco-Mongol customs and laws. There was a distinct opposition between the sedentary population of Central Asia, who shared a shariat-oriented Perso-Islamic culture, and the nomadic Turks who were still in the process of being Islamicized.[12]

When we hear Sirhindi and other *ashrafi* Muslims in India complain about the non-Islamic nature of Akbar's government, one of their frames of reference is prior precedent in Transoxiana where Naqshbandis and jurists had more influence in the political realm. They expected their comfort and welfare as *ashrafi* Muslims to be the first and foremost priority. The government's job was to discourage and abolish customs of non-Muslims. From Akbar's point of view, an expanding Mughal empire was too vast and required a leadership unfettered by a special *ashrafi* interest group touting their interests in the name of Islamic legalism. It did not make political, economic, or military sense just to think of Muslims when *ashrafi* Muslims were less than three percent of the population.[13] With very few exceptions, rulers of all times have put political expediency and maintaining political power before anything else. Thus, it is no surprise that, for the Mughals, political expediency almost always trumped religious concerns. A good example of this is the fluidity of religious identity among the Mughal elite. Babur converted to Shi'ism in order to gain support of the Safavid Shah and

10. See Alam, "The Mughals," 144.

11. See Hamid Algar, "A Brief History of the Naqshbandi Order," in Marc Gaborieau, Alexandre Popovic, and Thierry Zarcone, eds., *Naqshbandis: cheminements et situation actuelle d'un ordre mystique musulman* (Istanbul/Paris: Éditions Isis, 1990), 14.

12. See Hamid Algar, "Political Aspects of Islamic History," in Gaborieau *et. al.*, *Naqshbandis*, 126.

13. Urban population was 15% of the estimated 110 million population of the Mughal Empire, that is, 16.5 million. Even if one inflates the population of *ashrafi* Muslims by counting them as 20% of the urban population, that is only 3.1 million out of 110 million.

recapture Samarqand. His son Humayun followed his example, as we have already seen. Both reverted to being Sunnis after their short-term goals were achieved.

Akbar inclined to a way of ruling that focused on reason and commonsense political ethics instead of blindly following the precedents of another time and place, which some jurists have defined as Islamic governance. Abu'l-Fadl regularly read Nasiruddin Tusi's (d. 672/1274) *Akhlaq-i Nasiri* to Akbar. Through this process Akbar learned that to be a just king he needed to balance diverse interest groups. Insofar as jurisprudence and shariat guidelines intersect with political leadership, the bottom line is for a Muslim ruler to be just. Going beyond the letter of the Law, to the spirit of the Law, the moral lessons of the poetry of Hafiz, Sa'di, and Rumi, recited by Abu'l-Fadl to Akbar, brought home the need to treat all people with understanding tolerance regardless of different religious expressions and traditions.[14] This Nasirean ethic clashed with at least three centuries of an *ashrafi* "triumphalist" approach to Muslim rule, as we will see below. In a predominantly Muslim country, perhaps Akbar could have successfully ruled more in accordance with Ahrari and prior Islamic precedents, but India was exponentially more complex religiously, ethnically, and culturally. An unprecedented level of justice was required. The Nasirean approach advocating peace to all (*sulh-i kull*) held Akbar in good stead.[15]

But the devil is in the details. Sirhindi and many other pious Sunni Muslims could not understand how Akbar could be a just *Muslim* ruler and be married to a Rajput princess, or how he simply abolished taxes on non-Muslim young men who did not want to do military service (*jizya*) and invited Hindus and Shi'is to be among the Mughal elite. There were even non-Muslim rituals integrated into political culture. This was only the beginning. The wives of Mughal emperors, like their courtiers, were not expected to convert to Sunni Islam, so in imperial palaces one could find Christian chapels, Hindu temples, and mosques. If we look at Jahangir's memoirs, there are regular references to Mongol Chinggis law (*yasa* and *tamgha*), and visits to sufi shrines, but hardly anything dealing with Friday

---

14. See Lisa Balabanlilar, "Lords of the Auspicious Conjunction: Turco-Mongol Imperial Identity on the Subcontinent," *Journal of World History* 18/1 (2007), 23. Abu'l-Fadl also read Nasiruddin Tusi's *Awsaf al-ashraf* to Akbar, which would reinforce *ashrafi* attitudes. See Abu'l-Fadl 'Allami, *Mukatabat-i 'Allami Abu'l-Fadl*, 3 vols. (Lucknow: Nawal Kishur, 1911), 3:248.

15. Muzaffar Alam explains these two approaches in his "*Shari'a* and Governance in the Indo-Islamic Context," in David Gilmartin and Bruce B. Lawrence, *Beyond Turk and Hindu: Rethinking Religious Identities in Islamicate South Asia* (Gainsville, FL: University Press of Florida, 2000), 216-245.

prayers and mosque visits.[16] The Mughal emperors of Sirhindi's time followed Timurid principles in their informality and pragmatism. Establishing personal ties with the elite and affirming their loyalty was part of the Mughal way of ruling effectively. To implement this in practice, there were regular drinking parties, a Timurid custom. The first four Mughal emperors Babur, Humayun, Akbar, and Jahangir were regular users of alcohol and/or opium. There was a special officer at the Mughal court to take care of imperial intoxicants.[17] For pious Muslims this was just not right. Using the same principles that worked so well with his disciples, Sirhindi thought that if the Emperor aligned his creedal beliefs with the Sunni Hanafi mainstream then all this would change (see the first letter in this book). Even if the recipient of Sirhindi's letter communicated its contents, Jahangir apparently was not affected. He marched to the drummer of political expediency.

Opponents of Mughal rule chronicled their complaints in religious terms. The most obvious example is 'Abdulqadir Bada'uni's *Muntakhab al-Tawarikh* where he is particularly hostile toward Akbar's religious activities.[18] His views were shared by most *ashrafi* Muslims. Right after Akbar died, 'Abdulhaqq Muhaddith Dihlawi (d. 1052/1642), who spent approximately five years in the Mughal court, sent a letter to Shaykh Farid Bukhari, a lineal descendant of Muhammad and paymaster general (*mir bakhski*) in the Mughal government. The letter uses religious terms to strongly censure Akbar for acting as if he were greater than the Prophet, making reference to the Egyptian Pharoah (who claimed to be God in the Qur'an). 'Abdulhaqq then performs a "sufi diagnosis" linking Akbar's actions with his ego-self (*nafs*), which has not separated from the spirit subtle center (like the relationship of a man and a woman).[19] It is noteworthy how he ends the letter.

> It has been said that the conduct of each group is according to its occupation. What that means is that each person in each occupation or job proceeds according to the manner of doing things [appropriate to the occupation]. Being summoned to the noble shariat is the most important manner of doing something. Likewise, the Prophet, God bless him and give him peace, never elevated anyone up from a person's business [in life] (*harfat*). He left farmers to agriculture, traders to their commerce, family men to keep care of the family and children, the unmarried to be apart; the rich to their riches, and the poor ones to their

16. See Balabanlilar, "Lords of the Auspicious Conjunction," 27.

17. See Ibid., 33-36

18. See 'Abdulqadir Bada'uni, *Muntakhab al-tawarikh*, 3 vols., trans. by Wolseley Haig (Calcutta: Baptist Mission Press, 1925).

19. This situation between the spirit and ego-self is explained in much more detail in letter 1.287 in this book.

> poverty and fasting. Each group had its well-established, regulated way of doing things so that they could do their work and not veer from the well-trodden, straight path. To deviate from this is covering up the truth of God (*kufr* often translated as infidelity) and disobedience.[20]

'Abdulhaqq is complaining about Akbar mixing up the social order by putting *ajlaf* (the common Indian-origin Muslims) and even classes that are beyond the pale (the Rajput Hindus) into elite positions in the government. This complaint is based upon 'Abdulhaqq's interpretation of Prophetic precedent, the sunnat, which Akbar has disregarded.

Social distinctions between foreign-born Muslims who are "the noble" (*ashraf*), and Indian Muslim converts who are "the commoners" (*ajlaf*) are often ignored when analyzing sixteenth-century Indo-Muslim life.[21] The sociological dimension provides a lens to understand some of Sirhindi's statements, particularly those that have been interpreted negatively by modern readers. As early as the fourteenth century (at least from the texts we have available) Muslim social strata evolved into four groups: sayyids, putative descendants of the Prophet; shaykhs, putative descendants of the Companions; mughals, putative descendants of Turkic origin; and pathans, putative descendants of Afghans.[22] Barani, a fourteenth-century chronicler, noted that Iltutmish (r. 607/1211- 633/1236) dismissed thirty-three persons from

---

20. See Khaliq Ahmad Nizami, *Akbar and Religion* (Delhi, Jayyed Press, 1989), 409. This is my translation from the original Persian letter written by 'Abdulhaqq. See Abu'l-Majd 'Abdulhaqq Muhaddith Dihlawi, *Kitab al-makatib wa-rasa'il ila arbab al-kamal wa'l-fada'il* (Delhi, Matba'-i Mujtaba'i 1867), 84-91 (letter 17). I have read *ahammtarin* for *ahammbarin*. Nizami Sahib has interpreted the message of the selection that I have translated to mean "The sphere of religion is not for the rulers." *Akbar and Religion*, 404. I translate it differently. The rest of the letter goes on to explain that deeds in this life have their fruits in the afterlife.

21. David Damrel aptly notes that Sirhindi's antagonism toward non-Muslim participation in government and overall antagonism toward Indian non-Muslims "more likely comes from his background in Indian Islam rather than from his membership in the imported Central Asian Naqshbandi order." However, there is no further elaboration in his article, "The 'Naqshbandî Reaction' Reconsidered," in Gilmartin, *Beyond Turk and Hindu*, 188.

22. Shaykh should only include those of pure Arab descent—so we have names of Siddiqi from Abu Bakr as-Siddiq the first successor to Muhammad, Faruqi from 'Umar al-Faruq the second successor, and 'Abbasi from 'Abbas, Muhammad's paternal uncle. By the early twentieth century shaykh had become "little more than a title of courtesy" used by Hindu converts to Islam. Mughals are usually Persian or Chaghatai descent, adding Mirza or Amirzada to their names. See Ja'far Sharif, *Islam in India: The Customs of the Muslamans of India*, translated by G. A. Herklots, edited by William Crooke (Delhi: Oriental Books Reprint Corporation, 1972), 10-11.

government service on account of their low birth.[23] In the same way, Balban (r. 664/1266 - 686/1287) removed the low-born (*ajlaf*) from all-important offices and sharply reprimanded the courtiers who had given Kamal Mohiyar, an Indian Muslim, a post as a tax collector (*mutasarrif*) of Amroha. Muhammad Tughluq (r. 725/1325 - 752/1351) consciously initiated the policy of giving preference to foreign-born Muslims in administration and government, and systematically ignored the claims of Indian Muslims.[24]

Being among the *ashraf* was an important consideration for sufi authority also, at least if one wanted to attract *ashrafi* disciples and get government "donations." For many centuries the Chishti lineage, which depended financially on voluntary government donations, included such *ashraf* as Mu'inuddin Chishti (d. 633/1236 in Ajmer), Nasiruddin Chiragh (d. 757/1356 Delhi), Qutbuddin Bakhtiar Kaki (d. 633/1235), Sayyid Gesudaraz (d. 825/1422 Gulbarga), and Sayyid Ashraf Jahangir Simnani (d. 829/1425 Jaunpur). An aspirant looking for a sufi teacher would probably want an *ashrafi* shaykh to be his guide. In addition, *ashrafi* sufis have greater status because they are perceived to be more shariat-minded and more pious in their formal Islamic practices, which are presumed to have taken the place of indigenous customs. By definition, all of those who Sirhindi corresponded with were among the *ashraf* because they could read Persian.[25] They usually had their non-Indian place of origin indicated in their name, for example, Badakhshi, Kishmi, and Bukhari. The "Faruqi" in Ahmad Sirhindi's name indicates that he is a lineal descendant of 'Umar al-Faruq, the second caliph to rule after Muhammad. In the Indo-Muslim context of the sixteenth century, ancestry was important.

South Asian sufis almost always avoided any identification with the trades or attaching professional attributions (*nisbat*s) to their names because tradesmen were considered to be at the lower rungs of Muslim social strata. One apt "*ashrafi*" translation of this lower strata, *ajlaf*, is "coarse rabble," which include the tradesmen such as weavers, cotton-carders, oil-pressers, barbers, and tailors. With this background we can see that Sirhindi is giving philosophers the ultimate put-down when he says, "weavers and barbers

23. See also Dia'uddin Barani's *Tarikh-i Firoz Shahi*, trans. H.M. Eliot, *The History of India* Vol. 14, 2nd Edition (Calcutta: Susil Gupta Ltd., 1953), 178, for his contempt toward "low-born men."

24. See Imtiaz Ahmad, "The Ashraf-Ajlaf Dichotomy in Muslim Social Structure in India," *Indian Economic & Social History Review* 3 (1966) 270. Indian in this context means people from families who did not trace their lineage to non-Indian Muslim regions.

25. Except the letter written to a Hindu addressed to Hardai Ram *Collected Letters,* 1.167.

have specialized creative skills just like cameleon-like philosophers."[26] In his perusal of prominent hagiographical compendia of South Asia, Riazul Islam notes that almost all of the major hagiographic works make a point of mentioning the high pedigree of the leading shaykhs.[27] From the textual evidence, there seems to be no doubt that this *ashraf/ajlaf* social stratification permeated Indo-Muslim life, politically, socially, and even spiritually. With this background, let's now take a look at Shaykh Ahmad Sirhindi.

Preconceived Perceptions of Pious People

As a person who saw his mission in life to renew Islam and who spoke out against the prevailing lot of jurists, rulers, and sufis, Sirhindi would have lost the popularity contest of the long sixteenth-century by a large margin. In fact, Sirhindi's lack of popularity reached such heights that Jahangir gave him a one-year jail sentence because of his alleged exaggerated claims. Many jurists and sufis, in India and in the Hijaz, declared him to be outside the fold of Islam. Jahangir's grandson and Mughal ruler, Aurangzeb (r. 1068/1658-1118/1707), even proscribed the reading of Sirhindi's *Collected Letters*. We can infer that Sirhindi had many detractors, since many felt compelled to defend him and his ideas. There has been at least one book written per decade since 1022/1613 defending Sirhindi or one of his controversial ideas.[28]

Until very recently if one wanted to know more about Shaykh Ahmad Sirhindi, there were either hagiographical works and apologetics, or tracts against him and his ideas. In the twentieth century, Ahmad Sirhindi became the sixteenth-century de facto "founder-figure" of Pakistan after being extolled by Muhammad Iqbal (d. 1938), the first person publicly to advocate the formation of an independent Islamic state in the Subcontinent. This identification of Sirhindi with modern political agendas has only continued

---

26. See letter 1.200 in this book.

27. See Riazul Islam, *Sufism in South Asia*, 204.

28. Not all of these treatises are extant. The first in 1022/1613 was by 'Abdulhakim Sialkoti defending Sirhindi as the renewer of the second millennium and the latest (though not explicitly written to defend Sirhindi or his ideas) is the massive eleven-volume encyclopedia (almost 7500 pages) of the Indian Mujaddidiyya (Muhammad Mas'sud Ahmad, ed., *Jahan-i Imam-i Rabbani*: *Mujaddid-i Alf-i Thani Shaykh Ahmad Sirhindi*, 11 vols. Karachi: Imam Rabbani Foundation, 2005-2007). See Muhammad Iqbal Mujaddidi, "Hadrat Mujaddad Alf-i Thani quddus sirrahu ke dafa' men likhi jane wali kitaben," *Nur al-Islam* 33 (Jan./Feb. 1988), 45-72. Some of these controversies and the sources thereof are discussed in Buehler, *Sufi Heirs*, 246-247.

to distort his image.[29]

Yohanan Friedmann wrote a balanced study in 1971 stating the obvious when it was not so obvious. As he explains, Sirhindi was primarily a sufi and concerned with the accurate interpretation of religious experience (in Friedmann's words "the exploration of Sufi mysteries").[30] Ter Haar, in a comprehensive study of Sirhindi's ideas two decades later, concurs with Friedmann, but in a qualified manner. He reminds us that Sirhindi, although first and foremost a sufi, also wrote letters to influential Mughal elite and on occasion *did* insist that Mughal India be made a more "Islamic friendly" place.[31] In this, I follow in ter Haar's footsteps by seeking to represent Shaykh Ahmad Sirhindi as fully accurately as possible. I have outlined the sixteenth-century Mughal context of Sirhindi's life for the reader to understand that Sirhindi was not alone in his opposition to Mughal rule. When Mirza Hakim's (Akbar's half brother) army came through Sirhind in 988/1580-81 to dethrone Akbar, there were many nobles in Sirhind who openly welcomed him. There were conventional rationales for this opposition. Less evident are the personal factors in Sirhindi's life that heretofore have not been considered in the western academic literature. These are discussed below.

From 'Abdulhaqq Muhaddith Dihlawi and Jahangir to the present day, the most common critique of Sirhindi has been his apparently exaggerated claims. Sirhindi claimed that he was the first to receive certain spiritual knowledge, that he was at a higher station than Abu Bakr (who as Muhammad's first successor Sirhindi had declared to be the most exalted non-prophet human being), and that he was on par with the Prophet Muhammad.[32] Sirhindi also declared himself to be the unique one (*fard*), having absolute authority from the empyrean to earth and implied that he was the renewer of the second millennium.[33] What can scholars make of this and similar kinds of claims made by sufis before Sirhindi? One of the best-known examples is that of Ibn al-'Arabi (d. 638/1240 Damascus), who had multiple visions showing him to be the Seal of God's Friends, the eternal

29. Friedmann exposes these distortions in the guise of scholarship in his *Shaykh Ahmad Sirhindi*. For a more detailed update see Arthur F. Buehler, "Ahmad Sirhindi: Nationalist hero, good sufi, or bad sufi?," in Clinton Bennett, ed., *Sufis in South Asia* (New York: Continuum Publishing, 2012), forthcoming.

30. See Yohanan Friedmann, *Shaykh Ahmad Sirhindi*, 115.

31. Ter Haar lists the government officials with whom Sirhindi corresponded and which letters were written to them. By his calculation there are about 66 letters. See ter Haar, *Follower and Heir*, 16-17.

32. See Friedmann, *Shaykh Ahmad Sirhindi*, 87-89.

33. See Ahmad Sirhindi, *Mabda' wa-ma'ad*, ed. Zawwar Husayn with Urdu translation (Karachi: Ahmad Brothers Printers, 1984), 9-11.

source of being a Friend of God (*walayat*).

A consideration of Sirhindi's situation will suffice for understanding sufis' apparently exaggerated claims in general. There are basically three possibilities here. The first possibility is that these claims were made in an altered state of ecstatic consciousness and deserve to be put in the category of what Carl Ernst calls "ecstatic utterances" or what William Chittick calls "unruly utterances."[34] Sirhindi understands that non-realized sufis can have altered states of consciousness (*ahwal*) where they mistakenly perceive themselves to be closer to God than they actually are. Sirhindi apologizes (in letter 1.220 in this book) for some of his own claims (made in letter 1.11 in this book), explaining that he was mistaken. Here we have the rare case of a sufi himself recognizing some claims as inappropriate and abrogating them. But that leaves the question open because most of Sirhindi's seemingly grandiose claims still remain.[35] The second and third possibilities are that these claims are either true or false (or both). The vexing problem is that scholars qua scholars have no way of verifying these claims. If the intersubjective consensus of the sufi community agrees or disagrees with a claim over time then that has some weight. But that seldom turns up in the literature. In Sirhindi's case, the Naqshbandi community, over time, revised his status as the renewer of the second millennium. By the eighteenth century, his successors recognized him as the renewer of the *first* century of the second millennium. This will be discussed later.

Friedmann says that Sirhindi "frequently speaks of the common people with undisguised contempt. . . [using] expressions such as 'common people who are like cattle'.[36] Most of the references to the common people in *Collected Letters* refer to common Muslims who follow the shariat to distinguish them from the contemplative elite (*khawass*). In the few instances Sirhindi compares common people to cattle, it is a description of common people's unawareness (*maqam-i 'awamm ka'l-an'am*) or of common peo-

---

34. See Carl Ernst, *Words of Ecstasy* (Albany, NY: State University of New York Press, 1985), 3; and William C. Chittick, *The Self-disclosure of God: Principles of Ibn al-'Arabī's Cosmology* (Albany, NY: State University of New York Press, 1997), 302.

35. Using primary textual translations, I demonstrate many of Sirhindi's claims in "Tales of Renewal: Establishing Ahmad Sirhindi as the Reformer of the Second Millennium," in Jack Renard, *Tales of God's Friends: Islamic Hagiography in Translation* (Berkeley: University of California Press, 2009), 234-248. These claims are discussed analytically by Friedman, *Shaykh Ahmad Sirhindi*, 28, 60-68, 87-91.

36. See Friedmann, *Shaykh Ahmad Sirhindi*, 50. Although my *Fiharis-i tahlili* are not concordances, of the ten entries for "common people" only two refer to them as cattle. *Ajlaf* is not a term used to refer to them.

ple being ruled by their stomachs.[37] This does not appear to be a typical *ashrafi* attitude or "undisguised contempt."[38] In fact, it is an example of Sirhindi's very high standards for what it means to be a real human being. He says, "The common people are outside this shared human reality since they are ruled by their animal natures."[39] From this perspective, Sirhindi is just saying that extremely few people have taken the time to tame their ego-selves.

Sirhindi reserves his more strident notes for the Hindus. In a letter addressed to Shaykh Farid Bukhari, Akbar and Jahangir's paymaster general, Sirhindi cites Qur'an 66:9, "Strive against those who cover up God's truth (*al-kuffar* commonly translated as infidels) and hypocrites, and be stern with them." Sirhindi goes on to say that anyone who honors infidels (*ahl-i kufr*) disgraces Muslims. One assumes that Sirhindi is simply talking about Hindus being employed in the ranks of the Mughal elite because the letter is addressed to Farid Bukhari. Sirhindi goes on to say that this honoring also means keeping company with non-Muslims and talking with them, which implies a larger context than government service. They should be kept away like dogs.[40] He says that the least harm from associating with these non-Muslim enemies is the weakening of the shariat injunctions and a strengthening of non-Muslim customs. If they had the opportunity they would kill all the Muslims. "The object of collecting a special tax (*jizya*) from them is to humiliate them to the point that they will be afraid to wear nice clothing."[41] On the other hand, Sirhindi appears not to have taken his own advice. He writes a letter to a Hindu,[42] discusses his experience with

37. See *Collected Letters*, 1.313.168 and 3.49.114.

38. An *ashrafi* attitude towards native-born Indian Muslims is that they are "unworthy, disgusting and importunate, most of them being showy, superficial, and disagreeable." See Foltz, *Mughal India,* 107.

39. See letter 2.67 in this translation, point 16.

40. There is an implication here of non-Muslims being impure since dogs' saliva is considered to be impure and requires washing of garments before prayer according to Hanafi jurisprudence.

41. See *Collected Letters*, 1.163.43-44. Where there are no quotation marks, I have summarized parts of the letter using Sirhindi's language faithfully. Note also in ibid., 3.41.93, in the only letter addressed to a woman (unnamed), she is urged not to attend Hindu festivals or to pray to Sitala for the alleviation of fevers or smallpox. These entreaties apparently had little effect on Indian Muslim women overall since they are repeated in the nineteenth-century reformist treatise by Ashraf 'Ali T'hanawi, *Bihisht-i Zewar* in partial English translation Barbara Metcalf, *Perfecting Women: Maulana Ashraf 'Ali T'hanawi's Bihisht-i Zewar* (Berkeley: University of California Press, 1990).

42. The letter is addressed to Hardai Ram. See *Collected Letters,* 1.167.

"lots of Hindus" (ones ecstatically attracted to God),[43] and associates with Miyan Mir (d. 1045/1635), the Qadiri shaykh who was invited by Guru Arjan to lay the foundation stone of the Golden Temple.[44]

It is very rare for Sirhindi to talk like this in *Collected Letters*, but there probably was more going on than simply a bad mood that day. There are echos of Barani's rhetoric almost four centuries earlier, whose "principles of governance revolves [sic] around *shari'a, kufr, jihad,* and *jizya*; all that is good originates from Islam and a non-Muslim is nothing but evil embodied."[45] 'Abdulquddus Gangohi, the paramount Chishti-Sabiri shaykh who Sirhindi's father met as a youth, declared that only Muslims "of pure and zealous faith" should have posts in the government and non-Muslims (*kuffar*) should not be employed in government positions. Forced to pay *jizya*, they should not be allowed to dress like Muslims nor should they be allowed to practice their faith openly and publically. He wrote the current Mughal emperor, Babur, to return to the shariat.[46] Baqibillah, Sirhindi's Naqshbandi shaykh, was extremely unhappy to see that a Hindu physician had come to visit him when he was sick. It was only to please his mother that he relented to be treated.[47] There is a clear four-century consensus of the Indo-Muslim religious elite on how to treat and govern the Hindu majority. Sirhindi's attitudes often fit the *ashrafi* profile.

His involvement in daily life, however, fits the Naqshbandi profile. Although Sirhindi's primary life activity was contemplative training, he did not isolate himself from society. From Ahrari precedents, Naqshbandis were involved in society, and have articulated this principle with the dictum "being in solitude in society" (*khalwat dar anjuman*), one of the basic eight Naqshbandi principles formulated by 'Abdulkhaliq Ghujduwani (d. 575/1179). Sirhindi thought that it was his responsibility to improve the lot of all humans through the religious, moral, and spiritual enhancement of its leaders,[48] which meant that, upon occasion, he entered the fray via his letters to government officials. Sirhindi quotes the adage, "People adopt the

---

43. See ibid., 3.121.119.

44. See Carl Ernst, "Lives of Sufi Saints," in Donald S. Lopez, ed., *Religions of India in Practice* (Princeton: Princeton University Press, 1995), 508-509.

45. See Alam, "*Shari'a* and Governance," 225.

46. See Damrel, "The Naqshbandi Reaction," 184. For more information on 'Abdulquddus Gangohi, see Simon Digby. "Abd al-Quddus Gangohi (1456-1537 A.D.): The Personality and Attitudes of a Medieval Indian Sufi," *Medieval India* (New York: Asia Publishing House, 1975), 1-65.

47. See Baqibillah, *Kulliyat-i Baqibillah*, eds., Abu'l-Hasan Zayd Faruqi and Burhan Ahmad Faruqi (Lahore: Din Muhammadi Press, ca. 1967), 49-50.

48. See the first letter translated in this book, 2.67.

religion of their kings" to bring home his point.[49]

In these letters to the Mughal elite, Sirhindi invoked the primary principle of social order. Without social order an individual cannot live in peace. Muslims (and those of many other cultures) have sacrificed individual freedoms and rights for what they have considered the greater good of social order. Like 'Abdulhaqq's plea to Jahangir via Shaykh Farid, Sirhindi expected the government to maintain the *existing* social order. In other words, everyone was supposed to be in his "proper place" according to prior precedent. These learned sufis were conservatives in that they preferred to preserve what they thought had worked in the past. Precedent dictated taxing young non-Muslim men who did not join the military, and generally humiliating non-Muslims. An assumed superiority of the conquerer automatically puts the subjugated in an inferior position who should be treated accordingly. This is social order in an Indian context with a Muslim flavor. The *ashrafi* Sirhindi talking about how he feels toward Hindus was almost identical to Brahmin attitudes toward untouchable, outcaste *mleccha* Muslims. All of this, with its derogatory and discriminatory black-and-white pageant of blatant inequality, was intended to preserve a stable social order. Much of this, if not all, is unpalatable to modern sensibilities.

The Mughals broke with prior Muslim precedent in India. Akbar initiated the practice of treating temples as state property and as such protected the physical temples and their Brahmin priests. "[B]y appropriating Hindu religious institutions to serve imperial ends—a process involving complex overlapping of political and religious codes of power—the Mughals became deeply implicated in institutionalized Indian religions, in dramatic contrast to their British successors, who professed a hands-off policy in this regard."[50] This involvement, and its implications, ran counter to what most *ashrafi* Muslims considered proper social order. Richard Eaton gives an example of someone taking refuge in a mosque to avoid punishment from the Mughal Emperor Aurangzeb (r. 1658-1707), which suggests, "mosques in Mughal India, though religiously potent, were considered detached from both sovereign terrain and dynastic authority."[51]

Sirhindi's stable social order was not a "Muslim only" affair. His worldview recognized different religions with different ways of living one's life (*shariats*).[52] It was a "live and let live" perspective exemplified by the Qur'anic verse he cites, "to you, your way of living (*din*) and for

---

49. See *Collected Letters,* 1.195.84.

50. See Richard M. Eaton, *Essays on Islam and Indian History* (Delhi: Oxford University Press, 2000), 116.

51. See ibid., 123.

52. See letter 2.55 in this book.

me, my way of living (*din*).[53] [Q. 109:6] He never concerned himself with trying to "convert" non-Muslims to Islam or preventing non-Muslims from practicing their religions or living their way of life. There was concern, however, that Muslims could not live freely as Muslims. He says, "the infidels enforced the injunctions of their religion while Muslims were prevented from implementing the injunctions (*ahkam*) of Islam. If they did, then they were killed."[54] The injunctions he is speaking about here are not the individual worship aspect of shariat injunctions (*'ibadat*), since Muslims could obviously pray, fast, give alms, and perform hajj. Instead Sirhindi is referring to injunctions in society (*mu'amalat*), which include the right to build mosques, slaughter cows, and have the government appoint the requisite Muslim judges. In his hometown of Sirhind there had not been a judge for years.[55] Some of Sirhindi's concerns reflect the high degree of tension between Hindus and Muslims in the region. Between 1025/1616 and 1028/1619, Sirhindi mentions Hindus destroying a mosque and tomb in the pilgrimage spot of Kurukshetra reservoir (near Thaneswar) and building a temple on the site. He reports that on the fasting day the eleventh day of each month, Ekadashi, Muslims were not allowed to bake bread or sell food, but during Ramadan Hindus were allowed to do these activities.[56]

Before this, Akbar's "upside-down social order" had mortally lasting effects on Sirhindi's family. Akbar's ordering the execution of Sirhindi's father-in-law, Shaykh Sultan, in the fifth Islamic month (Jumada al-awwal) of 1007/December, 1598, did nothing to endear Sirhindi to the Mughal regime or to Hindus. This was one of the very few public killings in Akbar's reign. Hajji Shaykh Sultan was one of the people assigned in Akbar's imperial service to translate the *Mahabharata*,[57] and at some point Hindus complained that he had slaughtered some cows in Thaneswar. This was against the law in the Panjab, so he was banished to Bhakkar. Farid Bukhari, the governor of Multan at the time, interceded for him and Shaykh Sultan ended up

53. See *Collected Letters,* 1.47.18.

54. See ibid., 1.47.14.

55. See ibid., 1.195.85.

56. See ibid., 2.92.93-94.

57. One suspects that Akbar knew of his intransigent attitude toward the Hindus. 'Abdulqadir Bada'uni, a Muslim theologian and translator in Akbar's court who disagreed with Akbar's including Hindus in the court elite, was also assigned to translate parts of the *Mahabharata*. There is a short biographical notice of Shaykh Sultan T'haneswari in 'Abdulhayy b. Fakruddin Hasani, *Nuzhat al-khawatir*, 8 vols. (Hyderabad, Deccan: Da'irat al-Ma'arif al-'Uthmania, 1976), 5:161-162 which confuses 'Abdurrahman Khan-i Khanan for Shaykh Farid. There is no mention of Shaykh Sultan's demise at the hands of Akbar.

becoming the tax collector (*karori*) of Thaneswar.[58] Later, in the words of Abu'l-Fadl, "he [Shaykh Sultan] renewed his old grudges and set himself to hurt the good."[59] No specifics are given other than Shaykh Sultan was summarily executed. In Sirhindi's worldview, there would be no strife if Hindus lived in their world and Muslims lived in their world, with the *ashrafi* Muslims authoritatively presiding over the Hindus politically. There was no place in his worldview for mutual understanding or shared meanings much less mutual resonance between these two religio-cultural worlds.[60]

Sufi contemplative practice (or any other pre-modern contemplative practice), focusing on subjective *individual* experience and development, was structurally incapable of making an inter-religious space for this to happen. Subjective contemplative development is almost always independent of this kind of intersubjective inter-religious development. It is only with the advent of modernity that a critical mass of people could rationally view the cultural ignorance that had perpetuated slavery, caste, ethnocentricity, and sexism.

Who was Shaykh Ahmad Sirhindi?

Ahmad Sirhindi was born on 14 Shawwal, 971, or 26 June 1564, the fourth son of 'Abdulahad (d.1007/1599), who traced his lineage from the second caliph, 'Umar al-Faruq.[61] His father's family was descended from Farrukh Shah al-Kabuli, the great-grandfather of the famous Panjabi Chishti shaykh Fariduddin Ganj-i Shakar (d. 664/1265). 'Abdulahad first became the disciple of 'Abdulquddus Gangohi's (d. 944/1537) son Ruknuddin (983/1575) of the Chishti-Sabiri lineage from whom he received permission to teach.[62]

---

58. See 'Abdulqadir Bada'uni, *Muntakhab al-tawarikh*, 3 vols., trans. by Wolseley Haig (Calcutta: Baptist Mission Press, 1925), 3:173-174. Farid Bukhari went on to become the future patron of Baqibillah's sufi lodge in Delhi and a recipient of twenty-four letters from Ahmad Sirhindi.

59. See Abu'l-Fadl 'Allami, *Akbar nama*, 3 vols., trans. By H. Beveridge (Delhi: Low Price Publications, 1993), 3:1118.

60. See *Collected Letters,* 1.167.

61. 'Abdulahad's family tree going back to 'Umar al-Faruq can be found in *Hazarat al-quds*, 27 but a corrected version is found in *Nur al-Islam* 33/1 (Jan.-Feb. 1988), 127-241, which is a revised version of Muhammad Hasan Mujaddidi's *Insab al-anjab.*

62. See Badruddin Sirhindi, *Hadarat al-quds*, ed., Mahbub Ilahi (Lahore: Maqama-yi Awqaf, 1971), 28-30, has Sirhindi's Qadiri lineages confused. The most detailed source on 'Abdulahad is Khurshid Husayn Bukhari, *Kamal: Sawanih Hadrat Shah Kamal Qadiri Kayt'hli* (Lahore: Al-i Bashir Printers, 1976), 143-148. I thank Professor Iqbal Mujaddidi, the doyen of Indian Mujaddidi studies, for pointing out this book to me.

At some point 'Abdulahad also started to visit Shah Kamal Kayt'hali Qadiri (d. 981/1573), who gave him permission to teach the Qadiri contemplative practices.

After Sirhindi had studied the Qur'an (but apparently not memorizing it all),[63] his father sent him to Sialkot for formal training in all the branches of religious knowledge, for example, hadith, Qur'an commentary, jurisprudence, and Arabic grammar. He studied with Mawlana Kamal Kashmiri (d. 1017/1608-9), the teacher of 'Abdulhakim Sialkoti (d. 1067/1656), the well-known hadith scholar who was said to be the first to recognize Ahmad Sirhindi as the renewer of the second millennium. While in Sialkot he also studied hadith with Shaykh Ya'qub Sarfi Kashmiri (d. 1003/1593-4), a successor of the Kubrawi Shaykh Husayn Khwarzimi.[64] This stage of his education ended when he was seventeen years old. Then he returned to Sirhind to study hadith with Qadi Bahlul Badakhshani and Shaykh 'Abdurrahman b. Fahd and ended up in the Mughal capital of Agra around the age of twenty-two to join the Mughal army.[65] At some point in his six years or so away from home, Sirhindi ended up working with two brothers, Faydi, Akbar's poet-laureate, and Abu'l-Fadl 'Allami (assass. 1011/1602), Akbar's vizier, historian, and confidant. It is said that Court culture was not to Sirhindi's liking.[66] He left after a heated disagreement with Abu'l-Fadl, who had categorically dismissed prophecy in preference to reason. Soon after this incident, he returned to Sirhind with his father 'Abdulahad. On the

---

63. In *Collected Letters,* 3.47.101, Shaykh Sirhindi tells his two sons how he had memorized the Qur'an while in Jahangir's custody in the Gwalior Fort.

64. Muhammad Hashim Kishmi, *Zubdat al-maqamat* (Istanbul: Işık Kitabevi, 1997), 128-130. This account has the books he studied, which ones he was authorized to teach, and actual hadith *isnad*s. Unless otherwise stated this Persian version is the source used as Kishmi, *Zubdat al-maqamat*. Badruddin Sirhindi, in his less reliable *Hadarat al-quds*, 33 states that Shaykh Ya'qub Sarfi initiated Sirhindi into the Kubrawiyya.

65. Ghulam Mu'inuddin 'Abdullah Muhammad Khishagi Qusuri, "Ma'arij al-wilayat," Punjab University mss, #7765, f. 588 cited in Saleem Akhtar, "Mawlana Muhammad Sadiq Kashmiri and Mawlana Hasan Kashmiri," *Journal of the Pakistan Historical Society* 25 (1977), 218 fn1.

66. The outer aspects of court culture would be enough to alienate a pious Muslim. 'Abdulhaqq Muhaddith Dihlawi (d. 1052/1642), who spent up to five years at Fatehpur Sikri, avoided all the ambitious people around him, and was "deeply scarred and ashamed of his experiences at the court." See Scott Kugle "'Abd al-Haqq Dihlawi, an Accidental Revivalist: Knowledge and Power in the Passage from Delhi to Makka," *Journal of Islamic Studies* 19/2 (2008), 210. His stay in the Mughal court, roughly 991/1583 – 996/1587, might have overlapped with Sirhindi's.

way back to Sirhind, he got married to a daughter of a prominent nobleman, Shaykh Sultan T'haneswari,[67] and sometime at the end of 1000/1592 his first son Muhammad Sadiq (d. 1025/1616) was born.

It was also around this time that Sirhindi probably wrote his *Epistle Refuting Shi'ism*, defending the first three caliphs and 'Aisha. Sirhindi explains that he wrote it in response to a letter written by the Shi'i jurists of Mashhad to the jurists of Central Asia,[68] after the Uzbek leader 'Abdullah Khan Shaybani had conquered Mashhad in the second year of Shah 'Abbas Safawi's reign (997/1588-89).[69] Prior to this, Sirhindi had already written *Epistle Confirming Prophecy*, apparently after his run-in with Abu'l-Fadl over this and other topics.[70] During this period in Sirhind, he studied at least two sufi texts with his father: Ibn al-'Arabi's *Bezels of Wisdom* and Shihabuddin Suhrawardi's *The Bounties of Inner Knowledge*. Right before his passing, 'Abdulahad gave him permission to teach the Chishti-Qadiri practices that he had received from Ruknuddin Gangohi.[71] Sirhindi's father passed away in the sixth Islamic month (Jumada al-thani) of 1007 or January 1599, within a month of his father-in-law's execution. Nine months later he left for Delhi with the intent of making the pilgrimage to Mecca. By that time, he had written a third short treatise, *The Epistle on Saying "There is no god but God.*"[72]

Then came the turning point of his life. In Delhi he met Hasan Kashmiri,

67. See Badruddin Sirhindi, *Hadarat al-quds*, 50. Shaykh Sultan's brother, Shaykh Zakariyya, is mentioned four times in *Collected Letters*. In the first two, written to Farid Bukhari, Sirhindi is asking for assistance because Shaykh Zakariyya is having difficulties with his job as revenue officer. Ibid., 1.43.9 and 1.50.22. By the third letter, Sirhindi is pleading with Khan-i Jahan for Shaykh Zakariyya's release from prison. Ibid., 1.72.54. The fourth letter, 1.98, is addressed to Shaykh Zakariyya's son.

68. See Ahmad Sirhindi, *Radd-i madhhab-i Shi'i*, ed. with Urdu translation by Ghulam Mustafa Khan (Karachi: Anjuman Press, 1974), 3-4. The translator renamed this "*Ta'id-i ahl-i sunnat*" as a chronogramic title. Ter Haar discusses the context and content of this epistle, correcting Friedmann's remarks that Sirhindi wrote this epistle as a "rite of passage." See ter Haar, *Follower and Heir*, 25-26.

69. See Muhammad Ikram, "*Hadrat-i Mujaddid-i Alf-i Thani Shaykh Ahmad Sirhindi quddus sirrahu*" in Muhammad Ikram Chaghata'i, ed., *Hadrat Mujaddid-i Alf-i Thani* (Lahore: Sang-e Meel Publications, 2009), 234. This carefully researched article is the best of all the biographies in the book.

70. In the introduction to this epistle, Sirhindi mentions the difficulties for Muslims living in India and his having a debate with an unnamed person whose characteristics match Abu'l-Fadl. See Ahmad Sirhindi, *Ithbat al-nubuwwat*, edited and translated into Urdu by Ghulam Mustafa Khan (Karachi: Ahmad Brothers, 1984), 10.

71. See Sirhindi, *Hadarat al-quds*, 33.

72. See Ahmad Sirhindi, *Risala-yi tahliliyya*, ed. and translated into Urdu by Rashid Ahmad (Karachi: Idarah-i Mujaddidiyya, 1983).

who in turn introduced him to Muhammad Baqibillah, a Naqshbandi shaykh from Kabul who was born in the same year as Ahmad Sirhindi. Instead of making the pilgrimage, Sirhindi moved into Baqibillah's sufi lodge in the Firuzabad fort near Delhi in the fourth Islamic month (Rabi' al-thani) of 1008, or November, 1599. According to Sirhindi, this was his true beginning in sufi training. He stayed with Baqibillah for two and a half months before returning to Sirhind. The letters that were written after this trip and his realizing the "Naqshbandi connection" during the month of Rajab, meant that Baqibillah had given him unconditional permission to teach aspirants after this first visit.[73] His second visit to Baqibillah was the following Ramadan in 1009/1600.[74] On one of his two return trips, he received permission to teach the Qadiri practices from the disembodied spirit of Shah Kamal Kayt'hali and from his (living) grandson and successor, Shaykh Iskandar (d. 1023/1614).[75] Sirhindi then returned to Sirhind and saw Baqibillah one more time before Baqibillah died in 1012/1603. Sirhindi was recognized by almost all of Baqibillah's disciples as the principal successor. Baqibillah is usually left out in western accounts of Shaykh Ahmad Sirhindi, but he deserves a closer look.

Muhammad Baqibillah Naqshbandi Uwaysi Berang was born in Kabul in 971/1563.[76] His mother, a descendant of 'Ubaydullah Ahrar, was from Kashmir. His father, a Qilich Turk named 'Abdussalam Samarqandi, worked as a judge.[77] Baqibillah first studied with a Naqshbandi, Khwaja 'Ubaydul-

---

73. The Naqshbandi connection occurring during the month of Rajab is mentioned in Sirhindi, *Mabda' wa-ma'ad*, 16. Sirhindi's experiences leading up to this are described in letter 1.290 in this book. If letter 1.290 describes a continuous set of experiences, then it appears that Sirhindi received unconditional permission to teach on his first visit because of a "completion and completion-bestowing knowledge." Letters in the first volume mentioning the training of others: 1,3,5,10,11,14,16. These are supposed to be in rough chronological order. See the introduction to letter 1.220 for a teaching certificate given to Hamid Bengali, and Buehler, *Sufi Heirs*, Appendix 4 for further examples of conditional and unconditional teaching certificates.

74. Letter 1.16 appears to be the first letter Sirhindi wrote to Baqibillah after returning from the second trip.

75. See Bukhari, *Kamal*, 140, 147; Ahmad Sirhindi, *Mukashafat-i 'ayniya*, ed. and Urdu translation by Ghulam Mustafa Khan (Karachi: Educational Press, 1965), 7; and Kishmi, *Zubdat al-maqamat*, 134-136.

76. *Berang*, literally meaning "to be without color," is to be at a level of no level without attributes or the station of no station. In Sirhindi's terminology it would be someone who is wayfaring in God's Essence, where there are no stages, states, or levels.

77. These details are important because later some have claimed Baqibillah's sons to be sayyids.

lah Kabuli,[78] and ended up going to Transoxiana studying religious sciences under the guidance of Mawlana Sadiq Halwa'i. After coming back for a short period in Kabul, he returned to Transoxiana in search of a spiritual guide. Many shaykhs in Samarqand refused to initiate him because of his youth. Then he went to Lahore and developed a friendship with the future patron of his sufi lodge in Delhi, Farid Bukhari. During this time he had an Uwaysi initiation by Baha'uddin Naqshband (d. 791/1389).[79] Baqibillah then went to Kashmir (possibly in 999/1591 when Farid Bukhari went there) and stayed with Shaykh Baba Wali Naqshbandi (assas. 1000/1592). After Baba Wali's death (by poisoning), he returned to Transoxiana, apparently guided by 'Ubaydullah Ahrar's spirit. There he was formally initiated into the Naqshbandiyya by Muhammad Amkanagi (in 'Ubaydullah Ahrar's lineage d. 1008/1600) and given unconditional permission to teach after spending three days and nights in retreat with him. Much to his dismay, and over his protests, Baqibillah was sent back immediately to India. He first stayed in Lahore and went to Delhi in 1007/1598-99 to settle down permanently until his death in 1012/1603.[80]

It seems that Sirhindi adhered to the Naqshbandi principles that Baqibillah articulated.[81] Baqibillah's twenty-three recorded discourses and 87 letters have the same flavor of teaching and training that one finds in Sirhindi's more extensive *Collected Letters*. Although there is not nearly as much detail, it appears that both shaykhs are using the same contemplative map of attributes, qualities (*shuyunat*), and origins. Much discussion is centered

78. His sublineage is from Makhdum-i A'zam, Khwajagi Kasani (d. 949/1542) of Bukhara whose successor was Lutfullah (d. 979/1571). See Muhammad Hashim Kishmi, *Nasamat al-quds*, Urdu translation by Mahbub Hasan Wasiti (Sialkot: Maktaba-yi Nu'maniyya, 1990), 267. Muhammad Hashim Kishmi is the author of the first biography/hagiography of Sirhindi, *Zubdat al-maqamat*.

79. See Muhammad Mandawi Ghawthi, *Adhkar-i abrar: Urdu tarjama-yi Gulzar al-abrar*, Urdu translation by Fadl Ahmad Jewari (Lahore: Islamic Book Foundation, 1975), 477.

80. If one makes allowances for too many incorrect footnote references and disorganization, the best biographical introduction for Baqibillah is Ghulam Mustafa Khan, *Baqiyat-i baqi* (N.p, 1989), pp 8-28. Through his painstaking research we know that the compiler of Baqibillah's discourses (*malfuzat*) is Muhammad Sadiq Kishmi, the unnamed "Rashdi." It appears that these discourses were written down for Baqibillah's wife and Shaykh Sirhindi encouraged a reluctant Baqibillah to give Muhammad Sadiq permission to record the discourses. Ibid., 25-26.

81. Ter Haar goes into detail analyzing content of the first twenty letters Sirhindi wrote to Baqibillah. See *Follower and Heir*, 30-42. In terms of their respective attitudes on Ibn al-'Arabi and the unity of being, see the corresponding section in this Introduction.

on distinguishing these realms. It is not surprising that the teaching is often identical, for example, on the necessity to separate the spirit subtle center (*ruh*) and the ego-self (*nafs*) before unveiling (*mukashafa*) can be considered a reliable way of knowing something.[82] Baqibillah often distinguishes wayfaring in the attributes, associated with ecstatic states (*jadhba*), from sober wayfaring in the Essence. Wayfaring is a common sufi expression for the experience of spiritual traveling in various realms while doing contemplative practice. He reprimanded Sirhindi for his heretical quatrains.[83] Sirhindi learned well from his teacher, as you will see from the letters translated in this book, which repeatedly deal with these issues.

After Baqibillah passed away in 1012/1603, there were some succession squabbles and not all of Baqibillah's disciples followed Sirhindi's leadership after his death.[84] Baqibillah's two sons became attracted to dance, music, and song, which Sirhindi reminded them, was not in line with their father's teaching.[85] Tajuddin Sanbhali went to Mecca and Sirhindi got on with his teaching, sending his authorized deputies to the major cities of northern India. Badi'uddin Saharanpuri was sent to counsel members of the army in Agra, the Mughal capital, and had to leave Agra against Sirhindi's instructions after being blamed for some unspecified disturbances. Soon after this, the Mughal ruler Jahangir accused Sirhindi of being an arrogant imposter who compiled a book of idle tales called *Collected Letters* that led people to heresy.[86] Jahangir called Sirhindi to Agra and imprisoned him from 1028/1619 to 1029/1620. Sirhindi was obliged to accompany the army for at least two more years before retiring in solitude to his home in Sirhind. Shortly after, he passed away in 1034/1624 at the age of 63 lunar years, the same age as Muhammad had died a little over one thousand years before. Shaykh Ahmad Sirhindi's well-kept shrine in Sirhind is less than a couple hundred meters from the Sikh Fatehgarh Gurdwara where the two young sons of Guru Gobind Singh were treacherously executed in 1117/1705 in what is now a predominantly Sikh area of the Panjab.

---

82. See Baqibillah, *Kulliyat*, 24, 32. Note 'Abdulhaqq Muhaddith's similar commentary above in his letter to Farid Bukhari.

83. See ibid., 122-123. The quatrains are in the footnote at the bottom of the page.

84. These are detailed in ter Haar, *Follower and Heir*, 42-46.

85. See ter Haar, *Follower and Heir*, 44. Cf. Baqibillah, *Kulliyat*, 75-77.

86. See Friedmann, *Shaykh Ahmad Sirhindi*, 83. We do not know the specifics about those who opposed Sirhindi. Dara Shikuh might have been one of those who informed Jahangir about the opposition. See Hamid Algar, "Imâm-ı Rabbânî," *Islâm Ansiklopedisi* 35 vols. (Istanbul: Türkiye Diyanet Vakfı, 1988-), 22:194-99.

Ahmad Sirhindi as the Renewer of the Second Millennium

> Certainly Allah will send to this community at the beginning [or end] of every hundred years one who will renew for it its religion.[87]
>
> *Sunan* Abu Da'ud

Before Muhammad prophets were renewers of religion. In the Islamic version of history, it was the prophetic function to renew the process of submitting to God, *islam*, so that people could live their lives in harmonious surrender to God as *muslims*. Adam was the first of 124 thousand or so prophets who were said to have been sent to people all over the world inviting them to the straight path to God. Over successive generations, a degradation of the prophetic message occured. When things reached a certain point, God sent a prophet to guide people back to the straight path. This is how Islamic tradition explains the succession of prophets from Adam to Moses to Abraham to Jesus to Muhammad. There is one catch: Muhammad is the last prophet. So no one, according to the Islamic construction of prophetology, can come along after Muhammad and claim to be a prophet.

People still have the proclivity to deviate from the straight path. Muhammad alluded to this process in a hadith, "The best generation was the one in which I was sent, then those who follow them, and then those that follow them." Instead of prophets, there are renewers (sing. *mujaddid*) every century whose work is to renew the practice of *islam*, as stated in the hadith above.[88] Who are these renewers? That depends on which group of Muslims one asks because of the geographical and religious diversity in the Muslim community. There are different lists, both Sunni and Shi'i, but the Sunni criteria are that the person revive the prophetic *sunnat* and eradicate any innovations (sing. *bid'a*), and that his contemporaries recognize the benefits of his activity. A renewer cannot be self-appointed nor retroac-

---

87. See Hamid Algar, "The Centennial Renewer: Bediüzzaman Said Nursi and the Tradition of *Tajdid*" in *Journal of Islamic Studies* 12/3 (2001), 292. This is Professor Algar's translation of the hadith. Ella Landau-Tasseron in "The 'cyclical reform': a study of the *mujaddid* tradition," *Studia Islamica* 70 (1989), 79-118, argues that this tradition was fabricated to legitimise the original teachings of al-Shafi'i.

88. The renewer is also supposed to "postpone" the Day of Judgment. The connection between the Mahdi and the centennial renewer in the context of the "hadith of centennial renewal" and the overview of prior material on this subject is discussed in detail by Samuela Pagani, *Il Rinnovamento Mistico Dell'Islam: Un commento di 'Abd al-Ghani al-Nabulusi a Ahmad Sirhindi* (Naples: Universita Degli studi Di Napoli "L'Orientali," 2003), 98-115. Friedmann discusses millennial concerns in India during this century in his *Shaykh Ahmad Sirhindi*, 13-21.

tively appointed.[89]

The earliest formal written notice of Ahmad Sirhindi as the "renewer of the second millennium" appears in the first hagiographical treatise honoring Sirhindi, *The Quintessence of Stations*, written four years after he died.

> As I [Hashim Kishmi] was writing, it occurred in my heart that, of the great jurists of the time, God had made [Ahmad Sirhindi] the renewer of the second millennium. I did not think any more of it until one day when in the presence of my shaykh [Ahmad Sirhindi] the thought came to mind again. He [Sirhindi] said, "Mawlana 'Abdulhakim Sialkoti (d. 1067/1656), who is known throughout India as a great jurist with many books, wrote me a letter." Smiling, he continued speaking. "One of his epistles of praise was that [my being the] "renewer of the second millennium" should not be kept a secret but actually declared." I looked at my shaykh as he recited a Qur'anic verse. After all this happened, I went back serving my shaykh.[90]

If one added up all the disciples of Sirhindi's numerous representatives who were authorized to teach scattered from Bukhara to Mecca, there would have been thousands who would have easily agreed with 'Abdulhakim Sialkoti's proclamation. Combine this with the remarkable synthesis of the prophetic sunnat and sufism that Sirhindi pioneered (or renewed), and Sirhindi could be certainly certified as a renewer. There are two catches. Practically speaking, the consensus of jurists who decide centennial renewers for a region do not pick controversial sufis. Otherwise Ibn al-'Arabi would have been on many lists as a renewer.[91] Secondly, the hadith says every hundred years, not a thousand years.

Ahmad Sirhindi was the first to be associated with renewing an entire millennium. How did this unprecedented situation come about? Accord-

---

89. Algar precisely examines the criteria for a centennial renewer in "The Centennial Renewer," 292-297.

90. See Kishmi, *Zubdat al-maqamat*, 176. This passage is preceded by a verbatim account of Sirhindi's spiritual experience found in *Mabda' wa-ma'ad*, 79, followed by *Maktubat*, 1.209.105-106.

91. There is a list of nine renewers for the eleventh century in Muhammad Zafaruddin Fadl Bihar, *Chud'dwin sadi ke mujaddid* (Lahore: Maktaba-yi Ridwiyya, n.d.), 16. Of these nine, Ahmad Sirhindi and 'Abdulhaqq Muhaddith Dihlawi are the last two. In Muhammad 'Abdulhakim Khan Akhtar Shahjahanpuri, *Tajalliyat-i Imam-i Rabbani* (Lahore: Maktaba-yi Nabawiyya, 1978), 36, 59, there are two lists for eleventh century renewers, one with just Sirhindi and 'Abdulhaqq, and one with four renewers, of whom 'Abdulhaqq is one. Although Ibn al-'Arabi may not have made it on any list, his name, Muhyiuddin, the enlivener of religion, may very well state his actual role, making such formalities superfluous.

ing to Sirhindi, the millennium signaled the disappearance of Muhammad's bodily attributes, which had been decreasing gradually over this thousand-year period of time during which Muhammad became a totally spiritual being disconnected from worldly affairs. The end of the first millennium marked the lowest point in decline and explained for Sirhindi why covering up the truth of God (*kufr* usually translated as infidelity) had seemed to peak during Akbar's reign. Normally a great prophet (pl. *ulu al-'azmi*) would have been sent to put things in order. That was no longer possible, so according to Sirhindi, the perfections of prophecy will resurface in the Prophet's heirs, the most notable of whom is the renewer of the second millennium.[92]

Sirhindi never explicitly said that he was the renewer of the second millennium. Otherwise he would have been formally disqualified. Instead, he explained how he became the unique one (*fard*). Then Sirhindi adds a nuance to the well-known sufi spiritual hierarchy consisting of one axial leader (*qutb*) surrounded by various hierarchies of subordinates.[93] In the second millennium, the reality of Muhammad will transform to the reality of Ahmad as a person emerges to become the Prophet's deputy, who is called the central axial authority (*qutb-i madar*). The renewer of the second millennium is also the central axial authority. Those are the pieces. Then Sirhindi claims the role of central axial authority, equates it with the rank of uniqueness (*fardiyat*), which connects the millennial renewer with the unique one.[94]

Sirhindi details the experiences leading to his becoming the unique one. After achieving "complete annihilation of the ego in the attributes of supporting the cosmos (*qayyumiyat*),"[95] he ascended as far as 'Ali b. Abi Talib (assas. 40/661), and continued ascending with the assistance of the disembodied presence of 'Umar b. al-Khattab al-Faruq (assas. 24/644), the second caliph. "I traveled even higher, beyond the first degree of capabil-

---

92. Friedmann has discussed this topic of renewal and the millennium in great detail in *Shaykh Ahmad Sirhindi*, 13-21. There is a missing piece in his exposition because he did not make the connection between the technical sufi meaning of *fard* (translating it instead as "common believer") and Sirhindi's spiritual claims.

93. See the introduction to letter 1.287 in the translation.

94. The full translated texts are in Arthur Buehler, "Tales of Renewal: Establishing Ahmad Sirhindi as the Reformer of the Second Millennium," in Jack Renard, *Tales of God's Friends: Islamic Hagiography in Translation* (Berkeley: University of California Press, 2009), 234-248.

95. There is another strand of this saga of renewing that is not discussed, that is, the person "who supports the universe" (*qayyum*), a perfect human mediating inner and outer perfections between God and humans. See *Collected Letters,* 2.74.69; and ter Haar, *Follower and Heir of the Prophet*, 153-155.

ity to the attributes of God. Then I ascended to an even higher station, the station of the Muhammadan axis, which manifested as God's Essence." Then he received the robe of axial guide (*qutb-i irshad*) after arriving at the station of the axial guides. "I was graced by that sovereign of religion and the world (Muhammad). In that way I was bestowed this exalted rank." Sirhindi was then guided by the spirit of the Supreme Helper (*ghawth*), 'Abdulqadir Jilani (d. 561/1166), and with the strength of his spiritual power he arrived at the origin of origins. "With each station I returned to the physical world. This dervish had received the essential connection of being a unique one."[96]

Later in the same treatise, Sirhindi discusses the events of the second millennium. "There will come a time after the passage of a thousand some-odd years after the death of Muhammad when the reality of Muhammad ascends from its station and unites with the station of the reality of the Ka'ba. At this time, the reality of Muhammad takes the name of the reality of Ahmad and becomes the manifestation of the unique essence of God. Both blessed names (Muhammad and Ahmad) are established [as the aggregate of the reality of Muhammad and the reality of the Ka'ba]."[97] Sirhindi explains this in more detail to Mir Muhammad Nu'man Badakhshani (d. 1058/1648), the first disciple whom Sirhindi authorized to teach.

> The perfections of the friends of God (*awliya'*) of this time (one thousand years after the death of Muhammad) resemble the perfections of the noble Companions, even though the Companions [of Muhammad] have precedence. Because of the perfect resemblance [between the Companions and the aforementioned friends of God], one cannot give preference to one group over another. From this the Prophet was able to say, "[My community is like the rain]; I do not know who is better, the first or last among them.[98]

Then he explains to his eldest son Muhammad Sadiq, who received permission to teach in 1021/1612, that after completing the perfections of greater intimacy with God (the intimacy of prophethood) and becoming worthy of high office, the person who perfectly imitates the Prophet will be honored by being the Prophet's deputy.[99] In a further letter to his eldest son, Ahmad Sirhindi also alludes to a renewer of the new millennium (instead of the

---

96. Quoted material in this paragraph is translated from Ahmad Sirhindi, *Mabda' wa-ma'ad*, 9-11. This passage continues with Sirhindi receiving blessings from the leading figures of the rest of the major sufi lineages.

97. See ibid., 79.

98. See *Collected Letters,* 1.209.105-106. This letter goes into a very technical explanation of the previous quote from *Mabda' wa-ma'ad*, 79.

99. See *Collected Letters*, 1.260.91, translated in this book.

customary renewer every hundred years).

> At the beginning of each century there is a renewer designated from the jurists of the community who enlivens the shariat. Especially [at this time] after the passing of one thousand years there would have been a great prophet sent to the community—but it is not possible now to send a great prophet [because Muhammad is the Seal of the Prophets so no prophets come after him]. In a time like this, a jurist having deep experience of God (*'alimi 'arifi tam al-ma'ruf*) is necessary, someone with the stature to succeed the preceding great prophets.[100]

The renewer of the second millennium is also tied in with the axial guide. Not only does it seem that Sirhindi is claiming this role, but he also equates it with the rank of uniqueness (*fardiyat*), connecting the millennial renewer with the unique one. "Consider how extraordinary the axial guide really is. He has the total perfections of uniqueness. After many centuries and the innumerable passage of time, this kind of jewel appears! The dark world becomes filled with light from the light of his appearance. His light of guidance encompasses the whole world—from the ocean of the heavenly throne to the center of the earth. Any guidance, belief, and inner knowledge that a person receives and benefits from, comes from his path. No one can get these benefits except by his mediation."[101]

Toward the end of his life, Sirhindi wrote to Hashim Kishmi (d. 1054/1644), the author of *The Quintessence of Stations*. He explained that Muhammad has two spiritual entifications, bodily-human and spiritual-angelic. As the bodily-human aspect of Muhammad diminished after his death, the spiritual-angelic aspect became stronger until no signs of the bodily-human aspect remained at the end of a thousand years. "One can say that Muhammad necessarily became Ahmad as Muhammadan intimacy with God shifted to become Ahmadi intimacy. Muhammad (lit. the two "m"s) means two aspects and Ahmad involves one aspect, period. The name Ahmad is closer to God and further from the world."[102] (Note the prophetic name of Ahmad and the Ahmad of Ahmad Sirhindi.)

About the same time, Sirhindi wrote to his son and eventual successor, Muhammad Ma'sum (d. 1079/1668). He talked about an individual (*fard*), but as we have seen above, the *fard* as "unique one" is a very high spiritual

---

100. The letter is from *Collected Letters*, 1.234.33. The great prophets (*ulu'-i 'azmi*) are generally considered in the Mujaddidi tradition to be Noah, Moses, Abraham, Jesus, and Muhammad since they established a shariat for their people. Note that they do not all qualify as messengers because Noah is not recognized as "bringing a book." David, who is recognized as bringing scripture, is not mentioned.

101. See ibid., 1.260.95.

102. See ibid., 3.96.58.

rank of uniqueness. To be spiritually polite Sirhindi used this ambiguous term whose technical meaning was only known by well-read sufis. Sirhindi explained that after perfecting the intimacy of friendship, the secret of Muhammad's situation was that the center of the circle of belovedness had been entrusted to him. The unique one returns to the world from the station of two great intimacies, that of being intimate with Muhammad and Moses, in order to protect and preserve the Muslim community. In the meantime, the Prophet regains his place in the retreat of Divine Mystery.[103] This is how Ahmad Sirhindi experienced himself as the pre-eminent sufi in the world and, by definition, the millennial renewer.

With the replication of prophetic perfections, via the station of belovedness, Sirhindi explicitly claimed the sixth degree of following the Prophetic sunnat out of the seven degrees he outlined in *Collected Letters*. In addition, he claimed that he had been able to transcend time through following the Prophetic sunnat to its ultimate (seventh) degree. "It is certain (from a conventional perspective) that the follower as uninvited guest and heir is other than the Prophet. Although (from a unitary perspective) they are both the same in the single-file process of imitation and following."[104] This path is open to all by cultivating the prophetic perfections through following the Prophetic sunnat assiduously and by performing the Mujaddidi contemplative practices. Muslims who are a thousand or more conventional years removed from the "golden age" of the Prophet's lifetime can partake of the same spiritual bounty as the Prophet's companions thanks to Sirhindi's sufi leadership.

The renewal process is an intensification of a common Muslim's access to the Prophetic bounty (the first degree of following the Prophetic sunnat in Sirhindi's schema). As Mircea Eliade has explained, humans are enabled to "collapse time" through religious ritual, creating a liminal timelessness, *in illo tempore*. The hajj ritual is a paradigmatic example in the Islamic tradition (incorporating the *axis mundi* of the Ka'ba). Living in accordance with the Prophetic sunnat is a way of re-enacting the sacred history of the Prophet and his companions. The sufi lodge, as I have explained elsewhere, is a ritual structure designed to intensify this re-enactment.[105] What Sirhindi has done is intensify the process of collapsing time through contemplative practice and restructuring one's life according to Prophetic guidelines.

Ahmad Sirhindi's mode of renewal paralleled that of Ibn al-'Arabi.

---

103. See ibid., 3.94.52-53.

104. See letter 2.54 translated in this book. In this letter he explains the seven levels of following the Prophet. It does not explicitly state that he has achieved the seventh level just like he never declared himself to be the renewer of the second millennium.

105. See Buehler, *Sufi Heirs*, 44-54.

These modes are revealed in Samuela Pagani's schema involving three modes of renewal: the *salafi* (from *salaf*, ancestor) mode of renewal; the *khalafi* mode of renewal (*khalaf*, descendant, successor); and its metahistorical variant, "*khalafi-sufi*" mode of revival. The *salafi* mode seeks to renew Islam via the sunnat using a "historicizing rationalism."[106] In its extreme form, *salafi*s ignore an entire millennium of Muslim experience by pretending that there was nothing of Islamic value since the standardization of the hadith literature in the ninth century. The *khalafi* mode of revival, following the consensus of Sunni jurists, values the continuous regeneration of the consensual values of Islamic societies in an expansion of Islamic tradition over time.[107] The *khalafi-sufi* mode of revival acknowledges that the Prophetic sunnat is "the metahistorical source from which all existent religious knowledge—even those "new" acquisitions which were not present at Muhammad's time—draws its ultimate origin and legitimacy."[108]

This third metaphysical *khalafi-sufi* mode of revival is not easy to comprehend. According to Sirhindi's formulation, the Prophet needs the help of his heir yet the perfection of the heir is only by virtue of the Prophet. This is a paradox, not only in terms of linear time, but also in how it overturns the explicit ontological superiority of prophets over non-prophets in Maturidi theology. Sirhindi's formulation is similar to Ibn al-'Arabi's, that is, Muhammad had to fully realize Abraham's intimacy to God, which occurred through the intermediary of the unique one.[109] Ibn Taymiyya's (d. 653/1255) linear response to Ibn al-'Arabi's paradoxical statement was, "Who comes before cannot 'take' from who comes later."[110] Both Sirhindi and Ibn al-'Arabi support their *khalafi-sufi* formulations by citing the precedent of Muslims increasing Muhammad's blessings through their supplication at the end of each ritual prayer. Sirhindi says,

> It is established that each perfection of the unique one [lit. follower (*ummat*)] will come easily to him and the prophet of that community will also realize that perfection. This is according to the dictum, 'Whoever puts a praiseworthy sunnat into practice.'[111] The Prophet, through

106. See Samuela Pagani, "Renewal before Reformism: 'Abd al-Ghani al-Nabulusi's Readings of Ahmad Sirhindi's Ideas on *Tajdid*" in *Journal of the History of Sufism* 5 (2007), 292, 307-308.

107. See ibid., 310-311.

108. See ibid.

109. See ibid., 313. The notion of a living person having an interdependence with the spirit of Muhammad also has Shi'i parallels. See ibid., 311.

110. Ibid., 313.

111. This is a shortened form of "Whoever puts a praiseworthy sunnat into practice will be rewarded for it as well as receive the reward of those who enact it." This longer form is cited four times in *Collected Letters*.

> the mediating of this unique one, will also benefit from the perfections of the circumference of this circle. He will also become perfected in the intimacy of friendship (*walayat-i khullat*). The supplication, "May God bless Muhammad as He has blessed Abraham" after a thousand years will be accepted and answered.[112]

In a similar way, the Prophet benefits from a praiseworthy sunnat being put into practice, underlining how the Muslim community increases the Prophet's blessings. In a paradoxical fashion, Muhammad relies upon his followers to become more perfected although no one can ever equal the Prophet because his perfection is always increasing as his sunnat is being put into action. In this context, Sirhindi is merely facilitating a *khalafi-sufi* renewal with principles common to all Sunni Muslims (ritual prayer and acting in accordance with the sunnat).

Examining Sirhindi's renewal efforts through the lens of *Collected Letters*, the picture is more straightforward. Sirhindi is seeking to "set things right." Part of that enterprise is for Muslims to follow, both inwardly and outwardly, the example of the Prophet. Sirhindi discusses minute details of Islamic orthopraxy, whether in ritual prayer or how to tie one's turban.[113] With ritual practice there is little wiggle room. Sirhindi wanted to preserve the prophetic heritage as he knew it while exemplifying the model of the juristic sufi. To be an authentic sufi, according to Sirhindi, one had to be a real jurist and vice versa. In the realm of sufi practice, Sirhindi did not want people to confuse any altered state of consciousness with being close to God. There was a shared established sufi consensus that carefully discerned and differentiated illusory shadows from the reality of the Essence. There were also precedents for less-than-optimal sufi practice. According to Sirhindi, too many contemporary sufis were fostering altered states of consciousness among their disciples and avoiding the necessary hard work needed to crush out-of-control egos. Sirhindi, over and over, in excruciating detail, explained and corrected sufi practice as Baqibillah had done for him. Much of this is the job of a qualified sufi shaykh, but Sirhindi felt himself called to speak out beyond his circle of disciples. This latter characteristic

---

112. See *Collected Letters*, 3.94.52-53.

113. For prayer details see ibid., 1.266.132-133 and 1.312. "[T]o leave the turban end untied and hang loosely is sunnat. There are many people, however, who have chosen to let the turban end hang on the left side. With this deed, it is intended to resemble a dead person. Many people have imitated this action without realizing that they are not only negating the sunnat, but replacing it with an innovation. They are even respected for it." Sirhindi, *Mabda' wa-ma'ad*, 85.

fits the profile of a renewer.[114]

Sirhindi's experience of the juristic establishment was largely that of self-aggrandizing, ego-driven jurists seeking to please their governmental patrons in order to acquire more power and money. Upright jurists, on the other hand, could and should pursue contemplative practice. In Sirhindi's juristic sufism, there was a seamlessness between post-rational experience and the dictates of Hanafi jurisprudence. Prophecy, prophetic hadith, and the prophetic path all had priority over ordinary intimacy with God (*walayat*) because the prophetic path was closer to God in Sirhindi's experience. Sobriety, following the sunnat at a higher level than common Muslims (second degree or above),[115] and correct creedal dogma became the touchstones of authentic spiritual experience. Juristic sufism was, as its name implies, friendly to upright jurists.

Joining shariat and sufism, Sirhindi endeavored to renew sufi practice by clarifying authentic practices and standards, which included adherence to scriptural norms and legal principles. This meant that jurists were to deepen their understanding and character through sufi practice. Sufis were expected to verify their contemplative experience and beautify their behavior by honoring shariat norms. Each of these realms of knowledge, juristic and sufi, were to be synthesized at a higher level of consciousness with correspondingly more beautiful behavior.

In addition, Sirhindi was a *sufi* renewer. There is a close connection with Sirhindi's perceived cosmic rank and being a renewer. The practice and realization of submitting to God involved the synthesis of the rational and the suprarational, the shariat and sufism. Sirhindi's synthesis can be symbolized by his emphasis on the unity of contemplative witnessing (*wahdat-i shuhud*) rather than the unity of being (*wahdat-i wujud*). The former was a formulation affirmed by Sirhindi's own experience, which he interpreted to be more harmonious and in accord with how things really were. Sirhindi opposed the marginalization of the shariat that he associated with narrow interpretations of reality in the guise of "unity of being." Thus, he apparently went against the Indian sufi consensus (which may or may not have been the narrow version of unity of being that Sirhindi opposed). In Sirhindi's sufi universe, one endeavored to integrate the Muhammadan Truth (*haqiqat Muhammadiyya*), the practical sunnat of the Prophet, and the Islamic shariat social norms that had been created over the last thousand years. In short, Sirhindi challenged the political, religious, and spiritual status quo. The prophetic parallel is clear.

---

114. It is easy to see why 'Abdulhaqq Muhaddith Dihlawi was also considered to be a renewer. His letters echo many of the complaints with the same Prophetic justifications as Sirhindi's. See his *Makatib wa-rasa'il* cited above.

115. Again referring to letter 2.54 in this book.

In his quest for pursuing the prophetic path, Shaykh Ahmad Sirhindi was always up against difficulties inherent in the quest itself. How can a non-prophet ever follow the prophetic path? How can one ever hope to ever be a companion of the Prophet if one is born one thousand years too late and four thousand kilometers too far away? In this regard, *khalafi-sufi* renewal provides the meta-historical and metaphysical realm to do things that confound juristic scholars like Ibn Taymiyya. Through contemplative practice and experiencing the Origin beyond space-time, one becomes like one of the Companions through traveling on the prophetic path and experiencing prophetic perfections.[116] The uninvited guest eats at the same table and partakes in their bounty. All are welcome, regardless of space-time constraints. As a hadith says, "[My community is like the rain]; I do not know who is better, the first or last among them."

After Sirhindi's death, Shah Waliullah (d. 1176/1762) reiterated eleven signs of renewal that "prove" Sirhindi to be the renewer of the seventeenth century. These include spreading many types of inner and outer religious knowledge, performing miracles, being recognized at the time as a renewer, explaining stations on the Naqshbandi path in unprecedented detail, bringing people to follow the shariat and follow the sufi path, being able to read the letters at the beginning of some Qur'anic verses, and his standing up for truth even if it meant being imprisoned by the ruler.[117] Shah Waliullah concludes by declaring Shaykh Ahmad Sirhindi to be the renewer of the eleventh century, which has been the consensus of Mujaddidi shaykhs ever since.

Dimensions of Ahmad Sirhindi's universe

In the translated letters to follow, the first section deals with relatively straightforward letters on shariat, sunnat, and jurists. The following sections include letters that detail Sirhindi's contemplative experiences and aspects of the sufi path. These latter sections include the most intricate and technical material in the book. Although each translated letter has an introduction corresponding to its level of complexity, the discussions assume a

116. The realization of prophetic perfections by following a prophet assiduously is also an element of Ahmadi prophetology. See Yohanan Friedmann, *Prophecy Continuous: Aspects of Ahmadi Religious Thought and its Medieval Background* (Berkeley: University of California Press, 1989), 105-119. Muhammad's companions and successors are written with a capital letter when preceded by the definite article.

117. See 'Abdulahad Wahdat Sirhindi, *Sabil al-rashad*, Urdu translation by Ghulam Mustafa Khan (N.p., 1979), 4-8. This is not Sialkoti's *Dala'il al-tajdid* as indicated by Iqbal Mujaddidi in "Hadarat Mujaddid-i Alf-i Thani ke dafa' men lik'hi jani wali kitaben," *Nur al-Islam* 33/1 (Jan-Feb, 1988), 47.

basic knowledge of the Naqshbandi path and cosmology. This section is a general overview for the more detailed discussions introducing the letters that follow.

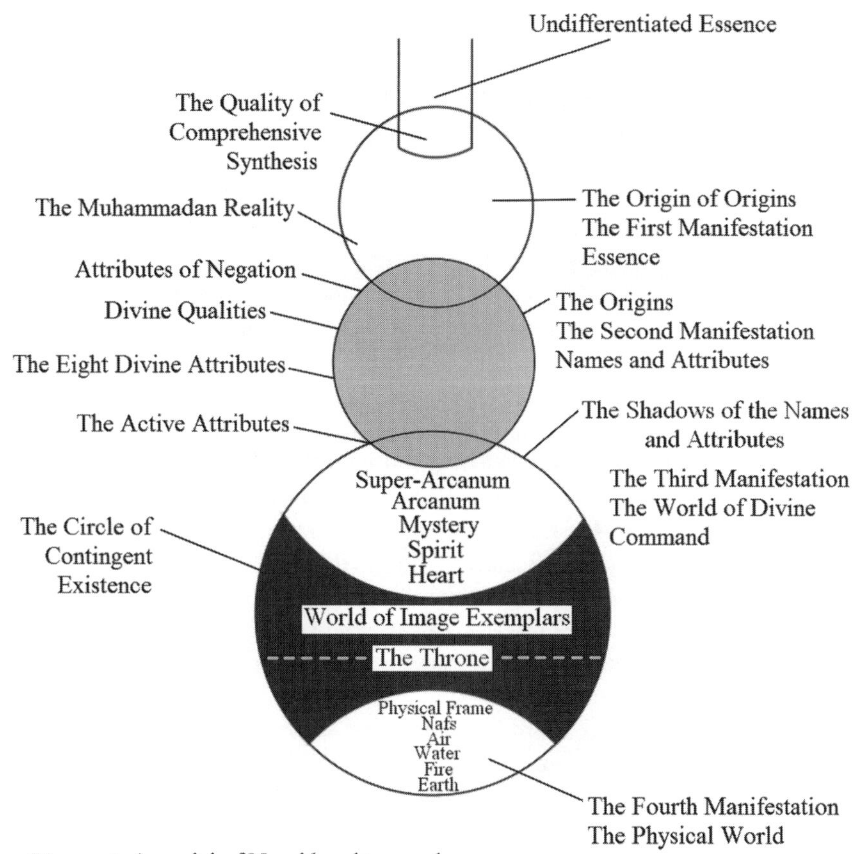

Figure 1. A model of Naqshbandī cosmology

The Macrocosm (see Figure 1)

A sufi aspirant is not a religio-cultural blank slate as she proceeds on the sufi path. Indeed, the Naqshbandi-Mujaddidi path is defined by the requisite articles of creedal faith and Islamic ritual practices in addition to the Mujaddidi cosmological conceptual map, pioneered by Ibn al-'Arabi.[118] Part of Naqshbandi wayfaring is having access to one's spiritual ancestors' wisdom and assistance, so there is good reason to stay connected and not veer too far from the well-trodden path of the Prophet Muhammad.

118. For a general overview, see William C. Chittick, "The Five Divine Presences: From al-Qunawi to al-Qaysari" in *Muslim World* 72/2 (April 1982), 107-128.

Contemplative witnessing is the method by which one transcends time and returns to the experiential roots of the Islamic tradition. It is a wide path in that it is open to all who agree with the assumptions and perform the practices. At the same time, it is a narrow path going directly to the goal. Guided Naqshbandi contemplative witnessing takes one to the metahistorical Prophetic source, Muhammad. Other paths go other places.

The Naqshbandi cosmological universe opens out from the Absolute undifferentiated Essence as the first entification (*ta'ayyun-i awwal*) emerges. It is also known as "the exalted pen," "the Muhammadan reality," and "the first Intellect." Also called the "relative essence," it functions as the source of divine energy for the spirit, mystery, arcanum, and superarcanum subtle centers associated with the human body and discussed below.[119] When Sirhindi talks about Essence (*dhat*) he means this first entification, the Muhammadan reality, sometimes called the divine world (*'alam-i lahut*).[120] It includes the interface (*barzakh*) between creation and undifferentiated Essence, the quality of comprehensive synthesis (*sha'n-i jami'*), which is collectively all God's attributes, qualities, and aspects. The second entification, sometimes called the world of omnipotence (*'alam-i jabarut*), contains God's names and attributes in addition to the active attributes which direct divine energy to the heart subtle center. Traveling in the names and attributes occurs in this entification. The third entification, usually called the world of divine command (*'alam-i amr*), is also called the world of angels or the world of sovereignty (*'alam-i malakut*). This is where the subtle centers associated with the human body are located. It is the domain of the shadows of the names and attributes.

The lower limit of this entification is the world of image-exemplars, the fourth entification and transitional intermediary zone between the world of command and the fifth entification, the world of corporeal bodies. The upper limit of the corporeal world is the Throne, below which are the two subtle centers of the physical frame and ego-self, the elements, humans, animals, plants, and minerals. The bottom circle is the circle of contingent existence and is the human realm, the confluence of the lower three entifications.

---

119. This is not obvious from Figure 1, which is misleading because about forty percent of the first entification overlaps with the second manifestation. The map is not the territory.

120. There is no fixed cosmological system. For example, Faqirullah Shikarpuri, whose modified diagram is Figure 1, equates non-differentiated Essence with the world of divinity. See Faqirullah Shikarpuri, *Maktubat-i Faqirullah,* ed., Mawlwi Karam Bakhsh (Lahore: Islamiyya Steam Press, n.d.), 30.

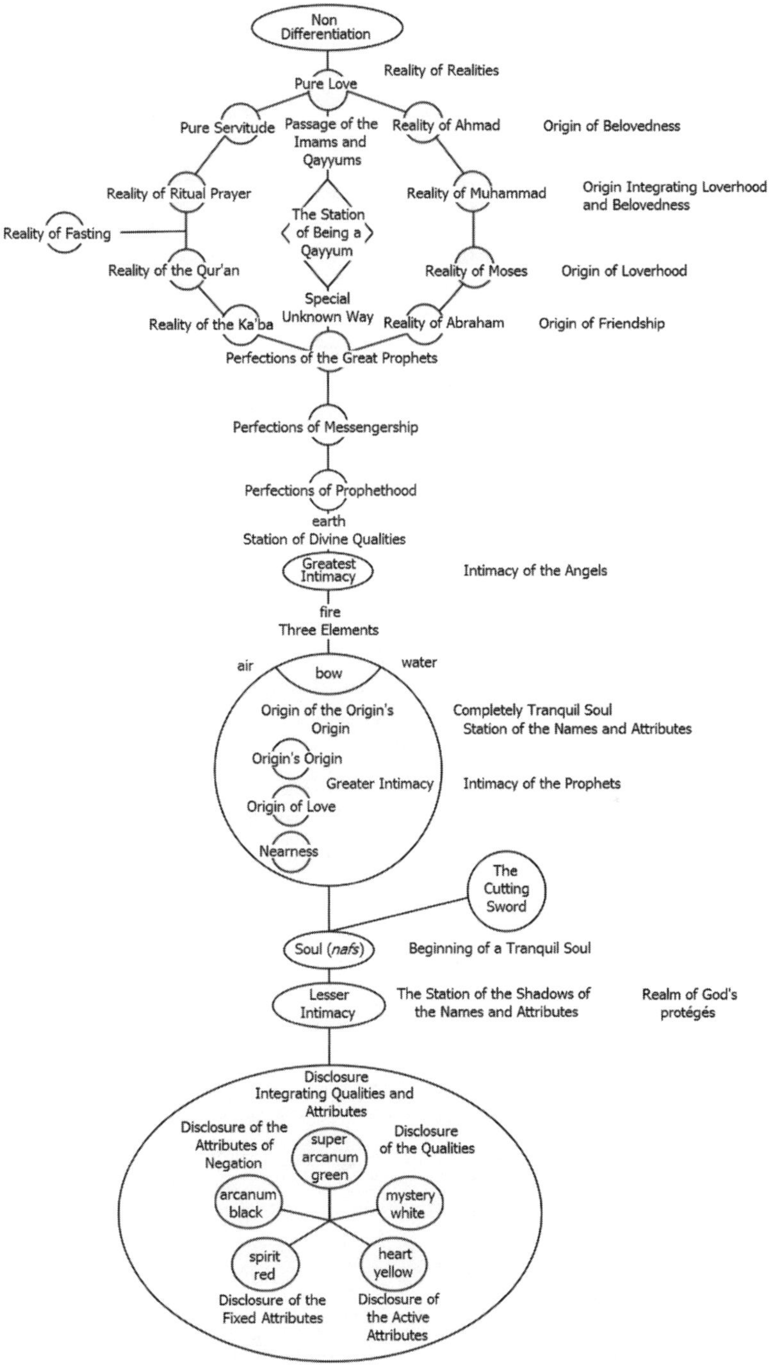

Non Differentiation
Reality of Realities
Pure Love
Pure Servitude
Passage of the Imams and Qayyums
Reality of Ahmad
Origin of Belovedness
Reality of Ritual Prayer
The Station of Being a Qayyum
Reality of Muhammad
Origin Integrating Loverhood and Belovedness
Reality of Fasting
Reality of the Qur'an
Reality of Moses
Origin of Loverhood
Special Unknown Way
Reality of the Ka'ba
Reality of Abraham
Origin of Friendship
Perfections of the Great Prophets
Perfections of Messengership
Perfections of Prophethood
earth
Station of Divine Qualities
Greatest Intimacy
Intimacy of the Angels
fire
Three Elements
air
bow
water
Origin of the Origin's Origin
Completely Tranquil Soul
Station of the Names and Attributes
Origin's Origin
Greater Intimacy
Intimacy of the Prophets
Origin of Love
Nearness
The Cutting Sword
Soul (*nafs*)
Beginning of a Tranquil Soul
Lesser Intimacy
The Station of the Shadows of the Names and Attributes
Realm of God's protégés
Disclosure Integrating Qualities and Attributes
Disclosure of the Attributes of Negation
super arcanum green
Disclosure of the Qualities
arcanum black
mystery white
spirit red
heart yellow
Disclosure of the Fixed Attributes
Disclosure of the Active Attributes

Figure 2 A model of the Mujaddidi path: the microcosm (adapted from Dhawqi, *Sirr-i dilbaran*, 201a)

The Microcosm[121]

The subtle realm associated with the human body, or what could be called subtle bodies, are expressed as *latifa*s, literally, subtleties. Two of them are located in the world of creation (the physical frame and the ego-self), and the other five are located in the world of command (heart, spirit, mystery, arcane, and superarcane). In a training environment, where aspirants need specifics, these subtle bodies are given locations on the body and are called "subtle centers" with colors associated with them. In reality, the locations and colors of these subtle centers varies widely from shaykh to shaykh. Faqirullah Shikarpuri (d. 1195/1781) explains that the five subtle centers of the world of command interpenetrate the physical body and are perceived according to the capacity of each individual wayfarer.[122] Each of these subtle centers is connected to a source of divine energy *(fayd)*, indicated in Figure 2.

The Mujaddidi Path[123]

To differentiate outer travel in the everyday world of form from its inner sufi counterpart in the subtle realms outlined above, sufis use a technical term "wayfaring" (*sayr*) which literally means "proceeding on the sufi path" or "wayfaring with beautiful behavior" (*sayr wa-suluk*). "Wayfarer" (*salik*) comes from the same Arabic root. Sirhindi has said that other sufis begin their wayfaring in the created world and end in the world of command, experiencing only lesser intimacy with God (*walayat-i sughra*). Naqshbandis begin in the world of command and end in the created world, hence their adage, "the end is included in the beginning." This is the prophetic path because the domain of the prophets is to invite others to God in the created world. The shariat is linked to the created world, and is brought to humans by prophets. The apparent "lowness" of the created world with respect to all the other, more subtle realms is only apparent. A person who returns from an ascent to the first entification is only outwardly in the world. Inwardly he is with God. This return to the world as the end of the path was already pioneered in the sufi world by Ibn al-'Arabi and 'Ala'uddawla Simnani.[124] The following

121. This brief section is so that readers can understand Sirhindi's letters. For a comprehensive treatment of the subject see Buehler, *Sufi Heirs*, 98-130. For some of the different locations of subtle centers see also Necdet Tosun, *Imâm-i Rabbânî Ahmed Sirhindî: Hayatı, Eserleri, Tasavvufî Görüşleri* (Istanbul: Insan Yayınları, 2005), 155.

122. See Faqirullah Shikarpuri, *Qutb al-irshad* (Quetta: Maktaba-yi Islamiyya, 1978), 565.

123. Though not technically a schema of the path, Letter 2.54 in this book deals with seven levels of sunnat that correspond to stages on the path.

124. See Hermann Landolt, "Le 'Double Èchelle' d'Ibn 'Arabi chez Simnani," in Mohammad Ali Amir-Moezzi, ed., *Le Voyage Initiatique en Terre d'Islam: As-*

description of the path is approximate because there are no discrete lines and points of arrival. If one looks at Figure 1, there are large overlaps between the entifications. These are examples of interfaces (sing. *barzakh*) that Sirhindi discusses in his letters. This means that there are many fuzzy boundaries, for example, between wayfaring to God and wayfaring in God, as well as between inner and outer wayfaring. The terms used and the figures in the book are only pointers. The map is not the experiential territory.

Before beginning spiritual wayfaring, a common person (by definition living in conventional consensus reality) is said to be in an ignorant state of abiding (*baqa'*). Everyday consensus reality is the mental realm preoccupied with linear, dualistic content. The inner and outer life of a common person does not go beyond the physical world. This is called the "first abiding." The Naqshbandi-Mujaddidi cyclical fourfold path begins by wayfaring to God (*sayr ila Allah*) in the world of command, the shadows of God's names and attributes. Wayfaring is nonlinear beyond time-space, eminently subjective and experiential, the realm of context that expands out to infinity. The first mode is outer wayfaring (*sayr-i afaqi*), going farther and farther, followed by inner wayfaring (*sayr-i anfusi*), going closer and closer. Finishing the latter mode roughly coincides with the completion of wayfaring to God (*sayr ila Allah*). Sirhindi associates much of this wayfaring to God with the wayfarer's experience of "unity of being" (*wahdat-i wujud*) where he says the majority of sufis get stuck. This is a place of ecstasy and often one is given conditional permission to teach at this point. Here the aspirant experiences God on the outside and the world on the inside.

Then one begins to proceed in the stage called "lesser intimacy with God" (*walayat-i sughra*), the closeness to God almighty attained by God's protégés along the path of "wayfaring in God" (*sayr fi'llah*), finally arriving at the end of the circle of shadows of the necessary names and leaving the circle of contingent existence. Continuing on, one arrives at the level of God's necessary names and attributes. This is the end of ascent in the "lesser intimacy of God" and is associated with what Sirhindi called "the unity of contemplative witnessing" (*wahdat-i shuhud*). The processes of annihilation and abiding in God (*fana'* and *baqa'*) are associated with this ascent.[125] At the summit of ascent one is with God both on the inside and outside. Sirhindi defines this as the end of the path of lesser intimacy with God (*walayat-i sughra*). If one continues, then there is only descent and the prophetic path begins.

The third part of the journey involves a descent "returning to the world of creation for God and by means of God" (*sayr 'an Allah billah*), the beginning of greater intimacy with God (*walayat-i kubra*). Now one begins to

censions cèleste et itineraries spirituals (Louvain-Paris: Peeters, 1996), 251-264.

125. See Ahmad Sirhindi, *Ma'arif-i laduniya*, ed. with Urdu translation by Zawwar Husayn Shah (Karachi: Idara-yi Mujaddidiyya, 1986), 63.

purify the spirit from the ego-self, associated with the station of separation after synthesis (*maqam al-farq ba'd al-jami'*).[126] This is when a person is once again able to recognize multiplicity (*farq* or separation of conventional objects) in conventional everyday reality after having the perception that "all is God" (called *jam'* or *jam'-i jam'*). The journey culminates in the fourth and last cycle, to live as an extraordinarily ordinary person in the created world (*sayr fi'l-ashya'*). Although one experiences the multiplicity of the world, it is experienced as a mirror of the One where unity is experienced in the multiplicity and multiplicity is experienced in the unity. This is the place where one is with God on both the inside and the outside, completely focussed on humanity. It is the "best of both worlds" where one can see with two eyes, the right eye of unity and the left eye of multiplicity.[127] It is following the prophetic path of inviting others to God and often called the second abiding in God.

KEY TO FIGURE 3.

1) Nasruddin in the market [the first abiding (*baqa'*)]
2) Nasruddin looking for his donkey [starting to deal with the ego-self]
3) Nasruddin finding footprints of the donkey [starting to work on the subtle centers]
4) Nasruddin finds the donkey [there is more awareness of the ego-self—the beginning of wayfaring to God]
5) Nasruddin catches his donkey though the donkey is recalcitrant [grappling full-on with the ego-self]
6) The donkey is calm following Nasruddin [the beginning of a tranquil ego-self]
7) Nasruddin is riding the donkey [a tranquil ego-self—the beginning of wayfaring in God]
8) This picture is just a white empty circle [beginning of separation of the spirit and ego-self from the heart—complete ascent and an experience of annihilation of the ego (*fana'*)]
9) Nasruddin walking back to town with no donkey [returning to the world of creation for God and by means of God]
10) The same picture as #1 [the second abiding—extraordinarily ordinary] in the bazaar

---

126. There is a discussion of this station in *Collected Letters*, 1.285.45-46 explaining how the spirit (*ruh*) is an interface between two aspects, form (*chun*) and formlessness (*be-chun*).

127. See Toshihiko Izutsu, *Creation and the Timeless Order of Things: Essays in Islamic Mystical Philosophy* (Ashland, OR: White Cloud Press, 1994), 19.

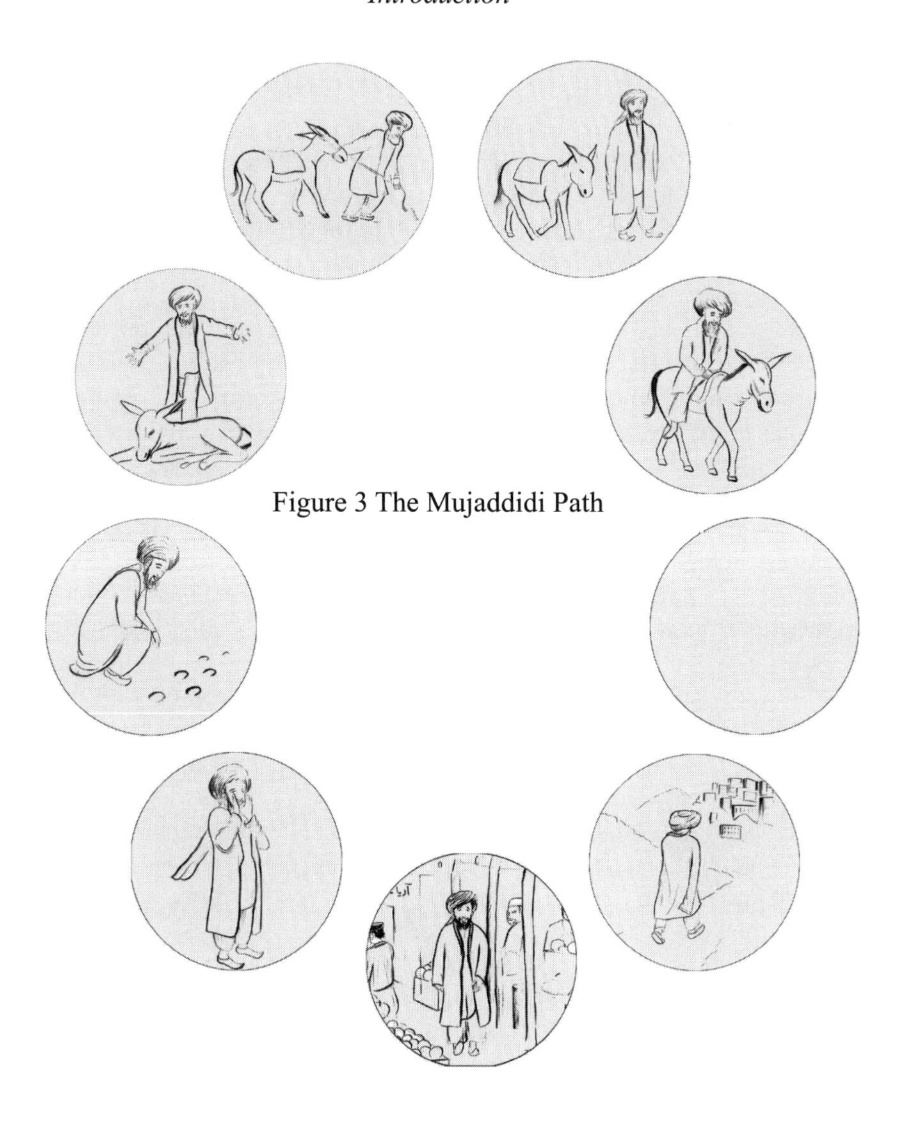

Figure 3 The Mujaddidi Path

> Perfected inner experiential knowledge is such that beyond it there is no inner experiential knowledge (*ma'rifat*).[128]
>
> Ibn al-'Arabi (quoted by Ahmad Sirhindi)

Ordinary knowledge and inner experiential knowledge

Shaykh Ahmad Sirhindi's precision of thought extends to epistemology. Throughout *Collected Letters* he differentiates two types of knowledge with

128. See Ahmad Sirhindi, *Ma'arif-i laduniya*, 23.

two distinct words: *'ilm* and *ma'rifat*. The first indicates a mental knowledge that is communicated through words, written or oral. The second is a kind of knowing stemming from one's own inner experience, which is further differentiated by levels of experience. Since these two words come up often in these letters, it is important to know how they are translated and why the distinction between them is so vital for Sirhindi. Hierarchical differences in reality are reflected in various modes of knowing. For Sirhindi there are qualitative differences between knowing at the level of mind and knowing at the level of spirit, though he uses another array of concepts and words to indicate the levels instead of "mind" and "spirit."

Long before Sirhindi, Dhu'l-Nun (d. 245/859) formulated a sufi epistemological framework based on inner non-linear experiential knowledge (*ma'rifat*) to differentiate it from the everyday linear knowledge (*'ilm*) of jurists.[129] Sirhindi continues this tradition by emphasizing the difference between ordinary everyday knowledge (*'ilm*) and inner experiential knowledge (*ma'rifat*), which he sometimes demarcates as acquired knowledge (*'ilm-i husuli*) and knowledge in the presence of God (*'ilm-i huduri*). Acquired knowledge is a rational, linear form of knowledge associated with the religious sciences transmitted down the ages from books and oral transmission. It is the knowledge of jurists. This is the knowledge concerned with the attributes of something, a transmitted knowledge that is "knowledge-about." We acquire this knowledge through the process of thinking about things, comparing propositions through internal dialogue, or contrasting images via internal vision. It is conceptual and representational knowledge, often called the knowledge of certainty (*'ilm-i yaqin*).[130] In an Islamic context, this is the received knowledge of shariat injunctions confirmed by juristic consensus. It is also the kind of knowledge that is generally taught in modern education, the received knowledge of a scientific-materialist paradigm.

Faith means that any doubt implied in received knowing has disappeared. The only way to eliminate doubt is to verify by experience. One has to know within. When one has come to really know and realize then faith arises. This is why I translate *ma'rifat* as inner experiential knowledge, often abbreviated as inner knowledge. Inner experiential knowledge is the knowledge of the thing in and of itself by experiencing its essential aspects (*i'tibarat-i dhatiya*). It is inner because one shuts out the outside world and turns off the incessant mental activity of the mind through the disciplined practice of contemplative witnessing. It is experiential because through contemplative witnessing one has an experience of post-rational, transpersonal aspects of being. Sirhindi specified two levels of this inner

129. Annemarie Schimmel, *Mystical Dimensions*, p. 6.

130. See letter 3.39 in this volume. Letters in this book also indicate alternate meanings of *'ilm-i yaqin* that go beyond the introductory material presented here.

experience: seeing something in a visionary experience with the eye of certainty (*'ayn-i yaqin*) and actually having the experience of *being* something with the reality of certainty (*haqq-i yaqin*). The former is the appearance of inner knowledge, and the latter is the reality of inner knowledge.[131] The eye of certainty involves "knowledge by acquaintance" with the quality of immediacy and direct encounter with the object of knowledge. The reality of certainty involves the three "upper realms" of God's attributes, qualities, and aspects.[132] In this domain, the inner knowledge of *ma'rifat* is that of utter bewilderment.[133] The person experiencing and the experience are one. Light fills the emptiness and there is no object. God is not an experience. Often Sirhindi calls people who have this kind of knowledge "verifiers" because they have found the truth within themselves and have verified it by witnessing and being it. He was very strict in this regard. For example, he asked forgiveness for saying something about the preference of the great prophets (*ulu' al-'azmi*) over other prophets, because it was something that he himself had not verified.[134]

Unlike seeing with one's physical eyes (*mushahada*), this witnessing is done contemplatively. Nor is it bearing witness to the oneness of God and Muhammad as God's messenger (*shahada*). Contemplative witnessing (*shuhud*) is experiencing in a post-rational state of consciousness. One is not using physical eyes because these are closed. Metaphorically one is using the eye of the heart. In physiological terms, perhaps we could say that the predominant beta brainwaves of everyday consensus reality are stilled, allowing theta or delta brainwaves to predominate. It is like stilling the ever-breaking waves of the mind and being able to perceive what is in the depths of the ocean through the surface stillness. There are many varieties of witnessing, but *contemplative* witnessing is a methodology that allows human beings to find out who they are. Contemplation is investigating what is all around with the mind stopped. It is the gateway to go beyond the mind (hence *post*-rational or *supra*rational) to what is said to be a universe incomparably vast when compared to the expanding physical universe. Contemplative witnessing is the methodology that allows every normally functioning human being to literally travel in the inner cosmos. Mind is the contents of consciousness and it identifies itself with these contents. This is part of the ego-self, the prison of identifying with the stuff of the mind. Contemplatively witnessing reminds us that we are not the mind/ego-self. It opens the human being to the content-less Infinite Context, commonly referred to as God.

---

131. See *Collected Letters,* 3.91.42.

132. See *Collected Letters,* 1.266.117.

133. See Sirhindi, *Ma'arif-i laduniya*, 30.

134. See *Collected Letters,* 1.209.108.

Both knowledge of certainty and knowledge of the eye of certainty are dualistic because there is a knower and something known. The reality of certainty, sometimes called "knowledge in the presence of God" (*'ilm-i huduri*), is also an inner experiential knowledge, but is a unitary way of knowing without a subject knowing an object. Sometimes a person with inner experiential knowledge is described as a "knower with God" (*'arif billah*). This carefully worded phrase means that one does not "have" knowledge of God but knows by being with and participating through God. One knows God only by means of God, or as Sirhindi says often in his letters, "Only the King's camel can carry the King's gifts."

The term "inner experiential knowledge," or *ma'rifat* as Sirhindi uses it, can overlap with both the eye of certainty and the reality of certainty. For example Abu Sa'id Abu'l-Khayr (d. 440/1049), "who experienced bewilderment, shows that he reached the station of inner knowledge (*maqam-i ma'rifat*). After realizing this station of bewilderment, there is the station of unitary knowledge (*ma'rifat*)."[135] Here I have translated *ma'rifat* differently because of the context. Although *ma'rifat*, is not a precise term, like many other words used in *Collected Letters* that point to inner experience, it clearly indicates that it is not rational knowledge communicated by others, whether through teaching or books. Instead, it is knowledge emanating from one's own inner post-rational experience, usually as a result of contemplative practice.

One can differentiate these three levels of knowing through the metaphor of fire. The first is knowing that there is a possibility of certainty (*'ilm-i yaqin*). This is equivalent to outer wayfaring (*sayr-i afaqi*). It is like seeing smoke and inferring that there is fire or hearing about fire. The next stage is perceiving certainty (*'ayn-i yaqin*). It is like seeing fire, but it is fleeting and does not stabilize. The final stage is the reality of certainty (*haqq-i yaqin*). It is *being* fire. These last two stages are in the domain of inner wayfaring (*sayr-i anfusi*). At the higher reaches of inner wayfaring one experiences the reality of certainty involving an abiding in God at the level of the Essence in helplessness and bewilderment. It is simply beyond physical human perceptual awareness.[136] This sufi structure of knowledge has little to do with the experiences of those involved in gnosticism(s), so-called "gnostics." Nor does it involve gnosis, all of which of which are markers of *dualism*. Since Islam is explicitly not a dualistic tradition, such terms do not have a place when studying a tradition like Islam, which focuses on declaring the oneness of God (*tawhid*).[137]

---

135. See letter 1.290 in this volume.

136. See Muhammad Sa'id Ahmad Mujaddidi, *al-Bayyinat*, 522-524.

137. See Ioan Culianu, *Tree of Gnosis* (New York: Harper Collins, 1992). He notes some of the many cases of confused usages of the term in Islamic Stud-

> One should never make the mistake of saying that one can dispense with the appearance and reality of the shariat and that there is no need to bother with the injunctions of the shariat. We say that shariat is the foundation of all that we do and how we interact with others.[138]
>
> Shaykh Ahmad Sirhindi

Shariat in Sirhindi's juristic sufism

Shariat has a root meaning of "the path to the water hole." For a herd of sheep or goats, there is usually never only one path to the water hole. Instead there is a maze of parallel paths all converging on the water hole. Shariat has also worked this way as independent jurists from various regions and locales have found many alternative legal solutions. Each Sunni legal school functions as an interpretive community that puts limits on how far one can stray on the way to the water hole. This is decided by the consensus of jurists of any given jurisprudential community over time.

In the context of *Collected Letters*, *shari'at*, the Persian version of the Arabic (and now English) shariah, has a range of multivalent meanings, which is why I have not translated it in its dictionary meaning as "canonical Islamic law." In an everyday context, shariat involves articles of faith (*i'tiqadat*) and guidelines for proper ritual and worldly behavior (*'amal*) that a consensus of jurists has formulated.[139]

After Muhammad died, there was a juristic vacuum and proto-jurists developed methodologies for future jurists to utilize in various cultures and times. These guidelines cumulatively became shariat in order to deal with situations that did not have a specific Prophetic precedent easily found in the Qur'an or hadith literature. There are four hierarchical sources in Sunni jurisprudence. The most authoritative are the Qur'an and the six canonical Sunni hadith collections.[140] If a jurist cannot find the legal solution there, he consults the third source, prior juristic consensus. If there still is no resolution, then, as a qualified jurist, there is the least authoritative fourth option,

---

ies, including Massignon and Corbin, in his definitive treatment of the subject in "Gnosticism from the Middle Ages to the Present" in Mircea Eliade, ed., *The Encyclopedia of Religion*, 15 vols. (New York: MacMillan, 1987), 5:574-578.

138. See *Collected Letters,* 2.50.138. Cf. the quote later in this section from Ibid, 1.172, translated in this book.

139. Here I am using Sirhindi's definition of shariat in *Collected Letters,* 3.17.29.

140. These are: *Sahih Bukhari*, *Sahih Muslim*, Nasa'i's *Sunan al-Sughra, Sunan Abu Da'ud, Sunan al-Tirmidhi*, and either Malik's *Al-Muwatta or Sunan Ibn Majah*. Bukhari's and Muslim's hadith compendia are considered the most authoritative.

making an independent legal judgment.[141] A jurist qualified to make that judgment will not linger too far off the path on the way to the waterhole of a legal decision.

Sirhindi's juxtaposes these juristic sources with four sufi sources of knowledge: inspiration (*ilham*), unveilings (sing. *kashf*), states (*ahwal* sing. *hal*) and ecstasy (*wajd*). These latter sources for sufism are not even half as trustworthy as shariat sources according to Sirhindi.[142] Any realization of inner knowledge (*ma'rifat*) acquired outside the shariat is only conjecture and guessing.[143] It is only when a sufi has progressed to greater intimacy with God (*walayat-i kubra*) that his inspirations and unveilings can be trusted because this is the level of prophetic intimacy with God.[144] He says, "The fruits of the reality of shariat are the perfections of prophethood; shariat comes from the level of prophethood."[145] If there are any conflicts between sufi sources of knowledge and juristic sources, the latter have precedence.

In Sirhindi's juristic sufism, the domain of the shariat expands to include the inner work involving the sufi path (*tariqat*) and reality (*haqiqat*). Conventionally, shariat, the sufi path, and reality are considered three different domains, but for Sirhindi they are one. These three domains fit together using the example of lying. Not lying is following the shariat. But not having the inclination to lie is the realm of the sufi path and reality. If the inclination not to lie comes with difficulty then one is still on the path to reality. If this inclination not to lie is effortless, then one is in the domain of reality. In this way, inner character development completes and perfects the outer shariat. Inner work needs to come first. How can someone be truthful or honest if she does not know what truth or honesty is? If someone is not in touch with the love in his heart where will the compassionate come from? Without the inner being prepared, for one to put on the appearances of truthfulness or honesty is hypocrisy. There is no way for change to come from the outside to the inside. By changing the inner, the outer changes automatically.

Sirhindi's juristic sufism has only one domain: the shariat, which is equal to the sum of submitting to God (*islam*), faith (*iman*), and behaving in a beautiful manner or being virtuous (*ihsan*). This is how Gabriel's hadith specified *din* (usually translated as religion).[146] The shariat is the organizing

141. See *Collected Letters,* 1.217.125.

142. See *Collected Letters,* 1.217.125.

143. See *Collected Letters,* 3.122.141.

144. See *Collected Letters,* 1.84.78. The reality of certainty (*haqq-i yaqin*) is the same level as greater intimacy with God.

145. See *Collected Letters,* 2.50.137.

146. Gabriel's hadith is discussed in Buehler, *Sufi Heirs*, 4-5.

principle for all of Islamic life. Nothing is outside of the shariat.[147] "Until these three dimensions of the shariat are experienced one cannot say that the shariat is confirmed. When it is, one reaches satisfaction of God."[148] Perfection of the shariat is acting in a beautiful manner (*ihsan*). Sirhindi notes that he was on the sufi path for ten years before he realized the reality of the situation (the multi-dimensionality of shariat).[149] "Reality (*haqiqat*) and the sufi path are the reality and the path of shariat. Shariat is not distinct from reality or the sufi path or vice versa. That is apostasy and infidelity," says Sirhindi.[150] The difference between shariat and reality is that shariat is associated with knowing the comprehensive nature of something (*ijmal*), using logical deduction, and concealing inner realities while reality is associated with knowing the detailed nature of things (*tafsil*), unveiling (*kashf*), and seeing inner realities.[151]

In Sirhindi's juristic sufism, the benefits of recollecting God (*dhikr*) are directly related to enacting the shariat injunctions, both obligatory acts and recommended ones (*sunan*) in addition to avoiding what is forbidden or doubtful.[152] Enacting shariat injunctions is ten times more important to sufi wayfarers than for others because a sufi's ascent is dependent on living fully in accordance with the shariat. Those who have inner knowledge and realization (*'arifan*) realize immediate tangible benefits from the shariat. The common people expect these benefits in the Hereafter.[153] In response to the sufi phrase that the shariat is the shell and reality is the kernel, Sirhindi asks, "What do people know of the perfections of the shariat? They parrot the dualistic clichés of kernel and shell (that is, the shariat being the shell and reality being the kernel) and are proud of intoxicated sufis and fascinated with states and stations."[154] "They deny the experience of the shariat that comes from the shariat's essence."[155]

Shariat is the joining together of the appearance and the reality. The ap-

---

147. See *Collected Letters,* 1.40.104.

148. See *Collected Letters,* 1.36.98. Note that the shariat is associated with the prophetic path of *nubuwat*, not the path of intimacy with God, *walayat.*

149. See *Collected Letters,* 1.36.98.

150. See *Collected Letters,* 1.57.30. Here is the tension between intoxication of annihilation in God, privileging an ascent beyond conventional consensus reality (*fana' fi 'llah*) and the sobriety of remaining in God (*baqa' bi 'llah*) involving a descent from the intoxicated heights, firmly rooted in everyday life.

151. See *Collected Letters,* 1.84.77.

152. See *Collected Letters,* 1.190.77.

153. See *Collected Letters,* 1.276.27.

154. See *Collected Letters,* 1.40.104.

155. See *Collected Letters,* 2.18.46. This passage does not specify what this essence is.

pearance is the outer aspect of shariat and the reality is the inner aspect of shariat. The superficial jurists (*'ulama'-i zahir*) are content with the outer aspect while the well-grounded jurists (*'ulama'-i rasikhin*) join the inner and outer.[156] According to Baha'uddin Naqshband (d. 791/1389, the founder-figure of the Naqshbandiyya), the goal of sufi wayfaring is that comprehensive inner knowledge becomes detailed, and that the logically proved juristic guidelines become revealed in one's unveilings. There is to be total harmony between shariat and sufi experience, a situation that occurs in the station of veracity (*maqam-i siddiqiyat*).[157]

Well-grounded jurists have the knowledge of both the appearance and essence of the shariat with a totally tamed ego-self (*nafs*).[158]

> Like the prophets they have achieved annihilation and abiding in God without attraction to God or following the sufī path. These jurists have verified the reality of the shariat, which is the reality of imitating the prophets.[159]

According to Sirhindi, Baha'uddin Naqshband did not say there was any special knowledge beyond that of shariat.

> From inspirations (*kashf* and *ilham*) one can learn about the shariat, like the prophets did with revelations. In truth, the opinions of jurists are more praiseworthy than the gibberish expounded by intoxicated sufīs. The jurists who are folk of God (*ahl-i haqq*) know the ineffability of God and do not confuse what they are experiencing in their imaginations with the Reality of God in the first entification (*ta'ayyun-i awwal*). Therefore, jurists are in a higher stage overall than sufīs.[160]

Sirhindi's emphasis on the shariat is mirrored by his focus on the superiority of the prophetic path. We can see that Sirhindi's perspective does not allow for separate notions of shariat, sufi path, or reality. They are hierarchical dimensions of the one reality. Sirhindi turned the common ideas of sufism upside-down. What is usually thought of as inferior can actually be superior, for example, the element earth. As one goes through the various levels of ascent,

> the element of earth is the most privileged element. In the stations of descent it becomes the lowest of all. So why is it that the element of earth becomes privileged at all when its natural place is to be the lowest

156. See *Collected Letters,* 1.276.27.
157. See *Collected Letters,* 1.41.4.
158. See *Collected Letters,* 2.18.46.
159. See *Collected Letters,* 2.54.7.
160. See *Collected Letters,* 1.130.82.

> element? In its fall to the lowest of low, calling people to God becomes perfected.[161]

Calling people to God occurs in the everyday world, the world where shariat organizes human life.

Typically, the goal of sufism is ascent to God, that is, becoming close to God. In Sirhindi's juristic sufism, this goal is only for beginners. The sufi goal for Sirhindi is to return transformed to this world because human completion/perfection is manifested in the material world.[162] At first glance, this is contradictory and paradoxical because the material world is cosmologically the farthest from God, and earth is the coarsest element of all (cf. Satan refusing to bow to a being of clay in Qur'an 38:71-85). Sirhindi's sufi goal is related to his emphasis on shariat. What appears to be reducing the scope of contemplative practice is actually setting higher standards for authentic realization. The realm of the body, the element of earth, is the last and most difficult aspect of a person to be transformed by contemplative practice. (It is as if he is addressing some new-age versions of sufism whose sphere of activity never goes beyond altered states of consciousness and the feeling of "being one with God.") According to Sirhindi, those having these types of ecstatic experiences, whom he called *wujudi*s, were in a deluded transcendental escape. Superficial jurists, without any connection to their hearts, were blinded by their petty concerns. Sirhindi expanded shariat to include contemplative practice as he grounded contemplative practice in everyday life—a juristic sufism synthesizing the best of both worlds.

Sirhindi rhetorically asks whether it is possible to go beyond the shariat. Predictably, he answers,

> The shariat consists of outward actions connected in this world to a person's inner being. Outer behavior is always occupied with the shariat, but the inner person also engages this matter. When the material world is the sphere of action, the inner person is of great assistance in outer deeds. The development of the inner person is tied to compliance with the shariat, which in turn is connected to outward behavior. In the material world, there is no way the inner and outer person can get around the shariat. Outer action is done in accordance with the shariat while the inner benefits result from adherence to the shariat. The shariat is the cause of all perfections and the basis of all the stations one passes through. The fruits of the shariat are not limited to this world.

---

161. See *Collected Letters,* 1.260: 81. Here the discussion is about the element earth, not the world (*dunya*). Letter 1.260 is translated in this book.

162. See Buehler, *Sufi Heirs*, 100. Ansari, *Sufism and Shari'ah*, 239-242 underlines how serving God by serving humanity (the prophetic path) is preferable to just experiencing "being at one" with God.

> The perfections of the next world and its eternal enjoyments result from the shariat.[163]

On the other hand, there are exceptions. Sirhindi asks rhetorically,

> So what does it mean to be independent of the shariat? The reality of the shariat does not pass beyond the spirit (*ruh*) and mystery (*sirr*) subtle centers nor does it reach to the arcane (*khafi*) or superarcane (*akhfa*) subtle centers. (Here he is referring to the cosmological locations of those centers through which one travels in the world of command; see Figure 1). Those who do go outside the shariat are in reality those who are [experiencing] the arcane and superarcane subtle centers. God almighty knows best the truth of the situation."[164] If one is in these subtle centers, following the shariat is no longer obligatory but praiseworthy (*mustahabb*). Since Naqshbandis do not neglect doing what is praiseworthy, this means that they strive to live in accordance with the reality of the shariat and advise others to do so also.[165]

If one cannot go beyond the shariat in the heart, spirit, and mystery subtle centers, then to what extent do the infinite non-linear possibilities of the inner world become limited by the necessarily finite boundaries of any set of linear creedal injunctions? Rationally, it does not appear that there is any relationship between subjective inner development, the result of contemplative practice, and a shariat that apparently deals with outer personal ritual behavior as well as outer interpersonal behavior. Baqibillah provides a clue, saying that shariat injunctions are not a rational matter. He states, "the mind (*'aql*) has difficulty with shariat obligations."[166] From sufi reports, including letters in this book, the Mujaddidi path has been formulated to use the shariat as a way to break down and tame the ego-self. Shariat is interwoven with Naqshbandi practice.

The sticky point, difficult to support in terms of human development or in terms of the infinite possibilities of spiritual experience, is the Sunni creedal emphasis on prophets being ontologically superior to other human beings. Ibn al-'Arabi responds to this doctrinal limit on consciousness development by saying, "This news is a terrible blow for the *awliya'*, for it

---

163. See *Collected Letters,* 2.46. 129. This letter is translated in this book. Ansari, *Sufism and Shari'ah*, 80-83, briefly discusses this aspect of shariat and sufism.

164. In letter 1.172 in this book.

165. Nasrullah Hutaki, *Sharh-i Maktubat-i qudsi ayat* (Peshawar: Taj Mahal Company, ca. 1976), 264.

166. Baqibillah, *Kulliyat*, p . 85.

implies the impossibility of experiencing total and complete servitude."[167] In addition, the Sunni consensus, in spite of the Qur'an stating that there is no preference between prophets [Q. 2.285], declares a special rank for Muhammad as the Seal of the Prophets. This means that Muhammad is the most perfect and complete human being that has ever been or will ever be. One of the many things that Ibn al-'Arabi and Sirhindi have in common is their pressing the boundaries of this creedal limitation, a cause of alarm for many jurists. For example, Sirhindi says that "[t]he distinction between the follower and the one being followed (Muhammad) basically is not seen."[168] This is like Ibn al-'Arabi differentiating legislative prophethood (which ended with Muhammad) from general prophethood (which is equivalent to Sirhindi's "greater intimacy with God").[169] Sirhindi, perhaps intentionally, avoided one aspect of controversy by explicitly honoring the prophetic path over the path of the protégés of God. His juristic sufism explicitly eliminated the possibility of any kind of prophethood being possible in the post-Muhammad era. Although Sirhindi sidestepped this kind of controversy, it simply morphed into other types of opposition.[170]

The goal of Sirhindi's juristic sufism was to get as many people as close to God as soon as possible and then to return to everyday life and invite people to God, the realm of the shariat. Unlike Ibn al-'Arabi who elucidated a comprehensive, exhaustive compendium of "all" perspectives, Sirhindi set up a mentoring infrastructure to continue his new sufi training methods throughout the eastern Islamic world. This juristic sufism operated in a straightforward manner, from emphasizing correct tenets of faith and daily Islamic practice to teaching a series of graded contemplative practices. Metaphorically, the Mujaddidi system is like a streamlined express train to get an aspirant closer to God. This express train is the shariat. It includes sincerely praying five times a day, without which, one will never have the opportunity to experience the heavenly ascension of Islamic ritual prayer.[171] There are no guarantees of quick arrival, but the necessary condition is to be on the train. Here is where the apparent narrowness and rigidity

---

167. Michel Chodkiewicz, *Seal of the Saints: Prophethood and Sainthood in the Doctrine of Ibn 'Arabi*, translated from the French by Liadain Sherrard (Cambridge, UK: Islamic Texts Society, 1993), 51.

168. In letter 2.46 in this book.

169. See Michel Chodkiewicz's excellent treatment of this subject in *Seal of the Saints*.

170. The controversy against Sirhindi in the Hijaz first occurred from within a Sufi environment. See Pagani, "Renewal before Reformism, 297.

171. See letter 2.46 in this book.

of the shariat come into play like train tracks.[172] In Sirhindi's juristic sufism, shariat is the vehicle and is intimately connected with the destination.

Sirhindi has formulated a method that integrates the domains beyond the phenomenal world, which go as deep/high as the Essence, with the domains of the phenomenal world, all the way down to the so-called lowest element of the lowest realm, earth. Not only is one developing subjectively through contemplative practice, but one is becoming a harmonious member of Islamic society (shariat orders society in an Islamic way) and transforming one's relationships within that society. The completion-bestowing person who is able to realize this goal *simultaneously* experiences the Essence where there is no differentiation along with experiencing the phenomenal world of rankings and hierarchies of context where one effortlessly commands the good and forbids evil. In *Collected Letters*, this is described as being with the world on the outside while being with God inside.[173]

Sirhindi explains the limitations of choosing either one of these paths rather than integrating both. On one hand, *wujudi*s privilege the Absolute, but it is only the merciful (*jamali*) attributes of God that suit them and fuel their intoxication. They perceive God to be the sum total of all created things (even though God existed before all these created things). According to Sirhindi, their delusional experience of God's immanence becomes an ego boost, as they disregard their servanthood in relation to the ultimate transcendence and mystery of God. In this lopsided preoccupation with the Absolute, they think the world is an illusion so one can behave as one desires. It is the ego-self running rampant. On the other hand, the superficial jurists preach hellfire and brimstone, emphasizing God's wrathful (*jalali*) attributes in an attempt to coerce people into following shariat guidelines through fear. Like the contemporary Salafi/Wahhabi enterprise, it collapses the multidimensional path to God into a flatland of rules and regulations to be obeyed.[174] Sirhindi's juristic sufism avoids these two unbalanced extremes by integrating the shariat, the sufi path, and reality in a grounded love under the canopy of the shariat. It is a juristic-sufi synthesis that is based on Sirhindi's own inspired contemplative experience.

---

172. The Naqshbandi path, in its glorious non-linearity, is trackless after the ego-self is reigned in.

173. Cf. a description of Ibn al-'Arabi's universe whereby "people are absent from God as long as they are present with creation." See William C. Chittick, "Presence with God," *Journal of the Muhiyuddin Ibn Arabi Society* 20 (1996) http://www. ibnarabisociety.org.uk/articles/presence.html accessed 30 May 2009. In Sirhindi's case the prophetic path is not an either/or proposition.

174. See Khalid Abou El-Fadl, *The Great Theft: Wrestling Islam from the Extremists* (San Francisco: Harper, 2005).

Sirhindi and the unity of God[175]

> Saying "All is God" is because of the various manifestations of God, not that it is the Essence of God in Reality, because the manifestations of God almighty are from God. So the meaning of "All is God" and "All is from God" become one. The differences in linguistic expression are because of the differences in perspective.[176]
>
> Shaykh Ahmad Sirhindi

Recognizing the unity and oneness of God, the unity of faith (*tawhid-i imani*), is the first part of the attestation of faith, "There is no god but God." This statement declares God to be one, and as such is a statement of *tawhid*, the verbal noun of the factitive form of the verb "to be singular/unique." This is a starting point to perceive things as they ultimately are, not as they appear to be in all their dizzying multiplicity. To become a formal Muslim one recites this attestation of faith verbally and in one's heart along with the second part, "and Muhammad is God's messenger." Sufis seek to go beyond this affirmation to actually experience this oneness, which in sufism is often called "the unity of being" (*wahdat-i wujud*).

Sirhindi's father 'Abdulahad had explained the ideas of the unity of being in the course of their mutual reading of Ibn al-'Arabi's *Bezels of Wisdom*.[177] 'Abdulahad had studied Ibn al-'Arabi's teachings with his Chishti-Sabiri shaykhs. In addition, Sirhindi's Chishti-Sabiri contemporaries in northern India avidly read and taught Ibn al-'Arabi's books.[178] [e.g., 'Abdurrazzaq J'hanj'hanawi (d. 949/1542),[179] 'Abdul'aziz Dihlawi (aka

---

175. Both ter Haar in his *Follower and Heir of the Prophet*, 117-136, and Tosun, *Imâm-i Rabbânî Ahmed Sirhindî*, 88-112, discuss these topics in much more detail.

176. Ahmad Sirhindi, *Sharh-i ruba'iyat-i Khwaja Baqibillah*, ed., Thana'l-haqq Siddiqi (Karachi: Educational Press, 1966), 36. This commentary was not written in the early stages of Sirhindi's sufi experience since it mentions *Mabda' wa-ma'ad*, written around 1019/1610.

177. Sirhindi probably studied Muhyiddin Ibn al-'Arabi's *Meccan Revelations*, the *Futuhat al-Makkiyya*, first printed in 4 vols. (Cairo: Bulaq, 1911). In *Collected Letters*, 2.58 Sirhindi comments on the hundred thousand Adams mentioned in Ibn al-'Arabi's *Futuhat*, 3: 348, 549.

178. For a very general overview, see William C. Chittick, "Notes on Ibn al-'Arabi's Influence in the Subcontinent," *The Muslim World* 82/3-4 (1992), 218-241. None of the following Chishti-Sabiris are mentioned except Muhibbullah Ilahabadi.

179. See Hasani, *Nuzhat al-khawatir*, 4:152-154.

Shakarbar) (d. 975/1566),[180] and Muhammad b. Fadlullah Burhanpuri (d. 1029/1620), and after Sirhindi, Muhibbullah Allahabadi (d. 1058/1648)].[181] In any case, Sirhindi would not have come upon the term *wahdat-i wujud* in any of Ibn al-'Arabi's books, because it was a term coined by later followers. After the time of Ibn Taymiyya (d. 653/1255), however, Ibn al-'Arabi's opponents latched on to that term to such a degree that Ibn al-'Arabi and *wahdat-i wujud* became synonymous. Sirhindi's perception of the unity of God is based upon his own contemplative experience and its subsequent interpretation in light of *other* sufis' experience of unity.[182] It is the later (mostly) non-sufi commentators who have reified this experience by associating it with a dogma, creed, philosophy, ideology, or doctrine. I have chosen the letters in this book to highlight Sirhindi's insights so that his experiences can be understood within their primary context, the post-rational domain of contemplative experience.

Under the tutelage of Baqibillah, Sirhindi finally had his own breakthroughs in contemplative experience that changed his life. He experienced the apparent ontological unity of being that his father had taught him from books. A common way of explaining this experience conceptually is to compare everyday consensus-reality consciousness with a dark night and a sky full of stars, representing multiplicity.[183] In the beginning stages of successful sufi practice, one is ecstatically confronted with bright sunlight, representing unity. With the resulting intoxication, the aspirant only sees the sun and thinks that there is nothing else in existence except the sun. Experientially, the multiplicity of the conventional phenomenal world disappears and one interprets God to be everything. With the collapse of the ego-self, one's consciousness becomes ecstatically drowned in the ocean of God. When the aspirant necessarily comes back to everyday consensus reality (though there are occasional instances of people not returning), the world of multiplicity is interpreted as illusion. From here, it is a very short

---

180. See Ibid., 160-162.

181. In the only published work of Muhibbullah Ilahabadi, *Manazir akhass al-khawass*, ed. Muhammad Tahir Ali (Santiniketan: Vishva Bharati Research Publications, 1993), there is mention of 'Ala'uddawla Simnani (p. 28) once. No mention is made of *wahdat-i shuhud*.

182. William Chittick has an intriguing idea that Sirhindi's emphasis on the unity of contemplative witnessing was to foil the opponents of *wahdat-i wujud*. I would rephrase this observation to say that Sirhindi's use of this perspective opened up the possibility of sufi practice for more jurists. See Chittick's "Rumi and *wahdat al-wujud*," in *Poetry and Mysticism in Islam: The Heritage of Rumi*, eds., Amin Banani, Richard Hovannisian, and Georges Sabagh (New York: Cambridge University Press, 1994), 90.

183. Sirhindi uses this metaphor in letter 1.43.6-7.

step to consider shariat practices superfluous. Sirhindi called the sufis who interpreted the phenomenal world as illusion and/or who mistakenly interpreted these experiences as experiences of God "*wujudi*s."

Baqibillah made sure that Sirhindi went beyond this stage as soon as possible.[184] From there, Sirhindi was able to experience both multiplicity and unity, in other words, he saw both the stars and the sun, and could discern between them. Finally he was able to see the sun and stars separately, as one does in conventional consensus reality. What had changed in the interim between these experiences was that he had become a transformed human being. With this realization, Sirhindi noted that large numbers of sufis were ending their journey thinking that the sun-only version of unity was the end of the path. It distressed him that they were interpreting their unity-of-being experience as an experience of God. Sirhindi had conclusively confirmed through experience what his mentor had told him, namely that they were merely experiencing the shadows of the attributes of God. Even more distressing was their increasing disregard for the shariat injunctions.

It is important to remember not to project Sirhindi's stance against *wujudi* sufis and *their* version of the unity of being on to Ibn al-'Arabi, who probably would have agreed wholeheartedly with Sirhindi's critique. On the practical day-to-day level, Sirhindi's main work, unlike that of Ibn al-'Arabi, was teaching and supervising the teaching of a large number of disciples. In that pedagogical context, Sirhindi perceived the learning challenges found in his disciples, one of which he called "asserting the unity of being" (*tawhid-i wujudi*). To deal with this learning impediment he emphasized the unity of contemplative witnessing (*wahdat-i shuhud*), namely that the unity one experienced was *subjective*, not ontological. In this way, the phenomenal world was not just trivialized as a figment of one's subjective imagination, along with the shariat. When one came out of contemplation, the world was the world. In contemplation God was God. This perspective of unity explicitly honored God's ultimate incommensurability, which might have attracted more jurists into learning about sufism.

The term "unity of contemplative witnessing" (*wahdat-i shuhud*) was first popularly used by 'Ala'uddawla Simnani (d. 736/1336). Sirhindi, however, uses this technical term in his own way on the basis of his own experiences and the needs of his students. When studies of Simnani and Sirhindi are sufficiently well advanced, we might be able to determine any affinity, if any, there is between the two. Sirhindi primarily objected to the perspective of the unity of being on the basis of his contemplative experience, while Simnani objected to this perspective for juristic reasons (see letter 2.42 in this book). There is a temptation to equate Simnani's and Sirhindi's thinking because of their differences with Ibn al-'Arabi (which are usu-

184. This is detailed in letter 1.290 in this book.

ally more apparent than real).[185] Citing Simnani in 'Abdurrahman Jami's (d. 898/1492) *Fragrances of Intimacy*, Baqibillah sardonically noted that Simnani had agreed with Ibn al-'Arabi when he had experienced what Ibn al-'Arabi had discussed, but disagreed with Ibn al-'Arabi over what he had not experienced.[186] Perhaps he is obliquely teaching Sirhindi, who might have been grappling with these two shaykhs' perspectives at the time.[187] Later, Baqibillah points out that the differences between Ibn al-'Arabi and Simnani were semantic.[188]

These two perspectives on unity are important for beginners to know because they function as markers on the path. One characteristic marker for aspirants experiencing the unity of being is intoxication and ecstasy. Before being tempted to bask in the experience of intoxication and ecstasy, they realize that they need to move beyond that point. Sirhindi evidently stayed in this intoxicated state for a long time (months to years). With his experiential insights and later reflection he devised training methods so his disciples did not get stuck there.[189] In terms of the Mujaddidi path, unity of being (*tawhid-i wujudi*) is associated with the knowledge of certainty (*'ilm-i yaqin*) and the unity of contemplative witnessing (*tawhid-i shuhudi*) is associated with perceiving certainty (*'ayn-i yaqin*).[190] This is the closest correlation between the two modes of unity and the various maps

185. Sayyid Ashraf Jahangir Simnani (d. 829/1425 Jaunpur), who studied with 'Ala'uddawla Simnani as a young man, responds to 'Ala'uddawla's ideas in *Lata'if-i ashrafi fi bayan-i tawaf-i sufi*, 2 vols. (Karachi: Maktabat-i Simnani, 1999) 2:129-150. His answer to 'Ala'uddawla begins on p. 144 of the 27th latifa. See also, Hermann Landolt, "Der Briefwechsel zwischen Kashani und Simnani über Wahdat al-Wujud," *Der Islam* 50 (1973), 29-81; and his "Simnani on *Wahdat al-Wujud*," in *Collected Papers on Islamic Philosophy and Mysticism*, edited by M. Mohaghegh and Hermann Landolt, (Tehran: Institute of Islamic Studies, 1971), 93-111.

186. See Baqibillah, *Kulliyat*, 28.

187. Sirhindi appears to be in this situation at the end of letter 1.11 in this book. His disciple Muhammad Sadiq Kashmiri Hamadani notes that Sirhindi was attracted to Simnani's perspective and tended to veer from Ibn al-'Arabi's. Perhaps this is because Muhammad Sadiq was a jurist and foregrounded Sirhindi's jurist side. See his *Kalimat-i sadiqin*, ed. Muhammad Saleem Akhtar (Lahore: al-Quraysh Publishers, 1988), 187 (Persian text).

188. See Baqibillah, *Kulliyat*, 37. Baqibillah explains that in the context of the absolute nondelimited (*itlaq-i mutlaq*), Simnani disagreed with Ibn al-'Arabi, understanding it to be "existence as negatively conditioned" (*bi-shart la shay'*) when Simnani really meant "existence as relatively non-conditioned" (*la bi-shart shay'*), which agrees with both Simnani's and Ibn al-'Arabi's perspective.

189. See ter Haar, *Follower and Heir of the Prophet*, 34. In letter 1.290 we get the detailed experiences that led him out of this state.

190. See *Collected Letters,* 1.43.6.

of the Naqshbandi path (discussed previously). The unity of contemplative witnessing, however, is not even close to the end of the path. In terms of certainty, the realization of certainty (*haqq-i yaqin*) lies far ahead,[191] as does the highest station of being a servant (*maqam-i 'abdiyat*) or utter bewilderment.[192] In Sirhindi's juristic sufism, the differences between these two perspectives are significant because the unity of contemplative witnessing is more jurist friendly. In addition, it would make it more difficult for a jurist's mind and ego-self to reject sufism. Such considerations have repercussions in a sufi training setting. Even so, the so-called "controversy" generated between these two formulations of unity has been vastly overstated in the scholarly literature. Those who criticize Sirhindi for not understanding Ibn al-'Arabi or for his not appreciating differing perspectives are doing a partial reading of Sirhindi's views on the subject. Appreciating the teaching context is critical in seeking to understand what Sirhindi is communicating. At the same time Sirhindi might very well have misunderstood aspects of Ibn al-'Arabi's writings.

The overall sufi consensus is that there is no real controversy. Indeed, both Ibn al-'Arabi and Sirhindi agree that these two valid modes of unity are simply two ways of perceiving the One. Sirhindi's mentor Baqibillah reminds us that differences in subjective experiences between protégés of God are like those between the imams of the legal schools. That is, the differences are in the understandings of their words, not in the basis of the actual case at hand (which in this case is declaring the unity of God, *tawhid*).[193] Sirhindi was well aware that the notion of unity of being was not Ibn al-'Arabi's formulation and that both the *Bezels of Wisdom* and *Meccan Openings* honor and encourage a Muslim to follow the shariat guidelines. Sirhindi seeks to reconcile many kinds of differences, including those between sufis and jurists and between these two experiences of unity.[194] He explains that the expressions, "All is God" and "All is from God," although semantically different, really are the same. The latter is preferable (to him) because it appeals more to jurists and it honors transcendence.[195] For Ibn al-'Arabi, the being side of the coin is the "God side" and the contemplative witnessing side is the "human side."[196]

---

191. These are discussed in letter 1.18 in this book.

192. For Ibn al-'Arabi see Qasim Kaka'i, *Wahdat al-wujud bi riwayat-i Ibn 'Arabi wa-Meister Eckhart* (Tehran: Intisharat-i Hurmus, 2007), 347. The station for Ibn al-'Arabi is being in servanthood (*'abudiyat*).

193. See Baqibillah, *Kulliyat*, 28.

194. In terms of reconciling sufis and jurists see letter 3.32 in this book.

195. See Sirhindi, *Sharh-i ruba'iyat*, 33-36.

196. See Kaka'i, *Wahdat al-wujud*, 255, 259-260. Ibn al-'Arabi says that for sufis there is annihilation of the injunction, (*fana'-i hukm*) not the annihilation of

The more one reads Sirhindi's works, the more one sees how he acknowledged other complementary perspectives. His writings did not encompass "all" viewpoints like Ibn al-'Arabi's,[197] but in the sufi environment of Mughal India his criticisms largely balanced out what he considered to be the extreme conditions of the time.[198] Sirhindi had his own unique role in his own time and place. He also had his own set of unveilings, some of which appeared to differ with those of Ibn al-'Arabi's, which he recognizes, like Baqibillah before him, are like the variant interpretations of imams of different legal schools.[199] But those differences are minor compared the overwhelming commonality between these great shaykhs. Rare for a sufi of any era, Shaykh Sirhindi publically acknowledged his errors.[200] He said:

> What can I do! Sometimes I war with shaykh Ibn 'Arabi—may God rest his soul—and other times we are at peace! He was the one who laid the foundations of the doctrine of the mystical knowledge of God (*ma'rifat*

---

the entity (*fana'-i 'ayn*). The former is the station of contemplative witnessing (*maqam-i shuhud*) not mere annihilation (*fana'*).

197. "Ibn al-'Arabi responds [to Ahmad Sirhindi] by pointing out quite rightly that in the *Futuhat*, he has already said everything such critics have said, because there he presents all valid points of view." Cited in William C. Chittick, "On Sufi Psychology: A Debate between the Soul and the Spirit," in Jalal al-Din Ashtiyani et. al., eds., *Consciousness and Reality: Studies in Memory of Toshihiko Izutsu* (Leiden: Brill, 2000), 343. Such a claim might seem to be extreme, but makes sense in the context of an interpretive community where Ibn al-'Arabi is an authority. Reading Kaka'i's voluminous *Wahdat al-wujud*, it is easy to see how Sirhindi affirms so many aspects of Ibn al-'Arabi's notions of sufism.

198. Here I am responding to William Chittick, noting the "unbalanced nature of Ahmad Sirhindi's criticisms." See "Spectrums of Islamic Thought: Sa'id al-Din Farghani on the Implications of Oneness and Manyness," in Leonard Lewisohn, ed., *The Legacy of Mediaeval Persian Sufism* (New York: Khaniqahi Nimatullahi Publications, 1992), 205 fn 2. Teaching has its own imperatives. Anyone teaching Islam in an upright manner in the contemporary West is going to teach it in an unbalanced fashion—emphasizing more of the positive aspects of Islamicate civilization than the negative aspects. This is because of the overwhelming negativity of the media and resultant attitudes prevalent in contemporary western culture.

199. One of Baqibillah's sons, Muhammad 'Ubaydullah, commonly known as Khwaja Khurd, kept needing clarifications about *wahdat-i wujud* and *wahdat-i shuhud*. See Muhammad Ma'sum, *Maktubat-i ma'sumiyya*, 3 vols., edited by Ghulam Mustafa Khan (Karachi: Walend Military Press, n.d.), 1:410-422. This letter is one of three letters over ten pages long out of 239 letters in the first volume of Muhammad Ma'sum's *Collected Letters,* (Muhammad Ma'sum was Sirhindi's son and formal successor).

200. See letter 1.220 in this book and 1.209.108.

> *wa-'irfan*) and thoroughly explained it. He is the one who spoke in detail of the Unity of God (*tawhid*) and the union with him (*ittisal*) and who explained the origin of multiplicity and multiformity. . . . Most of the Sufis who came after him chose to follow him and most used his terminology. Even I, miserable as I am, have profited from the blessings of this prominent man and have learned much from his views and insights. May God reward him for this from me. Because the moments in which a man makes mistakes necessarily alternate with moments in which he is right and because man sometimes says the right things and sometimes not, he—whoever he is and whatever he teaches—should regard the consensus of opinion of the majority of God's servants as the criterion for his being right and he should see the departure from this as proof of his not being right.[201]

The Indian sufi consensus after Sirhindi continued to appreciate Ibn al-'Arabi's vast contribution to the disciplined inquiry of post-rational human consciousness. Sirhindi's formulation of the unity of contemplative witnessing did not take the Naqshbandi world by storm, though Shah Waliullah (d. 1176/1762) and his son Shah Rafi'uddin Dihlawi (d. 1233/1818) both wrote short letters or treatises demonstrating that these two modes of experiencing unity were essentially the same. Any differences that arose were a result of semantics and terminology.[202] The sayyid Naqshbandi-Mujaddidi Mir Dard of Delhi (d. 1199/1785) deeply immersed himself in the books of Ibn al-'Arabi, along with those of Mulla Sadra.[203] One of the many unstudied jewels of Indian sufism, the Naqshbandi-Mujaddidi Faqirullah Shikarpuri (d. 1195/1781), wrote sophisticated sufi treatises, blending Ibn al-'Arabi's ideas, complemented by the ideas of his followers along with

---

201. From letter 3.79, translated by ter Haar, *Follower and Heir of the Prophet*, 130-131.

202. See Shah Waliullah, *al-Tafimat al-ilahiya*, 2 vols, Ghulam Mustafa al-Qasimi, ed., (Hyderabad, Sind: al-Matba' al-Haydari, 1967), 2: 261-284. This letter is translated into English by Fazle Mahmud, "Shah Walyullah's View on Wahdatul Wujud and Wahdatush Shuhud," *al-Hikma* 1 (1964), 42-64. The nineteenth-century Naqshbandi-Khalidi shaykh, 'Abdulqadir al-Jaza'iri (d. 1883) was a well known master of Ibn al-'Arabi's writings. He resolves these two perspectives (without mentioning them by name) clearly and concisely in less than two pages. See 'Abdulqadir al-Jaza'iri, *Le livre des haltes (Kitâb al-mawâqif)* 3 vols., trans. Michel Lagarde (Leiden: Brill, 2000), 1:552-553 (letter 191).

203. For the most detailed study of Mir Dard, see Homayra Ziad's "Quest of the Nightingale: The Religious Thought of Khwajah Mir Dard (1721-1785)," Ph.D. dissertation, Yale University, 2008.

Sirhindi's *Collected Letters* and his own sufi experience.[204] Even if most of the Naqshbandi-Mujaddidi shaykhs replaced Ibn al-'Arabi's *Bezels of Wisdom* with Sirhindi's *Collected Letters* as a required text, Ibn al-'Arabi's sufi framework and perspectives permeated Indian sufism.[205] The unity of contemplative witnessing as a way of interpreting the experience of unity was retained on the pages of Sirhindi's *Collected Letters*. These letters functioned as a detailed operating manual for a curriculum in contemplative practice showing how to verify ways of knowing about unity. Read and discussed in Mujaddidi circles led by learned and contemplatively experienced Mujaddidi shaykhs, Sirhindi's written and experiential legacy did make an impact. It was the jurist-friendly version of a renewed sufism.

The Collected Letters

> Glory to God who revealed such holy and ineffable [words] of God's Truth. His words are beyond human comprehension. In truth, the *Maktubat* are equal to divine inspirations . . . . What can I say? The description of this lofty gentleman [is difficult to express]. He is not a messenger but he has a book.[206]
>
> Ghulam 'Ali Shah Dihlawi,
> 19th-century Mujaddidi shaykh

Shaykh Ahmad Sirhindi began writing letters to his shaykh Baqibillah in 1008/1599. In 1025/1616, Muhammad Jadid Badakhshi Talaqani,[207] one of Sirhindi's disciples, compiled the first volume of these letters. There are 313 letters in the first volume corresponding to the number of Muslims fighting at the Battle of Badr with the chronogram title corresponding to the date of publication (that is, the sum of the numerical value of the letters equals the numerical value of the year), *The Pearl of Inner Knowledge* (*Durr al-ma'rifat*). Sirhindi's son, Muhammad Ma'sum, directed 'Abdulhayy b. Khwaja Chakar Hisari to compile a second volume of 99 letters, corresponding to the number of the most beautiful names of God with the

204. Two of his printed works are Faqirullah Shikarpuri, *Qutb al-irshad* (Quetta: Maktaba-yi Islamiyya, 1978) and *Maktubat-i Faqirullah,* ed., Mawlwi Karam Bakhsh (Lahore: Islamiyya Steam Press, n.d.).

205. See Hamid Algar, " Reflections of Ibn 'Arabi in Early Naqshbandi Tradition," *Journal of the Muhyiddin ibn 'Arabi Society* 10 (1991), 61.

206. See Ghulam 'Ali Dihlawi, *Malfuzat-i sharifa*, ed. Ghulam Muhyiuddin Qusuri, Urdu trans. Iqbal Ahmad Faruqi (Lahore: Maktaba-yi Nabawiyya, 1978), p. 135. The inspirations in the quote above are *ilham* (non-prophetic inspirations) not *wahy*, which are prophetic inspirations.

207. The "Jadid" here is to differentiate him from an older person of the same name, who has "Qadim" in his name.

chronogram, *The Light of Creation* (*Nur al-khala'iq*). This was published in 1028/1619. The third volume of 114 letters, corresponding to the number of suras in the Qur'an, ended up being compiled by Muhammad Hashim Kishmi Burhanpuri in 1031/1622 with the chronogram of *Inner Knowledge of the Realities* (*Ma'rifat al-haqa'iq*). Ahmad Sirhindi passed away before there were enough letters for a fourth volume, so the printed versions of the third volume include another eight or ten letters.[208]

The first complete lithographed edition of *Collected Letters* was printed in Delhi, in 1288/1871, with seven, almost exact, reprints after this.[209] Then Nur Ahmad (d. 1930) began to edit what has become the critical edition of *Collected Letters*. Born in the Sialkot district of what is now Pakistan, Nur Ahmad left for Mecca in 1881, becoming initiated by the famous Chishti-Sabiri shaykh Shah Imdadullah (d. 1899). Returning to India in 1890, he was initiated by the Naqshbandi-Mujaddidi shaykh, Shah Abu'l-Khayr (d. 1924 in Delhi), and began to work on the critical edition of *Collected Letters*. Using teams of able students, he gathered all available manuscripts and over a period of three years these manuscripts were compared with the lithographed edition. After all discrepancies were noted, Nur Ahmad went to Sirhind Sharif where Ahmad Sirhindi's family allowed him to compare his corrected copy with the manuscripts there.[210] Then he began a massive editing project, isolating and identifying Qur'an passages and Hadith, translating and/or defining difficult Arabic and Persian words and phrases, supplying biographical and bibliographical information on well known sufis, jurists, and their writing, defending Sirhindi occasionally against his detractors, and adding a subject index for each letter at the beginning of each of the nine fascicles that were published between 1909 and 1916. This publication was printed in four different paper qualities ranging in price from one rupee, four annas to two rupees, eight annas.[211] Until a 2004 Ira-

---

208. Ter Haar discusses the details of these latter letters in his "The collected letters," 41-42. For manuscript copies of Sirhindi's letters, see Munzawi, *Fihrist*, 3:2002-2008.

209. Professor Iqbal Mujaddidi made a very detailed list of each of these editions, which he graciously shared with me. The first lithograph was published by Matba'-i Ahmadi, followed by Matba'-i Murtadawi in 1290/1873, both located in Delhi. Nawal Kishur in Lucknow reprinted the next three. These five are identical in pagination. The next three reprints were from Nawal Kishur in Kanpur and are missing five pages in the third volume, which means that the last two letters, 3.123 and 3.124 are missing.

210. See Muhammad Musa Amritsari, "Sarguzasht-i Maktubat." In *Maktubat-i Imam-i Rabbani* (Lahore: Nur Company, 1964-1971), 4-12.

211. This is for the seventh fascicle printed in 1914. The most expensive was glossy, European paper and the cheapest was an off-white paper. The middle two

nian edition, just about all *Collected Letters* published in Persian after 1916 were facsimile versions of the original lithographed Nur Ahmad edition.[212]

Translations of *Collected Letters* appeared throughout the nineteenth century.[213] Sulayman Mustaqimzada's Otttoman translation of *Collected Letters* in 1751 was lithographed over a century later in 1860, predating the earliest Persian printing by eleven years.[214] Muhammad Murad al-Manzalawi's (d. 1934 Manzala is a township near Qazan) authoritative Arabic translation was subsequently published in 1899.[215] Known as Muhammad Murad Remzi in the Turkish world, he was an authorized Mujaddidi shaykh who probably had studied *Collected Letters* for many years with his Naqshbandi-Mujaddidi shaykh, Sayyid Muhammad Salih Zawawi.[216] The first complete Urdu translation of *Collected Letters* was done by Qadi 'Alimuddin in the nineteenth century using the original pre-Nur Ahmad Persian

---

qualities were white cloth paper. Professor Muzaffar Alam kindly deciphered the currency symbols.

212. See Ahmad Sirhindi, *Maktubat-i Imam-i Rabbani: Majmu'ah-i az namah'ha-yi 'irfani wa-adabi*, 2 vols., Muhammad Ayyub Ganji and Hasan Zari'i, eds., (Tehran: Intisharat-i Siddiqi, 2004). It is a typeset version of Nur Ahmad's edition without any notes.

213. This brief summary of translations is only for full translations. Professor Iqbal Mujaddidi has detailed partial translations in his introduction to Muhammad Sa'id Ahmad Mujaddidi, *al-Bayyinat: sharh-i Maktubat* (Lahore: Tanzim al-Islam Publications, 2002), 61-64.

214. See Ahmad Sirhindi, *Maktubat tarjaması*, translated into Ottoman by Sulayman Sa'duddin b. Muhammad Mustaqimzada (Istanbul, n.p. 1860).

215. See Muhammad Murad al-Manzalawi al-Qazani, *Maktubat: al-durar al-maknunat al-nafisa*, 2 vols. (Istanbul: Maktabat al-Mahmudiyya, n.d.). There is a newer Arabic edition of *Collected Letters*, Ahmad Sirhindi, *Maktubat al-Rabbaniya*, 3 vols., edited by Mustafa Hasanayn 'Abdulhadi (Beirut: Dar al-Kutub al-'Ilmiyya, 2004). It is not a new translation. However, it reproduces al-Manzalawi's Arabic text in a modern Arabic font with all the short vowels. There are some explanatory footnotes, mostly dealing with hadith.

216. 'Abdulhamid Daghistani (in Ghulam 'Ali Dihlawi's lineage) is Shaykh Zawawi's shaykh. See Ahmet Temir, "Do□umunun 130. ve Ölülümün 50. Yılı Dolayısıyla Kazanlı Tarihçi," *Türk Tarih Kurumu Belleten* 50/197 (1986), 495-505. For biographical details of Muhammad Murad see Muhammad Murad Ramzi Qazani, *Nafa'is al-sanihat fi tadhyil al-baqiyat al-salihat*, on the margins of Harawi, 'Ali bin Husayn al-Wa'iz, *Rashahat-i 'ayn al-hayat*, translated by Muhammad Murad Ramzi al-Qazani (Mecca: al-Matba'at al-Muhammadiya, 1890), 258-259. For Shaykh Zawawi, see Ibid., 140. Professor Necdet Tosun kindly brought these two sources to my attention.

edition.[217] This was followed by other Urdu translations from the Nur Ahmad edition in 1973 by Muhammad Sa'id Ahmad and by Zawwar Husayn in 1988-1993.[218] The first modern Turkish translation (from al-Manzalawi's Arabic translation) was by Abdulkadir Akcicek in 1977, followed by a team translation effort in 2004.[219] Shah Mohammad Muti' Ahmad Aphtabi, a Mujaddidi in the lineage from Musa Zai, Pakistan, has translated *Collected Letters* into Bengali.[220] In 2005 the full Chinese translation of *Collected Letters* from al-Manzalawi's Arabic translation was published, a collaborative effort involving the combined knowledge of experts in Arabic, Chinese, and Chinese mosque language.[221] Reference works in Persian and Urdu for *Collected Letters* include two commentaries, and two sets of indexes.[222]

It is not certain how many Mujaddidi shaykhs still use *Collected Letters*. When I was living in Pakistan it seemed to take about seven years for

---

217. See Ahmad Sirhindi, *Maktubat-i Imam-i Rabbani*, 2 vols., translated into Urdu by Qadi 'Alimullah (Lahore: Wafaq Press, 1988).

218. See Ahmad Sirhindi, *Maktubat-i Imam-i Rabbani*, 3 vols., translated into Urdu by Muhammad Sa'id Ahmad (Karachi: Medina Publishing Company, 1973) and *Maktubat-i Hadrat-i Mujaddid-i Alf-i Thani*, 4 vols., translated into Urdu by Zawwar Husayn (Karachi: Ahmad Brothers Printers, 1988-1993).

219. See Ahmad Sirhindi, *Mektubat-ı Rabbani*, 3 vols., translated into Turkish by Abdülkadir Akçiçek (Istanbul: Çelik Yayınevi, 1977); and *Mektubat-ı Rabbani*, 3 vols., translated into Turkish by Talha Hakan Alp, Ömer Faruk Tokat, and Ahmet Hamdi Yıldırım (Istanbul: Semerkand Yayınları, 2004). Professor Necdet Tosun kindly brought these two sources to my attention.

220. See Ahmad Sirhindi, *Maktubat Shariph*, 5 vols., translated by Shah Mohammad Muti' Ahmad Aphtabi (Dhaka: Chuphibad Pracar Sangstha, n.d.). Irshad Alam kindly gave me this information. I have used his transliteration of Bengali.

221. Yindu Yimamu Ranbani zhu, *Maketubate*, trans., Ma Tingyi, 3 vols. (Hong Kong: Tianma Publishing Co. Ltd., 2005). The story of this remarkable translating effort is in the forthcoming book by Eloisa Concetti and Thierry Zarcone, *Sufism in Xinjiang and Inner Asia in 19th-21th Century: Ahmad Sirhindî's Maktûbât and the Naqshbandiyya*. Thierry Zarcone graciously brought this Chinese translation to my attention.

222. A near-complete commentary, used for many of the introductions to the letters in this book, is Nasrullah Hutaki, *Sharh-i Maktubat-i qudsi ayat* (Peshawar: Taj Mahal Company, ca. 1976). A partial commentary is Muhammad Sa'id Ahmad Mujaddidi, *al-Bayyinat: sharh-i Maktubat* (Lahore: Tanzim al-Islam Publications, 2002). The only set of scholarly indexes is Buehler, *Fiharis-i tahlili*. The other set is a non-scholarly index. See Muhammad Na'imullah, *Ma'arif-i maktubat-i Imam-i Rabbani: tafsili fihrist maktubat-i Imam-i Rabbani Mujaddid-i Alif-i Thani* (Delhi: Shah Abu'l-Khayr Academy, 2002), which is written only for Urdu translations of *Collected Letters*.

a thousand-copy print run of Nur Ahmad's Persian *Collected Letters* to sell out. In 1991, they were printed in Peshawar. When that edition went out of print, another appeared in 1999 in Quetta. The publication of the first printed Persian edition in Iran, for the Sunni Kurds, and recent translations in modern Turkish, Bengali, and Chinese indicate the probability that *Collected Letters* is still being used for sufi training.

Pointers for reading this translation

Any brackets [ ] or parenthesis ( ) and their contents have been added by the translator. Except Qur'anic notations, for example [Q. 23:12], the contents of square brackets are to be read along with the text. Square brackets are there because of the need to break up sentences that may be a half a page long or to clarify the text. If there is a series of this-es and that-s where one cannot distinguish one from another and the whole point is to discern between the two, I replace the "this" and "that" with what is referred to. I have added death dates of the people involved and crucial explanatory material in parenthesis because there are already many footnotes. The Arabo-Persian equivalents of technical vocabulary are added in parenthesis so specialists can see how I have translated them. I have kept in most of the spiritual politeness formulae in their entirety so the reader can get a flavor of another set of priorities. Modern usage of English has been used as much as possible while retaining the flavor and nuances of the original. Any subheadings in the translation are in the original text. Anything added is noted in the footnotes. Except for one word, *shari'at*, which for Sirhindi is a multivalent realm onto itself, each of Sirhindi's words has an English equivalent (even though technically shariah has become an English word). Background material published after October 2009 related to the subjects of this book is not included.

On a more immediate and specific note, it is common knowledge, particularly to Muslims, that very influential groups have been spreading their ideology throughout the Islamic world for many decades.[223] Whatever their rhetoric may be, the effect is to rip the heart out of Islamic practice. Call it spiritual deforestation. This book is a small piece of fruit from a sufi tree of profound contentment and peace planted by a great sufi four centuries ago. God bless him and may his inner heart rest in peace. The blemishes are mine and I ask the reader's indulgence.

223. See Khalid Abou El-Fadl, *The Great Theft: Wrestling Islam from the Extremists* (San Francisco: Harper, 2005).

Chapter One
Shariat, Sunnat, and Jurists

Introduction to the basics of faith: Letter 2.67

This letter is written to Khan-i Jahan Lodi (d. 1038/1629-30), also known as Pir-i Khan. He was the son of Dawlat Khan Lodhi of the Shah Wakhil tribe and one of Jahangir's generals.[1] In 1015/1607, Jahangir gave him the rank of 3000 persons and 1500 horses (the highest rank being 7000), and the distinction of sonship (*farzandi*) with the name of Salabat Khan, saying that "Today there is not in my government any person of greater influence than he. . ." and later that year declared him to be "not less to me than my own sons. . ." He was given the new name of Khan-i Jahan.[2] In 1029/1620, Jahangir notes how Khan-i Jahan gives up a serious alcohol habit cold turkey.[3] When Shah Jahan took over after his father died, Khan-i Jahan fought against him and was killed in a battle against 'Abdullah Khan.[4]

Most of the letter is devoted to the dimension of revealed religion (*din*) known as faith (*iman*), one of the three dimensions of revealed religion clarified by Gabriel's hadith (the other two are submission to God, *islam*, and behaving in a beautiful manner, *ihsan*). In the Prophet's time, the articles of faith were having faith in God, God's angels, God's books, God's messengers, and the Day of Judgment. These have been expanded in this letter, according to a Central Asian version of the Hanafi school of jurisprudence (based on the founder-figure Abu Hanifa d. 150/767 Baghdad) and the Maturidi theological perspective (founder Abu Mansur al-Maturidi d. 333/944 Samarqand), into the nineteen points which Sirhindi considers most important.[5] Most of the

1. For his family particulars, see Afzal Husain, *The Nobility under Akbar and Jahangir: A Study of Family Groups* (Delhi: Manohar, 1999), 127-150.

2. See Jahangir, *Memoirs of Jahangir* (*Tuzuk-i Jahangiri*), 2 vols., trans., Alexander Rogers, ed., Henry Beveridge, 2nd ed. (Delhi: Munshiram Manoharlal, 1968), 1:87-89, 128, 139.

3. See ibid., 2:165.

4. See *The Tarikh-i Khan-i Jahani of Khawjah Ni'mat Allah*, edited by S. M. Imam al-Din, vol. 1 (Dacca: Asiatic Society of Pakistan, 1960). There are two letters addressed to him in *Collected Letters.*

5. The two other letters in *Collected Letters* dedicated to the subject of faith are letter 1.266, the longest letter in *Collected Letters*, addressed to Baqibillah's two sons, and letter 3.17 addressed to an unnamed woman. Generally the theological school of al-Ash'ari tends to rely on literal interpretation of prophetic revelation while the Maturidis give higher priority to the use of reason in ascertaining

articles of faith concern God (nine) and the Day of Judgment (four). Even though Sirhindi makes it clear that the rank, order, and legitimacy of Muhammad's successors have nothing to do with the principles of religion or articles of faith, he spends two pages discussing this subject for his reader as an interlude between the last two articles of faith.

An emphasis on the faith-dimension of religion runs through *Collected Letters* because these articles of faith are the starting point. Sirhindi says, "The first obligation (*fard*) for those of a sound mind (*'uqala'*) is to [have] correct articles of faith (*'aqa'id*) in accordance with the rightly guided mainstream (*ahl-i sunnat wa-jama'at*)."[6] 'Ubaydullah Ahrar (d. 895/1405) notes that there is only disaster if one's reality (*haqiqat*) is not formulated with the creed of the rightly guided mainstream, while if one's reality is in accordance with this creed, even if one is totally ruined, there is no need to be anxious.[7] Sirhindi recommends reading Fadlullah Shihabuddin Turpushti's *The Sanctioned Articles of Faith*,[8] but this is difficult reading for many readers even though it is written in Persian. Sirhindi's son Muhammad Ma'sum read Jurjani's *Commentary on the Way Stations*, the commentary of 'Adududdin al-Iji's *The Way Stations of Theology*, which is mentioned three times in *Collected Letters*.[9] Also recommended is Sa'duddin 'Umar al-Taftazani's *Commentary on Nasafi's Articles of Faith Concerning Religious Principles and Theology*, a commentary of Nasafi's *Instruction for Proofs of Religious Principles*, although Sirhindi disagrees with some of the commentary.[10]

---

knowledge of God's existence. For Sirhindi, the Maturidis are preferred because of their greater adherence to the Prophetic sunnat. In his view, the Ash'ari theology has been mixed with philosophical reasoning. See Ahmad Sirhindi, *Mabda' wa-ma'ad*, ed. Zawwar Husayn with Urdu translation (Karachi: Ahmad Brothers Printers, 1984), 55.

6. See *Collected Letters*, 1.266.106.

7. See *Collected Letters*, 1.193.81.

8. Mentioned in *Collected Letters*, 1.193.80 as *Risala-yi Turpushti*, recently published as Fadlullah Shihabuddin Turpushti, *al-Mu'tamad fi'l-mu'taqad* (Istanbul: Hakikat Kitabevi, 1990).

9. See *Collected* Letters, 1.251.57, 1.266.13, 1.306.153. See 'Ali b. Muhammad Jurjani, *Sharh al-Mawaqif*, 4 vols. (Cairo: Dar al-Basa'ir, 2008). Sa'duddin Mas'ud ibn 'Umar al-Taftazani, *Sharh al-'aqaid al-Nasafiyah fi usul al-din wa-'ilm al-kalam*, 2 vols., ed. Claude Salamé (Damascus: Wizarat al-Thaqafah wa'l-Irshad al-Qawmi, 1974). In *Collected Letters,* 1.251.57 Sirhindi also mentions Abu Shukur al-Salimi al- Kashshi's, *al-Tamhid fi bayan al-tawhid* in the context of justifying Mu'awiya's actions as mistaken ijtihad.

10. See *Collected Letters*, 1.266.131. See Abu'l-Mu'in Maymun Muhammad al-Nasafi, *Tabsirat al-adilla*, 2 vols., ed. Claude Salamé (Limassol, Cyprus: al-

There are many epistemological levels, or ways of knowing these articles of faith. For most common Muslims, these articles of faith are accepted as the way things are on the basis of the revealed sources of the Qur'an and Hadith. There is no questioning involved; the creed is simply believed and followed (*taqlid*) on the basis of religio-cultural transmission of knowledge. This is one reason why the word *iman* is often mistranslated as "belief." Specialists in philosophy, and to a lesser extent theologians (*ahl-i kalam*), go a step further by interpreting and investigating faith on the basis of rational inquiry. Sufis, in addition to acknowledging transmitted knowledge and rational inquiry, insist that the articles of faith can only be known through direct experience. In this letter, Sirhindi frequently implies his own experiential verification in his exposition of these articles of faith. In *Return to the Source*, he states how the Ash'ari creed appealed to him at first. Later, on the basis of the light of insight, he discovered that the Maturidi articles of faith were closer to the reality of how things really were.[11]

This letter is an example of Sirhindi seeking to religiously guide the Mughal leadership. In the very last section of the letter, the reader discovers that the nineteen points of Hanafi-Maturidi creed and related discussion outlined in the letter are intended for the Mughal emperor, Jahangir. Khan-i Jahan is supposed to convince Jahangir that these articles of faith outlined by the rightly guided mainstream are the only correct perspective and all other views are misguided.

Sirhindi's sincere conviction in writing this letter is based on transmitted Islamic scripture (the Qur'an and hadith), the rational knowledge utilized in formulating the Hanafi-Maturidi school of jurisprudence, and his own contemplative unveilings (sing. *kashf*). Correct creedal articles of faith are not to be taken lightly. As he states clearly, to be saved on the Day of Judgment one needs to share this creed. Anyone else will be doomed to eternal punishment. There is no indication that Sirhindi is acting out of self-interest here. Indeed, he says, "in striving to reform the Sultan one endeavors to reform all of humanity." This is the kind of task especially suited for a Renewer of the Second Millennium.

Jaffan & al-Jabi, 1990).

11. See Sirhindi, *Mabda' wa-ma'ad*, 55. Sometimes Sirhindi had an inner experience which disagrees with both the Maturidi and Ash'ari views, and with the views of Ibn al-'Arabi. For example, according to Sirhindi's experience, those who have never received a message from a prophet before the Day of Judgment will be rewarded or punished according to their deeds, after which they will be reduced to non- existence like animals. See Letter 1.259 and J.G.J. ter Haar, *Follower and Heir of the Prophet: Shaykh Ahmad Sirhindi (1564-1624) as Mystic* (Leiden: Het Oosters Instituut, 1992), 61. His discussion of orthodoxy and doctrine has informed my own treatment of the subject. Ibid., 59-68.

LETTER 2.67

In the name of God, the compassionate and merciful. Peace be upon those who have chosen to worship God. Your honorable letter arrived in which you respectfully and nobly had written about how certain sufis (*fuqara'*) have been dissatisfied. Thanks to God almighty. In this time of complete doubt and distress, the rich and happy ones have been held back because of their lack of affinity [with sufis]. But because of their innate goodness, they have humbly achieved faith in these sufis. It is a blessing that all the potential worldly connections that could have hindered this faith did not interfere with it. In all kinds of matters, these sufis' love and attention have not been concealed. One must be thankful for this great blessing and be hopeful because of the prophetic hadith, "The lover is with the Beloved."[12] God bless him and his family and give them peace.

O you who have the signs of nobleness and happiness! It is necessary that one's faith be aligned in accordance with the articles of faith (*'aqa'id*) and with the requisite views of the group who will be saved on the Day of Judgment (*firqah-i najah*), the rightly guided mainstream, the most outstanding and largest group. God almighty be pleased with all of them. This is necessary so that one can envision happiness and being saved on the Day of Judgment. Misguided articles of faith are those that oppose those held by the folk of the sunnat (*ahl-i sunnat*) and are fatal poison because they result in eternal death and punishment. Laziness and negligence in deeds [create] the hope that one has to be forgiven, but there is no capacity for forgiveness in laxness with regard to articles of faith. "God does not forgive associating others with God; God forgives whomsoever God wills." [Q. 4:48]

I will condense the [discussion of] articles of faith (*mu'taqadat*) of the rightly guided mainstream. One must act in accordance with this correction of articles of faith. With integrity (*istiqamat*) one must humbly ask God almighty concerning these articles of faith.

[1] One must know that God almighty exists with an Essence having no beginning or end.[13] All the rest of the things came into existence through the

12. This hadith is the most often quoted in *Collected Letters,* and mentioned twenty times. It can be found in the following hadith collections: al-Bukhari, *Adab*, 96; al-Muslim, *Birr*, 50; al-Tirmidhi, #2385, 2387, 3535; and Ibn Da'ud, #5127. All specific hadith references in this book come from *Mektubat-ı Rabbani*, 3 vols., translated into Turkish by Talha Hakan Alp, Ömer Faruk Tokat, and Ahmet Hamdi Yıldırım (Istanbul: Semerkand Yayınları, 2004). When I use *Mektubat-ı Rabbani* for further references it will be indicated by [MR].

13. The numbers in this letter corresponding to each article of faith are not in the original. I have followed the numbering outlined in the Urdu translation of Ahmad Sirhindi, *Maktubat-i Hadrat-i Mujaddid-i Alf-i Thani*, trans. Zawwar Husayn, 4 vols. (Karachi: Idarah-i Mujaddidiyyah, 1991), 2: 233-250.

being of God almighty. The creation of God almighty came from nonbeing to being. Therefore, God almighty is eternal and has no beginning. All created things come afterwards and manifest anew. God almighty is without beginning and eternally subsists without end. Whatever is newly created and manifest is transitory, that is, an occasion for non-being.

[2] God almighty is a singularity and nothing can be associated with God, neither in necessary being nor in being worthy of worship. Only God almighty has necessary being and is worthy of worship.

[3] Only God almighty has perfect attributes (these are the eight fixed divine attributes), knowledge, life, power, will, speech, hearing, sight, and origination. All of these are characterized by not having a beginning or end and are existent in God. Exalt God's sovereignty. The [worldly] connections of temporarily created things (*hawadith*) do not adversely affect the timelessness of the attributes nor is the eternal nature of the attributes hindered by the connections of newly created things. Philosophers, from lack of judgment, and Mu'tazilis, from blindness, confuse being connected with temporarily created things (*hawadith-i muta'allaq*, the passive participle) with connected temporarily created things (*hawadith-i muta'alliq*, the active participle).[14] They end up negating the perfect (divine) attributes and God's knowledge of the particulars. They do not know that [temporarily created things] are required to change because that is the nature of temporarily created things. They do not know that the [divine] attributes are eternal. The connections of the divine attributes with temporary connections are temporary.[15]

[4] God almighty does not have deficient attributes, that is, attributes that are not perfect. God almighty is free of the attributes of essences (*jawahir*), bodies, contingencies (*a'rad*), and the necessities thereof. Nor does God almighty have any capacity for space-time or directionality (*wijhat*), all of which are God's creations. It is ignorant for a person to think that God almighty is above the Throne or to think that the direction is up. The Throne and everything else [created] are all temporarily created things created by God almighty. What scope does something created and temporary have when the situation of the Creator is eternal and a mansion of Real-

14. The "being connected with temporarily created things" is a derivation of a divine attribute. For example, from knowledge, that which is known (*ma'lum*) or from power, that which is predestined (*maqdur*). According to Sirhindi they confuse the divine attributes with attributes of temporary things, which are incommensurable. Grammatically the example in the text involves the comparison between being connected (*muta'allaq*, the passive participle) and connected (*muta'alliq*, the active participle).

15. The general principle here is that the eternal is incommensurate with the temporal and should not be conflated with it.

ity? To some extent the Throne, the most honored thing in God almighty's creation, has more luminosity and radiance. Necessarily, the Throne has the injunction of being a mirror because the appearance of the greatness and majesty of the Creator is found here. Exalt God! It is clear why the Throne is called "God's Throne" from this association with its appearance. Otherwise the Throne and everything else compared to God almighty would have an equal [rank] because God created it. However, the Throne has the quality of being a mirror and other created things do not have this quality. It is the form of the person that appears [in the mirror]. One cannot say that a person is in the mirror. But relative to the person [reflected in the mirror] and the mirror, everything else in front of the mirror is the same. The difference is a function of acceptance. The mirror accepts [and thereby reflects] the form of the person and other things do not have the capacity to do this.

[5] God does not have a body, essences, or contingencies. Nor is God physical, limited, or finite. God does not have dimensionality or size. God is vast (*wasi'*), but not in our conventional way of understanding. God is encompassing, but it is not an encompassing that makes sense to our rational mind. God is close but it is not a closeness that we can understand rationally. God is with us but not in a way that we can [conventionally] recognize. In terms of faith (*iman*), we can say that God is vast, encompassing, close, and with us. But we do not know the quality of these attributes. Whatever we [think we] know [about God's Essence], we know that [our concepts] are grounded in corporeality.

[6] God almighty is not united with anything nor does anything become united with God. Nothing incarnates into God nor does God incarnate into any thing. It is impossible for God to become divided into parts or pieces. It is not possible for God to be assembled or broken up. God is incomparable to anything. God has no children or women. God's essence and attributes are incomparable and incommensurate, not resembling anything else. This much we do know: there is a God and that God has perfect names and attributes that glorify God and by which God is characterized. God is beyond our understanding and awareness and what we can rationally consider or imagine. God is beyond all of that as I have mentioned above. The senses (lit. eyesight) are not aware of it. The farsighted ones at the abode of *alast* have not entered any farther than this.[16] One should know that the names and attributes of God almighty cause one to understand, that is, they are apprehended by listening to one who follows the shariat. Each name designat-

16. To be in the abode of *alast* is to be at the dawn of waking awareness not yet in physical form. This is a reference to the Qur'anic phrase, "Am I not your Sustainer?" (*alastu bi-rabbikum*). [Q. 7:172] See also William C. Chittick, *The Sufi path of love: the spiritual teachings of Rumi* (Albany: State University of New York Press, 1983), 74.

ed in the shariat has emerged from God almighty and must be designated. The names that do not emerge from God do not have to be designated, even though the perfect name might be contained in that name. For example, God has been designated as "beneficent" (*jawad*) because this designation has come [in the Qur'an or Hadith] but one must not say that God is generous because this has not come.

[7] The Qur'an is God almighty's word, communicated by letters and sound as revealed to our Prophet. God bless him and his family and give them peace. Through the Qur'an, God' servants are enjoined [to do what is praiseworthy] and discouraged [from doing what is reprehensible]. It happens in the same way with our own mental speech, which manifests by means of our mouth and tongue that articulate letters and sound. We are able to manifest our hidden goals. It is like God almighty's own mental speech without the means of mouth and tongue. Through God's complete power, communicated with letters and sound, God sends God's message to God's servants. God's hidden affairs of enjoining [to do what is praiseworthy] and discouraging [from doing what is reprehensible] are communicated within letters and sound, adorned on the nuptial bed of appearance. Therefore, both kinds of speech are God's speech: mental (*nafsi*) and verbal (*lafzi*). The designation of God's speech in both cases is the way of the truth just like both kinds of human speech, mental and verbal, are ways of expressing the truth in our speech. It is not the case that mental speech is true and verbal speech is metaphorical just because metaphor negates what is conceivable (*ja'iz*). To deny verbal speech and say that these two kinds of speech are not God's speech is covering up the truth of God (*kufr*, commonly translated as infidelity). The other scriptures that were revealed to the prophets who preceded our prophet are all God almighty's speech, which is included in the Qur'an and in those scriptures. God bless them all. It is incumbent upon God's servants to follow God's injunctions.

[8] It is true that believers will ineffably see God almighty in Paradise without any direction, encounter, or encompassing. We can have faith in seeing God in the Hereafter without being concerned how this will happen because seeing God almighty is an ineffable experience. In this physical world, the truth of this is not evident to those who are limited to the world of form. They do not have faith. Oh! Through their blindness and exclusion, the philosophers, Mu'tazilis, and all the other heretical groups deny seeing God in the Hereafter. It is a logical deduction based on their not seeing God [in this world]. They do not have faith that they will be able to see God in the Hereafter.

[9] God almighty created God's servants. Their deeds, whether good or bad, are by God's decree. He is satisfied with good deeds and not satisfied with bad deeds, though both are from God's will and intention. But one

should know that evil is a result of bad etiquette with God almighty. One should not extrapolate and say that God is the Creator of evil, but should say that God is the Creator of both good and evil. The jurists say that one should say that God almighty is the Creator of everything but should not say that God is the Creator of impurities and pigs, which is not following the proper etiquette when speaking about God almighty.

The Mu'tazilis, from their dualistic stance, understand people to be the creators of their deeds. They attribute the good or evil of human action to the individual. The shariat and reason deny the Mu'tazilis. Indeed, authentic jurists (*'ulama'-i haqq*) acknowledge the power of a person in committing a deed. The resulting reward or punishment has been verified. The difference is clear between involuntary and voluntary action. In terms of power and reward or punishment, the person does not have anything to do with involuntary action but is involved with a voluntary action. There is such a difference of responsibility involved, and one can confirm the [resulting] reward and punishment.

Most people have doubt in the power and choice of a human being, thinking that a person is weak and compelled. They have not understood the meaning of the jurists. The evidence of human choice and power is not what most people think it is, that is, doing what one wants and not doing what one does not want to do. This is a far cry from being human. The meaning of power and choice is that a person does what he is religiously obligated to do. By taking responsibility for these obligations, appropriate behavior can emerge. For example, ritual prayer can be performed five times a day; one can pay 2.5% of one's surplus property in alms; one can fast one month (Ramadan) out of twelve; and one can perform the hajj once in a lifetime if there are sufficient resources. By analogy, the same applies for the rest of the injunctions of the shariat. God almighty, from God's complete benevolence, has guided [people] in ease [to perform] these injunctions. With respect to the weakness and lack of human will, God almighty has said, "God desires ease for you, not hardship for you" [Q. 2:185] and "God eases the burden for you, having created humans weak." [Q. 4:28] One cannot have patience for lustful tendencies nor can one tolerate difficulties in fulfilling religious obligations.

[10] Prophets have been the ones sent by God to all humans in order to invite them to God and set them on the straight path. God bless them. Whoever accepts their invitation will go to Paradise and whoever rejects them will be terrified by the punishment of Hell. Whatever has been conveyed by the prophets from God and communicated by them is all true. There is no room for disagreement here. The Seal of the Prophets is Muhammad, the messenger of God. God almighty bless and give peace to him and to all of his family. His religion abrogates all the previous religions. His book

(the Qur'an) is better than all the previous scriptures. No way of living in accordance with God's commands (shariat) supersedes the Islamic shariat. It remains until the Day of Judgment. Then Jesus will come and act in accordance with Muhammad's shariat, and be included in the Muslim community. God bless him and our prophet and give them peace.

[11] All that the Prophet has informed us about the conditions of the Hereafter is true: the contraction and punishment in the grave, the questioning of Munkar and Nakir in the grave, the annihilation of the world, the splitting of the sky and earth, the scattering of the planets, the raising of the earth and mountains breaking up into pieces, the Day of Resurrection from the graves and souls returning to their bodies, the earthquakes of the Last Day, fear of the Day of Judgment, the accounting of one's deeds, the testimony of one's limbs attesting to one's deeds, birds flying away, the naming of good and bad deeds, and putting them on the right and left sides of the scale respectively so that they can be weighed. From this, the lack or surplus of the relative good or bad can be determined. If it tips toward the right (the good deeds) then this is a sign of being saved and if it tips the other way it is a sign of loss. The heaviness and lightness measured by this scale is the opposite of the scale of the world. The pan of the scale that goes up is the heavy one and the one that goes down is the light one.

[12] It is confirmed that intercession, with God's permission, [will happen] first for the prophets and the pious and then for the sinners among the believers. Muhammad said, "My intercession is for those in my community who have committed great sins (*kaba'ir*)."[17]

[13] The narrow bridge (*pul-i sirat*) over the Fire that believers cross to reach Paradise [is the bridge] upon which infidels slip and fall into the Fire. This is true and confirmed.

[14] Paradise is arranged to put believers of God at ease and the Fire is prepared to punish those who cover up the truth (*kuffar* often translated infidels). Both are created and exist in the physical world and will remain for eternity, never to be annihilated. After the judgment on the Last Day, the believers who go to Paradise will stay there forever and never go outside Paradise. In the same manner, infidels who go to Hell will be there forever, being punished for eternity. It is not permitted for there to be any relief in what is due to them. God says, "Their punishment will not be relieved nor will there be any respite." [Q. 2:162] Whoever has a bit of faith in one's heart, even though he has gone to Hell for an excess of sins, the punishment will correspond to the extent of one's disobedience. Eventually this person will leave Hell and his face will no longer be black like infidels' blackened

17. This hadith is mentioned three times in *Collected Letters*, and found in the hadith collections of al-Tirmidhi, #2435, 2436; Abu Da'ud, #4739; and Ibn Maja, #4310 [MR].

faces. Due to the sanctity of his having faith, the sinning believer will not be chained up in irons like the infidels.

[15] Angels are the honored servants of God almighty who are not permitted the right to disobey God's orders. All they can do is do as they are commanded. They are beyond gender. It is impossible for them to be born or give birth. God almighty has selected a few angels to convey scripture (*risalat*). He has honored them to communicate revelation, books, and scriptures to the prophets. God bless them. This is because angels are protected from error, mistakes, and the Devil's (lit. enemy's) deception. Whatever has been communicated to them by God almighty is true and there is no possibility for them mixing the truth with what is not true. Through the greatness and the utter splendor of God almighty, these angels are in fearful awe. Angels have nothing else to do but obey God's commands.

[16] Faith is attesting in the heart and confirming verbally what has been reliably passed down to us concerning religion, both generally and specifically. What we do with the limbs of our bodies is outside the reality (*nafs* glossed as *haqiqat*) of faith but through faith [actions] can be completed and beauty created.

Abu Hanifa (d. 150/767 Baghdad), the great Imam born in Kufa, said that faith cannot increase or decrease because attesting in the heart means a clear certainty and conversion in the heart, so there is no capacity for differentiating more or less. God have mercy on him. When one accepts difference then one enters the circle of supposition and conjecture. Completeness and deficiency of faith are in respect to obedience and goodness (*hasanat*). To the extent that there is more obedience there is more completeness of faith. So the faith of ordinary believers (non-prophets) is not like the faith of prophets because prophetic faith, united with obedience to God, has reached the highest pinnacle of complete faith. God bless them. The faith of the common believers does not come close to that of the prophets. Still, these two types of faith overlap in the reality of faith. The faith of prophets, by virtue of being connected with obedience to God, has created a different reality. The faith of ordinary believers is not the incomparable faith of the prophets. There is no similarity between these two kinds of faith. The common people always share the same humanity with the prophets. God bless them. But the prophets have other perfections, have reached elevated degrees [of realization], and have confirmed another reality. That is, [the reality of] the prophets is higher than the common shared human reality. Humans are humans. The common people are outside this shared human reality since they are ruled by their animal natures.

Abu Hanifa said, "I am truly a believer." Imam Shafi'i (d. 204/820) said,[18] "I am a believer if God almighty wills." God have mercy on both of

18. Muhammad al-Shafi'i was the founder-figure of the Shafi'i legal school.

them. Whatever perspective one has, with respect to the state of one's faith a person can say, "I am truly a believer." From the point of view of the end one can say, "I am a believer if God almighty wills." But from whatever perspective one speaks, it is better to avoid the appearance of making an exception (that is, saying, "If God almighty wills.")

[17] Even if a believer commits serious sins (lit. is disobedient to God), a person does not go outside [the domain] of faith into the circle of infidelity (*kufr*). It is said that one day Abu Hanifa was sitting with a group of distinguished jurists. A person came and asked, "What verdict would you give an immoral believer who kills his own father for no reason, cuts off his head, puts wine in his skull, and drinks it? Then after drinking he fornicates with his mother. Is he a believer or an infidel?" Every jurist was off the mark in giving this person his due, treating him unjustly. Meanwhile, Abu Hanifa said that he was a believer and that he had not left his faith by committing those sins. The jurists were annoyed when they heard this, and spoke out malevolently against him, blaming and finding fault. In the end, when Abu Hanifa was vindicated, all of them accepted and acknowledged what he had said.[19]

[18] If a sinner repents before dying, there is a great hope of being saved because there is the promise of the repentance being accepted. If the person is not fortunate enough to repent, his situation rests with God. Exalt God's sovereignty. If he is forgiven then he will be sent to heaven. If not, he will be punished to the degree of his disobedience to God, that is, he will be sent to the Fire or not. In the end, he will be saved and will end up in heaven. This is because in the Hereafter infidels are deprived of God's mercy. Whoever has the slightest bit of faith can hope for God's mercy. If one does not get mercy for the weakness of sinning at the beginning, then by God almighty's divine favor it will be facilitated at the end. "Our Sustainer! Make sure our hearts do not go astray after you have guided us. Bestow your mercy on us from your presence, for you are the Bestower." [Q. 3:8]

The controversy concerning the succession and leadership [after the death of Muhammad], according to Sunnis, is not a part of the principles of religion whatsoever and has no connection with the articles of faith. God almighty thank them for their endeavors. Because the Shi'is have exaggerated this matter, by necessity authentic jurists (*'ulama'-i ahl-i haqq*) have investigated it in the context of the science of scholastic theology (*kalam*) and have clarified the truth of the situation. God almighty be pleased with these jurists. The principal successor after the Seal of the Prophets is Abu Bakr as-Siddiq (d. 13/634). After him is 'Umar Faruq (assas. 24/644), fol-

19. This is a polemic against the Kharajites who believed that committing a major sin put one outside the Muslim community.

lowed by 'Uthman (assas. 35/656), "the one with the two lights,"[20] and 'Ali b. Abi Talib (assas. 40/661). God almighty be pleased with all of them. Their preference is in the order of their succession. The preference of Abu Bakr and 'Umar (*shaykhayn*) has been established by the consensus of the Prophet's companions and the generation following them. Imam Shafi'i, a renown religious notable, the leader of those following the practice of the Prophet (*ahl-i sunnat*) according to Abu al-Hasan Ash'ari (d. 324/936 Baghdad), has transmitted this, saying, "The preference of Abu Bakr and 'Umar over the rest of the Muslim community is certain. Do not dispute their preference over the rest of the Prophet's companions. Otherwise one is ignorant or a fanatic supporter of 'Ali. God almighty honor him. For me, a person who gives precedence over Abu Bakr or 'Umar is a slanderer. I want to whip him the [legal] eighty lashes."

Shaykh 'Abdulqadir Jilani (d. 561/1166 Baghdad) transmitted a hadith in one of his books, *Sufficient Provision for Seekers of the Path of Truth*. God bless his inner heart. In this book Muhammad says, "I ascended and asked God himself whether 'Ali would be my successor. The angels said 'O Muhammad whatever God wants will come to pass; your successor is Abu Bakr.'" God bless Muhammad and give him peace. 'Abdulqadir reported that 'Ali had said that the Prophet did not leave this world until 'Ali agreed that Abu Bakr, 'Umar, 'Uthman, and 'Ali would succeed him in that order. God be satisfied with all of them.[21]

Imam Hasan, 'Ali's eldest son, has precedence over Husayn, his younger brother. God almighty be pleased with both of them. The jurists of the rightly guided mainstream give precedence in religious knowledge and exertion (*ijtihad*) to 'Aisha, Abu Bakr's daughter and Muhammad's favorite wife, over Fatima, Muhammad's daughter. God almighty be satisfied with both of them. 'Abdulqadir gives precedence to 'Aisha in his *Sufficient Provision for Seekers*. God bless his inner heart.

This poor one (Ahmad Sirhindi) believes that 'Aisha was more advanced in religious knowledge and striving (*ijtihad*), while Fatima excelled in asceticism, piety, and seclusion from people (*inqita'*). Therefore, Fatima is called "the virgin," which is a way of emphasizing a person aloof from worldly concerns. 'Aisha was a competent authority of the Companion's legal decrees. God almighty be satisfied with both of them. There was no problem of religious knowledge (*'ilm*) that confronted the companions of

---

20. "The one with the two lights" refers to 'Uthman's two successive wives, Ruqiyya and Umm Kulthum, both of whom were daughters of the Prophet. See the footnote 30 in letter 1.18 on page 127 for an inner interpretation of these two lights.

21. This statement put into the words of 'Ali is found in al-Daylami's *al-Firdaws* #5325 and Ibn Hajar's *Fath al-Bari*, 7:24 [MR].

the Prophet that 'Aisha could not answer.

The wars that happened between the noble Companions, for example, the Battle of the Camel and the Battle of Siffin, should be interpreted in a positive sense.[22] One must think of these events as not involving passion or fanaticism because the souls (*nufus*) of these notables were in spiritual companionship (*suhbat*) with Muhammad. They had become purified of passion, fanaticism, greed, and hatred. God bless him and them. Whatever they had that was beneficial was for Truth. If there was controversy and disagreement, that was for Truth. Each group acted in accordance with its own striving. They fought the opponent without getting involved in their own passion and fanaticism.

There is a saying, "Whatever turns out to be correct in one's own striving is rewarded (*thawab darad*) five times over." (that is, the double reward times five equaling ten times over) A person who is mistaken or misguided (*mukhti*) will receive one degree of reward, but in terms of being appropriately correct, he is very far from the station of the apparently blameworthy (*malamat*). However, in terms of degrees of religious merit, there is always hope for one degree of merit.

Jurists have said that in those [aforementioned] wars 'Ali b. Abi Talib was in the right. God almighty bless his face. His opponents' striving was not proper and correct. In spite of this, there is nothing to find fault with. They did not have the capacity to be apparently blameworthy because that is a place that is related to infidelity or sinfulness. 'Ali said that our brothers who rebel against us are not infidels or sinners because there is an explanation that prevents infidelity and sinfulness.[23] The Prophet has said "Avoid discussing the differences occurring between my companions."[24] God bless him and his family and give them peace. So all of the companions of the Prophet must be honored and remembered for their virtue. Not any one of these notables was bad and one must not suppose this.[25] Their disagreement

---

22. These battles do not reflect well on the supposed harmony of the Companions during the leadership of the rightly guided caliphs. In the Battle of the Camel, 'Aisha mounted on her camel and fought unsuccessfully against 'Ali. In the Battle of Siffin, 'Ali and Mu'awiyah's Syrian army sustained heavy losses without either side decisively winning the battle.

23. See al-Bayhaqi, *al-Sunan al-kubra*, 8:173; and Ibn Abu Shaybi, *al-Musannif*, #37763 [MR].

24. This hadith is mentioned twice in *Collected Letters*. A similar expression is found in Ibn Athir, *al-Nihaya*, 2:445 and al-Haythami, *Majma' al-zawahid* 7:248 [MR].

25. For the historically minded such a statement is problematic at best. The murders of three out of four of the first four caliphs are just the cover story for all the other kinds of behavior that mushroomed out of control after the Prophet

must be considered better than the reconciliation of others. This is the way of happiness and salvation because the love of the blessed Companions is on account of the love of the Prophet. Hating them becomes hating the Prophet. A notable once said, "One who does not have faith in the Messenger of God does not honor the companions of the Prophet."

[19] The signs of the Day of Judgment that the trustworthy Messenger (Muhammad) has reported are true. There is no possibility of disagreement. It is like the sun rising from the west, totally contrary to nature. [The signs of the Day of Judgment include] the appearance of the Mahdi (the divinely guided one), the reappearance of Jesus (lit. "God's spirit," *ruh-i Allah*), the coming of the Antichrist, the appearance of Gog and Magog,[26] the exodus of all the animals of the earth, and smoke coming from the sky. All the people will be taken under and be painfully punished. They will say in their agitated state, "Oh God take away this punishment because we have faith." The last sign of the Fire will rise out of Aden, Yemen.

There will be a group of ignorant people who will believe a person claiming to be the Mahdi, will come from India.[27] They claim that the Mahdi is in the past and that he has died. The evidence they give is that his grave is in Farah, Afghanistan (formerly Sijistan), [supposedly] indicated in well-known sound hadiths of uninterrupted hadith transmissions (*tawatur*). This is all the lying of the Mahdiwiyya because Muhammad outlined the signs of the Mahdi. The signs in the [aforementioned] hadiths detailing the signs of the claimant in whom the Mahdiwiyya believe [to have been the Mahdi] are absent from the prophetic hadith.

According to the prophetic hadith, the promised Mahdi sallies forth in rebellion. Over his head is a small cloud with an angel who cries out, "This is the Mahdi. Follow him!"[28] The Prophet said that there will be four rulers of the entire world: Dhu al-Qarnayn and Solomon from the believers,[29] and

---

died. Power struggles do not bring out the best in people. Sirhindi is reminding the reader that dwelling on negative past events is counterproductive.

26. Gog and Magog are mentioned in Qur'anic verses 18:94, as Yajuj and Majuj. They are ravishing the land and implore Dhu al-Qarnayn (often thought to be Alexander the Great) for assistance.

27. This is in reference to Sayyid Muhammad Jawnpuri (d. 910/1505) who claimed to be the Mahdi and the Mahdiwiyya who still existed in Sirhindi's time. See David Emmanuel Singh, *Sainthood and Revelatory Discourse: An Examination of the Basis for the Authority of Bayan in Mahdawi Islam* (Delhi: Cambridge Press, 1983).

28. This hadith is found in al-Tabarani, *al-Musnad al-shamiyin*, 2:71 [MR].

29. Dhu al-Qarnayn is mentioned in the Qur'an with an uncertain identity, that of Cyrus the Great or Alexander the Great.

Nimrud and Bukht-i Nassar from the infidels.[30] The fifth ruler will be from "Those of the Prophet's house," that is, the Mahdi.[31] The Prophet also said that that the Earth will not end until God sends a man from Muhammad's descendants (*ahl-i bayt*). His name will be Muhammad, whose father's name is the name of the Prophet's father, 'Abdullah, and whose mother's name is the same as that of the Prophet's mother, Amina. So the Mahdi will fill the world with justice in the same way as it is now filled with oppression.[32] In another hadith, it says that the Seven Sleepers of the Cave will help the Mahdi.[33]

Jesus will appear in the time of the Mahdi. Both will agree that the Antichrist should be killed. When the Mahdi's sultanate appears there will be an eclipse of the sun on the fourteenth of Ramadan.[34] At the beginning of that month there will be an eclipse of the moon, contrary to nature and astronomical calculations. To be fair, one must see whether these signs had appeared for the deceased Sayyid Muhammad Jawnpuri (d. 910/1505) or not. There are many other signs that the Prophet has indicated, God bless him and his family. Shaykh Ibn Hajar has written an epistle with two hundred signs of the Mahdi.[35] It is the utmost ignorance for a group to remain in error, in spite of the clear situation concerning the promised Mahdi. God almighty guide them on the straight path.

Muhammad has said, "In truth, there were seventy-one groups among the sons of Israel of which only one was saved from the Fire. Very quickly my community divided into seventy-three groups, and only one was saved from the Fire." He was asked which people were in the group that was saved. Muhammad replied, "The saved ones are in accordance with me and my companions.[36] The one group that will be saved is the rightly guided

---

30. Nimrod is the enemy of Abraham in the Qur'an. Nebuchadnezzar (Bukht-i Nassar) was a ruler of Babylon in the Chaldean Dynasty who died ca. 561 BCE.

31. This hadith is found in Ibn Hajar, *Fath al-bari*, 6:285 and al-Nawawi, *Tahzib al-asma'*, 224 [MR].

32. This hadith is found in Abu Da'ud, #4282; al-Hakim, *al-Mustadrak*, #8434; and al-Tabarani, *al-Awsat*, #1233 [MR].

33. The Seven Sleepers of the Cave (or The Seven Sleepers of Ephesus) are mentioned in the eighteenth sura of the Qur'an, The Cave (*al-Kahf*). This hadith is found in Ibn Hajar, *Fath al-bari*, 6: 503, 11:183; and al-Suyuti, *al-Durr al-mansur*, 6:345 [MR].

34. *Collected Letters*, 2.67.50 fn 10 states that this hadith, found in Daraqutni's hadith collection, is weak. MR does not mention it as a hadith.

35. This Ibn Hajar is probably Ibn Hajar al-Haytami (d. 974/1567) who has written an epistle *al-Qawl al-mukhtasar fi 'alamat al-Mahdi al-Muntazar*.

36. This hadith is found in al-Tirmidhi's hadith collection, #2641; Ibn Majah, #3992; Ahmad b. Hanbal, *Musnad*, 3:145, 4:102 [MR]. This hadith, condensed

mainstream that requires following the Prophet and his companions. God bless him and them. Oh God! Confirm us in the articles of faith of the rightly guided mainstream, have us die with their group, and be resurrected with them. "Our sustainer! Make sure our hearts do not go astray after you have guided us. From your presence bestow your mercy on us, for you are the Bestower." [Q. 3:8]

After correcting the articles of faith, it is necessary to pay attention to obeying the commands and avoiding the prohibitions outlined in the shariat, both of which are indispensably connected with deeds. One must perform ritual prayer five times a day in congregation calmly in all the movements without laziness. Prayer is the difference between submitting to God (*islam*) and denying God (*kufr*). When one performs prayer according to the Prophetic sunnat it becomes easier. This strong rope of submitting to God helps because ritual prayer is the second pillar of the five "pillars" (lit. principles) of Islam. The first pillar is faith in God and God's messenger, followed by ritual prayer, paying alms, fasting during the month of Ramadan, and performing the pilgrimage to God's House.

The first pillar is related to faith and the other four are related to deeds. The most comprehensive of all the acts of worship and most preferable is ritual prayer. On the Day of Judgment, the first accounting will be that of one's performing ritual prayer. If one's ritual prayer is satisfactory then the accounting will continue with the divine favor of God almighty. The accounting will also proceed with ease.

Whenever possible one must avoid doing what is prohibited by the shariat. What is not pleasing to God should be known as a deadly poison. Exalt God's sovereignty. One should always keep one's shortcomings in view. These should make one feel ashamed and upset, an experience of regret and sadness. This is the path of servanthood. God almighty is the Prospering One. A person who does something unpleasing to God, without batting an eye, and who is not ashamed or upset from that deed, is arrogant and obstinate. Persistent disobedience makes one close to not submitting to God, having him enter the circle of infidels. "Lord give us mercy from your presence and provide us right conduct in our affair." [Q. 18:10]

God has selected you for this blessing. People are heedless of this good fortune but it is possible that you too are unaware of this. It is [also a blessing] that the Mughal emperor (Jahangir), a Muslim for seven generations, is of the "folk of the sunnat" and a Hanafi. Although it is still some time before the Day of Judgment, it is far from the time of prophethood. Some students of the religious sciences have had the misfortune of greed created

---

in this rendition, has the Christians with seventy-two groups. Other hadiths have different numbers, for example, Beni Isra'il with seventy-two groups instead of seventy-one.

from the impurity of their inner selves. They have drawn near the rulers by way of flattery. In the firm religion, they have created doubts and disagreements. They have diverted the pure of heart from the straight path.

The great Emperor always listens attentively to your words and favorably accepts what you say. You have such divine favor that you can communicate, either directly or by allusion, the word of Islam that accords with the articles of faith of the rightly guided mainstream. God almighty thank them for their endeavors. You have the Emperor's ear, so petition to the best of your ability for the folk of God (*ahl-i haqq*). Moreover, continually be vigilant for a chance to get close to him. By means of discussing the schools of jurisprudence (sing. *madhhab*) and the Muslim community, the reality of Islam manifests. You can demonstrate the falseness and abomination of covering up the truth of God (*kufr*, commonly known as infidelity). Covering up the truth of God is the outer aspect of falseness. No intelligent person would be pleased with their falseness. Without batting an eye this must be exposed. One must unceasingly deny their false idols of worship. In reality, God does not fluctuate nor has any similitude [with anything else], and is the creator of heaven and earth. Exalt God's sovereignty.

Has anyone heard that their false gods have created a gnat, even if they were to gather everything together [to create a gnat]? If gnats were to bite them and harm them, they would not be able to protect themselves. It is preferred that another [is expected] to protect them. Thus, it is covering up the truth of God. They say that God will heal them, having observed the repugnant situation, and they will become closer to God.

They are out of their minds! How can they think that these inanimate objects have the capacity to heal, or that God almighty will accept the healing of idols, which are in truth God's enemies and the enemies of the idol worshippers themselves? It is like the Sultan kicking out the caretakers of his gardens who had rebelled against him. Some stupid people come up with a devious claim to help the gardeners in distress and reconcile them with the Sultan. It is ridiculous that they could be of service to the gardeners, ask the Sultan to forgive them, and have the gardeners gain access to the Sultan. Why don't these [stupid people] just serve the Sultan in reality and crush the gardeners? In that way, they could become the trusted "folk of God" and the "folk of nearness" (*ahl-i qurb*). Then they would experience security and faith. Fools take a rock and carve it with their hands. Then for years they worship it and have hopeful expectations from it. In short, the religion of those covering up God's truth (*kuffar*) is the outer aspect of falseness.

For Muslims, whatever is far from the path of Truth and the straight path belongs to the folk of passion and innovation. That straight path is the path of Muhammad and the same path of the rightly guided caliphs (the first four caliphs after Muhammad). God bless him and his family and give them peace. ʻAbdulqadir Jilani in his book *Sufficient Provision for Seekers of the Path of Truth* says that the nine heretical groups (in terms of basic principles) are the following: the Kharijiyya, Shiʻi, Muʻtaziliyya, Murji'a, Mushabbiha, Jahmiyya, Dirariyya (moderate Jabriyya), Najjariyya (al-Husayniyya), and Kulabiyya,[37] none of which existed during the time of the Prophet nor during the time of the first four caliphs, that is, Abu Bakr, ʻUmar, ʻUthman, and ʻAli. The controversies and divisions of these groups did not happen for years after the deaths of the Companions, Successors, and the seven jurisconsults (*fuqaha*) had occurred.[38] The Prophet said, "Anyone living after me will see much controversy, so you must adhere to my sunnat and the sunnat of my rightly guided caliphs. Hold tight to them. Keep yourself far from new events because every innovation is error.[39] Everything that is created after me [with respect to religion] should be rejected."[40] God bless the Prophet and his family and give them peace.

A school of jurisprudence (*madhhab*) created after the time of the Prophet and the rightly guided caliphs has deteriorated and is not a worthy perspective. (Here it is assumed that the rightly guided mainstream of the Hanafi-Maturidis is following the path of the Companions.) God bless him and them. Thanks to this great fortune, know that God's perfect blessing and preference have put us in the group that will be saved. We are in the rightly guided mainstream, which does not revert to passion and innovation nor take up corrupt articles of faith. The Muʻtazilis assert that God's servant participates in creating God's attributes, and that a person creates his own actions. This is a denial of the Day of Judgment, which is the source of good fortune in this world and in the Hereafter. They negate the existence of all the necessary attributes of God.

There are also two groups, the Kharijiyya and Shiʻi, who distort the [history of the] Companions and who think badly of religious notables.

---

37. There are articles concerning the Kharijiyya, Shiʻi, Muʻtaziliyya, Murji'a, Mushabbiha, Jahmiyya, and the Najjariyya (al-Husayniyya) in the second edition of the *Encyclopaedia of Islam*. The Kulabiyya are discussed in Huda bint Nasir ibn Muhammad al-Shalali, *Ara' al-Kulabiyah al-ʻaqidiyah wa-atharuha fi al-Ashʻariyah fi daw' ʻaqidat ahl al-sunnah wa'l-jamaʻah* (Riyad: Maktabat al-Rushd, 2000).

38. The Successors are the generation after the Companions. The seven jurisconsults of Medina are: Saʻid b. al-Musayyab, ʻUrwah b. al-Zubayr, Qasim b. Muhammad b. Abi Bakr as-Siddiq, Abi Bakr b. ʻAbdurrahman, Kharija b. Zayd b. Thabit, Sulayman b. Yasar, and ʻUbaydullah b. ʻAbdullah b. ʻUtbah b. Masʻud.

39. This hadith is found in al-Tirmidhi, *ʻIlm*, #2676; Abu Da'ud, *Sunnat*, #4607; Ibn Majah, #43,44 [MR].

40. This hadith is found in al-Bukhari, *Sulh*, 5; Muslim, *Aqdiyya*, 17; Abu Da'ud, 6; and Ibn Majah, #14 [MR].

They imagine themselves to be each other's enemies and accuse each other with hidden hatred. God spoke (Q. 48:29) about the companions of the Prophet. These two groups distorted God's word, and stirred up enmity and hatred between the Companions. God almighty grant them a happy outcome and have them return to the straight path. This group (presumably the Kharijiyya) also asserts that God almighty has directionality and location. They imagine God to be physical and assert that signs of accidents and possibility are necessary to God.

Let's return to the beginning of the discussion. You know that the Sultan is like the spirit (*ruh*). The rest of the human being is the physical body. If the spirit is sound then the body is sound. If the spirit is spoiled then so is all the body. So, in striving to reform the Sultan, one endeavors to reform all of humanity (lit. sons of Adam). In whatever time is available, use it for reform by explaining Islam. Then discuss the articles of faith of the rightly guided mainstream when you get an opportunity. You must catch the Sultan's ear, refuting conflicting schools of jurisprudence. If this good fortune becomes easy, it is an inheritance from the prophets who are helping you. God bless them. You have been given this good fortune freely. Know its value. Whether you do a lot or [whether you] exaggerate, whatever you do is praiseworthy. God almighty is the Prospering One.

Introduction to Shariat: Letter 2.46

This letter was written to Mawlana Hamid Bengali (d. 1050/1641 in Mangalkot, Bengal), otherwise known as 'Abdulhamid Bangali, a jurist who spent a year with Ahmad Sirhindi before receiving permission to teach others.[41]

This is one of the letters in which Sirhindi attempts to explain the paradoxical yet critical relationship of shariat to human realization and returning to God. Shariat for Sirhindi is much more than simply "Islamic Law," which is how the word is usually translated. Indeed, shariat is a multivalent word in *Collected Letters*, the main reason that it is not translated. Typically shariat is equated with a set of rules to blindly follow. This generalization applies in its outer form to the majority of common Muslims. On the other hand, shariat in Sirhindi's expanded context includes all the dimensions of Islam discussed in Gabriel's hadith, that is, submission (*islam*), faith (*iman*), and acting virtuously (*ihsan*). Until all these three dimensions have been verified, one has not verified the shariat.[42] In this letter, Sirhindi explains

41. Five letters were addressed to Hamid Bengali in Sirhindi's *Collected Letters*, including letter 1.292 and 2.46 included in this book. Part of this letter is translated in Muhammad Abdul Haq Ansari, *Sufism and Shari'ah: A Study of Shaykh Ahmad Sirhindi's Effort to Reform Sufism* (Leicester, UK: The Islamic Foundation, 1986), 231-233.

42. See letter 2.42 in this book and *Collected Letters*, 1.36.98.

that it is exceedingly difficult to reach God just by obeying shariat commands and prohibitions. Spiritual companionship (*suhbat*) and initiation are a part of following the sunnat and in this manner one can learn other, more continuous ways of remembering God that have been developed by the sufis. These same methods of remembrance cleanse the ego-self, which in turn makes it easier to follow the shariat.

A wayfarer begins to discover the truth of the shariat after the experience of annihilation in God (*fana'*) becomes wayfaring in God (*sayr fi'llah*). This is the experience of moving from negation to affirmation (*la illaha* to *illa Allah*) and going from wayfaring (*suluk*) to ecstatic attraction to God (*jadhba*), which is the station of abiding in God (*baqa'*). In terms of shariat, the appearance of shariat is associated with negation of *la illaha* and the reality of the shariat is associated with the station of affirmation and the level of perfected intimacy with God (*kamalat-i walayat*). At this point one is in the shadows of the levels of the Necessary. One should not think that the shariat is behind these shadows and reality is the kernel. The reality of these shadows and the kernel is only in the realm of contemplatively witnessing the shadows of the levels of the Necessary. The reality of the shariat is in the perfections of the intimacy of prophethood and arriving oneself at the levels of the Necessary. These levels are the attributes, qualities (*shuyunat*), and aspects (*i'tibarat*).[43]

The foundation of the shariat, indicated in the transmitted sources of the Qur'an, Hadith, consensus of the jurists, and the independent legal reasoning of qualified jurists (*ijtihad-i mujtahidin*), is reflected by sufis' sources of experiential knowledge, i.e., unveiling (*kashf*), inspiration (*ilham*), and altered states (*wajd wa-hal*).[44] As outlined in this letter, Sirhindi considers the sufis' ways of knowing to be inferior to the unquestioned authority of the transmitted sources. In addition, if there is any conflict between these two types of sources, transmitted or subjectively verified, then the transmitted sources are without question more reliable. The common person and beginning wayfarer have to blindly follow the transmitted interpretation of the sources, for example, articles of creed and school of jurisprudence. As one proceeds on the path, one is able to increasingly verify these transmitted sources to the point of performing one's own independent legal reasoning.[45]

---

43. See Nasrullah Hutaki, *Sharh-i Maktubat-i qudsi ayat* (Peshawar: Taj Mahal Company, ca. 1976), 603-604.

44. See *Collected Letters*, 1.217.125.

45. One example is Sirhindi not performing the common Hanafi practice of raising the right forefinger while reciting the affirmation of faith (*tashahud*) in the sitting posture of the prayer ritual. See letter 1.312. Sirhindi has not questioned the assumptions behind the infallibility of the Qur'an and Sunni hadith sources nor

As discussed in the Introduction, Sirhindi is seeking, through his emphasis on prophethood, to bring sufi practice back into balance by countering "transcendental escape." It is much more exhilarating to lose oneself in the ocean of Oneness than to deal with the ego-self. The path of prophethood is one that deeply encompasses all levels of reality while the path of intimacy with God (by Sirhindi's demarcation of the path) simply lacks the depth and intimacy of the prophetic path because one has not ascended as far. The path of intimacy, in Sirhindi's view, is like admiring the view of the plains from the Himalayan foothills but thinking that one is on Mt. Everest. It takes a lot more to get to Mt. Everest, which is a qualitatively different experience. The perfections of intimacy with God are incommensurate with the perfections of prophethood.

There are resonances in this letter of Mahayana Buddhist critiques of the Hinayana Arhat goal of achieving enlightenment for oneself. The Bodhisattva ideal of the Mahayana is to seek enlightenment to help others also reach enlightenment. Likewise, Sirhindi perceives those who simply strive for intimacy with God to be ego-centered. This brings to mind 'Abdulquddus Gangohi's (d. 944/1537) ecstatic utterance, "Muhammad Mustafa went within [the distance] of two bows or closer [to God] and returned. I swear to God that I would not have returned."[46] As discussed in the Introduction, Sirhindi is continually reminding the reader to follow the prophetic path, the path where shariat is first and foremost throughout the wayfarer's ascent and descent.

Just when the reader is beginning to think she understands what Sirhindi is discussing, he explains that there is a fourth incommensurate aspect beyond shariat, the path (*tariqat*), and reality (*haqiqat*). This is God's grace that deals with the great prophets (*ulu' al-'azmi*) and has nothing to do with performance of the shariat injunctions.[47] All of the prophets performed their shariat duties but only a few became great prophets. In this context, we are asked to imagine the shariat's outer form to be its inner reality and whose beginning is intimacy with God (*walayat*). This is an example of post-rational discourse, which is baffling to the rational mind yet understandable to one who has had this experience in a unitary state of consciousness.

---

has he disagreed with any sound Sunni hadith on the basis of his own subjective inspiration or unveiling. Perhaps his experiences have guided him to certain hadith rather than to others.

46. 'Abdulquddus Gangohi, *Lata'if-i quddusi*, ed. Ruknuddin (his son) (Delhi: Matba'-i Mujtaba'i, 1894), 65.

47. The great prophets are generally considered by Mujaddidis to be Noah, Moses, Abraham, Jesus, and Muhammad since they established a shariat for their people. This classification overlaps but does not coincide with those prophets designated as "messengers" who brought "books" to humankind.

The performance of shariat injunctions is directly related to reaching the furthest reaches of the world of command, but this is not the absolute end by any means. To reach the absolute end it is a *condition* to perform the shariat injunctions. It is like ritual prayer being the ascension (*mi'raj*) of the believer. A heavenly ascension is not guaranteed for each prayer but without doing ritual ablution, one cannot pray. If one does have the experience of ascension during ritual prayer it is not because of either ritual prayer or ritual ablution. Ritual ablution is a condition for ritual prayer and ritual prayer is a condition for the ascension in the same way that performance of shariat injunctions is a condition for reaching the absolute end of the path.[48]

Letter 2.46

Praise God. God give peace to those declaring "There is no god but God and Muhammad is God's prophet." This attestation of faith includes the path (*tariqat*), reality (*haqiqat*), and "God's law" (*shari'at*). The wayfarer begins the path at the station of negation, that is, "There is no god," and stays there until the negation of all other than God disappears from the perception. With this realization, the wayfaring stops as one arrives at the station of [the ego-self's] annihilation (*fana'*). After this, one comes to the station of affirmation, that is, "but God," under the influence of attraction to God (*jadhba*). At this point, one can verify that this level of reality, along with the experience of abiding in God (*baqa'*), has replaced that of annihilation. One arrives at what is called genuine intimacy with God (*walayat-i sadiq*). The culmination of negation and affirmation occurs by following the path to reality, by annihilation and abiding, by attraction [to God], and by wayfaring (*suluk*). As the unruly ego-self (*nafs*) is purified it becomes tranquil.

The perfection of being close to or intimate with God is connected to the first part of the attestation of faith, that is, "There is no god but God." The second part of this holy declaration (and Muhammad is God's messenger) confirms the messengership of the Seal of the Prophets. God bless him and his family and give them peace. These two aspects bring together and complete God's law in such a way that one acquires the elementary and intermediate aspects of the law, that is, the outward form, terminology, and rules. Realizing the reality of shariat is connected to reaching a certain level of intimacy with God. The perfections of prophethood, that is, the inheritance of the prophets, is also obtained by those who completely follow the prophets. God bless them.

One becomes intimate with God by traveling on the path towards reality (*tariqat* and *haqiqat*). Just as ritual purification (*taharat*) is a preparation and subsidiary precondition for ritual prayer (*salat*), there are conditions to

48. See Hutaki, *Sharh-i Maktubat*, 607.

realize the reality of the law and the perfections of prophethood. Closeness to God (*walayat*) is a precondition to actualize shariat. On the path to God one is distant from major impurities (*najasat-i haqiqiya*) while in reality minor impurities (*najasat-i hukmi*) are removed.[49] After a complete ritual purification, one becomes worthy of performing the injunctions of the Law. The ability to perform ritual prayer is one of the utmost degrees of closeness that one can have with God, in addition to being a pillar of religion and the "ascension of the believer."[50]

Thinking about the second part of the holy attestation (and Muhammad is God's messenger), I find an immense ocean that makes the first part appear like a drop.[51] Yes! The perfections of intimacy with God are insignificant compared to the perfections of prophethood. It is like an atom and the sun. Praise be to God. Some, in their distorted vision, give preference to intimacy with God over prophethood and relegate the shariat, the quintessence, to a position of secondary importance. What are they doing? Their tunnel vision is focused on the form of the shariat as they seize a part of the outer shell from the kernel (*maghz*). They belittle prophethood on the basis of its focus on humanity and consider it to be deficient because it focuses on the common people. Instead, they give preference to intimacy with God, concentrating on God. They say intimacy with God is preferable to prophethood without realizing that the perfections of prophethood involve turning toward God at the time of ascent toward God.

At the level of intimacy with God perfections of ascent begin to appear and are fully realized later at the station of prophethood. After returning to the world, one remembers a few of these appearances [of the perfections

---

49. Major impurities (*najasat-i haqiqiya*) are those that result from sexual intercourse, menstruation, and giving birth (among other things) and require a major ablution. Minor impurities (*najasat-i hukmi*) are those that result from such things as urination and defecation and require a minor ablution. In Hutaki, *Sharh-i Maktubat*, 604 the minor impurities involve being occupied in the shadows and the major impurities involve being occupied with the many things of the world (*mumkinat*).

50. Note the hadith often repeated by sufis, " Ritual prayer is the heavenly ascension of the believer" mentioned in *Collected Letters*, 1.260.88; 1:261.96; 1.293.117.

51. Here Sirhindi is turning things around for us to see things in another way. The conventional perspective is that the first sentence of the attestation is the ocean, that is, God, and the second part is the drop, Muhammad. Sirhindi is applying the attestation of faith to the path of the individual seeker, emphasizing that the *prophetic* perfections are oceanic compared to the drop of the perfections of those intimate with God (*awliya'*). The drop of the human being partakes of the ocean through following the prophets, not by stopping at the first rung of closeness to God, which is a pond in comparison.

of ascent]. At the time of the prophetic descent, as with intimacy with God, one is focused on humanity. The difference, however, is that intimacy with God involves focusing on humanity outwardly and with the Real inwardly. Praise God. In the prophetic descent, the focus on humanity is both inward and outward. [At the same time] one's entire being is with God as God's message spreads. Descent is more complete and perfect than intimacy with God because the verification is in books and other writings. This attention toward humanity is not like that of the common people as many imagine. The common people's preoccupation with others is a result of their all-encompassing bondage to the material world. Prophets have long since abandoned attachment to the world. Instead, they are attached to the Creator of humanity. Exalt God's dominion. These notables' attention is to guide humanity to the Creator of humanity for the pleasure of their almighty and holy Lord. There is no doubt that the goal of rescuing humanity from their servitude to the world is preferable to focusing on God for the sake of one's own ego-self.

Let's take the example of someone busy remembering God (*dhikr*). This person then comes across a blind person at the edge of a deep well. If the blind person takes one more step, he will fall in the well. Is it better to be recollecting God or to save the blind person? No doubt saving the blind person is better than just remembering God. God almighty does not need this individual or anyone else to recollect God. However, the blind person is God's servant and needs to be protected, especially when God has commanded to do so by putting the other person in a position to save him. Then saving the blind person becomes recollection of God and an act of obedience to God. One performs a duty in remembering God, which is affirming the existence of the truth of the Lord. Exalt God's power. In saving the blind person, there are two duties: the human obligation and the divine obligation toward the Lord almighty. One can say that just recollecting God at this time becomes a sin. Sometimes it is commendable not to simply remember God, just as there are days when it is prohibited to fast (for example, during the two Eids) and there are times when it is prohibited to pray (for example, when the sun is rising or setting over the horizon).

The goal of recollecting God is to avoid heedlessness in whatever form that may take. Remembering God should not be limited to the words of negation and affirmation, "There is no god but God," or repeating the name of almighty God, "Allah." Recollecting God includes obedience to God's commands and avoiding what God's law prohibits. Buying, selling, marriage, and divorce should be performed according to the injunctions of God's law. All these acts of obedience are considered remembrance of God as one keeps in mind the injunctions and prohibitions that God has enjoined. Exalt God's power. All deeds and the doers thereof are in God's full view.

By following the dictates of God's law, heedlessness can be avoided. However, a recollection of God in which one says the names and attributes of God is effective in reaching God quickly while increasing one's love for God.[52] A second way of remembering God is through obeying God's commands and avoiding what is prohibited. Except in rare cases, this latter type of recollection is not sufficient by itself to engender the attributes necessary to realize intimacy with God. Those who simultaneously actualize both ways of remembering God are even more uncommon.

The exalted presence of the master Baha'uddin Naqshband (d. 791/1389 in Bukhara) said, "The Presence of our lord Zaynuddin Tayibadi (also d. 791/1389) arrived near God from the path of religious knowledge (*'ilm*). God bless their inner hearts."[53] Another way of reaching God is through the recollection of God's names and attributes, a means of remembering God by acting in accordance with God's law. Yet it is not easy to follow the injunctions of God's law in all matters unless one has a strong love for the Establisher of the shariat (God). This encompassing love in turn is established through the recollection of the names and attributes of the Establisher. So that one can be honored by the fortune of remembering God through observance of God's law, first one must recollect God's names and attributes. The question of divine favor is another matter since there are no conditions and no special means. "God chooses whom God wills." [Q. 42:13]

Here we return to the original topic by saying that beyond these three aspects, that is, the path, reality, and shariat, there is yet another that is incommensurate with these three. At the level of reality the fourth aspect (lit. other aspect) has a connection with the affirmation "but God," which is the form. This fourth aspect is the reality of the form of the other three (the path, reality and shariat). For example, this fourth aspect first expresses itself through the shariat even though first acquiring the outer form of the shariat is connected with the level of the common people. After traversing the path and arriving at Reality, one can perceive the reality of the shariat's form. One should now imagine something whose outer form is its inner reality and whose beginning is intimacy with God (*walayat*). How can one explain this in ordinary conversation, even if forced to clarify it? This affair is the inheritance of the great prophets (*ulu al-'azmi*) who have a minute share in it, God bless them and give them peace. Since there are few roots

---

52. One example would be "In the name of Allah the most compassionate and merciful."

53. Zaynuddin Abu Bakr Tayibadi (Tabyadi in the text) received his "outer" religious education from Nizamuddin Harawi and his "inner" training via Uwaysi initiations from Ahmad Namaqi Jami (d. 536/1141-42). See *Collected Letters*, 2.46.128 fn. 8, which was based upon 'Abdurrahman Jami, *Nafahat al-uns*, 498-501.

in this affair, the branches will inevitably be even less.

Question: From this knowledge, it necessarily follows that a person of inner knowledge (*'arif*), at some levels of attainment, will abandon the shariat and ascend toward God outside of the shariat. Answer: The shariat consists of outward actions that are connected in this world to one's inner being. Outer behavior is always occupied with the shariat, but the inner person also engages this matter. When the material world is the sphere of action, one's inner being is of great assistance for [performing] outer deeds. The development of the inner person is directly related to complying with the shariat, which in turn is connected to outward behavior. In the material world, there is no way the inner and outer person can get around the shariat.

The shariat is the cause of all perfections and the basis of all the stations one passes through. The fruits of the shariat are not limited to this world. The perfections of the next world and its eternal enjoyments result from the shariat. The shariat is the pure tree whose fruit benefits humanity in both worlds. The benefits of many worlds are taken from there.

Question: In the perfections of prophethood, the inner person is oriented toward God (*batin bi-haqq*) and the outer focused toward humanity. Praise God. You have written in your own letters and treatises [and above in this letter] that in the station of prophethood, one is totally focused on humanity, inviting them to God. How do you reconcile these two statements?

Answer: This matter is related both to ascent and descent, the latter involving the station of inviting people to God. During ascent the inner person is with the most glorious Real, and the outer person oriented toward humanity so that one's deeds are in accordance with the noble shariat. While descending one is completely focused on humanity, guiding them to God with one's entire being. Exalt God's loftiness. There is no contradiction here. The verification of this station is the realization that focusing on humanity is the origin of concentrating on God. "Wherever you turn is the face of God." [Q. 2:115] This does not mean that the contingent is the Necessary Origin or the Necessary Mirror. Praise God almighty. What power does the lowly contingent have compared to the Necessary, almighty, and blessed Origin or God's mirror?[54]

One could say that the almighty and blessed Necessary is the mirror of the contingent, reflecting the material world in the mirror of God almighty like objects reflected in an ordinary mirror (that is, a mirror that reflects the outward shape of objects). Objects in an ordinary mirror do not penetrate the mirror itself or take on additional external forms. The material world

54. Sirhindi often uses "Necessary Being" (*wajib-i wujud*) or "Necessary" for God (the One). Its counterpart is the created "possible things" (*mumkinat*), or the many. I have usually translated the latter as "the contingent" to indicate their dependent relationship on the Necessary.

has the same relation when reflected in the mirror of God almighty. How can one conceive of an independent materialization when forms have no independent being at the level of the mirror? At the level of imagination forms do have a reality, but that is as far as it goes. From the perspective of a mirror, there are no objects and wherever there are objects, then reflection in the mirror is quite deceiving. Except for the imagination there is not a shred of evidence for the existence of these objects. Something can be imagined if it exists in time or space, but this is for non-existent objects. When God creates entities that are preserved from defect and from immediate perishing they become connected to eternity through eternal punishment and reward. Exalt God's power.

Know that what is viewed in an ordinary mirror is first thought of as form. Because of the mirror's presence, it is necessary to look at forms from another perspective. At first glance, the mirror of God almighty is just like an ordinary mirror, but because of the presence of material objects it is also necessary to look at the mirror from another reference point. In an ordinary mirror, the way forms are reflected is a function of the way the mirror is designed, for example, things can appear taller or shorter than they actually are. The mirror of the Necessary almighty Essence, on the contrary, is not designed to reflect material things because this lofty level is incommensurate with the material world. What kind of a mirror reflects material objects and what does it really show?

Indeed, it is in the levels of descent, the domain of verifying the names and attributes of God, where it is possible for the created world to reflect the form of God's necessary aspects. Thus, hearing, vision, knowledge, and power, which are reflected in the material world, are the outer forms of hearing, vision, knowledge, and power that are at the level of Necessary Being. Mirrors operate according to certain principles; for example, external forms appear in an ordinary mirror. As we said before, the mirror of God almighty (lit. the Necessary) first seems like an ordinary mirror because one sees things as [visible] forms in that mirror. A second perspective [given above] is useful [and with that let's] return to the matter at hand (ascent and descent).

Forms come into view [in the descent] after [having been] totally out of one's perception. Returning to the material world [after ascent] is arriving at the end of the path, far removed from wayfaring in the material world (the first *sayr fi'l-ashya'* before ascent, the state of most people). One becomes established in the center of the circle of possibility (the third and final stage). A transformation occurs in how one contemplatively witnesses the unseen, as faith in what is perceived in a contemplative state (*iman-i shuhudi*) becomes faith in transcendental realities beyond human perception (*iman-i ghaybi*). At this point one is completely involved in calling people to God and proclaiming the urgency of preparation for the next world. As this occurs, the unseen becomes distant and one can no longer witness a certain part of it. The contemplative witnessing after returning to the world, however, is more complete than before. Any contemplative witnessing that has a relationship to the next world is more complete than contemplative witnessing solely connected to this world.

Congratulations to those favored with blessings
And to the poor lover in pain and distress.

One should know from previous verification that the evidence of a form reflected in a mirror is only in the imagination. The mirror has an entirely independent existence from the actual form and the apparent form. One can say that the mirror is near to or encompasses the object. However, this is not the proximity or encompassing between two entities or between accidentally occurring substances (*jawahir bi-'ard*). Instead, there is a closeness and a permeating intimacy that the rational mind has difficulty comprehending. In this [paradoxical] way, this relationship [between the Necessary and contingent] is proved without knowing how it is so. "God is the highest ideal." [Q.16:60]

In this way, God has a closeness to the world, permeating and encompassing it. People believe this but do not know [rationally] how this is so. We do not know whether these attributes of proximity, togetherness, and encompassing are separate from mundane attributes or from the signs of possibility and occurrence. All of this involves resemblance and comparison in the world of metaphor, the bridge to reality. It has been made apparent using the allusion of the mirror and form so that the perceptive may be led with God almighty's favor from the metaphor of false appearance to truth. May they have a longing for the Essence instead of the form. Peace to the person who follows God's guidance.

Introduction to the seven levels of the sunnat: Letter 2.54

This is the only letter addressed to Sayyid Shah Muhammad.[55] In some ways, this letter contextualizes the previous letter (2.46) in that it outlines in seven degrees what had only been approximately explained before. For example, the realization of the fourth aspect mentioned in letter 2.46, the inheritance of the great prophets (*ulu al-'azmi*), is the fifth degree of imitating the Prophet in this letter.

The sufi path begins in the second degree where one is under the direction of a shaykh and begins wayfaring to God (*sayr ila Allah*). Between the latter phases of the second degree and the latter stages of the third degree the heart becomes connected to the origin of divine effulgence (*fayd*) and the

55. This letter has been partially translated by ter Haar, *Follower and Heir*, 56.

ego-self eventually becomes tranquil along with an increasing stabilization of the heart (*tamkin-i qalb*). It is the domain of lesser intimacy with God (*walayat-i sughra*). At the fourth degree, the level of the well-grounded jurists (lit. firmly established in the inner and outer religious sciences, *'ulama'-i rasikhin*), the ego-self is tranquil and one realizes the reality of the shariat and sunnat. It is the domain of greater intimacy with God (*walayat-i kubra*). At the fifth degree one experiences the perfections of the attributes and the Essence, as there is a transition to the intimacy of the prophets (*walayat-i anbiya'*). Beyond the great prophets, the sixth degree involves the stations of being the Beloved (*maqam-i mahbubiyat*) and of messengership (*maqam-i risalat*). The seventh degree is associated with descent and is a comprehensive integration of all the previous degrees of ascent.[56]

The main intent of this letter is to contextualize rankings of jurists. The role of jurists is primary for Sirhindi. Both Friedmann and ter Haar have outlined how Sirhindi criticizes the weak and bad jurists of the world.[57] Sirhindi does not have a high regard for most sufis either.

> Even though the jurists of the rightly guided mainstream (*ahl-i sunnat wa-jama'at*) have deficient behavior, the beauty of their creed concerning the Divine Essence and attributes illuminates them such that their deficiencies can be overlooked. So-called sufis doing all kinds of contemplative practices do not have the correct beliefs concerning the Divine Essence and attributes. They lack this beauty.[58]

Then Sirhindi goes on to express his love for jurists and their students.

> A protégé of God is always governed by a prophet. In disagreements between sufis and jurists, the jurists always end up being in the right because the views of jurists are a result of following prophets and they acquire the perfections of prophethood and prophetic knowledge. The sufi view is blocked by the perfections of intimacy with God. By definition, the knowledge from the lamp of prophethood is truer and more real than the level of intimacy with God.[59]

Well-grounded jurists have the knowledge of both the appearance and essence of the shariat with a totally tamed ego-self (*nafs*).[60] According to Sirhindi, Baha'uddin Naqshband (d. 791/1389) did not say there was any special knowledge beyond that of shariat. From inspirations (*kashf* and *il-*

56. See Hutaki, *Sharh-i Maktubat*, 625-626.

57. See Friedmann, *Shaykh Ahmad Sirhindi*, 47-48; ter Haar, *Follower and Heir of the Prophet,* 50-51

58. See *Collected Letters*, 1.8.16.

59. See Ibid., 1.266.123.

60. See *Collected Letters*, 2.18.46.

ham) one can learn about the shariat, like the prophets did with revelations.[61] This letter explains the criteria for a jurist to be considered "well-grounded" as Sirhindi ranks those who seek to imitate the Prophetic example.

LETTER 2.54

Praise to God. God give peace to those following Muhammad (lit. that Joy), who is the means of happiness in this world and the next. Imitating the Prophet has degrees and levels. The first degree is that of the common Muslims and involves the injunctions of God's law, the shariat. It is a stage of following the lofty Prophetic example, the sunnat, after one attests in one's heart that there is no god but God and Muhammad is God's messenger. This is prior to calming the ego-self, which is related to a degree of closeness with God. Jurists whose knowledge is from books (*'ulama-yi zahir*), pious individuals, and ascetics whose goal involves taming the ego-self participate and benefit equally in outwardly imitating the Prophetic example. The ego-self in this station is not saved from infidelity and rebellion. Nonetheless, this level of attainment is special. The outward imitation of the prophetic example resembles the reality of imitating the Prophet. This means that those outwardly imitating the Prophet have felicity and salvation in the next world, avoid the punishment of hellfire, and rejoice in the good news of entering heaven. Trusting in God's complete generosity, there are others who do not think it necessary to struggle against their ego desires. According to them it is enough to attest in one's heart that there is no god but God and Muhammad is God's messenger, since salvation only depends on accepting this.

Oh that a raindrop could form a pearl
And my tears could allow me to be received favorably

The second degree of imitating the Prophet involves acting in accordance with his sayings and actions so that one's inner self is involved. God bless him and his family and give them peace. This level corresponds to those on the sufi path who concentrate on refinement of character by avoiding disagreeable traits while eliminating inner deficiencies through [awareness of] their essential causes. An exemplary shaykh (*shaykh-i muqtada'*) leads them through the valleys and deserts of the path as they proceed to God.

The third degree involves imitating the states, visionary experiences, and ecstasies of those whose station is connected to special closeness to God. This level is especially for protégés of God who are "ecstatic ones wayfaring" (sing. *majdhub-i salik*) or "wayfarers ecstatically attracted to God" (sing. *salik-i majdhub*). When they realize this level of intimacy, the ego-self has become tranquil and free of struggle and rebellion. They have

61. Ibid., 1.30.82. See also in letter 1.18 in this book.

gone from denial to contentment and from covering up the truth of God to submission. From this point, all one's endeavors to imitate the Prophet will be real imitation, whether through prayer, fasting, alms, or any other injunctions of the shariat.

Question: What is the meaning of the expression "Ritual prayer is the door to reality"? Both ritual prayer and fasting involve many special ritual actions enjoined by the shariat. By fulfilling these requirements will the reality of the actions manifest? What about the form of the rituals? Is the reality of the ritual something beyond its form?

Answer: A beginner with a rebellious ego-self essentially denies the heavenly injunctions and therefore only performs the shariat requirements outwardly. The well-developed wayfarer with a tranquil ego-self accepts the injunctions of the shariat with contentment and satisfaction, performing the injunctions of the shariat in a way that exemplifies their reality. For example, a hypocrite and a *muslim* both perform ritual prayer.[62] The hypocrite, who inwardly denies the reality of prayer, only goes through the outer motions. The *muslim*, by means of inner obedience, is adorned with the reality of prayer. Thus, the form and the reality are a function of inner struggle and affirmation. The third degree of imitating the Prophet involves calming the restless ego-self and the real performance of pious actions, both of which occur after having achieved the perfections of special closeness to God.

The fourth degree of imitation is real imitation. Compare this to the first degree of imitation involving only the outer appearance of imitation. This fourth degree pertains especially to the well-grounded jurists (lit. firmly established in the inner and outer religious sciences, *'ulama'-i rasikhin*). After calming their ego-selves, they distinguish themselves by the good fortune of really imitating the Prophet. God almighty thank them for their endeavors. The friends of God have partially subdued their egos after achieving stability in their hearts. God almighty bless their inner hearts. Complete calming of the ego-self is only achieved, however, when one has acquired the perfections of prophethood. The well-grounded jurists have inherited these perfections and, through complete subjugation of their ego-selves, have acquired the reality of the shariat, that is, the reality of imitation of the Prophet. Other than the well-grounded jurists, no one else has these perfections, whether they have only achieved the form of God's law or whether they have reached the reality of the shariat. I will clarify this point about the well-grounded jurists so that an ignorant jurist (that is, one whose knowledge is only from the literal reading of books) will not claim to be well grounded or imagine his rebellious ego-self to be at peace.

62. Here both are outwardly Muslims but only one is a *muslim*, that is, someone who has truly submitted to God.

A well-grounded jurist is one who can interpret the ambiguous verses (*mutashabihat*) of the Qur'an and hadith and the isolated letters at the beginning of Qur'anic verses (*muqatta'at*).[63] The interpretation of the ambiguous verses results from concealed secrets. People who literally interpret the hand of God as God's power (*ta'wil-i yad*) or who literally interpret (*ta'wil-i wajh*) the face of God as God's Essence are devoid of inner knowledge. Whatever is derived from external knowledge will not be of any use. It is the prophets who know these secrets, symbols, and allusions. God bless all of them. Through the imitation and inheritance of these notables, anyone can be guided to this great fortune.

Realizing this degree of imitation of the Prophet is connected to calming of the ego-self and arriving at the reality of imitating the Friend of the shariat (Muhammad). It does not require the mediation of annihilation and abiding, wayfaring and attraction to God, or any intermediary of states, ecstasies, or manifestations. However, one can arrive at this good fortune more expediently by following the noble sunnat than by following paths leading one closer to God. God bless Muhammad and give him peace. This poor one (Ahmad Sirhindi) asserts the efficacy of following the sunnat while avoiding any trace of innovation. As long as one avoids beneficial innovations as if they were despicable innovations, the fragrance of this good fortune will grace one's mind and heart. These days this meaning is only understood with difficulty, since the world is drowned in an ocean of innovations. There is no peace from the gloomy oppression of these innovations. How can anyone who wants to get rid of innovations speak out and revive the sunnat?

Most contemporary jurists are practitioners of innovations and destroyers of the sunnat. It is known that innovations have become widespread practice because they are considered praiseworthy in their religious legal opinions. Innovations end up being used to guide people. What do the jurists say when something becomes a common practice after it is widely recognized as an error? They do not know that common practice is not an absolute proof for something being considered praiseworthy. A common practice is esteemed as praiseworthy when it comes from the practice of the Companions or when a general consensus among all people is reached.[64]

It is mentioned in *The Legal Opinions of al-Ghiyathiyya* that Shaykh Imam Shahid said,

---

63. The ambiguous verses in the Qur'an outnumber the clear, unambiguous verses (*muhkam*) and provide much scope for commentary. In Qur'an 3:7 it says that those who are not firmly grounded in religious knowledge should avoid trying to interpret the ambiguous verses.

64. The following paragraph is from the Arabic original.

> We do not consider something praiseworthy because the shaykhs of Balkh have declared it to be so in their legal opinions.[65] God bless him. Instead we accept the sayings of the revered Companions. God bless them. Common practice in Balkh does not indicate permissibility. When it actually does indicate permissibility, then it also demonstrates the continuity of the practice of the Companions. This is evidence for the shariat established by the Prophet. God bless him and his family and give them peace. People's actions are not proof of anything except if the people in all towns have a consensus, a recognized form of legal proof. Formulating a legal opinion does not make selling alcoholic beverages and charging interest legally acceptable.

There is no way of ascertaining the common behavior of everyone in all villages and towns. This leaves the genuinely established practices of Muhammad's companions. One can return to the Companions via his sunnat. God bless him and his family and give them peace. So where are the innovations and beneficial innovations? It was sufficient for the venerable Companions to acquire all the perfections through spiritual companionship (*suhbat*) with the best human (Muhammad). The jurists before us had the good fortune to be honored with well-grounded religious knowledge. Without choosing the sufi path with its ecstatic wayfaring, they traversed the path toward God by imitating the noble sunnat and by avoiding unpleasing innovations. God bless and give peace to Muhammad. God help us to follow the sunnat and keep us from acting out [deleterious] innovations. In this way, we can respect and venerate Muhammad.

The fifth degree involves imitating the perfections of Muhammad. Acquiring these perfections does not involve religious knowledge (*'ilm*) or deeds but instead depends entirely on God's favor and beneficence. Exalt God's majesty. The preceding degrees of imitation have no reality compared to this utterly lofty degree of imitation. These perfections are entirely the special domain of the great prophets (*ulu al-'azmi*). God bless them and give them peace. Following their example and benefiting from their inheritance enables one to be honored with these perfections.

The sixth degree of imitating Muhammad is the special domain of Muhammad's station of belovedness (*mahbubiyat*). God bless him and his family and give them peace. In the sixth degree, the grace of perfections is based only upon love (*mahabbat*), which is above the favor and beneficence of the previous degree of imitation. Very few people attain this level

---

65. These legal opinions are contained in 'Alim ibn 'Ula, *Fatawa-al-tatarkhaniyya*, 5 vols., ed. Qazi Sajjad Husayn (Hyderabad, Deccan: Da'irat al-Ma'arif al-Othmaniyya, 1984). The martyred shaykh may be Ibn 'Ula' al-Hanafi according to 2.54.8 fn. 3.

of imitation. After the first degree of imitation, the five further degrees, including this sixth level, are connected to stations of ascent.

The seventh degree of imitation involves descent and encompasses all the previous six degrees. The domain of descent involves attesting in one's heart,[66] an inner stability in one's heart, calming of the rebellious ego-self, and attaining harmony of the four elements of the physical body. The prior degrees of imitation are all partial; this one is comprehensive. In this station, a type of resemblance is created between the follower and the followed (Muhammad) that goes beyond imitation to the point of blurring the distinction between them. To the extent that they resemble each other, they are similar in a very fundamental way. One could say that they drank water from the same source, that they are in one embrace sitting on the same cushion,[67] or that they are like milk and sugar. Where is the follower and who is being followed? When there is a comprehensive connection with God (*nisbat*) there is no way that this relationship can change.

It is such a strange affair that if one deeply contemplates this station, there really is no imitation. The distinction between the follower and the one being followed basically is not seen. Still, a person realizes that he is a merely an uninvited guest (*tufayl*) and heir of the Prophet who might be received [as an honored guest].[68] God give the most favored blessings and the most complete salutations to him and all the other prophets. It is certain (from a conventional perspective) that the follower as uninvited guest and heir is other than the Prophet. (From a unitary perspective) they are both the same in the single-file process of imitation and following. It is helpful for the follower to differentiate him/herself outwardly from the one being followed, although as an uninvited guest and heir this is not required. The good fortune of sitting down with others as an uninvited guest and eating is by means of the prophets. God bless them. The felicity of the community comes from followers finding divine favor by being uninvited guests of the prophets and, after eating, taking some food and drink with them. God bless them.

Being in God's caravan, even knowing I will not arrive,
It is sufficient to hear the distant bell of the caravan's lead camel.

---

66. That there is no god but God and that Muhammad is God's messenger.

67. This felicitous rendition of "the one embrace on the same cushion" I owe to Naim Abdulwali, who had translated this same letter from the Arabic translation of *Collected Letters*.

68. In cultures with high standards of hospitality, like the cultures of the vast majority of those who would be reading this text in the Persian, uninvited guests regularly come along with the invited ones. There is no stigma of being an uninvited guest.

The completed follower of the Prophet is a person who has realized these seven degrees of imitation. Anyone else is a follower in some aspects, which depends on the degree of imitation attained. The ignorant jurists are happy at the first degree. If only that degree of imitation brought people to the final stage of accomplishment! Their conception of the form of the shariat limits their ability to follow the Prophet. They cannot imagine anything beyond that. So they consider the sufi path, a means to realize further degrees of imitation, to be useless. For most of them, there are no guides or exemplars except *Guidance in Applications of Hanafi Jurisprudence* and Bazdawi's book.[69]

For a worm hidden under a rock
The sky is the bottom of the rock.

God please make the reader and us aware of the reality of the most pleasing and favored imitation. Praise God. God bless and give peace to Muhammad and all of his brothers, the noble prophets, great angels, and all of their followers, until the Day of Resurrection.

Introduction to Islam and other religious communities: Letter 2.55

This letter is addressed to both Muhammad Sa'id (d. 1070/1660), Ahmad Sirhindi's second eldest son, who studied with Muhammad Tahir Lahori and Muhammad Tahir's elder brother, and to Muhammad Ma'sum (d. 1079/1668), his third eldest son and Sirhindi's formal successor (*sajjada nishin*).[70]

This letter outlines the principles for religious diversity between different religious communities and within the Muslim community itself. Sirhindi makes it clear that the Qur'an and the sunnat are infallible givens, and injunctions based on independent legal reasoning can be subject to error. All religious knowledge has its roots in the comprehensive Qur'an—the Hadith and sunnat are details thereof. Just as qualified jurists follow the commands of scripture and the sunnat of their prophet, prophets follow the commands

69. These are Burhanuddin 'Ali al-Marghaniyani (d. 593/1197), *al-Hidaya fi sharh bidayat al-mubtadi* (*Guidance in the Commentary of the Beginner's First Step*) (Beirut: Dar Ihya' al-Turath al-'Arabi, 1995) and Abu Hasan 'Ali al-Bazdawi (d. 482/1089) *Kanz al-wusul ila ma'rifat al-usul* (*The Treasure of Arriving at the Knowledge of the Principles of Jurisprudence*), both of which only deal with the outer performance of the shariat. The latter is found in print today along with its commentary, Abu al-Hasan 'Ali b. Muhammad Bazdawi with commentary by 'Abdul'aziz b. Ahmad Bukhari, *Kashf al-asrar 'an usul fakhr al-islam al-Bazdawi*, 4 vols. (Beirut: Dar al-Kitab al-'Arabi, 1974).

70. Ahmad Sirhindi wrote 24 letters to Muhammad Sa'id and 27 letters to Muhammad Ma'sum. One paragraph of this letter is paraphrased in Ansari, *Sufism and Shari'ah*, 235.

of the scripture revealed by the great prophets. Just as qualified jurists do not have to follow the independent legal reasoning of their prophet or other jurists, each prophet is not required to follow the injunctions of the great prophets based on great prophets' legal reasoning or their sunnats. This is because a prophet who is not a great prophet is only an authority for a special group. This is an explanation for the religious diversity existing in the world.

At the same time, the sunnat of one great prophet abrogates the sunnat of another great prophet. Thus Muhammad is the abrogator for all prior sunnat. For that reason, when Jesus returns right before the Last Judgment he will follow Muhammad's shariat and imitate Muhammad's sunnat, but Jesus will not necessarily follow the independent legal reasoning of Muhammad. Defending Jesus against detractors, Sirhindi then goes on to defend Abu Hanifa (d. 150/767 Baghdad), the founder-figure of the Hanafi school of jurisprudence. Although Jesus' rank is far above that of Abu Hanifa, he will not be a follower of Abu Hanifa's school of jurisprudence, though he will perform his religious duties in a Hanafi manner because that is following the Prophetic sunnat.

The letter ends reminding the reader that source of knowledge for shariat is separate from inspirations and unveilings. Knowledge from Khidr (a sage not mentioned by name in Qur'an 18:60-82) cannot assist a Muslim in shariat knowledge simply because Khidr is from a community prior to Muhammad's. Sirhindi noted that only a wayfarer in the beginning or intermediate stages sees Khidr. This is because realized seekers have their own unveilings (sing. *kashf*) and inspirations (sing. *ilham*) and do not need the intermediary of Khidr.

Advanced sufi verifiers and the common people are on equal footing before the expertise and rulings of qualified jurists. One realizes inner knowledge (*ma'rifat*) through the perfection of following the shariat, as noted in the previous letter. There is no logical reason for this, but that is apparently how it works. These secrets of the inner shariat become revealed through the outer shariat practices. After the Qur'an and sunnat, inspiration serves as a third source of guidance. It becomes a source of integrity, resembling what prophets used to guide their sunnat. It is, however, tentative, not conclusive like the prophetic sunnat.[71]

Letter 2.55

In the name of God, the compassionate and merciful. Praise God. God give peace to those honoring the glorious Qur'an. This holy book is the repository of all the injunctions of God's law and also contains all of the prior commands before Muhammad's prophetic mission. In brief, some of these divine dictates are such that anyone who knows Arabic, whether educated

71. See Hutaki, *Sharh-i Maktubat*, 632-633.

or not, can understand the meaning, allusions, proofs, and the requirements of the text.

There is a second kind of injunction that requires intellectual effort (*ijtihad*) and derivation to be grasped. This is a special understanding of qualified jurists who can make independent legal decisions (*mujtahidin*). By community consensus, the foremost of these leaders is Muhammad, followed by his noble companions and the qualified jurists of his community who followed them. God give peace to him and them. The time of the Prophet was the time of definitive revelation so the directives derived from the Prophet's independent reasoning [therefore] could not vacillate between accuracy and error. With authoritative revelation, truth and falsehood were easily distinguished from each other since the Prophet was not permitted to establish or to agree on errors. After the time of revelation, however, qualified jurists developed an imperfect method of deduction. That is why any injunctions derived from independent legal reasoning established at the time of revelation are certain to be beneficial guides for action and faith, as subsequent experience has demonstrated. For determining correct behavior after the era of revelation, thinking and reasoning is necessary and beneficial. For faith, thinking and reasoning are not necessary.

The third type of Qur'anic command is particularly difficult to understand. As long as one does not get a direct message from God, how can one know God's dictates? Exalt God's majesty. Only the Prophet can get such information. Although these commands are all taken from the Qur'an, it is the Prophet who displays these injunctions. God bless him and his family and give them peace. So the sunnat is necessarily and directly related to God's rules. Indeed, these commands manifest through the sunnat in the same way that the injunctions for independent legal reasoning are connected to analogical reasoning. Analogy reveals those injunctions. Therefore, both sunnat and analogical reasoning express God's guidelines even though there is a major difference between them. Reasoning is based on personal opinion subject to error. The sunnat is divinely and infallibly indicated and closely resembles its source, the Qur'an. Exalt God's loftiness. Therefore, the sunnat is considered an established command (on the conventional human level). Although in reality every established directive is only in the noble Qur'an. And that is that.

One should know that that there is scope for someone to disagree with the Prophet as long as that person is qualified to do independent legal reasoning (that is, a qualified jurist). But no one can differ with those commands that have proof and confirmation in authoritative scripture and are further affirmed through the sunnat. The entire community must follow these rules. The community's jurists who are qualified to do independent legal reasoning do not have to concern themselves with the injunctions derived from independent legal reasoning that conform to the Prophet's personal opinion. God bless him and his family and give them peace. They are at a station where there is merit in following their own personal opinions.

There is a subtlety here which one should be aware of. The prophets who followed the shariat of the great prophets (*ulu al-'azmi*) are only obligated to follow those commands established and verified in scripture. God bless them and give them peace. They do not have to follow injunctions derived from the great prophets' independent legal reasoning or their various examples (*sunnat*s) in the same way that qualified jurists do not have to follow the dictates derived from independent legal reasoning. How should a prophet be a follower? An injunction that prophets manifest is sunnat. The great prophets received such divine commands through direct signs from God. Prophets other than the great prophets also have confirmed these injunctions through God almighty's indications. What can "following" mean in this context when following does not make any sense? There are separate sets of divine commands depending on each era and the group involved. One time it is appropriate to make something permissible. Another time it should be prohibited. The great prophets were told that something was permissible, and the other prophets were told to forbid it. Both rulings were derived from the same divine source just as two qualified jurists come up with two contrary decisions using the same sources.

Question: These differences in independent legal reasoning are possible when one is dealing with personal opinion that can be either right or wrong. This does not make any sense. God Almighty's signs cannot vacillate between right and wrong. If something is permissible it cannot be prohibited and vice versa.

Answer: It is possible that something for one community is permissible and prohibited for another. God's ruling can be manifold in one situation depending on the number of different communities. Exalt God's loftiness. There is no inconsistency here. This means that there will be [diverse] opinions in the Muslim community. It is not going to happen that all people of this shariat are going to be subjected to one single ruling. According to God there are not two different rulings here for one situation. Exalt God's majesty.

Question: If the great prophets always judged something to be permitted and the great prophets following them prohibited it, then the second ruling abrogated the first. It is not permitted that the decisions of the great prophets can be abrogated by anyone other than them.

Answer: Abrogation is necessary when the second ruling applies generally to all people so that it removes the first ruling that pertains to one special group. Only another great prophet can do this. The second ruling stated above is not general because it prohibits only for one group. By definition, a prophet who is not a great prophet is only an authority for a special group. Thus, there is no conflict between the two rulings. In one situation, a qualified jurist can decide something to be permissible while another qualified jurist can decide the same thing in the same situation to be prohibited. There is no abrogation. Any attempt to prefer one of these rulings instead of another is futile. There is plenty of room for diverse rulings. Although for God's signs (the Qur'an), this is not the case. Many communities have found this diversity to be a viable solution.

In previous expositions of God's law (shariats), people understood the language of scriptural injunctions communicated by the great prophets. The prophets who followed them had no cause for disagreement. They communicated those divine commands pertaining to all the people. Each prophet belonged to the community he called to God. He did not advocate going against the injunctions already put in place by the previous great prophet. If something was permissible then it was permissible for all. If it was forbidden then it was forbidden for all. When another great prophet came and commanded a change of ruling then it was possible to think of abrogation.

One can abrogate according to these injunctions as long as one uses the language of revealed scripture. It is unthinkable to abrogate an injunction that has been established through independent legal reasoning and connected to the sunnat. The independent legal reasoning and the sunnat of one prophet cannot annul the independent legal reasoning and sunnat of another prophet because each pertains to a particular community. If this difference pertains to all the people or to one particular group then of course abrogation is possible (as explained above). In the shariat for Muslims, which gives rulings to the entire community, the second ruling abrogates the first.

Our prophet is the abrogator for all prior sunnat. God bless him, his family, all the prophets, and all the messengers and give them peace.[72] When the noble presence of Jesus comes back to earth right before the Last Judgment he will follow Muhammad's shariat and imitate Muhammad's sunnat. It is not permissible for anyone to abrogate the Islamic shariat. In a similar way, the ignorant jurists (*'ulama'-i zahir*) have refused to accept Jesus' abstruse and subtle knowledge, which they interpret as against the Qur'an and sunnat of Muhammad. As with the Spirit of God (Jesus) so it was with the Great Leader, Abu Hanifa (d. 150/767 Baghdad). God bless him.[73] Abu Hanifa,

---

72. Messengers in Islam bring books, for example, the Torah, Gospels, Psalms, and Qur'an, and prophets remind people of God's message that they have forgotten. Therefore, all messengers are prophets but only a small number of prophets are messengers.

73. Abu Hanifa is the founder-figure of the Hanafi legal school that guides Ahmad Sirhindi and most Indian, Turkish, and Central Asian Sunni Muslims.

through the blessings of avoiding what was unlawful (*war'*), piety, and following the sunnat, achieved a high degree of independent legal reasoning. Others who could not comprehend the subtlety of his meaning thought that his ideas conflicted with the scriptures. They considered him and his followers to be merely formulating their own personal opinions. This talk is from those who have not arrived at genuine knowledge and who do not have the intelligence or insight to understand it. Imam Shafi'i,[74] who shared some of Abu Hanifa's subtle knowledge, is known to have said, "All jurists are children of Abu Hanifa." It is sad that people project their own shortcomings from the rashness of shortsightedness.

If an incompetent accuses the Naqshbandiyya of shortcomings
(God forgive me if complain about that ignorant person in the future)
When all lions of the world have the Naqshbandi chain around their necks.
How will a fox's trick break the chain?

Concerning Jesus, Muhammad Parsa (d. 822/1420 Balkh) said in his *Six Chapters*,[75] "After the exalted presence of Jesus returns to earth, he will perform his religious duties in accordance with the legal school of Imam Abu Hanifa." Jesus' independent legal reasoning will agree with that of the Great Leader (Abu Hanifa). It does not mean that Jesus will be a follower of Abu Hanifa's legal school since Jesus' rank is too exalted to be following what jurists of the community dictate. God bless our prophet and him and give them peace.

Without any formality or partiality, it can be said that the luminous radiance of the Hanafi legal school is like a revealing vision in a great ocean. The rest of the legal schools appear like a bunch of small separated pools. Apparently a great number of Muslims follow Abu Hanifa. God be contented with them. This legal school is distinguished even among the diversity of legal schools, which employ many other principles and deductions. The Hanafis have a distinctive way of deriving legal injunctions based on the truth. It is a strange affair that Imam Abu Hanifa is superior to anyone else in adhering to the sunnat. He knows which hadith are weak, which hadith are worthy of following, and prefers his own personal opinion. It is like the Companion who said, as a result of extended conversation with the Prophet, the most preferred being, "I prefer my own personal opinion." God bless

74. Muhammad al-Shafi'i was the founder of the Shafi'i legal school.

75. Muhammad Parsa is a Naqshbandi shaykh whose guide was Baha'uddin Naqshband. *Risala-yi fusul-i sitta* concerns the science of hadith. It has yet to be published. See Carl Brockelmann, *Geschichte der arabischen Litteratur*, Supplement (Leiden: Brill, 1937-1942), 2: 283. There are three known manuscript copies indicated there.

him and them (the Companions) and give them peace. Others are not of this caliber. Therefore, their detractors call them "people of opinion" in addition to other things that are not polite to repeat. Abu Hanifa is blessed with complete knowledge, meticulousness, and piety. God Almighty make sure that Abu Hanifa's detractors call many people to Islam rather than contesting Abu Hanifa as the community's religious leader. "They want to extinguish God's light with their talk." [Q. 9:32] Praise God.

There are people who consider these religious notables of the Hanafi legal school to be "people of opinion," that is, that the Hanafis make rulings on the basis of their own personal opinion and do not follow the Qur'an and sunnat. According to their corrupt view, a large group of Muslims have gone astray and therefore have left the fold of Islam. Two kinds of people could have this belief. One is either a stupid person, unaware of his or her ignorance, or [the other] an unbeliever (*zindiq*) who wants to prove half of Islam to be false. The latter prefer not to follow any legal school but interpret hadith themselves. They have a faulty knowledge of the fundamental hadiths that the injunctions of the shariat are based upon. They negate whatever is not included in their partial knowledge and what they consider not to have sufficient proof.

For a worm hidden under a rock
The sky is the bottom of the rock.

A thousand cries of pain come from their cold fanaticism and corrupt views. Abu Hanifa was the founder of jurisprudence and he has authority over three parts of jurisprudence while all others share the fourth part. He is the owner of the house of jurisprudence and the others are his children. Given the necessity of the Hanafi school, I still have a personal love for Imam Shafi'i and consider him a notable authority. Therefore, I follow his juristic interpretations in some of my supererogatory practices. In spite of his ample knowledge and complete piety, compared to Abu Hanifa he is like a child. This affair should be left to God. Praise God.

Now we come to the essential matter that deals with conflicting injunctions derived from independent legal reasoning. If a difference occurs as a result of what a prophet said, then there is no need for abrogation. If there is a difference resulting from a discrepancy involving the Qur'an and the sunnat, then abrogation is necessary, as mentioned above. It has been established that the only authentic way to prove commands of the shariat is with the Qur'an and sunnat. Analogy performed by jurists qualified for independent legal reasoning and the consensus of the community also confirm injunctions. These four [Sunni] legal sources are the only basis upon which to verify legal injunctions. Inspirations cannot establish what is permitted and what is forbidden. Unveilings (sing. *kashf-i arbab-i batn*) cannot show what is obligatory (*fard*) and recommended (*sunnat*). Both protégés of God and common believers are equal in following the rulings of qualified jurists. Inspirations and visions do not give special favor to exempt one from following juristic guidelines.

The famous sufis, Dhu al-Nun (d. ca. 245/860), Abu Yazid Bistami (261/874), Junayd (d. 297/910), and Shibli (d. 334/945) are equal to any four common believers in the necessity to follow the independent legal judgments of qualified jurists.[76] Indeed, the distinction of these sufi notables is in other affairs, for example, divine visions and disclosures (sing. *tajalli*) that are the result of overflowing love of the true Beloved and being totally disconnected from anything other than God Almighty. Praise God and exalt God's majesty. They have become free of any vacillations of thought or vision. If they receive anything it is for God's sake and if they arrive anywhere it is near God. They are in the world yet not of the world. They are with their selves yet without them. If they live, they live for God, and if they die, they die for God's sake.

The beginners among the sufis achieve their goal through overpowering love. They gaze in the mirror of "every single atom in the world," each of which they discover to have all the perfections of the names and attributes of God. Advanced seekers give no outward indication of who they are. They start out forgetting anything other than God and end up beyond the inner and outer worlds. Their inspirations and what they themselves have to say is genuinely true. The most advanced of them get their knowledge and secrets directly from the Source. They are like the qualified jurists who follow their own opinion and independent reasoning. In their knowledge and ecstasies they follow their own inspirations and insights.

The presence of the master Muhammad Parsa was supposed to have received divine knowledge by means of the spirit (*ruhaniyat*) of the exalted presence of Khidr. God bless our prophet and all the other prophets and messengers and give them peace.[77] Such a report apparently indicates the kind of relationship a beginner or an intermediate seeker is able to develop. An advanced seeker receives such knowledge directly through clear, unambiguous visions. Shaykh 'Abdulqadir Jilani (d. 561/1166 Baghdad) has confirmed this. God almighty bless his inner heart.[78] One day while 'Abdulqadir was preaching at the pulpit, the exalted presence of Khidr appeared. The Shaykh greeted

---

76. Dhu al-Nun, Abu Yazid Bistami, Junayd, and Abu Bakr Shibli, are well known early sufis.

77. Khidr is variously interpreted to be a prophet who was never formally sent to humanity, an intimate of God, or an angel. *Collected Letters*, 2.55.16 fn. 5. Here it is implied that Khidr is a prophet.

78. 'Abdulqadir Jilani is a famous sufi and the founder-figure of the Qadiriyya sufi lineage, the most widespread sufi lineage in the world.

him by saying, "Oh Israel come and hear the words of a Muhammadan."[79] 'Abdulqadir understood that the exalted presence of Khidr was not a follower of Muhammad but instead came from an earlier community.

It has been verified that religious knowledge is one thing and what is behind the dictates of the shariat, the specialty of the "folk of God" (*ahl-i Allah*), is qualitatively another kind of knowledge. All religious knowledge, however, is the fruit and result of the injunctions of the shariat. The goal of the tree is to produce fruit. As long as the tree is standing one can expect fruit. Obviously it is unreasonable to expect fruit if the tree is cut down. If the goal is to get fruit, then to the extent that one takes good care of the tree it will yield fruit. However, this is only one aspect of the tree.

There is an analogy here between those who adhere to the requirements of the shariat and those who are lazy in adhering to the shariat. Those who adhere to the shariat have knowledge; the more they adhere to the shariat the more knowledge they have. A person who does not adhere to the shariat has no knowledge.

Introduction to Is there a place beyond the shariat? Letter 1.172

Sirhindi addresses this letter to Shaykh Badi'uddin Saharanpuri (d. 1040-41/1631) who was authorized to teach by his shaykh, Ahmad Sirhindi, and was sent to Agra to teach before returning to his hometown of Saharanpur.[80] This letter addresses a key issue in sufism, namely whether one can ever be exempt from the dictates of the shariat, or in Sirhindi's words, whether one is permitted to go outside the circle of the shariat. It is and it isn't.

First, there is the apparent form of the shariat (*surat-i shari'at*), the stage before one contemplatively confirms the reality of the shariat (*haqiqat-i shari'at*). In the first stage, one has faith (in the Day of Judgment, heaven, and hell for example) but after having contemplative confirmation, one *knows from experience* the reality of what was formerly taken on faith. Likewise the Qur'an and hadith are the outer form while the attributes and qualities of the words and knowledge are the reality. When the wayfarer ascends higher than the attributes and qualities (*shuyunat*), then the wayfarer contemplatively experiences himself higher than the shariat and outside the shariat. This occurs, for example, when the wayfarer is traveling in the arcane and superarcane subtle centers.

Pious jurists have not reached the places of the arcane and superarcane subtle centers, nor have they even heard of them. The only legal decision

79. Muhammadan in this sense means one who follows the sunnat of Muhammad. This is in clear contrast to mistaken orientalist notions of Islam being "Muhammadanism" in the same manner as the Christian notion of Christianity.

80. There are ten letters addressed to Shaykh Badi'uddin Saharanpuri in *Collected Letters*.

they could make if confronted with a place beyond the shariat is to declare that place to be one of covering up the truth of God (*kufr* commonly translated as infidelity). Those who have an elementary understanding of faith and rest in the appearance of Islam do not know about these things either. The origin of divine effulgence (*fayd*) for the attributes and qualities is the realm of the arcane and superarcane subtle centers, involving the comprehensive synthesis (*sha'n-i jami'*).[81] The form of shariat pertains to the physical body and the heart subtle center. The spirit subtle center undergirds the life of the physical body while the mystery subtle center follows the heart subtle center. Thus, both the spirit and mystery subtle centers are indirectly subject to the shariat and are connected to the reality of the shariat. The arcane and superarcane subtle centers are beyond the physical body and are not subject to the shariat simply because they cannot be. If one is in these subtle centers, following the shariat is no longer obligatory but praiseworthy (*mustahabb*). Since Naqshbandis do not neglect doing what is praiseworthy, this means that they strive to live in accordance with the reality of the shariat and advise others to do so also.[82]

LETTER 1.172

After praise and blessings, let it be known my dear brother that the shariat has a form and a reality. Explaining its form is entrusted to jurists whose knowledge is from literal reading of books (*'ulama-yi zawahir*). Exalted sufis are distinguished in elucidating its reality. The end of ascent of the form of shariat continues to the end of the chain of possibilities. After that, if wayfaring occurs in the degrees of necessity, form becomes infused with reality. This process of infusion continues until one ascends to the "quality of knowledge" (*sha'n al-'ilm*), which is the source of entification (*mabda'-i ta'ayyun*) of Muhammad. God bless and give peace to him and his family If there is further progress then one will go beyond both form and reality whereby the person of inner knowledge (*'arif*) experiences the "quality of life," (*sha'n-i hayawat*) a great quality having no connection to the world. It is one of the real qualities that do not yet have a relationship with the world until a connection [with the world] is engendered.

This quality of life is the doorway to the goal, introducing what is desired. In this realm, the person of inner knowledge (*ma'rifat*) finds himself outside the door of the shariat. Because he is protected, he does not neglect the smallest detail [in practicing] the shariat. There are very few people blessed with this great fortune. If one were to count them, extremely few would make the grade. There is a large group of sufis who have reached

81. See Buehler, *Sufi Heirs*, 114, 245; and *Collected Letters*, 1.260.75 and 1.287.62. Both of these letters are translated in this volume.

82. I have followed Hutaki, *Sharh-i Maktubat*, 263-264 very closely here.

the shadows of this exalted station. Since each exalted station has a shadow below it, [many sufis] suppose that they have stepped outside the circle of shariat from this high station, going beyond the outer shell and arriving at the inner essence. This is the station where sufis backslide. Many [sufis] of deficient [awareness] have arrived at heresy and unbelief in this way. They have taken their heads out of the noose of the splendid shariat. They have become lost and have led others astray.

There is a group of completed ones who have been honored with a degree of closeness to God (*walayat*). They have realized this inner knowledge in a shadow of this exalted station although they have not arrived at the origin (*asl*) of the station. Being protected, they do not seek to neglect any aspect of acting in accordance with the shariat even though they do not know the secret of this inner knowledge and do not understand the reality of the affair.

By the grace of God almighty and the charitable gift from God's Beloved (Muhammad), this poor one (Ahmad Sirhindi) has disclosed the secret of this difficult matter. The reality of the matter has become clarified, as it must. I have been able to explain a bit of what I have experienced. Possibly [this letter] will bring to the path those who are deficient and elucidate the reality of the matter to the perfected ones. One should know that the shariat obligations are connected to the physical body (*qalab*) and the heart subtle center (*qalb*) since purification of the ego-self depends on these two. The spirit (*ruh*), mystery (*sirr*), arcane (*khafi*), and superarcane (*akhfa'*) subtle centers are not involved in shariat. The two subtle centers associated with the shariat are always involved and the four that are not associated with the shariat are never involved. In short, before wayfaring the subtle centers are mixed together, not separate from the heart. This is because wayfaring (*sayr u suluk*) makes each one of them separate. Each reaches its original location. One knows which one is involved with the shariat and which one is not.[83]

Question. If a person of inner knowledge experiences both his heart and physical body outside the shariat, what is that all about?

Answer. This experience is not certain but is in the imagination. The source of imagination has imbued the heart subtle center and the physical body with the more subtle color of the subtle centers that are outside the circle of shariat. Some say that the obligations of the form of the shariat pertain to the heart and physical body, but the reality of the shariat also has capacity beyond that of the heart. So what does it mean to be independent of the shariat? The reality of the shariat does not pass beyond the spirit

83. Note that the physical frame and the heart subtle center are associated with the form of the shariat and the spirit and mystery subtle centers are associated with the reality of the shariat.

and mystery subtle centers nor does it reach to the arcane or superarcane subtle centers. Those who do go outside the shariat are in reality those who are [experiencing] the arcane and superarcane subtle centers. God almighty knows best the truth of the situation. God almighty help us and all other Muslims to remain firm in following the Prophet. God completely bless him and his family.

Introduction to differences between sufis and jurists: Letter 3.39

This letter is written to Mawlana Muhammad Sadiq Kashmiri, a well-known jurist and son of Kamaluddin Hanafi.[84] He is also the author of *Words of the Truthful* (*Kalimat-i sadiqin*). Muhammad Sadiq was called into court one day by Jahangir to dispute with a Shi'i, Mulla Habibullah, but Muhammad Sadiq remained silent.[85] This short letter simply states the epistemological differences between sufis and jurists. The sufi basis of knowing is unveiling and contemplative witnessing while the jurists use mental evidence and logical proof. Here the differences between sufis and jurists are more than just semantics.

Letter 3.39

Praise God. God give peace to God's servants whom God has chosen. According to sufis, the goal of the knowledge of certainty (*'ilm-i yaqin*) is having certainty. This certainty can be ascertained through logical deduction of cause and effect. Since this meaning [and method] is the same for jurists (lit. those who logically discern evidence), what is the difference between sufis' knowledge of certainty and that of rational thinkers (*ahl-i ma'qul*)? Why does the sufi understanding of the knowledge of certainty involve unveiling and contemplative witnessing (*shuhud*)? Which aspects of jurists' narrow perspective and thinking limits their understanding of knowledge of certainty?

One should know that, for both jurists and sufis, vision (*shuhud*) and impressions (sing. *athar*) thereof are necessary for the knowledge of certainty in order that one can detect a sign of the cause, which is not seen. In short, one figures out the connection between the cause and its effect. The reason for this is the movement from the knowledge of the effect's existence to the knowledge of the cause's existence. In the sufi understanding of certain knowledge (*'ilm-i yaqin*), this connection involves unveiling and contemplative witnessing, while for jurists the connection is theoretical because it requires thought and proof. For the sufis, therefore, the movement from the existence of the effect to the existence of the cause

84. There are five letters addressed to him in *Collected Letters*.

85. See 'Abdulhayy b. Fakruddin Hasani, *Nuzhat al-khawatir*, 8 vols. (Hyderabad, Deccan: Da'irat al-Ma'arif al-'Uthmania, 1976), 5:389.

is necessarily quick if not self-evident. For intellectuals and jurists, this movement is theoretical and mental. So the certainty of the sufis pertains to unveiling and contemplative witnessing while that of the jurists and intellectuals is confined to the narrowness of [sensory or mental] evidence. The sufi understanding of the knowledge of certainty is free from evidence based upon outward form and a [simple] movement from cause to effect.

In truth, it is the [methods of] unveiling and contemplative witnessing which run counter to jurists' inferential understanding of the knowledge of certainty. Because this is a subtle difference, it has remained hidden to most people. They must have become stuck at the level of bewilderment. There is a group of them who are incapable [of understanding] and who abusively criticize some notables of religion who have explained the sufi understanding of the knowledge of certainty [using experiential] evidence from an effect to the influence causing the effect. Because of all of that [intricate subtlety], they do not have an insight into the truth of these matters. God confirms the truth and God gives guidance on the path. God give peace to those who follow guidance.

Introduction to similarities between sufis and jurists: Letter 3.32

This letter is written to Maqsud 'Ali Tabrizi so he could discern appearances from the Essence.[86] According to Sirhindi, visions in spiritual practice are not the goal because they are usually mis-interpreted as disclosures of God (sing. *tajalli*). The letter opens with Sirhindi defining the frame of reference for the inquirer's contemplative visions. He explains that contemplative visions are the most elementary of preliminaries, and far from God. Elaborating further, Sirhindi explains that there is both truth and falsehood in these visions. Ultimately both of these aspects are useless because neither involve disclosure of the Essence. In other letters Sirhindi explains that the physical and mental austerities that Greek philosophers and Indian yogis perform to diminish the power of the ego-self (*nafs*) do not work because their effects only manifest in the outer realm.[87] Effective transformational practice involves knowing the relationship between the spirit subtle center (*ruh*) and the ego-self. Unless work is done in the world of command first, the journey back to God will take longer than a person's physical lifespan. Initially the spirit (*ruh*) is lost in the

86. There are three letters addressed to Maqsud 'Ali in *Collected Letters*.

87. Cf. the first level of following the sunnat in letter 2.54 in this book. Sirhindi also notes the non-effectiveness of non-Naqshbandi sufi practices that do not involve the world of command, the realm of purifying the heart. See letter 1.260 in this book. Sometimes he calls these people "folk of the practices" (*ahl-i riyada*). See letter 1.293 in this book.

ego-self and one has to do practices in the world of command in such a way that one can reach the station of difference (*maqam-i farq*) where the spirit ascends and the ego-self descends.[88]

Further in the letter Sirhindi corrects the misperceptions that have been communicated to Maqsud ʻAli. Sirhindi explains that fear and anxiety only block a person from God's grace. The real reason for the feeling of separation from God is having a misplaced goal in the realm of outer realization. Sirhindi finishes his straightforward appraisal of this unnamed "more experienced wayfarer" by a detailed critique of the quotation "And God encompasses everything" communicated to Maqsud ʻAli. The letter ends with Sirhindi acknowledging the illusory but actual existence of multiplicity in the universe and a note of appreciation to the jurists, whose differences with the sufis, he says, are only semantic.

LETTER 3.32

Give thanks to God. God give peace to God's servants whom God has chosen. You have written that a wayfarer told a more experienced wayfarer about his worry of sudden attacks of fear. The experienced wayfarer replied, informing him of the requirement of "And God encompasses everything." [He also explained that] fear, since it surrounds and includes what is desired, is known to be an indication of realization (*wasl*, lit. having arrived) and not a reason for being separated from God. [His situation according to the experienced person] is connected with the gates of visionary contemplation (*mushahada*) having to be open and the gaps of heedlessness having to be closed.

(Sirhindi's response) It is accurate [to say that] this discussion comes from the perspective of outward disclosure (*tajalli-yi suri*), the most elementary of the preliminaries on the path. In this realm, if there is realization, no matter how genuine, there is separation from God. That is how it appears from the standpoint of the outer form (*surat*). If there are contemplative visions (sing. *mushahada*) they are distant no matter how real they seem. It is like how one confirms viewing of outer forms. According to the notables of the path, this disclosure is considered to be worthless because it does not involve the annihilation of the wayfarer's [egoic] existence.

Truth (*muhiqq*) and falsehood (*mubtil*) are both involved in this disclosure. Indian yogis and Greek philosophers are aware of this disclosure and find good fortune and enjoyment from the inner and outer knowledge

88. An aspect of this principle is discussed in the context of sufi lineages in letter 1.260, where Sirhindi says, "Those of other sufi lineages purify their ego-self and perform strenuous exercises, traversing the beginnings of the appearance of the material world, saying that this is the beginning of the world of command."

(*ma'arif wa-'ulum*) of this domain. In short, the good fortune is that one can realize truth from the method of purifying the heart. The method of purifying the ego-self is for those realizing falsehood. To purify the heart one must have guidance while purifying the ego-self ends in error. Both [truth and falsehood] are entanglements of outer form and ignore the essence (*ma'na*) of the matter.

> A person who can only see the surface, heedless of the essence,
> What does he know of the majesty of souls?
> The person who is with the majesty of souls
> Has done what needs to be done.

But the person of truth (*muhiqq*) probably is saved from the appearance of existence. The person of falsehood (*mubtil*), not sticking to [the teachings of] the community of prophets, is overwhelmed by appearances and cannot be freed from his entanglements. Also, the outward disclosure is inside the circle of outward knowledge (*'ilm*). But since the condition and taste in the circle shoots out a ray of light, that outer knowledge can be called a state.[89] The outward disclosure can also be contemplatively witnessed as multiplicity. But it is a quite heavy and painful experience to see both oneness (*wahdat*) and multiplicity in every manner possible. Therefore, from the inner perspective of multiplicity and contemplatively witnessing multiplicity no name or sign can remain. Except for the True One (*wahid-i haqiqi* God), there is no contemplative witnessing (*mashhud*) until [one experiences] annihilation in God, which is the first step. On this path it becomes easy because annihilation involves forgetting everything but God in the heart.

Therefore, in this realm what scope does multiplicity have and what does it mean to witness multiplicity in that place? It has been said (above) that a feeling of fear is associated with the means of realization and with the gates of visionary contemplation. The goal of these realizations and visions is outward realization and visions, which is the origin of separation and distance. This is because realization, according to Naqshbandi notables, is authentic when one experiences the station of abiding in God (*baqa' billah*), which is after experiencing annihilation in God and forgetting all that is not God. The existence of fear is a negation of that good fortune. The experience of anxiety hinders that way station such that

89. On the 18th line of *Collected Letters*, 3.32.79 it reads *"an 'ilm hal-i tamami gardad"* (that knowledge completely becomes a state) which instead should read "*an 'ilm hal nama ast,*" (that knowledge is called a state) per the correction in Hutaki, *Sharh-i Maktubat*, 707. Apparently this is a typographical error in the Nur Ahmad edition since al-Manzalawi's Arabic translation, *Mu'arrab al-maktubat,* 2:46, has "that knowledge is like a state."

one is in the outer courtyard of the station of annihilation in God where fear becomes a kind of vanishing. One remembers things with difficulty, and then cannot remember them because one is forgetting everything but God.

It is written above in Arabic, "And God encompasses everything." (*wa-huwa 'ala kulli shay'in muhaytun*). The meaning of "encompasses" does not make sense in this phrase. Perhaps a non-Arab said it because the transitive of "encompasses" in Persian often uses the preposition "on." It is generally recognized in classical Arabic that the transitive of "encompasses" is preceded by the preposition "by means of." God almighty said, "God encompasses everything." [Q. 4:126] (*wa-kana Allahu bi-kulli shay'in muhaytan*) and "Does God not encompass everything?" [Q. 41:54] Apparently the phrase mentioned above was imagined to be from the Qur'an and quoted. It is not, however, since the explanation of the meaning in the Qur'an is another expression as it turns out.

You have also written that imagined multiplicity (*kuthrat-i wahmi*) and relative diversity (*ta'addud-i 'itibari*) are interpreted in such a way that most jurists fall into error concerning the multifold nature of being. You say that they are content to settle for the skin rather than the juicy fruit and accept the shell instead of the kernel. Although multiplicity and diversity are imagined and relative, they exist because they are a divinely designed creation, firm and stable, connected to religious affairs and the Hereafter. The objective effects (*athar-i kharaji*) of multiplicity and diversity are established. Even though imagination and a relative point of view can vanish, it is impossible to get rid of multiplicity and diversity. This is because the Prophet has warned of eternal punishment and reward in the Hereafter, which is dependent on multiplicity and diversity. God bless him and his family and give them peace. To make a legal judgment deciding that it is possible to get rid of multiplicity and diversity is to enter into apostasy and heresy. God almighty save us from that!

Thus, exalted sufis and noble jurists both declare the permanence of multiplicity and diversity with certainty. When one ascends on the sufi path this multiplicity vanishes because of a sufi's contemplative vision. Multiplicity is experienced as imagined and relative. In fact, it does not vanish even though it vanishes in a sufi's contemplative vision. Jurists know multiplicity exists. So the difference between sufis and jurists goes back to semantics. After agreeing on the meaning, each group has made a judgment on the basis of the their own [experientially] informed opinion. The sufis, from the approach of contemplative witnessing (*shuhud*), observe the vanishing of what they witness and declare [multiplicity] to be relative and imagined. Jurists observe the matter-of-fact firmness and stability [of multiplicity] and declare its existence. "Each has a direction towards which he faces."[90] [Q. 2:148]

This poor one (Sirhindi) has explained this meaning in detail in my letters and epistles, establishing that the difference between sufis and jurists is just semantic. If the meaning is not clear then I will review the topic. The jurists' perspective is closer to the truth of how it is in fact. The sufi perspective is from the viewpoint of an intoxicated and overpowered state. It is like stars are hidden during the day while in truth they are permanent. They are only hidden from daytime vision. Therefore, to declare stars permanent is more accurate than to declare that stars have no existence on the basis of [limited] observation.

Jurists, who declare the existence of multiplicity, have as their goal the durability of the shariat whose foundation is built upon diversity. The aspects of reward and punishment that accompany the shariat could not be imagined without multiplicity. Sufis also recognize this meaning even though they have difficulty applying their own experiences to the shariat. That which the jurists have said is true without any difficulty [of understanding], and has no need of corresponding artifices. There is no opaqueness or perplexity. Jurists do not prove the independent nature of existence in which there is room for disagreement. There is a necessity of God being involved with existence but jurists posit a weak sort of existence where there is emanation from something else, which is a position leading to error. However, on the scale of error, the jurists, who are the notables of religion, have made a minor and genuine error.[91]

Those of us who have come later have learned about religion and shariat from jurists and have joined our religious community (*millat*) and school of jurisprudence on the basis of their blessings. If it were possible to find fault with jurists, there would no longer be any confidence in shariat and the Islamic community. Therefore, it is said that finding fault with our predecessors is an innovation and error. It is considered a cause of error and doubt in religion and judged to be false.

You have written that they are content to settle for the skin rather than the juicy fruit. Perhaps you have imagined that appearances are the juicy fruit and the ineffable (*tanzih*) is the skin because jurists' involvement in calling people to God concerns the ineffable. Contemplative witnessing and the aspiration of one experiencing outward disclosures are appearances and forms. One must be just in saying who is occupied with the juicy fruit and who is involved with the skin. It has been clarified. "Either

90. "Each to his own viewpoint" would be a more suitable translation of the Qur'anic verse given the context of Sirhindi's letter. I have translated the Qur'anic verse in its own Qur'anic context which has to do with the direction of prayer.

91. The subtext here is Sirhindi seeking to refute the larger error of the *wujudi*s who seek to deny the objective reality of the outside world.

we or you are definitely rightly guided or manifestly in error." [Q. 34:24] "Lord give us mercy in your presence and provide us right conduct in our affair." [Q. 18:10] Peace from beginning to end.

Chapter Two
Contemplative Experience

Introduction to one of Sirhindi's early contemplative experiences: Letter 1.11

We begin this chapter with Ahmad Sirhindi writing to his shaykh, Baqibillah (d. 1012/1603),[1] concerning his second experience of a station.[2] Here we learn that passing through a station is not the same as being stabilized in a station. Naqshbandi-Mujaddidis ascending in their contemplative exercises (*muraqabat*) pass through the *reflections* of the stations of the prophets, but this is not the same as resting in those actual prophetic stations. Nor is passing through the stations of one's spiritual superiors the same as resting there. This point is important, for some have accused Sirhindi of implying his superiority to Abu Bakr as-Siddiq, the first successor to Muhammad.[3] Indeed, it is this letter that ostensibly caused alarm with Jahangir, who accused Sirhindi of having "also written a number of idle tales to his disciples and believers and made them into a book which he called *Maktubat*, [which] drag [people] into infidelity and impurity."[4]

In this letter, he describes his experience of the station of annihilation of the ego-self in God, with its respective attraction to God (*jadhba*) known as "wayfaring in God." Trying to make sense out of what happened, Sirhindi decides that his experience is probably what Khwaja 'Ubaydullah Ahrar (d. 895/1490 Samarqand) had experienced. It is this experience that moved him from the path of intentional, willful action to that of being in intimate spiritual companionship with Baqibillah. Throughout *Collected Letters* Sirhindi discusses a station and the center of a station, where the movement is from the periphery of the station to the center. From the center, one typically moves to the periphery of the next station.

When going inside, Sirhindi describes an abyss, the experiences of which resonate very much with what Christian contemplatives have called "the dark night."[5] This is a poignant reminder that inner wayfaring is not always a joyride. One of the experiences of the station of servanthood (*maqam-i 'abdiyat*),

1. There are twenty letters addressed to Baqibillah in *Collected Letters*.

2. This experience is detailed in letter 1.7.

3. Sirhindi addresses these issues further in letters 1.220, 1.257, and 1.292, all of which are translated in this book.

4. Jahangir, *Memoirs of Jahangir*, 2:93.

5. St. John of the Cross (d. 1591 Segovia, Spain) refers to the "dark night" and is the eighth of ten stages in his schema of spiritual ascent. In transpersonal psychology

the highest station of the stations of being near to God (*maqamat-i walayat*), is being yanked out of one's separateness. This happens in such a way that one is confronted with one's corporeal darkness and denseness as the subtle centers of the created world suddenly zoom very distant from the world of command.[6] This is the place from which Sirhindi says that he is worse than a foreign infidel or an apostate heretic, someone who has denied God and who will not have the benefit of God's mercy in the Hereafter.

Differentiating different levels of reality is a common theme for Sirhindi. One should not confuse the entity (*'ayn*) and the traces of the entity, the attributes. Since Sirhindi is of the Muhammadan disposition (*mashrab*), he and Shaykh Abu Sa'id Abu'l Khayr (d. 440/1049 Nishapur) have passed beyond contemplative witnessing (*shuhud*) of the attributes to contemplatively witness the qualities (*shuyunat*).[7] Sirhindi was able to verify his experience of the Essence by "comparing notes" with his predecessor, 'Ubaydullah Ahrar, and confirm that experiencing an absolute annihilation in God depends on experiencing the disclosure of the Essence (*tajalli-yi dhati*) first.[8] It was from this station that Sirhindi proceeded to further higher stations and was able to stabilize himself in the station of the disclosure of the Essence to experience "presence with God" (*hudur ma' Allah*). One outcome of this experience was his losing interest in reading about others' inner experiences and descriptions of the maps that guided such experiences. He is still very much in transition. Even with his inclination toward the ideas of Shaykh 'Ala'uddawla Simnani (d. 736/1336), Sirhindi wisely realizes that he does not have enough experience to jump to conclusions about experiences of the unity of being.

---

it refers to the relinquishment of a separate ego-self after many years of spiritual effort. I thank Bernard McGinn for clarifying St. John's exact terminology.

6. See Muhammad Sa'id Ahmad Mujaddidi, *al-Bayyinat: sharh-i Maktubat* (Lahore: Tanzim al-Islam Publications, 2002), 369. This is the best commentary on *Collected Letters,* but only goes up to 1.29. The author comments on this subject further in his commentary, ibid., 331-333 using Mazhar Jan-i Janan's letter mentioned below.

7. See ibid., 385. This is discussed further in letter 1.287 translated in this volume.

8. The information given about the disclosure of the Essence, including the necessity of having a Muhammadan disposition, in *Collected Letters* and in the commentaries, corresponds with the definition and explanation of the same term (*al-tajalliyat al-dhatiya*) given in 'Abdurrazzaq Kashani's *Lata'if al-i'lam fi isharat ahl al-ilham*, ed. Sa'id 'Abdulfattah (Cairo: National Library Press, 1996), 309-310. In terms of Sirhindi's experiences of abiding in God after the annihilation of the ego-self, such an experience characterizes the experience of an Essential disclosure of God. See Muhammad Dhawqi, *Sirr-i dilbaran*, 4th ed. (Karachi: Mashhur Offset Press, 1985), 115.

Toward the end of the letter Sirhindi chooses not to engage with Ibn al-'Arabi concerning their different perspectives. Instead he gives us a glimpse of a shaykh's life and activities beyond spiritual guidance, e.g., assisting disembodied spirits on their way and being spiritually and physically attacked. The next section concerns the age-old difficulties shaykhs have with their disciples: laziness, self-sabotage, and other ego strategies to prevent themselves from progressing. Given the experiences he describes in the first part of the letter, it appears that Sirhindi has only received conditional permission to teach. Baqibillah is still formally supervising Sirhindi's teaching. After discussing his teaching experiences, there is some technical discussion that makes sense only to Mujaddidi specialists. The reader can recognize that seekers "travel" in the various subtle centers and that they are in various stages of ascent to God or descent to the material world.

Sirhindi often mentions the attributes and Essence since the student often experiences the attributes as different from the Essence. How they experience the attributes/Essence is a litmus test for their progress and difficulties. The guiding Mujaddidi principle following Sunni-Maturidi creedal injunctions (see letter 2.67 in this book) is that the attributes of God are neither the Essence nor other than the Essence. Thus, when students experience the attributes/Essence in a manner described in this letter they have made significant progress. Sirhindi ends the letter in the bewilderment of experiencing something beyond oneness, and beyond will and desire. These have been annihilated as he engages in spiritual companionship (*suhbat*) with his completed and completion-bestowing shaykh.

Letter 1.11

When the lowest of servants, Ahmad, (Ahmad Sirhindi) was in a previously experienced station, in accordance with your noble instructions, he caught a glimpse of the first three caliphs. God almighty be pleased with them. They are [supposed to] appear in that station. I did not see them the first time because I was not stabilized in that station. I could only recognize Hasan, Husayn (the Prophet's grandsons), and Zaynul'abidin (Husayn's son) from the Prophet's family. God almighty be pleased with all of them. However, I did experience the Prophet's family passing through this station. By keen observation one can realize this.

At first I perceived that I did not have an affinity for this station. Lack of affinity or connection (*munasabat*) is of two kinds. [Temporary], that is, when no path appears and they show a path to him. Then there is a connection. [Secondly], Absolute, where there is no way to move. There are two paths that lead to this station, not three. That is, from the perspective of these two paths, another does not appear. The first path is seeing one's shortcomings and faults. With a strong attraction to God, one focuses all intentions on good works. The second path is spiritual companionship (*suhbat*) with a completed shaykh who is attracted to God and who has finished wayfaring/contemplative practice (*suluk*). God almighty, by means of your (Baqibillah's) favor, has blessed me with the first path to the extent of my ability.[9] Bless God.

No good deeds are happening even though I concern myself with this. But there comes a time that I no longer give any importance [to good deeds] and become agitated. One knows that there are no deeds being performed that are worthy of the angel above the right shoulder to record.[10] It is known that the book on the right has no good deeds written in it. Any writing is futile and useless. How could I be worthy of God almighty? Anything in the world is better than I, even a foreign infidel or apostate heretic. I can be considered worse than all of them.[11]

With respect to attraction to God, some requisites and related aspects of [attraction to God] remained although I had completed "wayfaring to God" (*sayr ila Allah*). This happened while experiencing annihilation of self in the center of the station of "wayfaring in God" (*sayr fi'llah*). All of this was complete. The states of annihilation of self occurred as I detailed to you in the last letter. It must be that this is the annihilation discussed by Khwaja 'Ubaydullah Ahrar when he said, "the end of this work." It must be the same annihilation that is verified after the disclosure of the Essence and ascertaining the realization of "wayfaring in God." The annihilation of intentionality is one aspect of this annihilation. As long as one is not annihilated in God, he will not be able to go to God's Majestic Court.

Those who do not have an affinity for this station are in two groups. One group focuses on the station and searches for a way to arrive. The other group does not even turn toward the station. Turning toward Baqibillah, according to the second path [of having spiritual companionship with a completed shaykh attracted to God], is a more effective way to arrive at this station than other paths. The affinity and connection of this path is evident

---

9. The first path is Sirhindi's situation during his first experience outlined in letter 1.7 because later on in the letter translated here (1.11) he goes on to thank his shaykh for being on the second path.

10. In the Islamic tradition each person has an angel over the right shoulder recording one's good deeds and another angel over the left shoulder recording one's bad deeds.

11. A very detailed explanation of this experience is found in Mirza Jan-i Janan's ninth letter in Ghulam 'Ali Dihlawi, *Maqamat-i mahzari*, Urdu trans. Iqbal Mujaddidi (Lahore: Zarin Art Press, 1983), 387-388. In short, Sirhindi was in such a place that when he looked inside himself all he could see was his "dark side" (lit. evil side *jihat-i sharr*) in such a way that it appeared that he was absolutely devoid of any perfections or admirable qualities.

because it is established with Baqibillah. It is all about obedience to his command. Sometimes there is arrogance and boldness, otherwise, I am this very Ahmad, your ancient servant.

The second time I observed from this station, other stations appeared, one higher than the other. After focusing on begging and grief, I experienced the station above the first station. I realized that this station was that of 'Uthman b. 'Affan (the third caliph, assas. 35/656),[12] and that the other caliphs also had passed through this station. This station is one of completion (*takmil*) and guidance. There are two stations above this one that I will discuss now. Above [the station of completion and guidance] another station came into view. When I arrived at that station, I became aware that this was the station of 'Umar Faruq (the second caliph, assas. 24/644) and that the other caliphs had also passed through [this station]. Above this, the station of Abu Bakr (the first caliph, d. 13/634) appeared. God almighty be pleased with all of them. I also experienced this station.[13] In addition, I was with the shaykhs of Baha'uddin Naqshband in the stations they had experienced.[14] The other caliphs (after Abu Bakr) also passed through this station. There is no superiority except [the difference] between passing through a station and being stabilized in a station. There is no station above that of Abu Bakr's except the station of the Seal of the Messengers (Muhammad). God bless him completely and perfectly.

Another station of light came into view opposite Abu Bakr Siddiq's station. God almighty be pleased with him. It was so exquisitely beautiful that nothing like this had appeared before. It was a bit higher than Abu Bakr's station like the height of a bench above the ground. Abu Bakr's station is the station of belovedness (*mahbubiyat*), variegated and colorful. I experienced the many colors reflected from this station. After this, in the same manner, I experienced a subtlety spread out on the horizon in all four directions like the sky or fragments of clouds. Baha'uddin Naqshband is in the station of Abu Bakr. God almighty be pleased with them both. I found myself in the station opposite to the station of Abu Bakr and experienced it in the same manner [with variegated colors and subtlety].

Another thing that happened was my giving up guiding others on the

12. In the text it has "the one with the two lights" referring to 'Uthman's two successive wives, Ruqiyya and Umm Kulthum, both of whom were daughters of the Prophet.

13. In the interlinear text it states that Sirhindi experienced the station by passing through it instead of being stabilized in this station.

14. Here the shaykhs refer to Baha'uddin's teachers, not everyone in the lineage preceding him. In note eleven in *Collected Letters,* 1.11.23 the editor states that Sirhindi was with these shaykhs as a son is with his father, as a seeker is with his spiritual master, or as a student is with his teacher.

path because it was not satisfying. It felt like I had become drowned and lost in the abyss of the world. How can a person who finds the inner strength to come forth from this abyss be able to forgive oneself? No matter how many other things a person may have to do, it is necessary and agreeable to guide others. But guiding others is conditional upon asking forgiveness if troubling, evil doubts occur while guiding others. Then one requests God's satisfaction. Without observing these conditions, satisfaction will not benefit the person, who will then remain at the bottom of the abyss. According to Baha'uddin Naqshband and 'Ala'uddin 'Attar (d. 803/1400 Hissar, Tajikistan), without observing these conditions one can guide others and have God's satisfaction. God almighty bless their inner hearts. This lowly one, without observing these conditions, found that sometimes there was God's satisfaction. Other times I was at the bottom of the abyss.

Another experience is in the book *Fragrances of Intimacy*. Quoting Shaykh Abu Sa'id Abu'l Khayr (d. 440/1049 Nishapur),[15] "When the entity (*'ayn*) does not remain where will the trace (the attribute) remain?"[16] "It does not leave one alone or spare one."[17] [Q. 74:28] These words at first glance are difficult to understand. According to Shaykh Muhyiddin Ibn 'Arabi (d. 638/1240 Damascus) and his followers, the entity (*'ayn*) is a part of what is known about God almighty and it is impossible to have an extinction of the entity. From ignorance, knowledge changes. When the entity is not extinct then the trace (associated with an attribute) does not go anywhere either. In this manner, it all makes sense to the mind.

Shaykh Abu Sa'id did not come up with a solution. After utterly concentrating [on this matter], God almighty revealed the secret of these words [to him]. He realized that neither the entity nor the trace remained. He found the meaning in himself and there was no longer any problem. [For me], the station of this inner knowledge (*ma'rifat*) also came into view. A very high [station] indeed! It was above the station that Ibn 'Arabi and his followers had spoken about. These two experiences (Abu Sa'id's and Ibn 'Arabi's) do not contradict each other. One comes from one place and the other from another place. To explain in detail requires a long discussion.

[Another topic] concerns the lasting nature of this experience [of the flashing disclosure of Essence (*tajalli-yi dhati-yi barqi*)]. Abu Sa'id said that it also becomes pertinent [to ask] about the meaning of the experience

15. This is 'Abdurrahman Jami's *Nafahat al-uns*.

16. See ibid., 308. The disappearance of the entity (*'ayn*) is discussed in detail in letter 1.287 in this volume.

17. The interlinear notes translate this Qur'anic passage as "neither Essence nor attribute."

and its lasting nature.[18] I found that this experience was lasting, although it rarely lasts.

Looking at books is another experience that is not at all gratifying except to describe what has happened to notables as they traverse the stations. It is commendable that one can read about this kind of thing. The states of former shaykhs are very interesting. [Theoretical] books about realities and experiential knowledge (*ma'arif*) cannot be comprehended [without actual experience]. This especially [applies to] talk about asserting the unity of being (*tawhid-i wujudi*), the ordered emanations (*tanzilat-i muratib*), and the subtle centers.[19] In this regard, I find a great affinity with Shaykh 'Ala'uddawla Simnani and we are in harmony concerning this matter both in personal inclinations (*dhawq*) and in first-hand experience. However, I am not going to deny the aforementioned knowledge [of unity of being] and oppose [those who assert the truth of unity of being].

Another experience involved me fighting diseases a few times, which had effects. In the same way, the conditions of some deceased persons appeared from the liminal world (*'alam-i barzakhat*),[20] and I alleviated their pain and distress. But now I have no more ability to concentrate on that or anything else. I had some misfortunes and ill treatment from people. There were many associated with me who were unjustly destroyed and forced to leave their homes. Basically no distress or affliction reached my heart, even where they had done harm.

Some companions who are in the station of attraction to God have talked about their inner knowledge and contemplative witnessing (*shuhud*) without having even made one step toward stations of the path. They do not have the slightest experience of the states of these way stations. It is hoped that God almighty will bless them with the good fortune of wayfaring (*suluk*) after all the aspects of being attracted to God [are finished].

Shaykh Nur (from these aforementioned companions) is stuck in this station. He has not arrived at the upper point in the station of attraction to God. He finds difficulty both in action and in rest and does not understand the harm [to himself]. Automatically he is stopped in his tracks. Likewise, most of his companions, due to a lack of guidance in behaving beautifully

18. It does not appear that Abu Sa'id discussed the disclosure of the essence in the *Nafahat al-uns*, though there are discussions of this subject by other shaykhs in Jami's, *Nafahat al-uns*, 410, 555. Footnote 11 on 1.11.23 in *Collected Letters* adds the technical description of the experience in question, that is, a flashing disclosure of Essence. There is a further discussion of this type of experience in 1.21 and 1.27 in *Collected Letters*.

19. These are the subtle centers and entifications mentioned in the Introduction.

20. This *barzakh* is the in-between place between this world and the next probably located in the world of the spirits.

(*adab*), have become stuck in their spiritual work. In this spiritual work it is surprising, from my point of view, how they get stuck when their intention is to develop themselves. It happens that they delay the spiritual work without intending to. Otherwise, the path is quite near. Shaykh Nur has gone to the lowest point. The activity of attraction to God has brought him to the end where he has arrived at the interface (*barzakh*) of that station. He was brought above, from the surface to the end [of the station] where the first attributes [appear] along with the constant light of the attributes. He sees himself separate from himself, and finds the shaykh to be annihilated. Then he sees the attributes separated from the Essence. Seeing that, he also arrives at the station of attraction to God. Now both he and the world are lost in a way that cannot be described in words. Whether outwardly in spiritual companionship or deeply hidden inside, one who is proceeding in [the level of isolation and absolute exclusive unity (*ahadiyat-i sirfa*)] will achieve nothing without bewilderment and confusion.

Sayyid Shah Husayn has also arrived near the end point in the station of attraction to God, and his mystery subtle center (*sirr*) has arrived at that point. Similarly, he sees the attributes separate from the Essence but he finds the Essence of the One (*dhat-i ahad*) everywhere. Outwardly he is happy and contented. Likewise, Miyan Ja'far has also arrived near the last point and appears to be very full of desire and lament, a lot like Shah Husayn. Among the other companions who have distinguished themselves are Miyan Shaykhi, Shaykh 'Isa, and Shaykh Kamal who have arrived at the upper point in the station of attraction to God. Shaykh Kamal is proceeding in descent [to the world of creation]. Shaykh Naguri has come below the upper point even though he has a lot of distance yet to go. There are presently eight or nine companions right here who have come up from the bottom point. Some have arrived at the center point facing descent [to the world of creation]. Some of the others are near and others are far.

Shaykh Muzammil finds himself lost and sees the attributes [emanating] from the Origin (*asl*) and the Absolute everywhere. He perceives things in the world like mirages without specific features and finds nothing. Concerning the Mawlana whom we know, it appears that his permission to teach people is a really good idea, but it should be permission suitable to one attracted to God, [that is, conditional permission]. There are some remaining matters, which he must benefit from since he has proceeded quickly without stopping. He will go to you (Baqibillah, lit. the Holy Presence), and you can tell him what you think will improve his situation. This poor one has reported whatever understanding he has had. The judgment is yours. Khwaja Diya'uddin Muhammad was here a few days. Overall he found presence of God (*hudur*) and tranquility.[21] In the end, due to a lack of income and not being at ease, he joined the army.

The son of Mawlana Sher Muhammad is also going into military service. Generally he is present with God and tranquil. He has not progressed due to some hindrances. He is quite arrogant. The servant must know his limits. After writing this letter, a feeling came over me and a state occurred that I couldn't explain in writing. I verified the annihilation of will (*iradat*) and just like before, the connection of the will became separated from desires. But the origin (*asl*) of the will remained like I have written before.

Now the will also appears from the origin. Neither desire nor will remain. As the form of this annihilation came into view, some knowledge appropriate to this station appeared. It was difficult to write this knowledge down because it was hidden and subtle. I should desist from writing about this knowledge. At the time of verifying this annihilation and overflowing knowledge, a special view beyond oneness (*wahdat*) appeared, although it is established that there is no view beyond oneness because there is not any affinity (*nisbat*). But I have reported what I have experienced. As long as I am not certain, I will not write boldly. The appearance of this station from beyond oneness is like seeing Agra beyond Delhi. There is no resemblance whatsoever. Whatever is in view is not oneness, nor beyond that, nor a station known by a title of reality, nor a truth known beyond that. Bewilderment and ignorance are the same. I do not feel any superiority from seeing this and do not know what to say. Everything seems to contradict everything else. Nothing comes for me to say. Surely this state resembles no other. God forgive me. I repent to God all that God dislikes—in speech, in deed, in thought, and in what is seen.

And also this time I have come to know that what I had thought to be annihilation of the attributes was in truth the annihilation of the characteristics of the attributes and their distinctions. [This happened] while the attributes became included in oneness and [other] characteristics became extinguished. Now the origin of the attributes has disappeared, as if one could be included in the other. Nothing remains of the predominance of exclusive unity. Nothing remains of any distinction from the level of comprehensive or detailed knowledge that I had realized. My entire vision has become focused on the outside world (*bar kharaj*). [According to the hadith], God was and with God there was nothing else.[22] He is now as God always has been. This time my knowledge corresponds with my state. Before, I mentioned knowledge with this meaning but without experienc-

21. Technically *hudur* means being present with God in the station of oneness. Ordinarily it can mean "ease."

22. This hadith is found in al-Bukhari, *Bad' al-khalq,* 1, *Tawhid*, 22; and al-Nasa'i, *al-Sunan al-kubra*, #11240 [MR].

ing the state. I hope that you will alert me to what is correct and what is in error. In addition, there is Mawlana Qasim 'Ali who has realized the station of completion as well as some companions here. God almighty knows best concerning the reality of my state.

Introduction to Sirhindi's further contemplative development: Letter 1.13

Ahmad Sirhindi is writing to his shaykh, Baqibillah.[23] He explains to Baqibillah how he had ascended to annihilation in God and descended while abiding in God. Transformed by his experience, Sirhindi has returned to the material world. He has completed his journey in lesser intimacy with God (*walayat-i sughra*) in the shadows of God's names and attributes. From the letter, it seems that he is still getting his bearings. Outwardly Sirhindi appears to be an ordinary person but inwardly his reality is extraordinary because inwardly he is with God. The five thousand year journey refers to the time it takes a non-Mujaddidi sufi, through the exercise of the personal will, to purify the elements and the ego-self through daily spiritual exercises. As outlined in the previous letter, Sirhindi had annihilated all will and desire to follow the path of spiritual companionship with his completed/perfected shaykh—which is the fast track.

The phrases "All is God." or "All is from God." have become shorthand for experiencing the (ontological) unity of being (*wahdat-i wujud*) or contemplatively witnessing the unity of being (*wahdat-i shuhud*). When Sirhindi uses the term "*wahdat-i wujud*" it is to designate the sufi experience of *wujudi*s who deny multiplicity in their assertion of the ontological unity of being. He proposes *wahdat-i shuhud* to balance this partial truth. Sirhindi experiences the unity of being as an elementary stage superseded by the experience of the attributes of creation being the shadow of God's attributes.

This letter has Sirhindi declaring that there is no contradiction between the outer shariat and his inner experiences. In the study of contemplative practice and religious experience, this is a significant move because it signifies that human-created-in-history shariat is the criterion to evaluate post-rational, inner experience. For Sirhindi, an inner experience is ultimately valid only if it conforms to the creedal and orthopraxic Muslim Sunni Hanafi dictates of shariat. Such a stance is quite appropriate in an environment where society is governed by the shariat, but in light of the apparently larger context of cross-cultural religious experience and consciousness studies, there are other issues involved. If the way to God is endless then it means that the shariat necessarily has to follow suit, for the infinite cannot be contained by the finite. Herein lies a much larger notion of shariat, as

23. There are twenty letters addressed to Baqibillah in *Collected Letters*.

discussed in the Introduction and in the previous chapter.

LETTER 1.13

The lowest of servants, Ahmad, exclaims one thousand and one 'ahs' of lament from realizing that the way to God is endless. Proceeding [along the way] has happened with such speed, with so many events, and with copious divine favor. Thus, the great shaykhs have declared that wayfaring to God (*sayr ila Allah*) is a journey of five thousand years. "The angels and the Spirit ascend to God in a day of fifty thousand years." [Q. 70:4] This verse alludes to when I feel discouraged in spiritual work and my hopes are extinguished. The Qur'anic verse, "It is God who sends down the saving rain after they have despaired and spreads out God's mercy" [Q. 42:28] gives me hope.

It has been a few days since I have experienced wayfaring in the world as an ordinary person (lit. wayfaring in the things of the world, *sayr fi'l-ashya'*). Again, people wanting sufi teaching have been flooding in, and generally I have begun teaching them. But still I do not find myself worthy of the station of completion to guide others. People's insistence causes me not to say anything because of shyness and politeness.

Previously, I have repeatedly told you about how I was bogged down with the issue of asserting the unity of being (*tawhid-i wujudi*) along with actions and attributes being connected with the source (*asl*).[24] When the truth of the matter became known I emerged from being stuck. I experienced the adage "All is from God" prevailing. I saw more completeness in this than the saying, "All is God." I knew God's creation (*af'al*) and God's attributes from a different perspective. Everything [was shown to me as it] passed above one by one, and my doubt completely disappeared. All that has been disclosed (*kashifiyat*) corresponds to the outer shariat without even the slightest contradiction. Sufis who contradict the outer shariat do so on the basis of what is disclosed to them, whether in sobriety or intoxication. There is no contradiction between the inner and the outer.

The contradictions that appear to those traversing the path need to be faced and resolved. The true realized one (*muntahi-yi haqiqi*) finds that inner experience corresponds to the outer shariat. The difference between the [superficial] jurists and the noble sufis is that jurists know [topics of shariat] by rational proof and the sufis know by their inner disclosures and by tasting. What is greater proof of sufis' sound condition than this correspondence (between their experience and the shariat)? "I will get upset and be quiet" [Q. 26:13] is how I feel now. I do not know what to say. I do not have the inclination to write about these states, nor is it possible to fit them

24. The text simply has *tawhid* but the context, and the interlinear note, clearly indicates that *tawhid-i wujudi* is intended.

in a letter. Perhaps there has been some wisdom in this. Please do not deprive this unfortunate one of your exceptional spiritual attention (*tawajjuh*) or leave me alone on the path. You were the starting point of these words. If there is verbosity then you are the cause. It is better not to show any more arrogance. The servant should know his limits.

Introduction to types of certainty and stations on the Sufi path: Letter 1.18

Ahmad Sirhindi is writing to his shaykh, Baqibillah.[25] Sirhindi alludes to the differences between the state of variegation (*talwin*) and the station of stability (*tamkin*). The former involves experiencing the states of the attributes while the latter has an experience of the realities of the attributes. Variegation, as the word suggests, brings upon all kinds of manifestations and events in the midst of fluctuating states. The seeker has not yet experienced the origin of the divine energy (*fayd*) flowing through the subtle centers. In contrast, stability means that the wayfarer has realized all of the subtle centers and has experiences of the Essence (*dhat*). It is the reality of certainty (*haqq-i yaqin*) with no overpowering attraction to God or bewilderment. After stability, the wayfarer proceeds to the level of Essence and the resulting experience of bewilderment.[26]

There are three levels of knowing expressed by the metaphor of fire. The first level is knowing that there is a possibility of certainty (*'ilm-i yaqin*). This is equivalent to outer wayfaring (*sayr-i afaqi*). It is like seeing smoke and inferring that there is fire. The next stage is that of perceiving certainty (*'ayn-i yaqin*). It is like seeing the fire but it is fleeting and does not stabilize. The final stage is the reality of certainty (*haqq-i yaqin*). It is *being fire*. The reality of certainty involves abiding in God at the level of the Essence in helplessness and bewilderment—it is simply beyond human awareness and perceptions.[27]

Sirhindi then details the relative positions of three stations: the station of intimacy with God (*maqam-i walayat*), the station of martyrdom (*maqam-i shahadat*),[28] and the station of truthfulness (*maqam-i siddiqiyat*).

25. There are twenty letters addressed to Baqibillah in *Collected Letters*. Hutaki suspects that this letter is actually 1.13 because it is the previous letter referred to in the beginning of 1.14. See Hutaki, *Sharh-i Maktubat*, 83.

26. This is discussed in ibid., 83-88.

27. See Ahmad Mujaddidi, *al-Bayyinat*, 522-524.

28. Logically one would think that this is the station of the "affirmation of faith" (or as ter Haar has translated "station of the (doctrinal) formula") since *shahadat* also has this meaning. Further investigation into the technical terminology and subsequent confirmation with Shaykh Ma'sum make it clear that "martyrdom" is the meaning here. It is not to be confused with the visible world of physical real-

According to Mawlana Khalid Baghdadi (d. 1242/1827 Damascus) these three levels have axial authorities (*qutb-i madar*) of 'Ali b. Abi Talib (assas. 40/661), 'Umar b. al-Khattab al-Faruq (assas. 24/644),[29] and Abu Bakr as-Siddiq (d. 13/634) respectively. The axial guide at the highest station, the station of prophethood, is Muhammad.[30] These three stations represent three degrees of intimacy with God and roughly correspond to lesser intimacy with God (*walayat-i sughra*), greater intimacy with God (*walayat-i kubra*), and greatest intimacy with God (*walayat-i 'ulya*).

In the station of martyrdom, characterized by knowledge, there is lesser martyrdom where one physically dies battling those who cover up the truth of God (*kuffar wa-mushrikin*), and a greater martyrdom where one's ego-self dies in the love of God. The first sword "carves two out of one" while the sword of love makes two into one.[31] The station of truthfulness is superior to this station because in the station of truthfulness there is total sobriety and its realization comes about not only from knowledge, but also from faith.[32]

Like in the previous letter, inner illumination and the principles of the shariat are necessarily in harmony. The difference between the "general" religious sciences and detailed inner experiences is like the difference between knowing the possibility of something and actually perceiving it. So scholars generally know about reward and punishment in the grave but realized sufis can actually *see* it. One kind of understanding is necessarily broad in nature and the other is quite detailed and self-evident. There is confirmation and detailed inner experience of what is outlined in the shari-

---

ity (*'alam-i shahadat*). The experience of "unity in multiplicity" noted in Letter 1.8 being the same experience as the "station of the (doctrinal) formula," indicated by ter Haar in *Follower and Heir,* 37-38 is not obvious. Neither of the commentators, Hutaki or Ahmad Mujaddidi, made this connection.

29. Note that 'Umar was assassinated while leading the morning prayers.

30. See Mahmud b. 'Abd Allah al-Husayni al-Alusi, *Ruh al-ma'ani*, 15 vols. (Multan, Pakistan: Maktaba-yi Imdadiya, n.d.), 3:76-77 [the fifth *juz* of the Qur'an]. He is commenting on "Whoever obeys God and the Messenger will be with those whom God favored among the prophets, truthful ones (*siddiqin*), martyrs, and righteous (*salihin*)." [Q. 4.69] When asked about 'Uthman's rank, Mawlana Khalid replied that 'Uthman had favor from both levels: martyrdom (he too was assassinated) and closeness to God. Ibid., 76. This is the inner meaning of 'Uthman's sobriquet, "the one with the two lights," mentioned above in fn 20 in letter 2.67 on p. 74.

31. See Ahmad Mujaddidi, *al-Bayyinat*, 528.

32. See ibid., 536 and al-Alusi, *Ruh al-ma'ani*, 3:77 [the fifth *juz* of the Qur'an]. Note that Abu Bakr's sobriquet, as-Siddiq, was given to him because of his utmost truthfulness and unquestioning faith.

at.[33] The comprehensive knowledge of the jurists is proved by the contemplatively witnessed shariat cases and commands.

In a brief discussion of free will and destiny, Sirhindi takes a clear middle path here. Fate and divine decree come from God's necessity, not by blind fate. People have choice and God knows what someone will choose ahead of time before any divine decree is written. Sirhindi then refutes those who assert the unity of being (*wahdat-i wujud*). They think (according to Sirhindi) that God is the union of both immanence and transcendence. He understands them to be intoxicated in the station of intimacy with God, while his perspective is from the sobriety of the station of martyrdom in harmony with the shariat.

In addition, they interpret the six ontological levels of being as necessarily being God.[34] Each of these levels has its own different reality and laws governing that reality so, according to Sirhindi's perspective, how can they all be the necessary absolute of the Essence?[35] Commenting on the Qur'anic verse mentioning God's speech and hearing, Sirhindi clearly states that human seeing and hearing is *not* God's seeing and hearing. God's hearing and speech are incommensurably transcendent. Human seeing and hearing is only a distant effect of God's seeing and hearing. The only power, life, and animating force in existence is God, who is incommensurably transcendent. Creation by itself is inherently dead. Only the being of God is alive as God is beyond existence-nonexistence. On the human level this

---

33. One can surmise that the inner experiences that confirm the shariat are culturally conditioned since contemplatives of other traditions do not have these experiences. In addition, there are no reports to my knowledge that sufis have had experiences that have indicated errors in the shariat. In addition, it is not obvious how a "rational and theoretical discipline of the shariat" can consistently conform to experiences that go far beyond the realms of the rational mind. Sirhindi continually reminds us of the incommensurability of the rational and his post-rational experiences. However, for him the shariat is a God-given reality and therefore there cannot be a contradiction between shariat and an experience of the Essence. From the letters in the previous chapter one can see that Sirhindi experiences shariat as both rational and post-rational.

34. The six necessary levels of Reality (*maratib-i wujubiya*) from top to bottom: 1) the undifferentiated Essence (*la ta'ayyun*) at the level of exclusive unity (*ahadiyat*); 2) the pure Essence (*dhat-i baht*) at the level of inclusive unity (*wahidiyat*) and comprehensive knowledge; 3) the level of unity (*wahdat*) and detailed knowledge; 4) the world of spirits/world of command; 5) the world of image exemplars (*'alam-i mithal*); and 6) the physical world. This is the formulation of Ibn al-'Arabi's followers. Figure 1 in this book is an approximate diagram of Sirhindi's variation with five levels.

35. See Hutaki, *Sharh-i Maktubat*, 88-89.

means that our bodies, minds, and ego identities are all ultimately dead in varying levels of nonexistence. Real life is beyond these shells.

Baqibillah's answer to this letter is found in his collected writings. He clarifies Sirhindi's experiences of closeness to God with 'Ubaydullah Ahrar's experiences and affirms that the contemplative witnessing of 'Ala'uddawla Simnani is superior to that of *wujudi*s. He quotes a saying by Ibn al-'Arabi (whom he addresses as the great shaykh but not as the greatest shaykh), "A state (an altered state of consciousness, *hal*) from the standpoint of knowledge (*'ilm*) can be controversial but someone in a state cannot say anything about knowledge." Then he quotes a saying by Abu Sa'id Abu'l-Khayr, "When someone asks a question from an altered state then the answer should be from an altered state."[36]

Letter 1.18

As long as there were various kinds of states and events of the heart happening, the lowest of servants, full of faults, Ahmad, son of 'Abdulahad, used to be arrogant and bold talking about these things. When God almighty, by the blessing of your exalted spiritual energy (*tawajjuhat*), freed me from the bondage of states, God honored me by [changing my previous state of] variegation to stability (*az talwin bi-tamkin*).[37] The outcome of this matter has only been bewilderment and worry. Instead of arriving there is only separation; instead of nearness there is only distance; instead of inner knowledge there is only the unknown; instead of knowledge there is only ignorance. Undoubtedly there has been a delay in writing letters, as I have not dared to talk about my daily states. Along with this, my heart has become cold in such an overpowering way that I do not feel like doing anything. I am hanging around with do-nothings and am not able to finish anything. I am nothing, and even less than nothing is too much. A person who is nothing and less than nothing can do nothing.

Now we come to the point of the letter. It is surprising that God has honored me now with the reality of certainty (*haqq-i yaqin*), since in that domain the knowledge of certainty (*'ilm-i yaqin*) and the vision of certainty (*'ayn-i yaqin*) do not cover one another. Annihilation and abiding are united

---

36. See Baqibillah, *Kulliyat-i Baqibillah*, eds., Abu'l-Hasan Zayd Faruqi and Burhan Ahmad Faruqi (Lahore: Din Muhammadi Press, ca. 1967), 123-124.

37. The experience of variegation (*talwin*) in an attribute is for one who experiences temporary states. The experience of stability (*tamkin*) in an attribute is for one who experiences the realities (*haqa'iq*). It appears that most sufis, along with Sirhindi, consider stability to be a higher station than variegation. For Ibn 'Arabi it is the most complete of stations. See Kashani's *Lata'if al-i'lam*, 346; and William C. Chittick, *The Sufi Path of Knowledge* (Albany: State University of New York Press, 1989), 108.

in the reality of certainty. In the eye of bewilderment and [the state] without any sign, knowledge and feelings are both in the reality of certainty. The absence of a sense of I-ness (*nafs*) is presence with God (*hudur*). Except for outer knowledge and inner knowledge (*'ilm wa-ma'rifat*), there is nothing but increasing ignorance and the unknown. Is it not strange that I have arrived and am still confounded?

God almighty, with God's own pure infinite divine favor, has facilitated progress in the degrees of completion. The station of martyrdom is above the station of nearness to God (*maqam-i walayat*). The connection (*nisbat*) of closeness to God and martyrdom is the connection between the outward disclosure (*tajalli-yi suri*) and the Essential disclosure (*tajalli-yi dhati*).[38] But the distance between these [two stations of martyrdom and nearness to God] is many times greater than the distance between these two disclosures. Above the station of martyrdom is the station of truthfulness. The distinction between these two stations is so great that it cannot be expressed or explained by allusion. There is no station above the station of truthfulness except that of prophethood. God bless those in this station.

It is impossible for a station to exist between the station of truthfulness and the station of prophethood. I know the ruling of this impossibility from direct and sound inner illumination (*kashf*). Some of the folk of God (*ahl-i Allah*) have verified [a place] between these two stations [of truthfulness and prophethood], which they have called close proximity [to God]. They were honored by this [experience], and were informed about the truth of this station after much concentration and endless supplications. Thus, in the beginning a station manifested between these two stations, as some notables had said, and afterwards they made the truth [of this station] known. Indeed! The attainment of this station is after reaching the station of truthfulness at the time of ascent. But being in the middle is a place to consider carefully. I will detail the truth of this station after we get together if God almighty wills.[39]

This station of [close] proximity is quite lofty. In the stages of ascent a station above this one is not known. The addition of being (*wujud*) to the Essence is experienced in this station as the authentic jurists (*'ulama'-i ahl-i haqq*) have established. God thank their efforts. Here being also remains

38. Various disclosures have connections to different realms. Between the outward disclosure with a connection to the physical world and the disclosure of the Essence with a connection to the divine Essence, there is the disclosure of light with a connection to the divine actions (*af'al*) and the essential disclosure (*tajalli-yi ma'nawi*) with a connection to the divine attributes.

39. Ibn al-'Arabi discusses both the station of truthfulness and the station of proximity. See Michel Chodkiewicz, *Seal of the Saints: Prophethood and Sainthood in the Doctrine of Ibn 'Arabi*, (London: Islamic Texts Society, 1993), 57-58.

on the path and above that there is ascent. Abu al-Mukarram Ruknuddin Shaykh ‘Ala’uddawla Simnani in some of his books said, “Above the world of being there is the world of the King of being.” The station of truthfulness is one of the abiding stations facing the world. The station of prophethood is lower than the station of truthfulness, although in fact it is higher, [a station of] complete sobriety and abiding in God.[40] The station of proximity to God has no way of being an interface (*barzakhiyat*) between the stations of truthfulness and prophethood because its face is one of absolute incommensurability (*tanzih-i sirf*) and complete ascent. How different and distant the station of proximity to God is [from the stations of truthfulness and prophethood]! (As Hafiz says), They have me in front of a mirror like a parrot. Whatever the Eternal Teacher says, I will say.[41]

The rational and theoretical discipline of shariat (*‘ulum-i shari‘iya*) is necessarily based on inner divine illumination and does not contradict whatsoever the principles of those who know the shariat. Comprehensive (*ijmali*) religious sciences are based on detailed (*tafsili*) experience, and are brought from needing proof to being self-evident. A shaykh asked Baha’uddin Naqshband what the goal of sufi wayfaring was. God almighty bless his inner heart. He replied that comprehensive inner experiential knowledge (*ma‘rifat*) should become detailed, and knowledge that can be proved should become that which [can be verified through] inner illuminations. He did not say that one should learn anything other than the religious sciences.

Indeed! On the path, one can experience a lot of inner and outer knowledge. One must pass from this [knowledge] and arrive at the utter end [of the journey], which is the station of truthfulness. One cannot arrive [just] from this inner and outer knowledge. I wish that I could figure out the folk of God who say they have realized this noble station, but yet [they] have no connection to the knowledge of this station or the inner experience. “Above those who know is the Knower.” [Q. 12:76]

I would like to advise you about the secret of the problem of fate and the divine decree. There must not be any contradiction in any way with the

---

40. The stages of descent face the world and the station of prophethood is one of these. So it is lower (being the lowest station in the stages of descent) but it is “higher,” that is, more advanced, in that it comes after all the stations of ascent.

41. The text has “behind the mirror” (*dar pas-i ayinah*) which I have interpreted as the poetic version of *dar pish* because the allusion is of a parrot being trained in front of a mirror while the parrot trainer speaks behind the mirror. There is another interpretation whereby the poet is behind the mirror like a parrot (in the role of a prophet) speaking what God says to the other parrots. See Husayn ‘Ali Harawi, *Sharh-i ghazalha-yi Hafiz*, 4 vols. (Tehran: Nashr-i Naw, 1991), 3:1568-1570 (ghazal #377).

outer principles of the illuminated shariat [when discussing this matter]. It should be free from the limitations of humans being able to totally ascertain God's decree (*ijab*) and from the flaw of predestined fate [so that it] appears like the full moon at night.[42] It is strange that this problem is hidden when there are no contradictions with the principles of the shariat. It would make sense to hide it if it were suspected to contradict the shariat. "God will not be asked about what God does." [Q. 21.23] Because of fearing You, who has the guts to open his mouth? One can only surrender to Your will.

Inner and outer knowledge pour down like rain that intellectual understanding is too weak to bear. Intellectual understanding is only an expression. Only the King's camel can carry the King's gifts. In the beginning, I had a desire to write about this rare knowledge (*'ulum*) but was not successful. For this reason, I had difficulties, but it ended in contentment. It is said that the goal of this knowledge flourishing [in a seeker] is to acquire an ability to do something, not simply to memorize it. [The difference is like that between students of religious sciences] who obtain knowledge to acquire the ability to practice jurisprudence (*mawlawiyat*), [and those who simply] memorize Arabic grammar and other things. Some of this knowledge is worthwhile.

God almighty and blessed said, "There is no thing comparable to God; God is the All-hearing, the All-seeing." [Q. 42:11] The first part of this verse is proof of God's utter incommensurability, the outer aspect. The second part of God's saying, "God is the All-hearing, the All-seeing," completes and perfects the incommensurability. The explanation is that people have the illusion that [God's] hearing and seeing are analogous [to their human experience of hearing and seeing].[43] God almighty has negated hearing and seeing to dispel this illusion. Only God is the Hearing and Seeing. The hearing and seeing in creatures has nothing to do with the listening and visual faculties. Like God almighty created hearing and seeing, God created the listening and visual faculties after the two attributes [of hearing and seeing] were created. This is according to the usual pattern of creating [the ability to] listen and visualize without the [necessary] effect of hearing and seeing. If we were to say that there is an effect of hearing and seeing, then this too is created.

Just as their essences (sing. *dhat*) are only inanimate elements without life, their attributes are also just inanimate elements without life.[44] It is as if God, through God's own power, were to create speech in a stone, one could

42. Such a formulation must allow for some human free will and not have actions predestined, otherwise humans cannot be accountable for their actions.

43. An interlinear gloss explains this cryptic sentence by saying that the second part of the Qur'anic verse clarifies the first part of the verse.

44. Human attributes are like (inanimate) inactive machinery that appears to "come alive" with electricity.

not say in reality that the stone speaks or that it has the faculty of speech. Just like a rock is inanimate, its faculty of speech is also inanimate if we assume that it can be present in a rock. The stone has nothing to do with pronouncing letters. All the [divine] attributes are like this.[45] In short, when the two attributes of hearing and seeing were more apparent, God almighty singled them out to negate them. It was necessary to negate the rest of the attributes in the same way.

God almighty first created the attribute of knowledge, and after that God focused on the attribute of knowledge until God created an [aspect of] the known (*ma'lum*). Then God created a relationship between the attribute of knowledge and the known. After that, God revealed what was known. Then after creating the attribute of knowledge, without the attribute having anything to do with it, God created the disclosure (*inkishaf*) within the attribute of knowledge. Then it became known that the attribute of knowledge did not have anything to do with its disclosure.

It is the same way with the attribute of hearing. First God created hearing, and then God focused on what was heard, and after that, listening. Finally [God created] the realization of what was heard. In the same way, God created seeing, the pupils of the eyes, after that, a focus on what is seen, then visualizing, then the realization of what is seen. Analogously [it applies to the rest of the attributes]. A person's hearing and seeing are such that the origins (sing. *mabda'*) of listening and visualization are in the two attributes of hearing and seeing. Whatever is not like [God] does not hear or see.

It is certain that human attributes and essences are absolutely inanimate. The intent of the second part (of Q. 42:11 above) is to completely negate human attributes, not to verify human attributes. Nor [is the intent to assert that] those attributes are only fixed (*thabita*) for God almighty so that God can be the union of transcendence (the first part of the verse) and the resemblance to God (*tashbih*) (the second part of the verse). The entire noble verse is to confirm transcendence and totally deny any kind of resemblance to God.

The first point is the verification of God's attributes and knowing that their essences (sing. *dhat*) are absolutely inanimate. It is just like a waterspout and a clay pot and knowing that water comes from [the spout]. This knowledge corresponds to the [first level of the] station of intimacy with God (*maqam-i walayat*).

The second point is to know that these attributes themselves are also inanimate, known to be completely dead. "You will die and they will die"

---

45. The attributes that Sirhindi refers to are the fixed, essential attributes (*sifat-i thubutiya dhatiya*) in the first entification: life, knowledge, speech, power, hearing, sight, origination, and will. See Buehler, *Sufi Heirs*, 115.

[Q. 39:30] is the knowledge corresponding to the station of martyrdom, [the second level of intimacy with God]. From this, one can understand the distinction between the two stations. A little bit of something is indicative of the whole like the drop and the pool from which it came. A good year is evident from a good spring season.

Likewise, those in this lofty station consider the actions of creatures as dead and inanimate. This is not to say that they attribute their actions to God almighty or understand God almighty to be doing these deeds. God almighty is beyond that. It is like a person throwing a rock. One cannot say that the person is moving, but [instead] motion exists "in" the rock and the rock is in motion. In spite of that, the rock is absolutely inanimate and its motion is also absolutely inanimate. If we assume that the rock's motion kills a person, one cannot say that the rock killed [the person]. However, we can say that the thrower killed [someone]. The verdict of shariat jurists is in agreement with this statement. God almighty thank them for their efforts. Jurists say that in spite of creatures initiating actions, whether it be with their intent and choice or not, the effects of their actions are created by God almighty. An action of creatures has nothing to do with creating these effects. Their actions involve some motion without it having an effect in bringing about an action. If one said on this basis that one could make these actions the focus of reward and punishment, it would be against reason. It would be like a rock being occupied with [doing] something and praise or blame resulting from its action.

I assert that there is a difference between a rock and those occupying themselves with doing something. The basis of legal obligations is power and will (*iradat*). A rock does not have will. Creatures' will is also a creation of God almighty and has no effect on what is desired, so the intention of creatures is also dead. The benefit of will is [the ability to] manifest what is desired after verifying the intention in the usual manner. If the power of the creature is influenced in one aspect, it is like the Central Asian jurists have said, "God has created that effect like God has created power." God almighty thank them for their efforts. In its effect there is no choice at all, so its effect is also inanimate. For example, a person sees a rock thrown down by someone that ends up killing someone. The observing person knows that the rock is inanimate, and that the thrower's action involves an inanimate movement. The resulting effect of that action, death, is also recognized to be inanimate. All the essences, attributes, and actions are absolutely inanimate and absolutely dead. God is Life Everlasting, the All-hearing, All-seeing, Omniscient, All-Knowing who does whatever God chooses. "Say: If the ocean were ink [to write] the words of my Lord, the ocean would dry up before the words of my Lord would be used up even if we were to bring another ocean." [Q. 18:109]

I have been very arrogant and bold. What could be done? Beautiful discourse comes from absolute beauty. It is necessary that speech be beautiful, no matter how long it is. Whatever God said also beautifies in spite of my having no connection to God, not even to speak of God or to say God's name. A thousand times I wash my mouth with musk and rosewater. But still I do not deserve to say your name. The servant must know his limits. I hope to receive your attention. What can I present to you about my ruined condition? What I say and whatever is within me is from the divine favor of the Origin (*mabda'*) of that great attention, even though I am the same old Ahmad, your devoted servant.

Miyan Shah Husayn is on the path of asserting the unity of being (*tawhid-i wujudi*), and is content with that. It has come to mind that he has emerged from there and is experiencing bewilderment, which is the goal. From childhood, Muhammad Sadiq (Sirhindi's eldest son) has not been able to keep himself under control. He will make good progress if we can go on a trip together. He made great progress on a trip we made together to Daman-i Kuh and became drowned in the station of bewilderment. In bewilderment with me there was a complete connection [with God]. Shaykh Nur also is in this station and has made much progress. There is a youth from the circle of this poor one (Sirhindi) whose state is very high. He is ready and close to the [experience of] flashing disclosures (*tajalliyat-i barqi*).

Introduction to Sirhindi's culminating contemplative experience: Letter 1.290

This letter is addressed to Mulla Muhammad Hashim Kishmi Burhanpuri (d. ca 1054/1644), compiler of the third volume of Ahmad Sirhindi's *Collected Letters* and the author of *The Quintessential Stations*.[46] It is a letter describing Sirhindi's contemplative experiences in detail that led up to his shaykh, Baqibillah, giving him unconditional permission to teach. Sirhindi clarifies these experiences by comparing his own experiences with other types of sufi experience. The reader can appreciate the *scientific* nature of the sufi path here. Sirhindi is first given tasks to perform in the "laboratory" of subjective experience. The "laboratory results" are checked with his mentor, who then verifies that Sirhindi's experiences do or do not coincide

46. Ahmad Sirhindi wrote thirteen letters to Muhammad Hashim. See also, Iqbal Sabir, "Khwaja Mohammad Hashim Kishmi: A Famous Seventeenth Century Naqshbandi Sufi" in Mansura Haidar, *Sufis, Sultans and Feudal Orders: Professor Nurul Hasan Commemoration Volume* (New Delhi: Manohar, 2004), 63-70; and the introduction to Muhammad Hashim Kishmi, *Zubdat al-maqamat*, Urdu trans., Ghulam Mustafa Khan (Sialkot, Pakistan: Maktaba-yi Nu'maniyya, 1987), 9-30. [Only the Persian edition is cited in the rest of the footnotes]

with the consensus of those "verifiers" who have used the same Naqshbandi methods. This is how serious contemplative practices operate.

Sirhindi started to experience more and more absence as a result of the sensation of the manifestation of disclosures (sing. *tajalli*) that overpowered his spirit subtle center (*ruh*). Since the spirit is connected closely with the body, this overflowing of the spirit subtle center caused him to lose contact with bodily sensations and feeling. The ocean that he saw could have been the shadow of the divine disclosures revealed to him.[47] An annihilation where one forgets everything but God comes naturally because one loses contact with the material world without sensory contact with it. This is the technical meaning of annihilation. Likewise, as the sensory mechanisms activate, the material world "returns" to consciousness, and the experience recedes. When this realization of annihilation disappears then one experiences the annihilation of annihilation. Continually Sirhindi is being taught by his mentor that what he thinks is God or annihilation in God is just one of many states in the shadows of the attributes.

Throughout *Collected Letters* Sirhindi continually reminds his readers that what the *wujudi* shaykhs think they are experiencing as God is something else in the shadows very far from the origins (sing. *asl*). An essential awareness of the presence of God (*'ilm-i huduri-yi dhati*) involves contemplative witnessing (*shuhud*) and inner awareness (*'ilm-i khud*). In the station of unity of being, God is seen as encompassing the world. Even though the knowledge of God encompassing the world is one thing, in reality God is beyond comprehension. Unfortunately those who are in a state of spiritual intoxication, who Sirhindi classifies as *wujudi* sufis, cannot differentiate between essential encompassing and the knowledge of encompassing. This is why they confuse the two.

In the detailed account of Sirhindi's experiences Baqibillah asks him to forget the point that appears. As the wayfarer is contemplatively witnessing and passing through an attribute, that point is only an *imagined* point still in the world of possibility appearing to be connected to God's knowledge. In reality, the knowledge of God that one thinks is connected to the world actually originates in the imagination of the seeker because there is no connection between the world and God's knowledge other than God knowing about the world. It is like a mirror with the reflection of an object. There is no connection to the mirror whatsoever.[48] One only sees the Essence (lit. the Necessary world) with the eye of contemplative witnessing, not with the human physical eye.

The "Naqshbandi presence" discussed in the letter is experiencing attraction to God at the beginning of the path and the continual experience of

47. See Hutaki, *Sharh-i Maktubat*, 465.

48. See ibid., 466-467.

essential disclosures (sing. *tajalli-yi dhati*). Naqshbandis experience "real annihilation in God" while *wujudi* sufis who are wayfaring in the details do not realize the inner knowledge (*ma'rifat*) that is imparted with the experience of "real annihilation in God." Further in the letter, Sirhindi explains that people can experience what they consider to be the "reality of certainty" (*haqq al-yaqin*) but that does not mean it actually is. There is the certainty that arises from an essential divine disclosure (*tajalli-yi ma'nawi*) and there is the certainty arising from the appearance of a divine disclosure (*tajalli-yi suri*). For Naqshbandis, this reality of certainty, also called the comprehensiveness of union (*jam' al-jam'*), is being able to see both the world of possibility and the Necessary world (*'alam-i wajib*) together and to be able to distinguish between the two. The *wujudi* sufis experience just union (*jam'*) and cannot distinguish between these two worlds. The next stage, of separation after experiencing the whole (*farq ba'd al-jami'*), is when one experiences imagining the world of possibility and seeing it separately from the Necessary world. Sirhindi is seeking to show throughout his letters that there are verifiable ways of knowing about unity, whether it is from the Necessary world, the mirrorness of being manifest (*mir'atiyat-i mazhariyat*), shadowness, or the contemplative witnessing of oneness (*wahdat*) in multiplicity.[49] This is not "armchair sufism" but a set of very precise directions for aspirants to evaluate their experiences and discriminate the real from the shadow of the real.

People travel in the locus of manifestation of a certain name (*mazhar-i ism*) depending on their prophetic disposition. For example, those following Adam are in the shadows of the attribute of physical formation (*takwin* or engendering creation), while those following Jesus are in the shadows of power (*qudrat*). At this level, the wayfarer only is traveling to God since the wayfaring is in the shadow of the attributes. Traveling *in* God is in Essence. When Sirhindi says the name is above the fixed entity (*'ayn-i thabita*), he means that the seeker is in the shadow and has knowledge of the outer form.[50]

Concentrating on God (*yad dasht*), experiencing the continual presence of God is not the absolute end but just the end of contemplative witnessing (*shuhud*). The absolute end is ineffable. Contemplative witnessing can happen in the mirror of form and/or the mirror of Essence or beyond either or both of these. Witnessing in the mirror of Essence is the real contemplative witnessing of realized wayfarers. There is also the possibility of contemplatively witnessing beyond both form and Essence, but this is usually intermittent. When it is continuous then one experiences "being present [with God] while not being absent to oneself" (*hudur-i bi ghaybat*). Realized wayfarers have a continuous penetrating experience of God while not

49. See ibid., 470.
50. See ibid., 475.

being absent to themselves.[51]

Throughout *Collected Letters* Sirhindi indicates that sufis of the past had achieved significant progress on the path. He uses these examples to indicate the degradation of sufi practice he perceived all around him. Abu Sa'id Abu'l-Khayr was "one desired by God" (*murad*) who experienced bewilderment without any awareness, which shows that he reached the station of inner knowledge (*maqam-i ma'rifat*). Continuing in this analysis, 'Ubaydullah Ahrar had knowledge of unity unveiled to him while Baqibillah had the same experience of knowledge but with intoxication at the same time. One who really knows (*'arif*) sees the reflections of the disclosures of God's attributes in sobriety. Ahrar was among the "top twelve" of the spiritual hierarchy of his time who were responsible for the well being of humans.[52]

Sirhindi looks back at two of the "rightly guided caliphs," Abu Bakr and 'Ali, and distinguishes them according to the kind of attraction to God that they each had. Abu Bakr had the attraction to God associated with self-abiding being (*qayyumiyat*) while 'Ali had the attraction of God associated with togetherness (*ma'iyat*).[53] It is another example of Sirhindi's going beyond simple outward doctrinal formulations, in this case, Sunni-Shi'i, and discerning differences based on his experiences of the inner situation involved. The Naqshbandi lineage stems from both these caliphs, and Sirhindi appreciates them both.

Letter 1.290

In the name of God, the most compassionate and merciful. Praise God, the Lord of the worlds. God bless and give peace to the Master of the Messengers (Muhammad), his family, and his pure and noble companions. Know that the exalted Naqshbandi path is the closest to God, the fastest [to reach the goal], the most in harmony with the Qur'an and sunnat, and the most firm and stable. It is the way that allows one to submit the most to the will of God, who is the wisest, the most sincere, the best guide, the highest and most exalted, the most majestic, and the most patient in suffering. God almighty bless the spirits (sing. *ruh*) of its members and the inner hearts of its masters.

All the greatness of this path and the exaltedness of these great shaykhs is by virtue of their assiduous following of the sublime sunnat and by their

51. See ibid.

52. See ibid. Typically these twelve include a spiritual hierarchy that is traditionally headed by an axial leader (*qutb*) with three nobles (*nujaba'*), four pillars (*awtad*), seven pious ones (*abrar*), and forty substitutes (*abdal*). The numbers do not add up here but there are many variations of the preceding schema. See the introduction to letter 1.287 for more background information on this spiritual hierarchy.

53. See Hutaki, *Sharh-i Maktubat*, 477.

avoiding unacceptable innovations. That is, [the Naqshbandis followed] that which was in conformity with the noble Companions. May they have the goodwill of the Benefactor. [Like the Companions], the end of the task has become included in its beginning. The presence and awareness of the Companions continues to be engendered [in such a way] that after arriving at the pinnacle of completion [one arrives at yet] another, higher awareness beyond that.

Oh Brothers! God almighty guided all of you to the narrow path. This poor one (Ahmad Sirhindi), when he became attracted to this path, God became the guide to his work.[54] This guiding path serves as a refuge of intimacy with God (*walayat*) and an awareness of Reality. [It is a path characterized by] "the end is included in the beginning" and arriving at degrees of intimacy with God (*darajat-i walayat*), which leads to the most satisfying revealed religion (*din*).

Our shaykh, lord, and leader, Shaykh Muhammad al-Baqi (Baqibillah) is an important successor in the family of notable Naqshbandi holy presences. God sanctify their innermost beings. He taught this poor one (Ahmad Sirhindi) the recollection formula involving the name of the Essence (*Allah*).[55] Using an established [Naqshbandi] method, [my shaykh] showered spiritual power (*tawajjuh*) on me until its savory taste completely permeated my being. I started crying from intense yearning. A day later, a feeling of being dazed and having a feeling of not being in control of myself (*bikhudi*) [occurred], which according to these notables (*buzurgan*) is an authentic [experience] called "absence to oneself." (*ghaybat*).[56] I set out in that "absent state" and saw a limitless ocean with shapes of the world like shadows [in it].[57] I began gradually to be overcome more and more by this feeling of absence, sometimes for six hours, sometimes for twelve hours, and at times the entire night.

When I went in this condition to my shaykh, he said that I had realized

---

54. From this point Ansari translates a part of this letter in *Sufism and Shari'ah*, 202-206. My translation has benefited from his pioneering effort.

55. *Dhikr-i ism-i dhat* is typically sitting in ritual purity towards Mecca with total concentration on the heart, experiencing the heart saying, "Allah, Allah. . ." See Buehler, *Sufi Heirs*, 127-129.

56. According to Shaykh Ma'sum Naqshbandi, *bi-khudi*, *ghaybat*, and *istihlak* are different experiences. *Bi-khudi* is not being in control of oneself; *ghaybat* is the experience of "everything disappears except the face of God" referring to Q. 2:115 where one loses contact with the sensory world; and *istihlak* is the annihilation of the ego-self, the *nafs*. The experience of *ghaybat* also is the result of love and ecstatic attraction to God (*jadhba*). See *Collected Letters,* 1.200.89-90.

57. Zawwar Husayn adds in his Urdu translation that the black-colored forms look like the reflections of objects when they are under water. Sirhindi, *Maktubat,* trans. Zawwar Husayn, Vol. 1 (part 2), 406.

a kind of annihilation in God (*fana'*) and forbade me to recite any more recollections of God (*dhikr-i ism-i dhat*). He ordered me to observe my awareness (*nigahdasht*). Two days later, I realized what the Naqshbandis call annihilation in God and he had me continuing to observe my awareness. After that annihilation in God, I realized the annihilation of annihilation in God. He asked if I saw the entire world as one and connected together. When I replied yes, he said that it was considered to be "annihilation of annihilation" and a worthy experience. In spite of seeing that state [of the entire world as one], it was a superficial [experience] of union.[58] That very evening I experienced the annihilation of annihilation superficially and reported this to him. Then I experienced a state after annihilation in God. I said [to him] that I was experiencing the knowledge itself directly.[59] [This experience was] such that the attributes that I had thought were mine [actually] were those of God. Praise God. After that, an all-expansive light appeared and I thought that it was the black light of the Real.

When I told him about this, he said that I had contemplatively witnessed (*mashhud*) the Real but in a veil of light. He added that the expansion (*inbisat*) appearing in this light is in [the realm of] knowledge itself (not in what is known). This light expansively shines on everything that manifests in the world, high and low, by virtue of its connection with the Essence. Exalt God's affair. He told me that I had to reject this expansion. After that, the expansive black light gradually dimmed and narrowed until it became a point. He said that I had to also reject that point in order for me to experience bewilderment. So I did it just like that. The imagined point disappeared from the middle, resulting in bewilderment. In that realm [of bewilderment] there was contemplative witnessing of the Real without any veil.

When I reported [this experience], he said that the direct experience of God's presence (*hudur*) that I had was the "Naqshbandi presence," also called "the Naqshbandi connection" [to God]. This direct experience is also called "being present [with God] while not being absent to oneself" (*hudur-i bi ghaybat*).[60] "Including the end in the beginning" (*indiraj-i nihayat dar bidayat*) is realized in this station and the aspirant acquires this con-

58. Superficial here means that it appeared that way but was not real union.

59. This kind of knowledge, knowledge-by-identity, is juxtaposed to transmitted knowledge (*'ilm-i husuli*), which is knowledge received through an intermediary, usually a teacher of some kind.

60. *Ghaybat-i suri* is associated with the essential presence (*hudur-i ma'nawi*) and a disassociation from sensory feeling. See *Collected Letters,* 1.200.90. Technically *hudur* means being present with God in the station of oneness (*wahdat*) as one experiences absence (*ghaybat*) from physicality and ego-consciousness. Experiencing the presence of God while being with people (*hudur-i bi ghaybat*) is another

nection. Other lineages [have their aspirants] perform remembrance of God and litanies given by the sufi guide so that they can arrive at the goal.

My view of springtime is from my rose garden.

This poor one (Ahmad Sirhindi) realized this connection of noble being (the Naqshbandi path) a little over two months after learning remembrance of God. After deepening this connection [with God], I experienced another annihilation [in God], which is called "the real annihilation." (*fana'-i haqiqi*) My heart expanded so much that the entire world from the Throne to the center of the earth was tiny in comparison.[61] After that, I saw myself as God along with every individual in the world and even every small particle. Then I saw each small particle in the world, one after another, as separate individual entities (sing. *'ayn*). I experienced myself to be identical with everything until the entire world became lost in a small particle. After that, I saw myself, indeed every small particle, so extensive and expansive that the entire world, indeed numerous worlds, could be contained [in this vast expanse]. I experienced myself and each small particle as light. The light was so extensive that in each flowing atom forms of the world were annihilated in that light. Then I experienced myself, indeed each small particle, sustaining the whole world.

When I mentioned this [to my mentor Baqibillah] he said that this [experience] was the level of "the reality of certainty" (*haqq al-yaqin*) in affirming the oneness of God (*tawhid*).[62] The comprehensiveness of union (*jam' al-jam'*) is [another way of explaining] this station.[63] Afterwards, I experienced God in the forms of the world like I had before [but] this time what I saw was [all] imagined (and therefore illusion). Each small particle that I experienced as God was indistinguishable from every [other] small particle that I had imagined. While in total bewilderment, I remembered the

---

way of "being in solitude in society," (*khalwat dar anjuman*), one of the basic eight Naqshbandi principles articulated by 'Abdulkhaliq Ghujduwani (d. 575/1179).

61. According to Sirhindi, the Throne is separate from the traces of the heavens and earth and is one of the noblest "parts" of the macrocosm, acting as an interface between the world of creation and the world of command. See *Collected Letters,* 2.21.49-50, 1.44.95. The heart subtle center is the throne of the human microcosm. See ibid., 2.11.34.

62. Shaykh Ma'sum Naqshbandi has explained certain truth (*haqq al-yaqin*) as experiencing truth by being that truth (knowledge-by-identity); *'ayn al-yaqin* is the actual experience of something (knowledge-by-acquaintance); and *'ilm al-yaqin* is merely hearing about something from reliable transmitted knowledge (knowledge-about).

63. *Jam' al-jam'* is truly seeing both creation and God. See Dhawqi, *Sirr-i dilbaran*, 128. In Shaykh Ma'sum's words, this station is the integrated culmination of all the previous levels.

interpretation of [Ibn al-ʿArabi's] *Bezels of Wisdom* that I had heard from my learned father. God's compassion be with him.[64]

> If you want to say that the world is God and if you want to say that the world is created then you can say that from one perspective it is created and from another perspective it is God. You can also say in bewilderment that you cannot differentiate between the two.[65]

These words totally relieved my anxiety. When I went to my shaykh, I told him about my experiences. He said that my being in God's presence (*hudur*) was still not clear and that I should work on the exercises [he had given me] so that I could distinguish existence (*mawjud*) from illusion. Concerning the interpretation of the *Bezels of Wisdom* indicating the absence of distinctions (between existence and illusion) that I read to him, he said that Ibn al-ʿArabi had not explained the state of a completed person even though some had verified the absence of distinctions. Accordingly, I got working on my exercises.

After two days, the presence of God manifested through the exalted spiritual energy (*tawajjuh*) of my shaykh (Baqibillah) enabling me to realize the difference between existence and illusion. Thus, I was able to distinguish clearly between true existence (*mawjud-i haqiqi*) and the illusory imaginary. I realized that the attributes, traces, and signs appearing to proceed from the imaginary [world] actually were from the Real. Praise God. I realized that these attributes and traces were merely imaginary [although they were *from* the Real]. In the outside/objective world (*kharij*) I did not see even a speck of the Essence. When I reported this state to my shaykh, he said that this is the stage of separation after experiencing the whole,[66] and up to this point it is the end of the endeavor. After this, whatever happens is a result of the nature and potential of each person. The shaykhs of the [Naqshbandi] path say that this stage is the station of bestowing completion (*maqam-i takmil*).

You should know that this poor one (Ahmad Sirhindi) was brought from intoxication to sobriety in the first stage and honored [to proceed] from annihilation [in God] to abiding [in God]. I observed only the Real in each and every small particle of existence, as each small particle became a mirror reflecting God. From that station I was taken to bewilderment. When I came back to my senses, I found God (lit. presence of the Real) [encompassing and included] *with* each and every small particle of my being, but

64. The best English translation of *Fusus al-hikam* is Ibn al-ʿArabi, *The Bezels of Wisdom*, trans., Ralph Austin (Mahwah, NJ: Paulist Press, 1980).

65. Translated from the Arabic.

66. *Farq al-jamiʿ* is the profuse appearance of the qualities of the Essence. See Dhawqi, *Sirr-i dilbaran*, 275.

not [discretely] *in* each small particle of it.[67] The previous station appeared lower compared to this second station. Then I went into bewilderment again and came back [to sobriety]. At this stage (the second station), the Real was not connected to the world, nor separate. It was neither in the world nor outside it. In comparison to the togetherness (*ma'iyat*), encompassing, and penetrating [way God appeared in relation to the world] that I experienced at the first stage, everything completely disappeared. Praise God.

In spite of experiencing that same mode of being, God appeared to become visible again. I saw everything [like before] while also palpably feeling it. I observed the world during this time, but unlike my previous experience there was no connection with the Real. Then I experienced total bewilderment again. I realized, after returning to the state of sobriety, that the Real has a direct relation (*nisbat*) to the world and beyond that connection [with the world] there is an ineffable quality of affiliation (*nisbat-i majhul al-kayfiyat*). Praise and Exalt God. I realized one could contemplatively witness God almighty in an ineffable way. Again, I went into bewilderment and experienced a kind of contraction. When I came back to my senses I witnessed God without any experience of that ineffable connection. There was no connection of God to the world, neither knowingly nor ineffably. During this time I observed the world in a very special way and was favored with a special kind of knowledge [through which I realized] that there was no relationship between the created world and God almighty, even though I had contemplatively witnessed both God and creation.

At this time I was informed that the form of the attribute that I had contemplatively witnessed was not the immanent Essence of the Real. Instead, it was the imaginal form (*surat-i mithali*) linked to God's engendering creation in such [a way] that it is beyond the relationships of the created universe. Praise God. Whether one knows or does not know how things come about, it is beyond words and impossible to express.

Forget it. How can you ever be with the Beloved?
When climbing to the mountain summit is so dangerous?

O dear one! If I were to write about my states in detail and to explain my experiential knowledge of the Divine (*ma'arif*), then it would end up being very long and wordy. This is especially the case with experiential knowledge of the unity of being (*tawhid-i wujudi*) and the outer knowledge of

67. The principle here is that as one transforms and experiences more subtle aspects of reality there is a continuous process of inclusion and encompassing such that one increasingly feels/experiences God. This is expressed explicitly (emphasized by my added italics) to indicate that God cannot be limited by confinement to the material level of existence (*hulul*), so-called incarnation.

objects.[68] If an explanation were to be given, those who have spent their lives [experiencing] the unity of being would know that they have not even received a drop from that endless ocean. It is odd that this same group does not think that this poor one [Ahmad Sirhindi] to be among those experiencing the unity of being but instead classify him with jurists who deny the unity [of being]. In their shortsightedness, they think that insisting on their experiences of divine unity is [an indication of] being completed and that further development beyond that station is [a sign of] deficiency.

> A few who do not know themselves and judge others
> Though there is beauty, they see it as a shortcoming.

To prove [their claims] this group presents sayings by prior sufi shaykhs who have experienced the unity of being. God, blessed and exalted, render justice to this group. Where could they have learned that the shaykhs who had preceded them had remained stuck and had not advanced from that station? This is not a discussion about experientially realizing the unity of being, which obviously has occurred, but talking about developing from that station. If they say that a person who has advanced beyond that station is a denier of the unity of being and they remain fixated on a certain technical term (*wahdat-i wujud*), what kind of debate is this?

Let's get down to business. It is said that a little [of something] signifies that there is more [of it] like a drop can indicate an ocean. Thus, I will be brief. A drop suffices [to make my point]. O brother! When all the other students were gathered around, the holy presence of the Master (Baqibillah) declared my knowledge as completed and completion bestowing, and he granted me a certificate to teach the [Naqshbandi] way. At that time I was reluctant to accept myself as completed and completion bestowing. Baqibillah replied that there was no place for reluctance. The great shaykhs had declared [the culmination of] these stations to be the station of being completed and bestowing completion. Any hesitation concerning this station necessarily calls into question the perfections of those shaykhs.

Accordingly I began teaching the [Naqshbandi] path and turned my attention to looking after seekers' needs. Many among them had such amazing experiences that they achieved in hours what normally would take years. For a while, I became very diligent in this work but eventually discovered that I had a deficiency in knowledge. None of the seekers had experienced the flashing disclosure (*tajalli-yi dhati-yi barqi*) of the Essence that prior leading shaykhs had declared to be the end [of the path] nor did they have any idea about [the experience of] wayfaring to God or wayfaring in God. It is, however, necessary to realize these kinds of perfections. During this

68. In a *wujudi* context, *tawhid-i wujudi* could also be translated as asserting the "unity of objective being."

period my own deficiency in knowledge flared up again. I gathered the seekers who were there at the time and confessed my own deficiency, wanting to bid farewell to all of them. The seekers, however, did not accept this interpretation and with humility kept their faith in me [as a completion-bestowing shaykh]. Afterwards, God by means of God's dear one (Muhammad), brought about the expected states [of wayfaring to God and wayfaring in God]. God bless him and his family and give them peace.

Section 1

Know that attaining to the path of the presences of the Masters involves [adhering] to the tenets of the rightly guided Sunni mainstream and following the sublime sunnat of Muhammad (*sunnat-i saniya-yi Mustafawiya*). God bless and give peace to its master. [One also should] avoid innovation and base desires, act with firm intention as much as possible, and not take the easy way out [*'amal bi-rukhsat*].

With respect to spontaneous attraction to God (*jadhba*), first there is an experience of no self (*idmihlal/istihlak*),[69] which has been considered to be non-being (*'adm*). The subsequent experience of partial stabilization (*baqa'*) verifies the [prior] experience of no self.[70] This is interpreted as the existence of non-being (*wujud-i 'adm*). That is, there is an existence and a partially stabilized abiding (*baqa'*) arranged in a certain way with non-being that involves an experience of no self. Note that this experience of no self does not mean an absence of sensory input. Some believe that it does, others do not. It is possible for the person experiencing this [type of] partially stabilized abiding to return to human attributes and to a sensual character. On the other hand, when one experiences abiding in God following an annihilation of the ego-self in God (*fana'*) one cannot return. The Grandmaster (Baqibillah) expressed the same meaning when he said, "one can return to being in human nature (*wujud-i bashariyat*) from the existence of non-being but one can never return from the existence of annihilation of the ego-self in God (*fana'*) to being in human nature. God sanctify his innermost being. This is because abiding in the existence of non-being means that one still has further to go on the path while [a person who has experienced] the existence of annihilation of the ego-self in God

69. The text is clear that *idmihlal/istihlak* (also called *fana'-i wujudi*), which I have translated as "an experience of no self," is not the same experience as *fana' fil-lah*, that is, annihilation in God, characterized by bewilderment. See the interlinear gloss in *Collected Letters*, 1.290.96 line 11 and 1.240.41.

70. The process here is progressive dissolution (*idmihlal/istihlak/ fana'*) of everyday consensus reality/ego and a re-integration or stabilization at increasing levels of awareness. Technically this partial *baqa'* is called *baqa'-i wujudi* and is the abiding which follows *fana'-i wujudi*. Cf. *Collected Letters*, 3.100.68.

(*fana'*) has arrived at the end and cannot return [to being in his or her human attributes]."

A notable said, "No one returns [to human attributes] after returning [to the Source] except if one is [still] on the path. After arriving there is no return." One should know that one who has experienced the existence of non-being, although [still] on the path, is aware of the conclusion of the endeavor according to the dictum, "The end is included in the beginning." The fully realized person (*muntahi*) finds it easy at the end because he has realized the essence (*khulasa*) of the connection comprehensively (*ijmalan*) through this prior awareness. This connection to God (*nisbat*) has been actualized because it has been completely engendered in the realized person. The general trace of that [transformation] is experienced in the realized person's entire being.

[For one experiencing the] existence of nonbeing, this [connection to God] is restricted to the essence of the heart. If [only] this connection were complete and if [only] the path were comprehensive. Undoubtedly the fully realized person is one who is aware of the details [in the context of comprehensiveness]. It is not possible for him to return to his bodily attributes. This is because [after] that connection to God has permeated throughout the physical levels, the body gets rid of its attributes, and one is annihilated in God. This is a total gift. To take back such gift is not appropriate for the holy almighty and blessed Majesty.

On the other hand, one who has [only] experienced the existence of non-being (*wujud-i 'adm*) is blocked [from that connection to God] permeating his reality. In short, because these levels [of physical, human attributes] pertain to the heart, that [aforementioned] connection to God is generally flowing in a natural way through these physical, human attributes. It is enough to move the outer form aside and overpower it, but not to the point of [complete] annihilation. It is possible that a person who has experienced the existence of non-being can return to human attributes because sometimes obstacles overwhelm him, but one who has arrived does not return the way he came.

Know that some of the shaykhs of this exalted lineage (the Naqshbandiyya) have experienced the no-self mentioned above and the corresponding partial abiding (*baqa'-i wujudi*). God almighty bless their spirits. Moving beyond this [partial] annihilation and abiding in God, [these shaykhs] have proved that the disclosure of the Essence and the contemplative witnessing of the Essence are also at this level [of experience]. They know that this [total] abiding in God is [the experience] of one who has arrived. It is associated with concentrating on God (*yad dasht*),[71] which is continuous

71. *Yad dasht* is continually experiencing nothing else but God. See Hutaki, *Sharh-i maktubat*, 465.

awareness of the Majesty. They know for certain that in this station everything is related to the end being included in the beginning. There is no [total] annihilation and abiding in God except for the fully realized seeker who has arrived and who is specially [honored with] disclosures (sing. *tajalli*) of the Essence and the continual presence of God. Bless God. This is only for the fully realized person who has arrived and cannot return [to human attributes] under any circumstances. This initial going beyond [partial annihilation and abiding in God] along with the aforementioned expression [of the end being included in the beginning] are valid [experiences] and have a firm basis [in sufi experience].

The same kind [of topics such as] annihilation and abiding in God, disclosure of the Essence, contemplative witnessing of the Essence, arriving at the goal (*wasl*), and concentrating on God are found in *Passages* written by Khwaja 'Ubaydullah Ahrar.[72] God sanctify his innermost being. One notable said that this book, consisting of letters and writings sent by Khwaja Ahrar to some sincere friends, is based upon experiential inner knowledge (*ma'rifat*) and insights of the people writing him.[73] One should speak to people according to what they can understand and guide them accordingly. The same situation happened with the *Epistle of the Ahrari Lineage* concerning the way the holy presence of Khwaja Ahrar discussed topics. It was the same story when the presence of our master, the support of the favored religion, our shaykh and lord Baqibillah wrote a commentary on [Ahrar's] *Quatrains*.[74] God almighty bless him.

Every abiding experienced in ecstatic attraction to God points toward asserting the unity of being. Therefore, some shaykhs have interpreted the experience of certainty (*haqq-i yaqin*) in such a way that the end result is unity of being. Some imagine that this interpretation is incorrect. For them, the experience of certainty is the goal of the outward disclosure of form and the whole affair ends in blame and reproach.[75]

In reality, the experience of certainty for those [who equate it with the outward disclosure of form] is experienced in the aspect of ecstatic attrac-

---

72. 'Ubaydullah Ahrar, *Fiqarat* (Hyderabad?, Deccan: Matba'-i 'Ayn, 1890s). An Arabic translation is in the margin of Sirhindi, *Mu'arrab al-maktubat*, trans. al-Manzalawi, 1:281-355.

73. Presumably this is in response to questions they had addressed to him. Ahrar, like other sufi shaykhs, answered beginners differently than advanced seekers.

74. See Baqibillah, *Sharh-i ruba'iyat: risala-yi sharh-i ruba'iyat-i silsilat al-Ahrar* in his *Kulliyat-i Baqibillah*.

75. *Tajalli-yi suri* is associated with outer wayfaring (*sayr-i afaqi*) and knowledge of certainty (*ilm al-yaqin*). See *Collected Letters,* 1.30.79. These are both considered to be preliminary at the beginning of the path. Cf. *Collected Letters,* 3.32.79.

tion. This experiential inner knowledge is suitable for that specific station, [but] the outward disclosure of form is something else. You cannot hide something from those who possess it. Seeing the unity in the mirror of multiplicity happens in a way that the mirror becomes completely hidden and nothing remains visible except the unity [of objective existence]. Thinking that this station corresponds to concentrating on God, they apply themselves to concentrating on God at this level. They assert that the station of beautiful action (*ihsan*) or sincerity is the disclosure of the Essence and contemplative witnessing of the Essence.[76] These lost ones are united in their interpretations. Union with God is just losing oneself in God.

This technical term (presumably *maqam-i ihsan* or *maqam-i ikhlas*) is particular to the holy presence of Nasiruddin Khwaja ‘Ubaydullah [Ahrar]. Even the shaykhs who have followed [the practices] of this [Naqshbandi] lineage have not spoken about this technical term. Whoever performs good deeds is good. Ahrar's holy words reflect his attributes. Language is a mirror of the heart and the heart is a mirror of the spirit. The spirit is a mirror of the human truth and human truth is the mirror of the Real. Bless God. The hidden realities are a long way from the hidden Essence in terms of language. There the linguistic form, having been accepted [by the person], will arrive at ears ready [for these] realities.

Ahrar also said that he had served some notables who had favored him with two things. The first was that [for them] whatever he wrote was new, not old. The second was that whatever he said was accepted [by them], not rejected. From these holy words, his greatness and the exalted way station of his knowledge can be understood. It is clear that he had nothing to do with his words. They came from [inspired interior] reflection.[77] God knows better the truth of Ahrar's state and the lofty degree of his accomplishment. He recited these couplets (from the opening lament of the reed flute in Rumi's *Mathnawi*),[78] which reflect his state.

Everyone has become my intimate friend from his own projections.
No one is aware of my inner secrets.
My secret is close to my lament.
But no eye or ear has this light.

---

76. In the *maqam-i ihsan* one is in the station of doing each act and thinking each thought as if God were intently looking as outlined in Gabriel's hadith when Muhammad answered Gabriel's question about *ihsan*.

77. The text of *Collected Letters,* 1.290.97 is unclear. Al-Manzalawi al-Qazani's Arabic translation, *Mu‘arrab al-maktubat*, 1:337, clarifies this point.

78. See Jalaluddin Balkhi/Rumi, *Mathnawi-yi ma‘nawi*, ed., Reynold Nicholson and Nasrullah Purjawadi, 4 vols. (Tehran: Mu'assasa-yi Intisharat-i Amir Kabir, 1985), 1:3 (In the six-volume *Mathnawi*, Vol. 1 verses 6-7).

This poor one (Ahmad Sirhindi) will only write a little about the reality of his erudition and experiential inner knowledge. As I get to the end of this letter I realize my limited understanding. It is in God's hands. If God had honored some of them with the gift of contemplative practices (*suluk*) after their having completely realized spontaneous attraction to God by God's complete divine favor, then they could have proceeded a long way aided by this attraction. It is [a journey] equivalent to fifty thousand years. Bless God. The Qur'anic verse, "The angels and Spirit ascend to God in a day spanning fifty thousand years" [Q. 70:4] is a symbolic reference to the small measure of time [it could take] to realize real annihilation in God (*haqiqat-i fana'fillah*) and its corresponding real abiding in God.

The end of contemplative practice (*suluk*) is at the end of wayfaring to God (*sayr ila Allah*), which is called absolute annihilation in God (*fana'-i mutlaq*). After that, there is another station of spontaneous attraction to God, wayfaring in God (*sayr fi'llah*), which is also called abiding in God. Wayfaring to God means going to a name [of God] of which the wayfarer is a locus of manifestation (*mazhar*). Wayfaring in God is wayfaring in that name (the name that governs the seeker) because each name encompasses the infinity of God's names. Then wayfaring in that name [which is also wayfaring in God] must also be without end. This poor one (Ahmad Sirhindi) realized special divine experiential knowledge in this station. I will say more about this later if God wills. In the levels of ascent, this name is above the fixed entity (*'ayn-i thabita*) because the fixed entity of the wayfarer is this name's shadow and its outer cognitive form (*surat-i 'ilmiya*). Those who have been blessed [in this way] by God's favor are special. Exalt God's affair! Wayfarers also ascend from this name and advance without limit if God desires.

> After explaining this, there is something subtler.
> Hidden, more auspicious and beautiful.

Those of other lineages who arrive [at the end of the path] have other practices while sharing the verification of annihilation in God and its corresponding abiding with the Naqshbandis. It takes them a long time, however, to traverse the path and arrive at the end by means of [their] exercises and exertions. Naqshbandis [lit. the notables of this great family], with the pleasant flavor of being favored with contemplative witnessing and the taste of having realizing the goal, traverse the long distance to the end in a short time. They arrive at the Ka'ba of their desire. After arriving, they will continue progressing forever, but there are few who are fortunate to have such development and closeness to God as accomplished practitioners. The preference for spontaneous attraction to God in contemplative practice is related to the meaning of belovedness (*mahbubiyat*). As long as someone is not "desired by God" (a *murad*), he will not experience attraction to God.[79] When one who is desired by God is pulled [toward God], each mirror [of the heart] becomes closer and he experiences more closeness with God. There is a large difference between one who is desired and one who desires (*murid*). That is God's favor which God bestows as God sees fit. God is the great generous master.

> The love of beloveds is hidden and covered.
> The love of lovers is announced with the clamor of two hundred drums and flutes.
> The love of lovers saps the strength.
> The love of beloveds wholesomely nourishes.[80]

It is said that those desired by God in other lineages also share this development and closeness because attraction to God precedes their contemplative practice. What is [going on] in preferring the Naqshbandi method (*tariq*) to others and what is the [rationale] of saying the Naqshbandi method/way is closest? The answer is that those using other methods are not in a position to realize [what Naqshbandis] mean [by the goal]. While some [non-Naqshbandis] receive this good fortune by chance, the Naqshbandi method is [explicitly] structured to realize this good fortune.

According to the expressions of the leaders of this exalted lineage, concentrating on God (*yad dasht*) occurs after experiential verification of both aspects, that is, after attraction to God and after contemplative practice come into existence.[81] When Naqshbandis say the end of the path, it means the end of the levels of contemplative witnessing and awareness, except for the absolute end that is beyond the beyond. Specifically, this means witnessing the letter *y* in the mirror of the exterior form, the "letter *y* in the mirror" signifies "beyond the exterior form and meaning." This contemplative witnessing, without being concealed [by the exterior form and meaning], is called a "flashing disclosure" (*tajalli-yi barqi*), that is, the experience of this witnessing comes in flashes.

Then it becomes concealed. Through divine grace as a person experiences continuous contemplative witnessing and completely emerges from the restrictions of veils, then [it can be said] that one is concentrating on God or presence (*hudur*) without being absent to oneself (*ghaybat*).[82] Exalt God's dominion! This is because the presence of veils while contemplatively witnessing verifies that one is absent to oneself. As long as one does not

---

79. For more detail concerning *jadhba* and *murad*s see Buehler, *Sufi Heirs*, 122.

80. The last two lines are from Balkhi/Rumi, *Mathnawi*, 2:251 (In the six-volume *Mathnawi*, Vol. 3 verse 4394).

81. These two *jadhba*s are discussed previously in this letter.

82. Cf. footnotes 56 and 60 above.

experience veils on a continual basis, [the term] "concentrating on God" is applicable.

Here one should know a subtle point. The inner heart (*sirr*) of each person who arrives will not return.[83] His awareness is continual. But the permeating of that connection to God is like a flash in a person's inner and outer being. On the other hand, beloveds' (*mahbuban*) spontaneous attraction to God in their contemplative practice puts them ahead [of others] with a permanent connection to God, totally governed by the inner heart. The inner heart does its work by regulating their inner and outer beings. An allusion to this is the saying, "Their bodies have calmed down like their spirits until their outward appearances have become like their inner beings and their inner beings have become like their outward appearances."

Undoubtedly there is no place for absence (*ghaybat*) in their awareness, and this connection to God is superior to all other connections. The meaning [of the Naqshbandi connection to God being superior to all others] is widespread in the books and letters of the Naqshbandi shaykhs because this connection stems from [a corresponding level of] awareness. The culmination of the levels of awareness is attained without veils and having continual [recollection of God]. The shaykhs of this lineage know this connection in a special way. In order to realize the benefit [of continually aware presence], it is important to establish the method, as has already been done. It is possible that some notables of other lineages might find it easy [to progress] and even achieve [the goal].

The model of the distinguished protégés of God, Abu Sa'id Abu'l-Khayr, provided a symbol of this awareness through what his teacher Abu 'Ali Daqqaq (d. 405/1014) had verified. Abu'l-Khayr asked what this talk of continual [aware presence] was all about. His teacher replied that there was no such thing. He asked again and got the same answer. The third time he asked, his teacher replied that if it was possible, it was rare. Abu'l-Khayr started dancing [in ecstasy] and said that this [also] is from those rarities.

This is what I had said, namely, the absolute end is that which is beyond the beyond. If one ascends after verifying this awareness then a wave of bewilderment happens.[84] As one leaves this awareness behind, like all the [previous] levels of awareness, it has the same feel (lit. color) as the rest of the levels of ascent and will return. This bewilderment is called the "greater bewilderment" (*hayrat-i kubra*), a special [experience] of the greatest shaykhs. It is like what is found in their books. One notable in this station said, "Your beauty has turned me upside down like this. No news remains of your mole, your soft beard, or your curly locks."

83. This is not the mystery subtle center.

84. According Nur Ahmad's footnotes, ascent comes after the verification of continual awareness. See *Collected Letters,* 1.290.100.

Another said,

> Love is beyond infidelity or religion.
> I saw love superior to doubt or certainty.
> Infidelity, religion, certainty, and doubt,
> All four sitting together on the bench of the rational mind.
> When the world's rational mind passes away from me,
> Then I will understand the truth of infidelity and religion.
> Whatever it is, anything can block the way.
> Just like Alexander's wall.[85]

Another notable said,

> Negation and affirmation are from God's court.[86]
> As they returned with empty pockets.

After realizing this station of bewilderment, there is the station of unitary knowledge (*ma'rifat*). Whenever someone is honored with the good fortune of realizing true faith (*iman-i haqiqi*) after true infidelity (*kufr-i haqiqi*), which is the station of bewilderment, then they are [truly] favored.[87] The final aspiration of those who have verified Reality (*muhaqqiqan*) is the reality of faith. The station of inviting others to the revealed religion of submitting to God (*maqam-i da'wat*) and perfection in following Muhammad (lit. the holy presence of the master of shariat) is in this station. It is represented by the Qur'anic dictum, "I call on God with discernment, I and whoever follows me." [Q. 12:108] Muhammad (lit. that pleasure of the religion and world) searched for this [true] faith, saying, "O God give me true faith."[88] Surely after this there is no infidelity (*kufr*) or [even] true infidelity, which is the station of bewilderment. For protection, [Muhammad] used to say, "I ask Your protection from poverty and infidelity."[89] This level is at

---

85. Dhu al-Qarnayn, mentioned in Q.18:83-94, built a wall to protect the world against Yajuj-Majuj or Gog and Magog. Alexander is often associated with Dhu al-Qarnayn, hence Alexander's wall.

86. The negation and affirmation here refers to the expression, "There is no god but God."

87. There is also infidelity of the sufi path (*kufr-i tariqat*), which for Sirhindi is superior to a practice of Islam that only involves the form of the shariat but is deficient with respect to submitting to the sufi path (*islam-i tariqat*). See *Collected Letters,* 3.91.45 and 2.95.100.

88. A hadith found in Ibn Khuzayma's *al-Sahih*, #1119 and al-Tabarani's *al-Awsat*, #3696 [MR]. It is only mentioned once in *Collected Letters.*

89. A hadith found in Abu Da'ud's hadith collection, #5090; al-Nasa'i's hadith collection, #3:73, 8:262, 267; and Ahmad b. Hanbal's *Musnad*, 5:36, 39, 42, 44 [MR]. It is only mentioned once in *Collected Letters.*

the end of the levels of the experience of certainty (*haqq al-yaqin*). Here knowledge and vision/experience (*'ayn* referring to *'ayn al-yaqin*) are not veiling each other.

> Congratulations to those being graced by this felicity
> And to the miserable lover with suffering woes.
> That says it all.

You should know that God almighty guided you [to realize] that these dear ones experience two kinds of spontaneous attraction to God. The first kind is that experienced by Abu Bakr as-Siddiq (lit. the holy presence of the greatest upright person). The method [of the Naqshbandis] is associated with Abu Bakr. God almighty be pleased with him. This spontaneous attraction is a special spiritual power (*tawajjuh*) [transmitted through Muhammad] that undergirds all of creation. One experiences no self (*idmihlal/istihlak*) [in the process].

The second type [of spontaneous attraction to God] begins to appear in the method of the holy presence of the master of Naqshband (Baha'uddin Naqshband). It comes about from the path of essential togetherness (*ma'iyat-i dhatiya*). This type of spontaneous attraction to God was transmitted from Baha'uddin to 'Ala'uddin 'Attar (d. 803/1400). While 'Ala'uddin 'Attar was the axial guide (*qutb-i irshad*), he clarified a method to achieve this [second] kind of spontaneous attraction to God. This method is famous among his successors, the 'Ala'iyya lineage.[90] Their writings indicate that the closest of all the paths is the exalted 'Ala'iyya path. Although the basis of this spontaneous attraction is from Baha'uddin Naqshband (lit. the holy presence of the master of Naqshband), the founder of the technique to achieve this [attraction] is specifically from master 'Ala'uddin. God sanctify their innermost beings. The truth is that this method has many blessings. Some [aspects] of this method are more effective than many other methods. Even now the successors of the 'Ala'iyya and Ahrariyya are fortunate to have this great benefit as they [continue to] train aspirants in this way. The holy presence of master Ahrar received this [training] by virtue of Mawlana Ya'qub Charkhi (d. 851/1447) who is one of the successors of the holy presence of master 'Ala'uddin.

The first kind of spontaneous attraction to God, associated with the holy presence of Abu Bakr as-Siddiq is a separate method to realize the

---

90. This is the same lineage as that of Ahrar and Ahmad Sirhindi. See Buehler, *Sufi Heirs*, 87 for a genealogical chart. See Necdet Tosun, *Bahâeddîn Nakşbend: Hayatı, Görüşleri, Tarîkatı* (Istanbul: Insan Yayınları, 2002), 313-316, for the relationship of *tawajjuh* and *rabita* in the 'Ala'iyya practice. See Buehler, *Sufi Heirs,* 135 for an exposition concerning visualization of one's shaykh and spontaneous attraction to God.

goal. This method is counting how many times one recollects God (*wuquf-i 'adadi*). A contemplative practice (*suluk*) beyond achieving this [kind of] spontaneous attraction has been verified. There are more than [just] two kinds [of spontaneous attraction to God]. Abu Bakr used one of these methods to realize the goal. God almighty be pleased with him. Muhammad (lit. the holy presence of the message of finality) also experienced the same attraction to God with the same method.

The holy presence of Abu Bakr as-Siddiq, because of the complete sincerity he experienced with Muhammad and because of his annihilating himself in Muhammad,[91] has become distinguished from all the other Companions with this special method. God almighty be pleased with and sanctify all of them. This same connection to spontaneous attraction to God and contemplative practice with this special method continued up to the holy presence of Imam Ja'far as-Sadiq (d. 148/765). This is because his mother was one of the blessed offspring of the holy presence of Abu Bakr's elder son.[92] God almighty be pleased with them. Imam Ja'far had the two sides [of his family in mind] when he said, "Abu Bakr gave birth to me two times." Since the presence of Imam Ja'far has a separate affiliation from his blessed ancestors (on his father's side), he brought together both methods.[93] He combined Abu Bakr's attraction to God and contemplative practice with ['Ali b. Abi Talib's way] of doing contemplative exercises to reach the goal. The difference between the contemplative practice of 'Ali and Abu Bakr is that 'Ali was doing outer wayfaring (*sayr-i afaqi*) while Abu Bakr's contemplative practice had little relationship with this.[94] There is a similarity in that [metaphorically] one makes a hole in the realm of attraction to God, which leads one to the goal.

In 'Ali's type of contemplative practice, one experiences inner knowledge while in that of Abu Bakr, one is overcome by love (*mahabbat*). Undoubtedly the holy presence of 'Ali is the door to the city of knowledge, just as the holy presence of Siddiq experienced the capacity of sincere friendship (*khullat*) with Muhammad. God bless him and give him peace. Muhammad said, "If I were to take someone as a sincere friend then I would

91. The text has "*fani dar ihsan,*" which in later sufi texts has often been called annihilation in the messenger or (*fana' fi-rasul*).

92. Qasim b. Muhammad b. Abi Bakr.

93. This other lineage is that of the first five Shi'i Imams from 'Ali b. Abi Talib – Hasan – Husayn – Zayn al-'Abidin – Muhammad al-Baqir – Ja'far as-Sadiq.

94. In Letter 2.42 (in this book) Sirhindi explains, "outer wayfaring (*sayr-i afaqi*) is with respect to the person holding the mirror. Therefore, it is called outer wayfaring not wayfaring in the outside world." See *Collected Letters,* 2.42.102.

take Abu Bakr as a sincere friend."[95]

The holy presence of Imam Ja'far brings together an attraction to God based on love and a type of outer wayfaring that is the source of transmitted and inner experiential knowledge. He has acquired the luxuriant good fortune of love and unitary knowledge. After this, Imam Ja'far delegated this combined connection to God as a trust to the Sultan of the Knowers (*Sultan al-'arifin*), also known as Abu Yazid Bistami (d. 261/875).[96] God sanctify his innermost being. That is, the load entrusted [by Imam Ja'far] rested on the shoulders of Abu Yazid so that gradually those ready [for a practice involving both love and unitary knowledge] could benefit from it. The appearance of Abu Yazid's spiritual power (*tawajjuh*) took on another aspect. Before carrying that trust, Abu Yazid had no relation to [Imam Ja'far's] connection to God.[97]

There is wisdom in carrying [this trust]. Even though people having this connection to God did not get much [from it themselves], the light of this connection provided luxuriant good fortune [to others]. For example, one kind of intoxication associated with this connection is from the traces of Abu Yazid's lights. For beginners, this intoxication is without sensory awareness, gradually becoming hidden afterwards. Because sobriety overcomes this connection, one [ends up] in the [various] levels of sobriety. Outwardly one is sober and inwardly one is intoxicated. These lines explain this condition.

---

95. A hadith found in al-Bukhari's *Sahih*, #455, 3456, 3457, 3691, 3904 and in al-Muslim's *Sahih*, *Fada'il al-sahaba*, #532, 2383 [MR]. It is mentioned once in *Collected Letters*. 'Ali as the door to the city of knowledge is also mentioned in the Sunni hadith.

96. Imam Ja'far as-Sadiq (d. 148/765) could not have met Abu Yazid Bistami (d. 261/874) in physical form. These types of experiences are known as an "Uwaysi connections" because Uways al-Qarani had an experience of Muhammad from his home in Yemen that was acknowledged by Muhammad. See Buehler, *Sufi Heirs*, 85-89.

97. Abu Yazid is typically associated with transgressive ecstatic utterances that are associated with attraction to God, for example, "Glory be to me!" (*subhani*) instead of the orthopraxic "Glory be to God." Often Abu Yazid is contrasted with the "sober" Junayd (d. 297/910) who is perceived to represent abiding in God (*baqa'*) after annihilation in God. Shaykh Ma'sum Naqshband has commented that even though Abu Yazid outwardly exhibited attraction to God his inner inclination could easily have been that of abiding in God just as Junayd's outer sobriety could be balanced by his inner intoxicated attraction to God. Note Junayd's response to Nuri's criticism of his sobriety: "You see the mountains and think they are solid but they move like clouds." [Q. 27:88] Cited in Annemarie Schimmel, *Mystical Dimensions of Islam* (Chapel Hill, NC: University of North Carolina Press, 1975), 181.

Come from the heart while being non-attached on the outside.
The beauty of living like this is rare.

This is the frame of reference! Each notable [in the lineage] passed down the light of this connection among his own group until it reached the holy presence of the divine knower, Master 'Abdulkhaliq Ghujduvani (d. ca. 575/1179), the head of the circle of holy presences of the Masters (*hadrat-i khwajagan*).[98] God sanctify their innermost beings. At the time of 'Abdulkhaliq, this exalted connection again was renewed from the beginning and it manifested openly. Then in this manner 'Abdulkhaliq proceeded in outer contemplative practice (*suluk-i afaqi*) until this connection again became hidden. After realizing a spontaneous attraction to God, he took different paths in his contemplative practice, [eventually] experiencing an ascent until Baha'uddin Naqshband appeared.[99] God sanctify his innermost being. That connection to God, with both an attraction to God and an outward contemplative practice, manifested again with both the aspects of unitary knowledge and love being completely combined. With this combination another kind of attraction to God arose from the path of togetherness (*rah-i ma'iyat*), and was again given to Baha'uddin Naqshband as explained above.[100]

From Baha'uddin's perfections, 'Ala'uddin 'Attar realized the luxuriant good fortune of being Baha'uddin's vice-regent. With the good fortune of both kinds of attraction to God and being honored with outward contemplative practice, 'Ala'uddin arrived at the station of being the axial guide (*qutb-i irshad*). Likewise Muhammad Parsa (d. 822/1420 in Balkh), from Baha'uddin's perfections, realized complete favor. Baha'uddin, looking back on his life, said that all that he had longed for could be seen in Muhammad Parsa. It is also related from Baha'uddin that the goal of his existence was to manifest Muhammad Parsa and have him in his service. By virtue of his perfections, Muhammad Parsa received the connection of uniqueness (*nisbat-i fardiyat*) late in his life from 'Arif Riwgari (d. 616/1219).[101] This overpowering connection prevented him from being a shaykh and from completing

98. For a detailed genealogical chart from Abu Yazid Bistami to 'Abdulkhaliq Ghujduvani see Buehler, *Sufi Heirs*, 87. See ibid., 58 fn. 6 for a discussion of Ghujduvani's death date.

99. Here is another example of an Uwaysi connection whereby a disembodied spirit becomes involved in one's sufi training.

100. This is the path of essential togetherness (*ma'iyat-i dhatiya*) discussed above.

101. This is another case of an Uwaysi connection since 'Arif Riwgari died in 616/1219 and Muhammad Parsa died in 822/1420. *Maqamat-i fardiyat* is also the station of belovedness (*maqam-i mahbubiyat*). See Dhawqi, *Sirr-i dilbaran*, 174, 176. Note the discussion of the perfections of uniqueness and the axial guide in Letter 1.260 in this book.

the training of aspirants even though he had a high degree of completion and bestowing completion. The holy presence of Baha'uddin Naqshband said that if Muhammad Parsa became a sufi guide and director, the world would be illuminated from him. Our lord 'Arif Riwgari realized the connection of uniqueness from his grandfather, our lord Baha'uddin Qushlaqi.[102]

One should know that the connection of uniqueness has a complete focus on the Real. It has nothing to do with guidance in contemplative practices, bestowing completion, or calling people to God (*da'wat*). If the connection of uniqueness is compared to the connection of the axial guide, which is the station of bestowing completion and calling people to God, then for the connection of uniqueness to prevail, guidance and completion bestowing in this form are weak and overpowered. On the other hand, the person who has both of these connections is in balance and his exterior will be completely focused on humanity while his inner being is totally focused on the Real, almighty and holy. The highest degree is in the station of calling people to God. One who is in this station has both of these connections to God. Although the connection of being the axial guide is also unique, it is sufficient for [someone to] call people to God. But notables in this station of calling people to God are at another level [of awareness]. Their gaze can heal diseases of the heart and their spiritual companionship prevents disagreeable character traits.

The Master of the Assembly (*Sayyid al-ta'ifa*), Junayd Baghdadi (d. 297/910), was assisted by this great fortune and became honored by this way station. Junayd realized the connection of being the axial leader (*qutbiyat*) from Shaykh Sari Saqati (d. 253/867), and [he experienced] the connection of uniqueness from Shaykh Muhammad Qassab (d. 275/888). Junayd indicates this [lineage] when he says that people imagine that he is a disciple of Sari but [instead he asserts that] he is a disciple of Muhammad Qassab.[103] The connection of uniqueness prevailed [to such an extent] over the connection of being the axial leader that the latter was forgotten to the point of being considered non-existent [compared to the connection of uniqueness].

After the successors of the holy presence of the master of Naqshband, the guiding lamp of this notable lineage, there was the holy presence of the Master 'Ubaydullah Ahrar. Completely traversing the Masters' station of

---

102. Qushlaq is about 75 km. (twelve farsangs) from Bukhara according to fn 1 in *Collected Letters*, 1.290.104. Baha'uddin Qushlaqi was 'Arif Riwgari's father-in-law and a successor of Amir Kulal (d. 772/1370), one of Baha'uddin Naqshband's shaykhs, in addition to being Baha'uddin's hadith teacher.

103. This saying of Junayd's comes from 'Abdurrahman Jami, *Nafahat al-uns*, 81.

attraction,[104] Ahrar set out in outer wayfaring (*sayr-i afaqi*) until he reached the name without entering into the name. He experienced a special annihilation in the name and he again entered the state of attraction to God before experiencing a feeling of no self and an abiding, both in the same aspect of attraction. All in all he had a great experience in this aspect of attraction. The transmitted knowledge and inner knowledge from his own experience as a result of the annihilation and abiding helped him to realize this station. He did, however, experience a feeling of absence in [the realm of] knowledge caused by changing between the two aspects of knowledge, [that is, inner experience and outer transmitted knowledge]. One of the times he felt absent there was a proof of the unity of being (*tawhid-i wujudi*) followed by its non-existence. That is how it is when one tries to confirm matters dealing with the unity of being, for example, essential encompassing nature, diffusion, and togetherness. Contemplative witnessing of oneness in multiplicity with the multiplicity being hidden by the whole is such that the wayfarer can never say "I." Knowledge that is subordinate to abiding after absolute annihilation is apart from that. This knowledge is not like the [partial] knowledge resulting from the perspective of unity of being. This knowledge is according to the true sciences of shariat, free of needing to take on burdens, constraints, or demands, and having to respond to them.

In general, an abiding that [occurs] along with the aspect of spontaneous attraction to God unavoidably involves intoxication and is incapable of sobriety. Therefore, the notion of "I" does not return to the abiding wayfarer experiencing the presence of abiding. Nor does any allusion to "I" occur because in attraction to God one is overpowered by love, and for love to overwhelm there must be intoxication. Thus, every aspect of intoxication is associated with spontaneous attraction to God [or an abiding mixed with spontaneous attraction]. Any knowledge of this is necessarily mixed with intoxication. It is like saying that the oneness of being is based on intoxication and love in such a manner that nothing remains in the gaze except the Beloved. One decides to negate everything other than the Beloved. If one goes [from intoxication] to sobriety, then witnessing the Beloved does not prevent one from looking at something else nor prevent one from making a judgment on the oneness of being.

An abiding that is after an absolute annihilation is the end of contemplative practice, the foundation of sobriety, and the beginning of unitary knowledge. Intoxication has no place in this realm and the wayfarer loses his knowledge, both transmitted and experiential, in the state of annihilation. It returns but is imbued with an essential consciousness (lit. color). This is the meaning of abiding in God. Then one's knowledge has no room

104. The Masters or Khwajagan referred to here are the lineage from Muhammad up to and including 'Abdulkhaliq Ghujduvani.

for intoxication. Instead, the person's knowledge is in accordance with the knowledge of the prophets. God bless them and give them peace until the Day of Judgment.

I heard from a notable that the holy presence of master Ahrar had a connection from his mother's side of the family who had [a proclivity] for strange states with a strong spontaneous attraction. Ahrar also realized [these states], and was graciously blessed from the station of the twelve axial leaders (*maqam-i aqtab-i ithna'shar*), which is connected with his invigorating of religion and the great love he had. It was from this station that he strengthened the shariat and supported religion. The sweet scent from his precious states has been mentioned above [in this letter]. After that, he renewed the Naqshbandi path and propagated their way of behaving in a beautiful manner (*adab*), especially in India where the inhabitants had been deprived of his perfections. All of this became verified with the appearance of the guidance, protection, divine knowledge, and awareness of the renewer of the satisfying religion, our shaykh and lord Baqibillah. God almighty grant him peace. I hope that a bit of Baqibillah's perfections has also been preserved in this letter. Since it is not known whether he would be satisfied with this chapter, I have refrained from boldness.

Introduction to realization of unity with God: Letter 1.291

This letter is addressed to Mawlana 'Abdulhayy.[105] He is the son of Khwaja Chakar Hissari (Hissar is in Tajikistan), the compiler of Ahmad Sirhindi's second volume of *Collected Letters*. Here the focus is on the experiences of those claiming to have the experience of "unity with God" (*tawhid-i wujudi*). Throughout *Collected Letters*, Sirhindi is not denouncing the experience of "unity of being" (*wahdat al-wujud*) but just explaining, from his own experience, that it is merely a preliminary stage and *not* ontological union with God, though it may be perceived as such. His analysis, which is repeated many times in *Collected Letters*, is that those who have these type of experiences are still in the realm of the heart and have not yet reached the origins of the divine effulgence (*mabadi-yi fayd*), nor have they experienced the separation of the subtle centers. Their experiences have come from what they have unreliably experienced in altered states of consciousness (*ahwal*) in ecstatic attraction to God (*jadhba*) and overflowing love. Instead of finishing their ascent to the origins, they prematurely start their descent, thinking that they have already reached the Essence when they have mistaken the world of the spirits for the Essence. Therefore, when they start their descent they see the Beloved in each atom but without really experiencing the Beloved. They re-

105. He had four letters addressed to him in *Collected Letters*. There is some biographical information about him in *Collected Letters,* 1.277.29. Ansari translates a part of this letter in his *Sufism and Shari'ah*, 250-254.

main in the station of the heart facing the shadows.[106]

Sirhindi does not deny these experiences of perceived union with God because they are involuntary. His primary objection is their misperception that they have arrived at the levels of the Essence when they are still in the shadows. There is contemplatively experiencing unity (*tawhid-i shuhudi*) that Naqshbandis experience, which is not involved with temporary states of ecstatic attraction. Metaphorically, the world and the sun are perceived as identical. Nothing appears to exist except the sun. In this kind of continual presence they experience Oneness in the multiplicity. This is not the same experience as those who are at the stage of the heart because the Naqshbandis have arrived at the Invigorator of the heart, though it is difficult to sustain this presence.[107] For Sirhindi, this is a good example of how one can subjectively witness and experience oneness contemplatively, which is not objectively one's experience in the outside world. There is incommensurability between subjective and objective ways of knowing/experiencing. Those who experience this kind of unity arc at the level of the "eye of certainty" (*'ayn-i yaqin*). Those who are in the station of the heart are at the level of "knowledge of certainty" (*'ilm-i yaqin*) because they have not forgotten the world and because they consider the spirit (*ruh*) to be the Real ineffable realm, which it is clearly not.[108] Sirhindi also discusses briefly a third kind of unity (*tawhid-i 'ala'i*), the highest kind of experience of unity, which helps relieve those who are overpowered by their love and attraction to God.

There are two types of those who have seen the goal: those who get involved with devotional music and ecstatic dance (*sama'*) and those who do not waver from their contemplative witnessing (*shuhud*) without any chance of rest. The Naqshbandi notables are in this latter group and continue to see the oneness in multiplicity in the mirror of the world until they can rest in contemplative witnessing of the Beloved.[109]

Letter 1.291

In the name of God, the compassionate and merciful. Thanks to God, the Lord of the worlds. God bless and give peace to the master of messengers (Muhammad) and to all of his family and companions.

God almighty has guided you. Know that for the first group [of those claiming unity with God] the basis of the unity of being comes about after long meditation [focused on] the idea of the unity of God (*tawhid*) until they understand the meaning of the attestation of faith, "There is no god but God"

---

106. See Hutaki, *Sharh-i maktubat*, 478.

107. See ibid., 480.

108. See ibid., 481.

109. See ibid., 482-483.

as "[There is] nothing existent but God." They experience this as a kind of unity with God (*tawhid*) after deceiving experiences, deliberation, and imagination from the overpowering domination of their mind.[110] This idea of unity persists in their mind because after constant [meditative] practice the impression of this inner knowledge becomes strongly established [in their mind] through the power of imagination. It is a defective [perspective] because [this kind of unity] is the creation of the person's mind. A person experiencing this kind of unity is not one who has experiences of [altered] states (sing. *hal*) because those [who experience altered states] are centered in their hearts. This person has no idea about the station of the heart during this time. He is aware of nothing more than [preconceived] knowledge. Knowledge comes in degrees, some aspects transcending other aspects.

For a second group, the basis of their unity of being is spontaneous attraction to God (*injidhab*) and heart love (*muhabbat-i qalbi*). The people in this group begin working with recollection exercises and contemplations (*muraqabat*) free of imaginary meanings of unity with God. Through the effort of practicing or merely through divine favor, they reach the heart station and experience a spontaneous attraction to God. In this station, if the beauty of the unity of being manifests to them, it is by the overpowering of love for the Beloved where they see nothing other than the Beloved.[111] They do not know anything except the Beloved. This kind of unity is [known through] states [as opposed to an experience of unity based on preconceived knowledge] and is far removed from the traces of imagination and illusion-like visions.

If this second group at the heart station were to return toward the world from this [heart] station, they would observe contemplatively that the Beloved itself is in each small particle of the world.[112] They would know that the creatures of the world are in the Beloved's mirror reflecting the Beloved's beauty and elegance. Through the grace of God, if these people of the heart leave the station of the heart and turn towards the Holy Majesty, the One who enlivens hearts (lit. He who makes hearts fluctuate, *muqallib al-qulub*, that is, God), then this inner knowledge of unity with God (*ma'rifat-i tawhidi*) that they cultivated in the station of the heart begins to disappear. Exalt God's affair. To the extent of their ascent they find that this inner knowledge to be so unsuitable that some of them [even] find fault with and deny someone like Ruknuddin Abu'l- Mukarram 'Ala'uddawla

---

110. In a juristic/theological context *tawhid* means the declaration of God's unity. In an experiential context it refers to what many report to be the experience of a feeling of oneness with God.

111. The following sentence exactly repeats the meaning of this sentence and is omitted here.

112. Cf. Sirhindi's experiences of annihilation in the preceding letter, 1.290.

Simnani (d. 736/1336),[113] who has had that contemplative experience of unity of God. Others, after this inner knowledge disappears, do nothing and neither affirm or deny this knowledge.

The writer (Ahmad Sirhindi) avoids those who deny Simnani's knowledge of unity and stays away from their fault finding. There is scope for denying [this state] as long as those in this state have intentionality and choice when that state appears. But those in this state [of denial] are unintentionally overcome by this state so they can be totally excused. There is no rebutting or finding fault in a person who is forced [to do something]. He is excused. But I know this much, and it has been verified, that above this inner knowledge there is another [more encompassing] inner knowledge and beyond this state there is another state. Those constrained in this [heart] station are shut off from many perfections and numberless stations. This poor one (Ahmad Sirhindi), with little to offer and without pursuing the meaning of "asserting the unity of God," did meanwhile exert himself performing contemplative practices (*muraqabat wa-adhkar*).

Through God's grace, I entered the service, guidance, and overflowing refuge of realities and inner knowledge of awareness of the presence of the supporter of the satisfying religion, our shaykh and lord, Muhammad al-Baqi (Baqibillah). God sanctify his innermost being. After learning how to recollect God, I was brought to this inner knowledge of the station of the heart by his focusing spiritual energy (*tawajjuh*) on me, giving me all kinds of transmitted and inner knowledge of this station. The intricacies of this inner knowledge were revealed as I spent some time in this station. Finally, I gracefully left the station of the heart as the knowledge of the unity of being began to decrease until gradually it was completely gone. The objective of discussing one's states is [so others] realize that talking about this subject is based upon actual experience, not preconceived mental concepts. Some protégés of God (*awliya'*) have only communicated the inner knowledge of unity that has appeared to them at the beginning of the state and in the station of the heart. So it is not their deficiency at this point on the path [because it is natural to have these kind of experiences at the beginning]. This poor one (Ahmad Sirhindi) also wrote letters about the inner knowledge of unity at a similar stage of development. Since some friends distributed

113. Note the correspondence initiated by 'Ala'uddawla Simnani involving three questions to his Khwajagan counterpart, 'Ali Ramitani (d. 721/1321), who was Baha'uddin Naqshband's great-grandfather shaykh (his shaykh's shaykh's shaykh). Apparently this was when the Khwajagan still did loud remembrance of God (*dhikr*), while Simnani is reported to have done silent dhikr (which subsequently became a prevalent Naqshbandi practice). See 'Ala'uddawla Simnani, *Musannifat-i Farsi*, ed. Najib Mayil Harawi (Tehran?: Shirkat-i Intisharat-i 'Ilmi wa-Farhangi, 1991), 363.

these writings it has been difficult to collect them so I have left them scattered about. Deficiency is when a person does not go beyond this station.

There is a third group of those who experience unity with God and experience an extreme [feeling of] non-being (*istihlak*) in their contemplations. They experience [everything] continually disappearing such that no trace of the requisites of [ordinary] existence manifests. They think that returning to their ego-self (the sense of I-ness) is infidelity [because] for them the ultimate goal is annihilation of ego-self and the experience of no self (an experience of *tawhid-i wujudi*). They conceive of contemplatively witnessing God in the world as an entanglement. Some of them say, "I want an absolute annihilation such that I never return to existence." They are slain by love.[114] The divine hadith (*hadith qudsi*) "I am the ransom (lit. blood money) for the person I kill" refers to this. They are always under the weight of their experience. They do not have a moment's ease because ease involves heedlessness and in continuous annihilation there is no possibility of forgetting or being heedless [of God].

Shaykh 'Abdullah Ansari Harawi (d. 481/1089) said that if anyone were to make him forget God, even for a moment, hopefully that person's sins will be forgiven. Forgetting is necessary for human existence. God almighty, in God's complete generosity, keeps people busy with different activities to divert themselves according to their individual circumstances so that the weight of existence generally becomes bearable for them. [For example], one group gets pleasure from listening to music and dance while another group writes books expounding transmitted and inner knowledge.[115] Others are busy with ordinary permissible affairs (*umur-i mubah*). 'Abdullah Istakhri (actually 'Abdurrahim Istakhri), along with some dog keepers, used to go out in the forest. A person asked 'Abdullah [why he was traveling with dog keepers] and he answered that it was to relieve the weight of existence.[116] Some of them have found comfort in knowing the unity of being and contemplatively witnessing the unity in the multiplicity so that they have some ease from that heavy load.

From this [third] group, there are those Naqshbandi shaykhs who have

---

114. Cf. 'Abdulquddus Gangohi's (d. 944/1537) ecstatic utterance, "Muhammad Mustafa went within [the distance] of two bows or closer [to God] and returned. I swear to God that I would not have returned." See 'Abdulquddus Gangohi, *Lata'if-i quddusi*, ed. Ruknuddin (his son) (Delhi: Matba'-i Mujtaba'i, 1894), 65.

115. The Nur Ahmad edition has *shi'ar* on *Collected Letters,* 1.291.108. *Shi'ar* is not found in Qadi 'Alimuddin's Urdu translation nor in al-Manzalawi's Arabic translation, which both rely on copies of *Collected Letters* written or published prior to the Nur Ahmad edition of *Collected Letters*. I have followed these latter two translations instead.

116. This story is from 'Abdurrahman Jami, *Nafahat al-uns*, 242.

experienced unity. God sanctify their innermost beings. These notables (*buzurgan*) have become connected to God through absolute transcendence (*tanzih-i sirf*).[117] They have nothing to do with the world or seeing God in the world but instead focus on inner knowledge that gives protective guidance and an understanding of inner knowledge and realities. Nasiruddin 'Ubaydullah Ahrar (d. 895/1490) has written about knowledge of the unity of being and the contemplative witnessing of unity (*shuhud-i wahdat*) in multiplicity. Asserting the unity of God is discussed in the latter category (contemplative witnessing of unity in multiplicity). His book, *Passages*,[118] includes [a discussion about] the knowledge of unity and, in addition, the foundation of this knowledge. The goal of inner knowledge is a loving and intimate rapport with the world. Our master Baqibillah has the same view of inner knowledge and he favorably responds in some of his letters to ideas in *Passages*.[119] This knowledge about unity is not based upon ecstatic attraction to God (*jadhba*), nor from being overpowered by love. Ahrar's visions do not have a connection to the world and what he sees in the [mirror of the] world [only] appears to resemble what he sees in [objective] reality.[120]

This is, for example, like a person who is captivated by the beauty of the sun, losing himself completely in complete love [of the sun] forsaking any name or trace of himself. If this lost one desires, he could get a little rest by experiencing the loving attachment to something other than the sun. In not being overcome by the rays of the sun, he could breathe normally for a while. The sun radiates beauty in [the mirror of] this world, which engenders love and intimacy with this world. Sometimes they are informed that this [earthly] world is identical with the sun and except for the sun nothing else [really] exists. Other times [they say that] one can see the reflection of the sun's beauty in the mirror of the small particles of the world. No one ever asks at this point how the world could be the same as the sun. Their understanding the sun to be the earth goes against actual fact.

This is because human beings have certain common experiences [of reality] while in other experiences they differ. In some affairs where there are differences [of perspective], God almighty, with God's complete power,

117. Absolute immanence is associated with a complete ascent. See *Collected Letters,* 1.18.39. Prophets calling people to God is also associated with it because one needs complete ascent before descending to properly call people to God. See *Collected Letters,* 1.272.5.

118. See 'Ubaydullah Ahrar, *Fiqarat*.

119. See Letters #8 and #19 in Baqibillah, *Kulliyat*, 78, 88.

120. From here until the end of the paragraph the pronoun "they" (*ishan*) could refer either to the Naqshbandi shaykhs mentioned at the beginning of the paragraph or to Ahrar. I have used the singular "he" after Ahrar is mentioned, realizing that the points Sirhindi is making also refer to the aforementioned Naqshbandi shaykhs.

sometimes clouds people's perceptions concerning the basis of legal rulings (sing. *hukm*) and what is beneficial for the general welfare. Thus, some only view common parts [of the whole], which is how they can make a ruling on the unity of the sun and earth. In the same way, they are able to experience the sun to be identical with the earth. They experience God with the world although in truth they are incommensurate. Yet, the resemblances of a name make this unity (*ittihad*) correct for them.

For example, God almighty exists and so does the world even though, in truth, between these existences there is no commensurability. In the same way, God almighty is knowing, hearing, seeing, living, able and desiring.[121] Some also attribute the world with these essential/necessary attributes of God, even though necessary attributes are separate from contingent attributes. But because the particular quality (*khususiyat*) of contingent being (*wujud-i imkani*) and the deficiencies of incipient attributes (*sifat-i muhdathat*) are hidden from their view, they can pass judgment on the unity [of the necessary and contingent].

There is a third type of asserting the unity of God that is the highest. In truth [that type of unity is for] those with inner knowledge who are not overcome by their states and whose intoxication is not a result of their inner knowledge. They experience these states in order to benefit. By means of their inner knowledge, they want to be able to transform intoxication to sobriety for solace and comfort. In the same way, some listen to devotional music and dance to find comfort and others occupy themselves with permissible activities [for the same reason]. You should know that there are people in these groups who derive satisfaction by occupying themselves with their conflicting visionary experiences (sing. *mashhud*). On the other hand, [other] notables do not focus on the differences in their visions nor are they comforted.[122] So this latter group of notables cannot help but to perceive the world as the origin of their visions or to ascribe a splendor to their visions in the mirror of the world until they experience that load lightening up.

This poor one (Ahmad Sirhindi) did not know the basis of this third kind of unity through the methods of unveiling and having the actual experience. I only knew about the two other aspects of unity (*tawhid-i wujudi* and *tawhid-i shuhudi*). This third kind of unity was only an idea in my mind and for this reason [it was not mentioned] in epistles and letters. Of the two aspects [of unity I expected to be found] only the second was mentioned and the unity of being was contained in this.

---

121. For more background on essential/necessary attributes see Buehler, *Sufi Heirs*, 115.

122. Reading *aram namigardand* instead of *ram namigardand* in *Collected Letters,* 1.291.110.

After the death of the refuge of guidance, the pointer to the direction of prayer (Baqibillah), I went to visit his noble grave in Delhi, which happened to be on Eid.[123] While approaching his grave, a spiritual power manifested from his holy grave with focused attention from his holy disembodied spirit. With complete kindness I was graced with a special connection to the holy presence of the Khwaja Ahrar. When I experienced that connection within myself I necessarily discovered the truth of transmitted and inner knowledge by means of tasting the experience myself. I found out that the foundation of the unity of being for them was not being attracted in the heart nor overpowering love. Instead the goal of that inner knowledge was to relieve that overpowering [feeling].

For a long time, some people will not see the manifestation (*izhar*) of this meaning properly. When the two aforementioned aspects of unity (*tawhid-i shuhudi and tawhid-i wujudi*) were mentioned in some epistles, people of little understanding became deluded or suspicious. This explains why some began to think less [of Baqibillah and Khwaja Ahrar], even though they have experienced the unity of God. The message of these rebels has gone so far that this delusion has come to affect some weak-willed students by weakening their states. Seeing the need to correct the evidence of this type of unity (the third type) and in order to attest to the remembrance of that event (that is, at Baqibillah's tomb mentioned above), it is proper for this to be known by proclaiming it in writing.

One of Baqibillah's sincere disciples related that Baqibillah had said that people imagine that our connection to God is from reading books but it is not like that. The purpose [of the information from books] is to become heedless of ourselves for a while. This repeats what has been said above. The saving grace of Shaykh 'Abdulhaqq [Dihlawi] (d. 1052/1642), who was a sincere disciple of the holy presence of our master (Baqibillah), said that right before Baqibillah's death, Baqibillah said "We have come to know the certainty of certainty (complete certainty), such that [experiencing] unity with God (*tawhid*) is a narrow alleyway. The main highway is another way. We are also aware of what came before (less than complete certainty) but this kind of certainty is what has come to manifest now."[124]

From this discussion, one can understand that at the end of Baqibillah's life he did not have an affinity for experiencing unity with God. If that kind of unity had manifested when he was beginning to experience states it no

123. There are two Eids, one after Ramadan and the other after the hajj.

124. Sirhindi is referring to the last group session recorded before Baqibillah's death. Baqibillah says, "It has been verified that there is a way beyond the path of *tawhid*. [It is] wide. Compared to that wide road (lit. king's highway) the path of *tawhid* is a narrow alley." Baqibillah, *Kulliyat*, 64.

longer remained [at the end of his life].[125] Most shaykhs experience that kind [of unity] at the beginning, but by the end they have gone beyond it. After realizing the station of spontaneous Naqshbandi attraction to God, the method of Baha'uddin Naqshband (d. 791/1389) is different from the methods of 'Ubaydullah Ahrar (lit. holy presence of master Ahrar), as are the [resulting] knowledge and inner experiences. The overpowering [nature] of Ahrar's spiritual energy is the result of an inner connection stemming from the long line of notables from his mother's ancestors.[126] This annihilation of self and no self that has been discussed above is from the inherent nature of those notables' affiliation (*nisbat*). This poor one (Ahmad Sirhindi), by means of the goodwill of my contemporaries, has been chosen to train students in the path of the holy presence of the master Naqshband. This includes teaching the transmitted and inner knowledge of that path having a great affinity for the outer religious sciences of the shariat.

In this very corrupt time, people are very lazy in performing the basic elements of the shariat. Seeing that it is proper to manifest [these elements], this path was designated to benefit seekers. If God wants me to spread Ahrar's method then those lights will illuminate the world because both of these notables (Baha'uddin Naqshband and Ahrar) have been given the complete method and both have demonstrated the method of bestowing completion (*tariq-i takmil*). "Favor is in God's hand to give to whom God desires. God is the greatest Benefactor." [Q. 57:29]

> There is a King with such generosity
> That he gives a beggar both heaven and earth.
> If a king comes to the door of an old woman
> O master (*khwaja*), in disappointment of missing it,
> Don't pull your moustache out!

In accordance with the Qur'anic dictum, "Let the bounty of God be [expressed] by your words" [Q. 93:11] hidden secrets are revealed. God (lit. the Truth) almighty bestows his favor on the seekers of Truth. Even though deniers [of the aforementioned perspectives] will not get anything [from what I have said] except even more denial, the intent is to benefit seekers not in debate with deniers and those who aspire to different goals. "[God] leads many astray and [God] guides many." [Q. 2:26] Those with insight can see that after a person chooses a path on the basis of its benefits, the superiority of this path and the deficiencies of the other paths will preclude their pursuing any other path.

---

125. Reading *baqi nist* instead of *baki nist*. *Collected Letters,* 1.291.111.

126. Ahrar's mother was a descendant 'Umar ibn al-Khattab, the second caliph.

City gates can be shut.
But the mouths of deniers are never closed.

Thanks to God, who possesses the greatest kindness and strength, from beginning to end. God bless and give peace eternally to the messenger, his excellent family, and his pious companions.

Chapter Three
Aspects of the Sufi Path

Introduction to getting beyond the ego-self Letter 1.52

This letter is addressed to Shaykh Farid Bukhari (d. 1025/1616), a lineal descendant of Muhammad and paymaster general (*mir bakhski*) in the governments of both Mughal emperors, Akbar and Jahangir.[1] When re-confirming him to the post of *mir bakhski*, Jahangir honored Shaykh Farid by saying, "I regard you as both a warrior and a scholar." (*sahib al-sayf wa'l-qalam*).[2]

The main topic of this letter is how to get beyond the human conditioning of I-ness, the false sense that one is separate from God and God's creation. To get beyond the ego-self means to have a well-developed ego-self to begin with because any contemplative practice for taming the ego-self presupposes a healthy ego-self to tame. Mental illness is usually associated with an *underdeveloped* ego. Sirhindi reminds the reader of the wily nature of the ego-self that is amazingly adept at preserving itself at any cost. Long before the advent of "New Age" casual "feel good" spirituality and practices, Sirhindi points to the egoic nature of doing practices in a way that does not challenge the ego-self and thus entrenches the ego-self even further. In the context of a mentor who teaches contemplative practices and who facilitates ethical/character development, these same practices have been shown to be quite effective for transformation. Herein is where the shariat plays such a critical role in post-rational spiritual development. It is a path that fosters development both subjectively and intersubjectively.

Sirhindi cites examples of shariat injunctions such as alms, prayer, and fasting that do not conform to one's desires of the moment nor to the rational mind. They are to be done because they are God's commands. Modern scholars can document the apparently man-made construction of shariat laws. On the other hand, pious Muslims, whether sufis or not, assert the divine inspiration involved in formulating the shariat. In terms of dealing with the ego-self these concerns are secondary. Obeying the shariat commands is obeying the shariat commands. Obeying the sufi master is obeying the sufi master. Even if one is asked to do something patently absurd, one does it. This is a methodology for taming the ego, and it often operates counter to common sense and rational thought. There is ample room for abuse by

---

1. Shaykh Farid has twenty-four letters addressed to him in Sirhindi's *Collected Letters*.

2. See Jahangir, *Memoirs of Jahangir*, 1:13.

an unscrupulous guide here, especially if the mentor is still operating out of the egoic-self. Contemplative practice and transformation of the ego-self are not strolls in the park. If they were, what kind of transformation would occur? Here Sirhindi emphasizes the necessity of purifying the heart and cleansing the ego-self instead of reinforcing the ego. Following the shariat is central to that process, and the remembrance and recitation of "There is no god but God" is a pivotal practice.

Letter 1.52

> God almighty increase your reward, raise your rank, expand your heart, and ease your affairs in reverence to the grandeur of your ancestor. God give the most favored blessings and perfected greetings to him (Muhammad) and his family. God almighty hold us firm in following God, outwardly and inwardly. God have mercy on a servant whose supplication is "amen."[3]

Again, I am writing a few phrases complaining of a bad and ill-tempered companion. Please hear them with acceptance. Respected sir, the human ego-self inciting to evil (*nafs-i ammara* hereafter in this letter translated as ego-self) is innately endowed with a love of social status and domination. The ego-self's intention is feeling superior to others. Essentially, it desires that creatures be dependent on it for everything, obeying its orders and prohibitions, and not needing anyone or being under anyone's command. This is a pretense to being God and to sharing God's incommensurability. Exalt God's sovereignty. But the ego-self is neither happy nor satisfied in sharing; it wants to rule over God. That is it. A divine saying (*hadith-i qudsi*) was revealed for all those ruled by the ego-self.[4] "Consider your ego-self to be an enemy since it rises up repeatedly against Me." This means that one's own ego-self is the abode of the enemy because the ego-self certainly is rising up as God's enemy.

3. This last sentence is taken from the famous poem of Layla and Majnun. One version is that Majnun's father took him to the Ka'ba to bring Majnun back to consensus reality. His father asked him to supplicate to God so that his love for Layla would subside. His supplication (the first hemistitch of the line) is "Oh Lord may my love for Layla never leave me!" to which the crowd, in sympathy with Majnun's love for Layla, exclaimed, "Amen."

4. Divine sayings are considered as God's words but not a part of the Qur'an. See William A. Graham, *Divine Word and Prophetic Word in Early Islam: A Reconsideration of the Sources, with Special Reference to the Divine Saying or Hadith Qudsi* (New York: Walter De Gruyter Inc., 1977). A similar hadith can be found in al-Bukhari's hadith collection, *al-Adab al-mufrad*, #590; al-Muslim's hadith collection, *Birr*, 38, #2620; Abu Da'ud, #4090; and Ibn Majah, #4174 [MR].

So, letting the ego-self grow by giving it what it desires, for example, status, domination, superiority, and pride actually helps and strengthens God's enemy. Thus, one should realize the repulsiveness of this matter explained in the divine saying, "Grandeur is my mantle and greatness is my loincloth. Whoever argues with me concerning either of these two things, I will throw into the fire. I do not care." The lowly world is accursed and detested by God almighty because worldly gain supports the fulfillment of the ego-self's desires. Whatever assists an enemy is accursed. Poverty becomes Muhammadan pride.[5] This is because neither poverty nor realizing weakness [of the ego-self] is a desire of the ego-self. One goal of sending prophets and the underlying reason for shariat obligations is to weaken and destroy the ego-self. The prescriptions of the shariat have been revealed to alleviate egoistic desires. People's egoistic desires become extinguished to the extent that they act in accordance with the shariat. Therefore, declaring one legal judgment from the shariat is better at eliminating an egoistic desire than a thousand years striving to do inner practices to tame one's own ego-self. Moreover, these inner practices do not have the light of complying with the requirements of shariat since they assist and reinforce egoistic desires.

Hindus and yogis persist in doing inner practices but nothing useful results from this except a strengthening and cultivation of the ego-self. For example, giving one dinar in alms, enjoined by the shariat, is more useful in destroying the ego-self than spending one thousand dinars voluntarily without any injunction from the shariat. Eating food on the Eid after Ramadan according to an injunction of the shariat is more beneficial than personally deciding to alleviate egoistic desires by fasting for years. Two cycles (sing. *raka'*) of [morning] ritual prayer performed in congregation, established as a preferred practice by the Prophetic sunnat, is qualitatively superior to spending the entire night doing supererogatory prayers (*salawat-i nafila*), (that is, prayer not mandated by the shariat) and not doing the morning ritual prayer in congregation.

Generally, as long as one does not purify the ego-self at all nor purify oneself of the impurity of one's delusions of grandeur, it is impossible to be saved. It is continually necessary to be concerned about getting rid of this disease so that one does not have an eternal death. The attestation of faith, "There is no god but God," situated to negate gods outwardly and inwardly, is the most beneficial and suitable [way] of purifying and cleansing the ego-self. The notables of the path have chosen this very attestation of faith to purify the ego-self. God almighty sanctify their inner hearts. Unless the broom of "no god" sweeps the way, you will not arrive at the palace of "but God."

5. This is a reference to a hadith, "Poverty is my pride" (*faqr fakhri*).

Wherever the ego-self is in the station of rebellion and violating the agreement [between God and humans] one should repeat, "There is no god but God" to renew one's faith. Muhammad said, "Renew your faith by saying 'There is no god but God.'"[6] It is necessary to repeat, "There is no god but God" all the time because the ego-self is continually in the station of impurity. In a hadith, it is mentioned that the benefits of "There is no god but God" are such that if the heavens and planets were placed on one side of a balance and "There is no god but God" on the other side, certainly the balance would tip to the side of "There is no god but God."[7] Peace to the one who follows God's guidance and the obligation of following the Chosen One (Muhammad). God bless him and his family.

Introduction to "Encouraging a youth to the sufi path" Letter 1.73

This letter is addressed to Qilichullah bin Qilich Khan, a prince during Jahangir's reign who was not one of Sirhindi's disciples.[8] From the narrative, it is clear that Sirhindi exalts the inner world, the world leading toward God, while cautioning against the trappings of the outer world, which he perceives as leading one away from God. In Sirhindi's view, any activity that is not directly involved with salvation is useless human activity. This is based on a very strict interpretation of Islamic law in which permissible actions (the majority of human life) needs to be restricted so that more time can be spent in prayer and meditation during the day. Indeed, if one's increased efforts in this regard accelerate one being close to God, then to do mundane activities with worldly results is a waste of time. Sirhindi is being consistent in coaxing this young man to follow the dictates of the shariat in order to tame his ego-self. He is urging him to do what pleases God instead of what is pleasing to himself. Toward the end of the letter, Sirhindi's advice is what one pious Muslim would give to another Muslim while inviting him to associate more with Naqshbandi shaykhs.

Letter 1.73

May God almighty keep you on the straight, wide path of Muhammad's

6. Mentioned twice in *Collected Letters* and found in Ahmad b. Hanbal's *Musnad* 2:359; al-Daylami, *al-Firdaus*, #2564. [MR]

7. In al-Bukhari's *al-Adab al-mufrad* (and in other Sunni hadith collections) it is related in a hadith that the prophet Noah said to his son, "I command you with two things . . . I command you with *La ilaha illah Allah*. If the seven heavens and the seven earths were placed on one side of a scale, and *La ilaha illah Allah* were placed on the other side of the scale, they would give in to *La ilaha illah Allah*. . ." See also Ahmad b. Hanbal, *al-Musnad*, #6583; al-Haythami, *Majma' al-zawahid*, 4:220; and al-Hakim, *al-Mustadrak*, #154 [MR].

8. There are three letters addressed to Qilichullah in *Collected Letters*.

shariat. God eternally bless and give peace to its companions. Oh son! The world is a place of trials and tribulations. Outwardly it is adorned with all kinds of lies and falsehoods, the appearance of which is made beautiful by imagining it to be the mole, cheek, tress, and face of the beloved, seeing the imagined sweetness, moistness, and freshness. But in truth, it is a perfumed corpse, a heap of garbage filled with flies and worms, a mirage appearing as water, poison tasting like sugar, and entirely devoid of good qualities. The world treats those in it so disgustingly that it is beyond words. Those enamored of the world are crazy, put under its spell and deceived. Whoever is seduced by its appearances is stained with an eternal loss and whoever views the world as sweet and fresh will have the ill fortune of eternal penitence. The Prince of the Worlds (Muhammad), the Beloved of God said, "The world and the Hereafter are like fellow wives; if one of them is happy the other is angry."[9] God bless him and his family. So whoever is pleased with this world will experience wrath in the next world and be miserable and without hope there. God almighty save us and also save us from loving the world and from those who love the world.

Oh son! Don't you know what the world is? It is what keeps you from God almighty. Therefore, women, children, wealth, status, power, amusements, and being occupied with worthless pursuits are all aspects of the world. Any knowledge not applicable to the Hereafter is also an aspect of the world. If learning astronomy, logic, engineering, mathematics, and other useless knowledge were worthwhile, then philosophers would be saved in the next world. Muhammad said, "The sign of God turning away from the servant is the servant's occupying himself with what does not pertain to God."[10] (As Rumi says), Everything except God's love, even if it is sugar-coated, is painfully bitter.[11]

They say that learning astronomy is useful in knowing the prayer times. This does not mean that the prayer times cannot be known without knowing astronomy, but that knowing astronomy is one way of knowing the prayer times. There are many people who do not know astronomy but know the prayer times better than astronomers. Similarly, the same justification is given to learn logic, mathematics and other knowledge, that is, in general they are useful in some of the religious sciences (*'ulum-i shari'i*). Overall, after many contrivances, they find it permissible to learn these disciplines. If the goal of studying these disciplines is to know the obligations of the

9. This hadith is mentioned three times in *Collected Letters,* and is found in Ibn Hibban, *al-Sahih*, #6019 and Ibn al-Mubarak, *al-Zuhd*, #594 [MR].

10. This hadith is mentioned twice in *Collected Letters,* and is in al-Bayhaqi, *al-Zuhd*, #72 and Abu Nu'aym al-Asbahani, *Hilyat al-awliya*, 9:343 [MR].

11. See Jalaluddin Balkhi/Rumi, *Mathnawi-yi ma'nawi*, 1:226 (In the six-volume *Mathnawi*, Vol. 1 verse 3686).

shariat and supporting theological proofs, then it is another matter. Otherwise it is entirely impermissible. One should consider whether doing something permissible which necessitates neglecting religious obligations goes beyond the limits of permissibility or not. There is no doubt that occupying oneself with these disciplines keeps one from being involved in the requisite religious sciences.

O son! God almighty, in God's complete, unremitting divine favor, has blessed you from the beginning of youth with the success of repentance and with your return to the hand of a Naqshbandi dervish. God almighty sanctify his inner secret. I do not know whether or not you have resolutely repented from the grip of the ego-self (*nafs*) and Satan. Integrity (*istiqamat*) is difficult. When you are in the prime of youth, the means for realizing religion are easily available, while most of your companions are inappropriate and undesirable. My advice to you is that you are a novice on the spiritual path and there are a lot of temptations.

O son! The task is to avoid the unnecessary permissible acts and act in accordance with just the necessary [permissible acts] in order to perform acts of worship with the intention of tranquility (*jam'iyat*). For example, the purpose of food is to have the strength to worship God obediently; the purpose of clothing is to cover the private areas of the body and protect one from heat and cold. All that is necessarily permissible should be done in the same manner. Naqshbandi notables have chosen to act decisively [in accepting the hardships of strictly following the shariat], avoiding the easy way out [that is, doing just what is technically permissible (*rukhsat*)] whenever possible. God almighty sanctify their inner hearts. It is sufficient to perform the required religious acts (*'aza'im*) that are compulsory. If one cannot perform the required religious acts, one should not step outside of the circle of the permissible and do what is prohibited and doubtful. From a perfected munificence, God almighty has completely allowed ease in what is permissible, expanding this wide circle of ease. Apart from these favors what could equal the [feeling of] gratification of God being satisfied with one's behavior and what could equal the [feeling of] discontent if God were angry with one's conduct? God almighty's satisfaction in heaven is better than heaven and God almighty's anger in hell is worse than hell.

A person is a servant subject to God's commands. He was not created to do whatever he pleases and ignore [the consequences]. One must think deeply about the urgency of the task or only shame and loss will be there tomorrow. The time to do the work is when one is young. A brave young man does not let this time slip away. He realizes the great opportunity. It is probable that he will not reach old age, and if he does, he might not attain tranquility. If he does [attain tranquility] he cannot do the work because it is a time when weakness and laziness prevail. The blessings of God almighty include all the available means to realize tranquility along with the presence of parents who bear the burden of supporting their young son. It is a time of opportunity, strength, and possibility. What excuse is there to postpone until tomorrow what can be done today? Muhammad said, "[God] destroys those who procrastinate [in repenting].[12] God bless him and give him peace. Yes! It is praiseworthy to leave the lesser, worldly things to do tomorrow and today finish the deeds [related to] the next world. To reverse these priorities is strongly disapproved. Now at the prime of youth, enemies of religion, the ego-self and Satan, dominate. A few good deeds at this time have so much more value than twice as many good deeds when these enemies do not dominate. In a military context, soldiers fighting when the enemy is in a dominant position are quite important. Even the slightest hesitation on their part is so critical and apparent that the threat of enemies during peacetime is unimportant in comparison.

Oh son! The goal of creating humans, the apex of creation, is not amusement and games nor eating and sleeping. The goal is total worship (lit. performing the acts of servanthood), that is, submissiveness, humility, weakness, poverty, and continual supplication to God. The goal of worship, explained by the Muhammadan shariat, is the whole-hearted and grateful worship of God in total submission and obedience to God. God bless him and give him peace. This worship is for the welfare and benefit of God's servants. None of these actions pertain to God. One must struggle to enact the commands of God and avoid prohibited actions. Glorify God's affair.

God almighty, in spite of God's absolute self-sufficiency, has honored God's servants with commands and prohibitions. We needy ones should thank God for this most perfect blessing and should gratefully endeavor to comply with religious precepts (*ahkam*). You know that if someone with high worldly status gives a job to a subordinate then what happens in that job is in the interests of the person who offered it. The subordinate highly respects the authority [of his superior], knowing that a powerful person had given him the job, and that [he should perform it] with the utmost of gratitude.

One should realize what a calamity it is when the greatness of God is valued less than the greatness of the aforementioned worldly person such that the person does not strive to obey God's religious precepts. Exalt God's sovereignty. One can only feel shame and must awaken oneself from the dreams of a fool. Not complying with God's commands results from two things. First, one considers the precepts of the shariat to be lies and does not believe them; or second, one considers the greatness of God almighty's

12. This hadith is mentioned three times in *Collected Letters,* and is in al-Daylami, *al-Firdaus*, #2420 and Abu Nu'aym al-Asbahani, *Hilyat al-awliya*, 3:338, 6:55, 9:283 [MR].

command to be less [important] than that of worldly people. Exalt God's sovereignty. One has to notice this sad state of affairs.

O son! If a persistent liar says that the enemy is going to launch an all-out night attack on such-and-such people, then the wise people of that group would protect themselves by defending against this misfortune even though they know the informant is a liar. One could say that suspicion of danger according to the wise is a necessary precaution.

The Truthful Messenger (Muhammad) has explicitly announced the punishments in the Hereafter, but no one takes notice. God bless him and give him peace. If they were aware, then they would take care to avert [punishment] since they know how to ward off punishment from what Muhammad has said. So what kind of faith (*iman*) is it whereby the reports of the Truthful Messenger are equivalent to liars' words of no value? One will not be saved by the appearance of submitting to God (*islam*). Inner certainty (*yaqin*) must be realized. There is certainty when there is neither belief (*zann*) nor conjecture. All those who are wise also acknowledge conjecture in the face of danger just like God almighty says in the Qur'an [lit. God's glorious words], "God sees what you do." [Q.49:18]

In spite of this, people still manage to act in a disgusting manner. If they knew that a poor, wretched person observed these [vile] deeds, they would never commit them in front of him. Thus, there are two conditions of these people: First, they do not believe what God almighty has told them; or second, they do not believe that God is omniscient. Therefore, this kind of attitude is either from faith or from infidelity. It is incumbent upon you to renew your faith anew as Muhammad said, "Renew your faith by saying 'There is no god but God.'"[13] God bless him and give him peace.

One should also repent sincerely of what displeases God almighty and completely refrain from what God has forbidden. Pray the five ritual prayers in congregation. If one is awake and able to do additional night prayers (*namaz-i tahajjud*), this is a great blessing. Paying alms, one of the pillars of Islam, should of course be done. The easiest way to pay alms is to put each year's alms aside from one's property with the intention of giving alms. Over the year, distribute what you have set aside for alms. In this way, it is not necessary to renew one's intention to pay alms every time [one distributes it]. It is sufficient for one to put money aside each time.

One knows each year how much will be spent on the poor and deserving but because there is no intention of alms it is not counted as alms. In the aforementioned case, one gives alms and is relieved of unexpected expenses. Assuming some money was left over from the money set aside to spend on the destitute, one should take care to set that money aside from

13. Mentioned twice in *Collected Letters,* and found in Ahmad b. Hanbal's *Musnad* 2:359; al-Daylami, *al-Firdaus*, #2564. [MR]

one's own property [and spend it on alms the following year]. Each year one should do the same because alms should be separated [from one's own property]. If today one does not have the good fortune to give to the poor, tomorrow the blessing will come.

O son! Since the ego-self is essentially very selfish and rebels against complying with God's dictates my words by necessity are emphatic. Exalt God's sovereignty. All possessions and wealth come from God almighty. What right does a person have to delay in complying [with God's guidelines]? He must pay alms very gratefully. Likewise, for the rest of one's worship there are no excuses of any kind. One should encourage people to perform their religious duties well and make sure no one has any outstanding obligations. In the world it is easy to fulfill one's duties. With politeness and flattery one can alleviate [duties to others]. In the Hereafter the task is difficult with no solution. One must ask the jurists about matters in the next world and about the legal judgments of the shariat. Their words have an effect, perhaps because of their blessed souls and the deeds to match. One must keep away from the worldly jurists whose knowledge is a means to acquire property and status. If one has a need [to consult a jurist] and cannot find a pious jurist, then one can consult a [worldly jurist] on the basis of this need.

Where you are Miyan Hajji Muhammad Uttara is a pious jurist and you already know Miyan Shaykh 'Ali Uttara. Both of these esteemed men are a godsend to the region. It is best to go to them for any investigation of legal matters. Oh son! What connection is there between us poor ones and worldly people such that we [are in a position to] talk about their good and bad? Advice about the shariat in this regard is absolutely complete and perfect. "God has the conclusive proof." [Q. 6:149]

But since you have gone to the poor ones for repentance, the heart will usually become focused on your state by means of that connection [with them]. It is the same focus that is the reason for this discussion. I know that you have already heard most of this advice and questioning, but the goal is to implement this in action, not just knowing. A sick person who knows the cure for his disease will not recover until he takes the medicine. Just knowing about medicine is of no benefit. All of this insistence and urgency is for action. Knowledge just proves itself correct. Muhammad said, "The person punished most on the Day of Judgment will be the one who knows and has not reached God from his knowledge."[14] God bless him and give him peace.

Son, know that even though your previous repentance has not been suc-

14. This hadith is mentioned two times in *Collected Letters,* and is in al-Darimi's *al-Sunan*, #262; Ibn al-Mubarak, *al-Zuhd*, #40; and al-Tabarani's *al-Saghir*, #507 [MR].

cessful because of lack of spiritual companionship (*suhbat*) with those of a tranquil heart (*jam'iyat*), it shows the exquisite jewel of your willingness. With the blessing of that repentance, it is hoped that God almighty will eventually favor you with the prosperity of doing deeds that satisfy God, thereby ensuring your salvation. In any case, may your link of love with this group (the Naqshbandiyya) continue and may you make supplication and humbleness with this group a habit. It could be expected that God almighty will bless you with God's love by means of your love of this group, totally attracting you to God and release you from the distractions of the world.

Love is a fire that, once kindled, burns up everything except the Beloved.

> After the sword of "*no God*" kills everything other than God,
> there is nothing left to see.
> All is annihilated "*except God.*"
> Bravo! You have seared away the love of anything not associated
> with God.

INTRODUCTION TO "THE EXPANSE OF THE HEART" LETTER 3.45

This letter is written to Mawlana Sultan Sirhindi to explain the special nature of the heart.[15] Sirhindi begins the letter with a down-to-earth moral teaching to treat each person's heart in a gentle manner. The heart of common people, although not integrated, is the closest aspect of their beings to God, and should be honored. Then the context shifts to the meaning of an integrated heart. In this letter, the heart is not the physical heart nor the heart subtle center but a simple integration (*jami'-i basit*) whereby all the subtle centers are included in this integrated heart after they have become purified. This is the consolidation of subtle centers (lit. unitary form, *hay'at-i wahdani*) discussed in Naqshbandi-Mujaddidi literature.[16] The reason why the integrated heart is so close to God is because God almighty is also integrated in a basic manner. God in essence is undifferentiated (*'adm-i tarkib*). It is through such an integrated heart that one has inner knowledge (*ma'rifat*) of the divine Essence.[17] An integrated heart is one of the outcomes of purifying all the subtle centers, going to their origins, the name governing them, and then to a universal name (one of the eight essential attributes).[18] The enigmatic reference to "a place beside the heart" is another way of saying

15. There are two letters addressed to him in *Collected Letters*. This letter was originally written in Arabic.

16. See Buehler, *Sufi Heirs*, 251-253.

17. See Hutaki, *Sharh-i Maktubat*, 715.

18. These eight essential attributes are: knowledge, life, power, will, speech, hearing, sight, and origination. See Buehler, *Sufi Heirs*, 115.

that after knowers (*'arifin*) have purified and consolidated their subtle centers, then it is only through God's grace not knowing how (*bi-la kayf*) that one arrives at the Essence.

Letter 3.45

Praise God, the Lord of the two worlds. God bless God's messenger, Muhammad, and all of his family and give them peace. It is known that the heart [subtle center] is a neighbor of God almighty and nothing else is closer to the Holy Presence than the heart. Take care not to injure any heart, whether it is obedient or disobedient, because a neighbor is protected even if he is disobedient. Fear that [you may injure someone's heart]! After covering up the truth of God (*kufr*), which is the way to offend God almighty, there is no greater sin than injuring someone's heart. This is because the heart is the closest of all to God almighty. All of creation worships God almighty. Damaging and disdaining God's servant is necessarily like injuring his Lord. So by analogy consider when there is a Lord with absolute authority. One should only act in God's creation to the extent that one is entrusted, so this precludes harming others. However, there is obedience to God almighty's command like a virgin unmarried woman being lashed one hundred times [for adultery]. If someone were to hit her one more time, then it would be oppression and harm.

Know that the heart is the most preferred and noble of God's creation. Human beings are the most favored entity in the macrocosm because of their comprehensiveness (*ijmal*). Likewise, the [integrated] heart is the most preferred entity in the human microcosm due to its complete simplicity and fullness. Anything that is more comprehensive and integrated is closer to God almighty.[19] In the human being, the heart is the interface (*barzakh*) between the created world and the world of command.

In the levels of ascent, the human subtle centers ascend to their origins (sing. *asl*). For example, one ascends first to the origin of water, then to the origin of air, then to the origin of fire, then to the origins of the subtle centers, then to the partial name that rules over the origins of the subtle centers, then to the complete name. Then, if God wills, one goes to [a place] beside the heart because the heart does not have an origin to ascend to. In the beginning, the ascent is from the heart, toward the almighty Essence. Certainly the heart is the door of the hidden unseen Reality (*ghayb al-huwiya*).[20] But arrival is difficult from the path of the heart alone without fulfilling

19. This is another way of saying that the larger the context, the closer to God, who is the Context beyond context.

20. This is glossed in the Nur Ahmad edition as the separate Essence not including the attributes, qualities (*shuyunat*), or aspects (*i'tibarat*). See *Collected Letters*, 3.45.107 fn 2.

that condition [of going to a place beside the heart]. It is easy after fulfilling this condition. Don't you see the union and expanse that is in the heart after traversing the detailed levels? The goal of the heart in this station is an integrated heart, the simplest of the simple, not a small chunk of meat.

Introduction to shadows versus the Essence: Letter 2.42

This letter is addressed to Khwaja Jamaluddin Husayn Kulabi,[21] whose father, Mirza Husamuddin Ahmad Badakhshi (d. 1043/1643), was a devoted disciple of Baqibillah's married to one of Abu'l-Fadl 'Allami's daughters. He was in charge of the education of Baqibillah's two sons after Baqibillah had passed away.

The main theme in this letter is one of discriminating the shadows from the Essence and of recognizing what is authentic wayfaring. Paradoxically, realizing the goal does not depend on inner and outer wayfaring because these two types of wayfaring are in the shadows of the shadows of the attribute. But unless one does this inner and outer wayfaring, one will not benefit from annihilation in God (*fana'*). One reason for mistaking shadows for Essence is that after purifying the subtle centers, the shadows of disclosures of the Essence become reflected in the ego-self (*nafs*) of the wayfarer. The mistake is seeing the appearance of the Beloved in the outer mirror and imagining it to be the actual Beloved.

The Real is ineffable and formless because it is beyond inner and outer worlds. For Sirhindi, it makes no sense to say that outer wayfaring (*sayr-i afaqi*) is wayfaring to God (*sayr ila Allah*) or that inner wayfaring (*sayr-i anfusi*) is wayfaring in God (*sayr fi'llah*) because even the shadows of the names and attributes are beyond this. In inner and outer wayfaring one sees the disclosures and lights from the active attributes (*sifat-i fi'liya*). The active attributes and fixed attributes (*sifat-i thubutiya*) are still ahead on the path in closer wayfaring (*sayr-i aqrabiyat*) along with the attributes, qualities (*shuyunat*), aspects (*i'tibarat*), and the lifting of the veils of light.[22]

Inner wayfaring is still in the realm of lesser intimacy with God (*walayat-i sughra*). Two common misperceptions in this wayfaring are 1) perceiving the Necessary world at the level of possibility in the contingent world and/or 2) perceiving a likeness of the Necessary at the level of the contingent world. The intimacy of the prophets, greater intimacy (*walayat-i kubra*), is in the eight essential attributes, far beyond inner or outer wayfaring. One goes from the shadowy manifestation of appearances to the enlivening experiences of the levels in the Necessary.

---

21. Ahmad Sirhindi wrote six letters to Jamaluddin Husayn.

22. See Hutaki, *Sharh-i Maktubat*, 591.

Letter 2.42

In the name of God, the most compassionate and merciful, thank God, the Sustainer of the two worlds. God bless and give peace to the Lord of the Messengers (Muhammad), his noble family, and his great companions from now until the Day of Judgment.

Dear son, God almighty help you in both worlds. Listen very carefully. The wayfarer, after rectifying intentions and purifying desires, should busy himself with recollection of God in addition to learning how to perform difficult contemplative exercises and austerities. Having cleansed his vile characteristics with praiseworthy character, he realizes a transformation. Repentance and returning to God become easy for him while love of the world leaves his heart. He achieves patience, reliance on God, and satisfaction. Experiencing these subtle essences (*ma'ani*) within himself, he gradually witnesses thc order of the image-exemplar world (*'alam-i mithal*).[23] After discerning his purity from human foulness and their vile attributes, he completes outer wayfaring (*sayr-i afaqi*).

One group of sufis exercises caution in this station, ascertaining that each and every one of the seven human subtle centers in the image-exemplar world [corresponds] with its respective appearance of light.[24] This indicates that each subtle center is purified. They go along in outer wayfaring beginning in the heart subtle center and gradually and in order finish with the superarcane subtle center, which is the last. For example, the indication that the wayfarer has purified the heart center is the manifestation of the heart center as an appearance of red light. For the spirit subtle center (*ruh*), there is a yellow light, and so on for the rest of the subtle centers.[25]

Achieving outer wayfaring is when the wayfarer witnesses his character attributes changing in the mirror of the image-exemplar world and feels his shadow of darkness and impurities in the physical world until there is certainty that one has purified [his heart subtle center] and cleansed [his ego-self] completely. The wayfarer has realized outer wayfaring when he can continually contemplatively witness his actions and states in the image-exemplar world, which is the totality of the outside world, and when he can see in himself the shifting appearances of the physical world. Although this wayfaring in reality takes place in the wayfarer's ego-self, it is a qualitative (*kayfi*) transformation of personal characteristics and character. But from

---

23. The world of image exemplars (*'alam-i mithal*) is the lower level of the world of command. It serves as an intermediate zone between the world of command and the physical world.

24. See the Introduction for background on the subtle centers (*lata'if*).

25. The color of lights associated with each subtle center is not uniform. See *Collected Letters*, 2.42.101 fn 4 and Buehler, *Sufi Heirs*, 106-108.

afar the wayfaring appears to be outer, not inner [wayfaring], so this wayfaring is also attributed to inner wayfaring (*sayr-i anfusi*). By completing an inner wayfaring, which is attributed to be wayfaring in the inner world, sufis have also completed wayfaring to God. Annihilation in God, the typical expression used in sufi practice (*suluk*), is also connected to this [type of] wayfaring. Wayfaring after this is wayfaring in the inner world, [which others call] wayfaring in God (*sayr fi'llah*). Abiding in God (*baqa' billah*) is also verified in this realm. In this station, one also experiences attraction to God after wayfaring. It occurs when the subtle centers of the wayfarer become purified from human impurities during outer wayfaring. In the mirror of these subtle centers, shadows and reflections of the comprehensive name governing the wayfarer appear.

These subtle centers are the originating places of manifestations of particularities (*juzi'yat*) of the comprehensive name. This wayfaring is named inner wayfaring because the inner world is the mirror of the shadows and reflections of the [divine] names, not because the wayfarer's travel is in the ego-self.[26] For example, when one is doing outer wayfaring it is with respect to the person holding the mirror. Therefore, it is called outer wayfaring not wayfaring in the outside world. In reality, this wayfaring is shadows-of-God's-names wayfaring in the inner mirror (*maraya-yi anfus*). Therefore, this wayfaring is called the wayfaring of the Beloved in the lover.

The form is far from the mirror.
For one who can hear the form, it is from light.

This wayfaring is wayfaring in God. With this in mind one can say that the character of God molds the wayfarer. He is transformed from one way of being (lit. set of habits) to another way of being. This is because he takes part in some outer characteristics associated with a locus of manifestation of one of God's names,[27] even if it is in a general way.[28] So, in this manner, wayfaring in God's names is verified. This is the end of the realization of this station, and corrects what people say about wayfaring. What kind of states could someone in the station have experienced and what is the speaker's meaning? Each person talks in accordance with his own understanding and perception. [Often] the speaker has an intended meaning associated with his words and the listener understands a different meaning from the

26. Sirhindi's comment is so that the reader does not conflate the *nafs* with *sayr-i anfusi* where *anfus* is a plural form of *nafs*.

27. For an exposition of Ibn al-'Arabi's use of *mazhar* as a loci of the manifestation of God's names, see Chittick, *Sufi Path of Knowledge*, 89-90.

28. The Arabic *fi'l-jumla* here overlaps with a concept that Sirhindi uses, namely *ijmal*, having a meaning of comprehensive without being specified. Both ideas contrast with *tafsil*, a particularized aspect of a name or attribute.

same words.

Shaykhs, without difficulty, say that inner wayfaring is wayfaring in God. Without even batting an eye they also say that inner wayfaring is abiding in God. They imagine their arriving-station and union. I find this sloppiness quite troublesome. Inevitably in correcting and orienting this enterprise, stratagems and formality are necessary, some of which are taken from the words of shaykhs and some of which comes from elaboration of topics and inspirations.

Outer wayfaring is basically the process of eliminating bad character traits. In this process, inner wayfaring is gloriously manifesting praiseworthy character traits.[29] Elimination corresponds to the station of annihilation in God, and gloriously manifesting [praiseworthy character traits] corresponds to abiding in God. Shaykhs have determined that inner wayfaring does not have an end and does not stop even if one were to continue wayfaring forever. They have said that the good qualities (*shama'il*) and the characteristics of the Beloved do not have an end. So God's good qualities will always be shining in the mirror of the wayfarer, attribute by attribute, as God's perfections manifest one by one. Therefore, they say that there is no interruption. How could an end [to the process] be conceivable? If a particle is big or small—who cares after spending a lifetime at the bottom of oneself?

Then there is annihilation in God and abiding in God realized by outer and inner wayfaring. They call this being free from the limitation of the name of being close to God (*ism-i walayat*), and perceive this as the complete end up to here. If there is any wayfaring after this, according to them, it is returning [to the physical world] and interpreted as returning to the world of creation for God and by means of God (*sayr 'an Allah billah*) or a fourth kind of wayfaring, which they call "returning to live as an apparently ordinary person" (*sayr fi 'l-ashya'*) and associated with descent. They have established that these latter two types of wayfaring are for completion and guidance just as inner and outer wayfaring are for the same closeness to God and completion. One group of shaykhs has said that there are seventy thousand veils that are known to exist, for example, the hadith, "God has seventy thousand veils of light and darkness."[30] In outer wayfaring, these veils are burnt because tens of thousands of veils are burnt in each of the seven subtle centers. When outer wayfaring is completed all of the veils are lifted and the wayfarer becomes certain that he is wayfaring in God (*sayr*

29. Specifically this latter process involves a connection with God such that God's attributes shine in the mirror of the wayfarer.

30. This hadith is quoted six times in *Collected Letters,* and is in al-Tabarani, *al-Kabir*, #5802; al-Haythami, *Majma' al-zawahid*, 1:79; Abu Ya'la, *al-Musnad*, #7487; al-Daylami, *al-Firdaus*, #3074; and al-Ruyani, *al-Musnad*, #1055 [MR].

fi'llah). He has come to the station of arrival. This is the (mistaken) realization of those on the sufi path who are close to God and a replica of all of their completion and completion bestowing.

My concerns in this subject will be demonstrated by means of God's favor and magnanimity. Exalt God's sovereignty. Having set out and proceeded on the path, manifesting blessing and thanksgiving, I will write about it. Those of you who have discernment learn a lesson. You should know that God almighty has guided you on the straight path. God almighty is ineffable and incommensurate (*bichun wa-bichigun*), just as God is beyond the inside and outside worlds. So they say that outer wayfaring is wayfaring to God and inner wayfaring is wayfaring in God. This does not make any sense. Both inner and outer wayfaring are wayfaring to God and wayfaring in God is many stages removed from inner and outer wayfaring, beyond the beyond of inner and outer wayfaring.

It is a strange affair when they determine that wayfaring in God is inner wayfaring. For them, it does not have an end and it is inconceivable that one could traverse the path even if one were to live forever, like it was said above. Since inner wayfaring is like outer wayfaring, both are in the circle of possibility. So with these suppositions it is not possible to traverse the circle of possibility. Surely then there will be nothing but continual disappointment and eternal suffering, Eternal annihilation in God will never be verified nor [on these suppositions] can abiding in God be imagined. So how can anyone arrive and be united [with God], and how can one realize closeness and completion?

Praise God! Whenever notables (*buzurgan*) confuse a mirage with actual water, imagine that "going to God" is "being in God," conceive of possibility as necessary, or interpret quality with beyond quality from their small mindedness, what kind of a complaint can one make? What a calamity for them to call the inner world (*anfus*) Reality (*haqq*) because they imagine their wayfaring to be endless when an end exists. They have determined that the appearance of the names and necessary attributes of God in the mirror of the wayfarer to be inner wayfaring. Exalt God's sovereignty. That appearance is the appearance of a shadow of the shadows of God's names and attributes, not the appearance of the origin of the names and attributes. One will find the verification of this written at the end of this letter if God wills.

What can I do? How can I reconcile these bad-mannered people with the majesty of God almighty and knowledge and discrimination? How can I participate in God's kingdom without God almighty? Although the rights of these notables are their own responsibility, I am required to educate them in many ways. God sanctify their innermost beings. The rights of God are above all of their rights as is the education by God almighty above education by anyone else. With the elegance of God's education, I have been saved from this ruin and have not participated without God while being in God almighty's holy kingdom. "Thanks to God who has guided us. We would never have been guided if God had not guided us." [Q. 7:43]

God almighty is incomparable. Whatever is colored with quality or quantity has a designation and is far from God almighty. God cannot be contained in the mirror of the outside world and what is manifested in the inside world. Whatever appears in the inner and outer worlds is like the manifestations of quantity and quality, so one must pass beyond the inner and outer worlds and look for God almighty beyond these worlds. Likewise, the inner and outer aspects of the circle of possibility, the Essence, God's names, and God's attributes cannot contain God almighty. Nor can anything appearing there [contain God almighty] such as the shadows and reflections of the names and attributes of God almighty or any resemblance to them. The shadows of the names and attributes and whatever resembles them are outside of the inner and outer worlds. In this shadow place, one cannot do more than embellish or design. So to whom do these manifestations (*zuhur*) occur, and just where are these disclosures (sing. *tajalli*)? This is because the names and attributes of God are like God's Essence, without quality, quantity, resemblance, or example. Since you do not go out of the inner or outer worlds, you do not know the meaning of the shadow of the names and attributes of God. So how can you arrive at the names and attributes of God almighty?

It is a strange affair! If I were to speak about the definite openings of unveiling (*mukashafat*) and what is known with certainty, it would not agree with the perceptions of shaykhs nor would it agree with what has been unveiled to them. Who will believe my certain experiences or accept them? If I do not speak out, hiding [what I know], it is like I have recommended the mixing of Reality with what is false. [In the past], I have found ways of getting out of doing that which God, the almighty and sanctified, makes incumbent. Therefore, by necessity, I am presenting that which is Real and that which is worthy of God's almighty holiness, while negating what is not appropriate to God's holy majesty. I am not afraid of opposing others nor do I lament doing this. There used to be fear of others' opposition when I was hesitant and doubtful to act on what had been disclosed to me. Then the truth of the matter was confirmed like the dawn constantly breaking in the morning. Like the full moon, the origin of the affair was clarified. The shadows passed away completely, their shapes and resemblances disappearing into thin air. There were no longer any doubts.

Baqibillah said that the sign of healthy states was achieving certainty with completion. God sanctify his innermost being. How is it that doubts and misgivings are created? With the endless divine favor of God almighty, insight into the details of the established states of these notables has become easy. The inner knowledge of asserting the unity of God and unity (*ittihad*), encompassing, and penetrating has become disclosed. The reality of what they see and contemplatively witness, linked to realization, and the intricacies of inner and outer knowledge [associated with] these experiences has evidently reached its conclusion. For a while they have endeavored to reside in the station and have attained more or less, except if God almighty wills otherwise. The end of this matter has become apparent through the grace of God. God's sovereignty be exalted. All these strange events and visions are in the shadows, trapped in shape and resemblance.

We aspire to that which is beyond the beyond of that. The real goal is way beyond all of that. Having to disregard everything else, I turned toward the ineffable Divine Majesty. All that had been specified and imbued with quality or quantity became free of quality and quantity. "I have turned my face toward God who created the heavens and the earth, as one of pure faith, and am not one of the idolaters." [Q. 6:79]

If the matter had not been like this, I would have never spoken out against the shaykhs nor would I have opposed them on the basis of assessment and assumptions. I would have never brought up this disagreement if there had not been a connection with the necessary Essence and attributes of God and speaking about God's divinity and transcendence (*tanzih*). God's sovereignty be exalted. It would never have occurred for me to oppose what had been disclosed (*makshufat*) to these shaykhs nor to speak against their knowledge connected to realization. This is because I am a humble gatherer of the harvest of their riches. I am the worthless leftovers at the seat of their tables of favor.

I will repeat the proof that they have fostered in me through the many ways that they have educated me. With various kinds of magnanimity and behaving in a beautiful manner (*ihsan*), they have benefited me. But what can be done when the rights of God are greater than their rights? Exalt God's sovereignty! This is because the inquiry of God almighty's Essence and attributes began to happen. It became known that it is impermissible to abandon some matters concerning God's holy majesty. In this realm, endeavoring to be quiet and fearing to oppose others is far from the dictates of religion and integrity (*din wa-diyanat*). One in the station of servanthood and obedience cannot turn away from this [task]. Jurists and sufis disagree on controversial matters like the issue of the unity of being and other topics involving philosophical speculation and inference. God almighty have mercy on them. My opposition to them is based on the methods of unveiling (*kashf*) and contemplative witnessing (*shuhud*), which jurists are strongly against.

But the condition of discussing these affairs is to bring out their positive side. It is understandable how Shaykh 'Ala'uddawla Simnani (d. 736/1336) is opposed to unity of being in the same way as jurists and he sees the shamefulness of that perspective. Whenever people experience this kind of unity from unveiling, they do not consider the unity of [objective] being to be reprehensible. The reason is that strange states and peculiar types of inner experience are involved. In short, it is not preferable to remain in this domain. Being satisfied with [these kinds of] states and inner knowledge is not a beautiful way of being.

Question: With this supposition, are the shaykhs false shaykhs (*batil*) and is Reality beyond what is disclosed and contemplatively witnessed by them?

Answer: "False" means that there is no truthfulness (*sidq*). We are what we are. The origin of these states and inner knowledge is the overflowing love of God almighty. The overflowing of love for God almighty happens in such a manner that in their perspective and vision nothing is left of the name and sign of that which is not God (*ma siwa*). They annihilate the other and otherness of [the designations of] name and sign. At this time they inevitably consider that which is not God to be annihilated because of intoxication and an overpowering of their state. They will not see the presence of what is other than God almighty! What is false here? Where is the falseness? In this realm, it is the overpowering of God and the falseness of the false. These notables, in their love of God the exalted, have abandoned themselves and what is other than themselves. They have not relinquished [the designation of] the name and sign from themselves or other than themselves. It is possible that the false has fled from their shadow. Here it is all God and for God. What do the superficial jurists (*'ulama-yi zahir*) understand about these notables' truth? Other than shallow disagreements, what do these superficial jurists understand? What can these jurists attain from their perfections?

Speaking of this, other perfections are beyond these states and inner knowledge. Comparing these states and inner knowledge to perfections is like comparing a drop to an ocean.

> The sky is low compared to the Throne.
> It is only high relative to the Earth.

Returning to the main topic, I will talk about rending the veils. They say that in outer wayfaring the veils of light and darkness are raised up completely, as has been mentioned above. According to this poor one (Ahmad Sirhindi), this is a doubtful assertion because it goes against what has been proved and contemplatively witnessed. This is because rending the veils of darkness is related to traversing all the stages of the circle of possibility, which includes both inner and outer wayfaring. The rending of veils of light is related to traversing the necessary names and attributes of God, almighty and holy. As long as name, attribute, quality (*sha'n*), and aspect (*i'tibar*) do not remain in the wayfarer's vision, it is possible for him to completely rend the veils of light and be honored with a naked arrival. Although this arrival is a small attainment, it is exceedingly rare.

So in outer wayfaring it is not even known whether half the veils of darkness have been torn away. How is there any rending of the veils of light? In short, with the veils of darkness there are different levels, which is the reason [people] have become mistaken. In the darkness, the veils of the ego-self (*hujub-i nafsani*) are above the veils of the heart.[31] For example, in a little darkness, a person imagines the darkness to be light if something appears like light. In truth, darkness is darkness and light is light. A person with sharp vision does not confuse one with another. Having found the origin of the error this person has not decided that darkness is light. "That is God's bounty which God gives to whom God desires. God is of great bounty." [Q. 62:4]

They have honored me with a path on which I have proceeded. It is a path that combines attraction to God and wayfaring. Eliminating [bad character traits] and gloriously manifesting [praiseworthy character traits] are unified here. The purification (*tasfiya*) of [the worlds of creation and command] and cleansing [of the ego-self] (*tazkiya*) are associated with each other in this realm. Inner wayfaring in this station is included in outer wayfaring. Cleansing originates in purification. Unburdening oneself of the ego-self originates in gloriously manifesting [praiseworthy character traits]. Essential attraction to God brings about wayfaring. The inner includes the outer, but the precedence of the Essence is for gloriously manifesting and attraction to God. Purifying has priority over cleansing with respect to the Essence. The inner world is regarded more than the outer. Therefore, it became inevitable that this [Naqshbandi] method has become the shortest path, making it easier to arrive at the goal. Moreover, I assert that this [Naqshbandi] path certainly brings one to the goal. There is no possibility for one not to arrive. There is a question of integrity (*istiqamat masa'lat*) in that one must ask and one must request the opportunity from God almighty.

As for what I have said, that is, that this is certainly a path leading one to the goal, the first step on this way is attraction to God, which is arriving at the outer courtyard. Staying in the places of other stations, in other way stations on the path, or in stations of attraction to God is not included in [this type of] wayfaring. With this method, obstacles arise because wayfaring is like being an uninvited guest (*tufayli*) since attraction to God is connected to attainment. Therefore, it is not pure wayfaring here or reprehensible attraction to God that blocks the way.

---

31. This could also be read that there are more veils of the ego-self than veils of the heart.

This is the King's Road of the prophets. God bless them. The prophets have arrived by stages of arrival according to the distinction of the degrees of their ranks. Traversing the inner and outer in one step, they have proceeded with another step beyond the inner and outer. The affair is carried upward from wayfaring and attraction to God because the end of wayfaring is up to the end of outer wayfaring. The end of attraction to God is up to the end of inner wayfaring. When outer and inner wayfaring are completed, the matter of wayfaring and attraction to God is finished. After that, it is neither wayfaring nor attraction to God. This meaning is not worthy of understanding for each attracted-to-God wayfarer or wayfarer attracted to God. According to them, there is no place to step beyond the outer and inner. Assuming one had an eternal life and did nothing but inner wayfaring, even then he would not be able to complete it. A notable has said, "If a particle is big or small, who cares after spending a lifetime at the bottom of oneself?" (as said above) Another person has said that self-disclosure of God (*tajalli*) only occurs by virtue of the form in which it discloses itself (*bi-surat al-mutajalli*). One can only see the form of its disclosure in God's mirror, not the self-disclosure of God in the mirror. It is not possible to see God.

One should know that through the petitions to God from my shaykhs and my guides to God, my eyes were opened to this path. It is through their mediation that I speak out this way. I have learned the basics of the aforementioned path from them, and have obtained knowledge of the religious sciences (*mawlawiyat*) from their noble attention. If I have any knowledge, it is because I was their uninvited guest. If I have any inner knowledge, it is also a result of their favor. By virtue of these great sufis (*buzurgan*), I have been immersed in the path of "including the end in the beginning." I have received the connection of attraction of being a *qayyum* from them,[32] and have seen in one of their glances that which people do not see after a forty-day retreat. After one of their words, I have experienced that which others do not experience in years.

> One finds from a glance of Shams-i Tabrizi, the light of religion
> What is not in ten-day or forty-day retreats.

That was eloquently spoken.

> The Naqshbandis are strange leaders of the caravan.
> They take the caravan by a secret way to Mecca.

---

32. The *qayyum* is the living person having the highest spiritual rank of all sufis on earth. See tract one in Sirhindi's *Mabda' wa-ma'ad*, translated in Arthur Buehler, "Ahmad Sirhindi's Indian Mujaddidi Sufism," in *Journal of the History of Sufism* 4 (2005), 209-228; and *Collected Letters*, 2.76.69-70.

With a lofty inner nature and high aspiration, Naqshbandi shaykhs have established the beginning of the path from inner wayfaring and have traversed outer wayfaring, which is included in the inner wayfaring. "Traveling in the homeland" (*safar dar watan*) is a Naqshbandi expression and a metaphor for this wayfaring. With the method of these notables, it is the shortest path and the closest one for attainment. The end of others' wayfaring is the beginning for Naqshbandis. That is why Naqshbandi shaykhs have said, "the end is included in the beginning."

Briefly, these notables' path is higher than the paths of other shaykhs. God sanctify their innermost beings. This is an extremely high path and the presence and awareness of Naqshbandis is beyond most of the other sufis. It follows that they have said that their connection to God (*nisbat*) is higher than that of others. From this connection to God, they have had their desired presence and awareness. But still there is no place to step nor passage beyond inner and outer wayfaring, attraction to God, and the closeness of God's protégés. Inevitably these Naqshbandi leaders have not reported anything outside of the inner and outer. Nor have they spoken about anything beyond attraction to God and wayfaring. They have spoken with the measure of complete intimacy with God (*kamalat-i walayat*). The folk of God are after annihilation in God and abiding in God (*fana' wa-baqa'*). Whatever they see, they see within themselves and whatever they have discerned, they have done so within themselves. Their bewilderment is within their own existence. "Can't you see what is in yourselves?" [Q. 51:21]

Give thanks to God almighty. These notables, even though they have not reported anything other than the inner, they do not want to become captive to the inner either. They want to negate the inner like the color of the outer. By reason of the otherness of God (*ghayrat*), they negate the inner. Baha'uddin Naqshband said that all that was seen, heard, and known was all other than God. God sanctify his innermost being. With the truth of the word "No" one must negate it [also].

> They are heart-engravers but they do not constrain the heart.
> Every moment they adorn another heart from a wonderful thing beyond.
> Engravers pure of heart engraving.
> Although our heart engraving is pure and of the earth.

Here one should know that there is a secret: the negation of the otherness of God is something else and the non-existence of the otherness of God is yet something else. How different these two are!

As I said before, there is no place to step outside of attraction to God, wayfaring, and inner or outer wayfaring because what is beyond these four pillars of closeness to God are the sources and basics of prophetic perfections. The hand of closeness to God is small compared to that lofty tree. A majority of the companions of the prophets, and a minority of the rest of the peoples who followed them, ended up being guided to the good fortune of following the prophetic inheritance. On this path, which combined attraction to God and wayfaring, they traversed distant way stations. They have stepped into what is beyond wayfaring and attraction to God and have gone completely outside of the circle of shadows, returning to [the place where] the inner is just like the outer. In this station, the flashing disclosure of the Essence, which for others is like a flash of lightning, is continual for them. The matter for these notables is above disclosure, whether flashing or not, because disclosure calls up a kind of shadowness. For these notables, the dot from the shadowness resembles a great mountain.

These notables' work begins with attraction to God and divine love. God's sovereignty be exalted. With God's endless favor, this love overflows moment-by-moment, creating strength and overpowering. By necessity, love of anything other than God vanishes step by step, and related unknown entanglements are gradually removed. The person who experiences this overpowering love of God finds that the love of anything but God totally disappears. Love of God and being a captive of God replaces everything else. Inevitably one's vile personal habits and corrupt character will be completely removed. [These] vile character traits become adorned with praiseworthy ones such that the ten stations are confirmed.[33] Whatever is associated with outer wayfaring becomes trouble-free and any difficult wayfaring and strenuous contemplative practices become easy. This is because love requires a demanding obedience to the Beloved. Perfected love is realized when one arrives at complete obedience. When obedience to the Beloved gradually becomes complete, one realizes a measure of human strength and [wayfaring through] the ten stations becomes easy. One realizes wayfaring in the Beloved, just like with outer wayfaring. Inner wayfaring also comes to an end because the Prophet said, "The lover is with the Beloved."[34] God bless him and his family and give them peace.

Since the Beloved is beyond the inner and outer, the lover must pass the inner and outer in conformity with being together with God (*ma'iyat*). Therefore, the wayfarer must leave behind inner wayfaring and realize the good fortune of being together with God. These notables, with the good fortune of loving God, deal with love, not the outer or inner. However, the inner and outer are within the competence of these notables' affairs. Wayfaring and attraction to God are uninvited guests of their work, but love is

33. The ten stations are (in order): repentance, trusting in God, poverty, patience, gratitude, fear, hope, love, inner knowledge, and satisfaction.

34. This hadith, in the collections of Bukhari and Muslim, is the most often quoted in *Collected Letters*, mentioned twenty times. See the footnote at the beginning of Letter 2.67.

their stock in trade. Obedience to the Beloved is incumbent upon them and is related to performing the dictates of the shariat, which is the way of life (*din*) preferred by God almighty. God bless its friend (Muhammad) and give him peace. The sign of perfection/completion of love comes from their perfection in [performing] the shariat. Perfect performance of the dictates of the shariat is dependent on knowledge (*'ilm*), deeds, and sincerity. This is a sincerity that is realized in all speech and action and in all conditions of rest and action imaginable. It is the good fortune of a sincere person (*mukhlas*).[35]

Returning to the original discussion, I assert that the goal of wayfaring, purification, and attraction to God is cleaning the ego-self from corrupt character traits and vile personal habits. The chief of all base qualities is bondage (*giriftari*) of the ego-self along with [trying] to attain the desires of the ego-self. Therefore, inner wayfaring is necessary, as is transforming bad [character traits] to praiseworthy attributes. Outer wayfaring is outside the goal, and there is no worthwhile aim associated with it because outer bondage is a function of inner bondage. Whatever a person desires, he desires by means of desiring itself. If he wants money and children, he desires it for his own profit and enjoyment. With inner wayfaring, his desiring vanishes by means of the overflowing of love of God almighty. Desire for money and children is included in his desiring and also vanishes. So inner wayfaring is necessary and outer wayfaring, like an uninvited guest, is included in inner wayfaring and becomes easy.

Therefore, the wayfaring of the prophets became restricted to the inner. The outer, by virtue of being included in the inner, became cut off. God bless them and give them peace. Yes! Outer wayfaring is good if one is given an opportunity to traverse [that path]. Without delays one arrives at the end of outer wayfaring. If one does not have that opportunity to traverse [the path] and is impeded by delays, it is possible that outer wayfaring should be considered as something of no benefit and as a hindrance to achieving one's aspiration. Inner wayfaring is valuable, to the extent one is able to traverse, since it is going from badness to goodness. Inner wayfaring is a great blessing because it takes one to the end that is outside of the circle of inner wayfaring. What necessity is there for a wayfarer to contemplatively witness his inner sinful qualities and personal changes in the outer mirror? This is just like purifying one's heart being made known in the imaginal mirror. This attribute is seen in the form of a red light. Why doesn't one make use of one's inner strength and recommend purifying the heart with one's intuition (*firasat*)? There is a famous proverb that says, "What need

35. The commentary explains that *mukhlis* is an enigma to understand and to be a *mukhlis* is to be in great danger. The *mukhlis* has a troublesome kind of sincerity because the ego-self is intact. See Hutaki, *Sharh-i Maktubat*, 595.

is there to spend twelve years at the doctor's?" With true ecstasy (*wijdan*),[36] one will experience the changing of one's states. With intuition one's own health and sickness will be known.

Very well! There is much inner and outer knowledge, disclosures of God, and manifestations (*zuhurat*) in outer wayfaring but all of this goes back to shadows. There is a lot of consolation in resemblances and examples. Inner wayfaring constantly has a connection to shadows according to what has been verified in [my] epistles and letters. Outer wayfaring must be connected to the shadow of the shadow because the outer is like the shadow of the inner and the mirror of the inner appearance.

One should know that the inner states are contemplatively witnessed, while purification, and glorious manifesting [praiseworthy character traits] are made known from there in the outer mirror. An example of this is a person, whether awake or asleep, seeing himself to be a king in the imaginal world or observing himself to be the axial leader of the age (*qutb-i waqt*). In truth, there is no [actual] king or axis [in sleep]; they only exist in the objective world (*dar kharij*). In short, from both waking and sleeping, one can conceive of the potentiality of being a king or axis. A soul (*jani*) should come into alignment so that the matter comes into being from strength, like going from an exchange of messages to an embrace.[37] We are what we are.

Cleansing the ego-self and manifesting gloriously are connected to inner wayfaring. That which is seen in outer wayfaring is the capability and readiness of unburdening oneself of the ego-self and then manifesting [praiseworthy character traits] in a glorious manner. In the objective world, as long as one does not see oneself purified while inner wayfaring or in ecstasy, then one is not purified. In truth, [when one is not purified] one does not have the good fortune of being annihilated in God or having experienced and verified the ten stations. From the seven subtle centers, one obtains nothing but the outer shell. By necessity, inner wayfaring is included in wayfaring to God. Completing wayfaring to God, which is the station of annihilation in God, is connected to the completion of inner wayfaring. Wayfaring in God, which is a few stages after inner wayfaring, [then] becomes manifest.

How can one arrive at felicity? Watch out!
The mountains become sparse.
Beware of fear.

---

36. Here "inner strength" is glossed in Nur Ahmad's interlinear notes.

37. There is an unclear usage of words in the beginning of this sentence in the Nur Ahmad edition. The Arabic translation has, "One must be with humility of spirit (*ruh*) until the matter emerges from strength to deed." See al-Manzalawi al-Qazani's *Maktubat: al-durar al-maknunat al-nafisa*: 2:68.

Oh felicity-affected one! In inner wayfaring, the knowledge and love attachments connected to the essence (*dhat*) of the wayfarer vanish. As the bondage in oneself grows to include bondage of others, it also includes the shadow of the bondage in one's essence. That too vanishes because the bondages of others arise from one's own bondage in oneself, like was explained above. Thus, it is correct that outer wayfaring is traversing within inner wayfaring so the wayfarer only experiences one mode of wayfaring. In the same way, the wayfarer is saved from both self-bondage and the bondage of others. Therefore, according to the extent of this inquiry, the meaning of both inner and outer wayfaring becomes clear without any difficulty because in truth there is both wayfaring in the inner and outer worlds. Wayfaring in the inner world consists of gradually cutting the inner connections. Cutting the outer connections contained in inner wayfaring manifests while wayfaring in the outer world. On the contrary, others' inner and outer wayfaring necessitates difficulties, as explained above. Indeed! Everywhere there is truth one is free from constraint. God almighty is the prosperous one!

Listen carefully! It is said that the appearance of the names and necessary attributes of God is in the mirror of the wayfarer, which is in inner wayfaring. Exalt God's sovereignty! They say that gloriously manifesting [praiseworthy character traits] is known after unburdening oneself of the ego-self. In truth, this is not the appearance of the names and attributes of God nor is it the glorious manifesting after unburdening of the ego-self. Instead, that appearance is the appearance of a shadow of the names and attributes, which is the reason for unburdening oneself of the ego-self and for facilitating cleaning and purification. The explanation is that the beginning is on the side of God, which is appropriate for being the causative origin (*mabda'iyat*). First, the appearance of a shadow of the goal is experienced in the mirror of the seeker so that the darkness of the seeker vanishes and purification and cleaning are realized.[38] When all this happens, then one has completed inner wayfaring.

When the ego-self becomes released, then the capability of glorious manifesting and the possibility of the appearance of God's names and necessary attributes arises. So, with inner wayfaring comes the realization of glorious manifesting [praiseworthy character traits], which is connected to cleaning and purification. Unburdening oneself of the ego-self, which has been imagined to be in outer wayfaring, is only the form of ego-release rather than the reality of ego-release. Up to here in inner wayfaring, realizing the unburdening of the ego-self and appearance of the names and attributes in the mirror of the seeker can be imagined as the shaykhs have said.

From this explanation, it necessarily follows that the shadow's con-

38. The goal here is for a manifestation of the names and attributes of God.

nection breaks off first. As long as a shadow of the goal is not reflected in the mirror of the wayfarer, one cannot conceive of breaking off from what is other than the goal. But after the realization of breaking off, one is connected with the origin (the names and attributes). According to the shaykhs, a person having a connection has precedence. They must mean a shadowy connection. [Another group says that] a person who has broken connections is preferred [to one having connections]. In this case, they must mean a connection with the origin. The dispute between the two groups comes back to one of words.

Shaykh Abu Sa'id al-Kharraz (d. 277/890 or 286/899) was delayed in this station saying, "As long as we do not see it we do not experience it, and as long as we do not experience it we do not see it.[39] I do not know which was first." God sanctify his innermost being. It is known that experiencing the shadow is before liberation [from the shadows], and experiencing the origin is after liberation. There is no doubt. It is like in the morning before sunrise, and the appearance of shadows [created by] the rays of sunlight until the darkness recedes from the world and it becomes clear. The sunrise happens after the vanishing of the darkness and realization of clarity. So the appearance of the sun's shadows happens before the darkness vanishes just as darkness vanishes before the sunrise. It this way, the rise of kings is beautiful after being unburdened from the ego-self and subsequent purification. Without any foreshadowing of ego-release and subsequent purification, it is hard to imagine. However, one cannot imagine that the being unburdened from the ego-self and purification do not precede their rise. The truth appeared. Controversy and doubt disappeared. God almighty is the Inspired One.

Introduction to the sufi path: Letter 2.71

This letter is written to Muhammad Sa'id (d. 1070/1660), Sirhindi's second son who studied with Muhammad Tahir Lahori and Muhammad Tahir's elder brother.[40] In this letter, Sirhindi clarifies some of his own interpretations of contemplative experiences. He deftly explains how, from the perspective of intoxication, something appears as an ocean while from the larger context of sobriety after intoxication it appears as a dot. Again, he emphasizes the difference between the path of intimates of God (*awliya'*) and the prophetic path. It is easy to associate ascent with intimacy with God along with the phrase "There is no god but God" and descent with prophet-

39. The Urdu translation has "as long as one does not cut oneself off from other than God then one will not realize the goal, and as long as one does not realize the goal then one will not be able to cut oneself off from other than God." See Sirhindi, *Maktubat,* trans. Zawwar Husayn, 2:151.

40. There are twenty-four letters addressed to Muhammad Sa'id in *Collected Letters*.

hood along with the phrase "and Muhammad is God's Messenger." But this is not the case. *Both* protégés of God and prophets are involved in both ascent and descent. The difference, not explained explicitly in this letter, is that the prophets ascend much higher and achieve genuine perfections of Essence before descending, while the intimates of God only realize perfections of the shadows before their descent.[41]

Letter 2.71

There is no god but God and Muhammad is God's Messenger. The first part of this phrase, "There is no god but God," includes an affirmation of the level of the Necessity [of Being] (*martaba-yi wujub*), who is almighty and holy. The appearance of the level of Necessity in imaginal form (*surat-i mithali*), which is contemplatively witnessed in the form of a dot, is closer than the appearance of the level of Necessity seen in a long and wide form. Although at the level of Necessity, the dot and the circle cannot be contained. Nor is there scope for length, breadth, or depth. This is why in the disclosed appearance (*surat-i kashifi*) the phrase "There is no god but God" appears just like a dot.

The phrase "and Muhammad is God's Messenger," alludes to calling people to God, which is related to physical bodies and essential natures (*jawahir*),[42] where space (lit. length and width) is tangible. The imaginal form of this station, from the perspective of disclosure, is necessarily experienced as having length and breadth. In this station the wayfarer, because of the remaining intoxication, experiences the phrase "and Muhammad is God's Messenger" like an ocean. The phrase "There is no god but God" is imagined to be like a dot next to that ocean.

It is from there that this poor one (Sirhindi), because of the remaining intoxication [in me], has asserted and written that the phrase "and Muhammad is God's Messenger" is an ocean. Because next to that, the phrase "There is no god but God" is like a dot. In this station Ibn al-'Arabi has said, "The Muhammadan union (*jam'*) is more whole (*ajma'*) than a divine union without end. Exalt God's sovereignty." Because of God almighty's favor and the expanse of incomparableness on the level of Necessity, a ray is emitted. An ineffable encompassing of the level of Necessity manifests. In spite of the extent of space, the entire world is created, ordering both its individual and indivisible aspects. The things that were like an ocean without end, [that the wayfarer] first experienced as a dot, now are experienced as an ocean without end. The ocean [of the world] appears smaller than the individual and indivisible aspects.

41. See Hutaki, *Sharh-i Maktubat*, 650.

42. Zawwar Husayn's Urdu translation has outward appearances (*zawahir*) instead of *jawahir*, which appears to fit the context better.

From this place, one should not suppose that intimacy with God (*walayat*) is preferable to prophethood because intimacy with God pertains to "There is no god but God" and prophethood pertains to "and Muhammad is God's Messenger." I assert that prophethood consists of the realization of both holy phrases. The prophetic ascent is associated with "There is no god but God" and the descent is associated with "and Muhammad is God's Messenger." So the aggregate of these two phrases is the realization of the station of prophethood, not just the second part like most people imagine. It is [also mistakenly] believed that "There is no god but God" especially pertains to intimacy with God. That is not so. In the station of intimacy with God, one realizes both phrases because there is both ascent and descent. One also achieves the station of prophethood through ascent and descent. In short, the station of intimacy with God is the shadow of the station of prophethood. The perfections of being intimate with God are the shadows of the perfections of prophethood.

Whatever one says in the station of intoxication is excused. I have shared intoxication with them and therefore in some of my letters I have written that "There is no god but God" pertains to the station of intimacy with God and "and Muhammad is God's Messenger" is associated with the station of prophethood. Intoxication is also a great blessing if it ends up in sobriety and in true submission to God after infidelity of the path (*kufr-i tariqat*). "Oh Lord do not blame us for what we have forgotten or have done in error." [Q. 2.286] With the alms of your lover, Muhammad, God bless him and his family and give them peace. God have mercy on God's servant who says "amen."

Introduction to Reprimanding a beginner Letter 2.77

This letter is written to Mawlana Hasan Baraki, a student of Ahmad Baraki before becoming a disciple of Sirhindi and being authorized to teach by him.[43] Shaykh Hasan has misunderstood the nature of sufi experience, has criticized sufi shaykhs on this basis, and in turn is being strongly reprimanded by his shaykh Ahmad Sirhindi. Hasan thought that both the inner and outer worlds would be annihilated when experiencing annihilation in God, and one would be unable to speak. In annihilation it is the five subtle centers that are annihilated not the outer senses. He also criticizes other *wujudi* shaykhs for thinking that the physical world is simply a manifestation of God because they perceive it to be so through their contemplative witnessing. Sirhindi explains that at a certain stage of practice this is natural way of perceiving their experience. They have to go through this stage. When they mature, they will be with God inside and with the world outwardly, realizing that these are two

43. There are three letters addressed to Mawlana Hasan Baraki in *Collected Letters*.

different realms. In any case, Hasan is not in a position to be critical of others; he has enough work to do on himself.

The commentator, Nasrullah Hutaki, aptly remarks how a person who reaches the shadow of an attribute, the person who reaches an attribute, the person who reaches the qualities and aspects, and the person who reaches ineffability are all called "realized" (*muntahi*). He then illustrates the point by saying, "Two knees of a mouse are quite different than the two knees of a camel although they both have knees."[44]

LETTER 2.77

God be praised and God give peace to the servants whom God has chosen. A noble letter from my brother Shaykh Hasan arrived. It had the fragrance of describing the shariat regulations and the integrity of the shariat. God almighty better his condition. May you be pleased.

You had written that a well-known way of proceeding on the sufi path, believed by sufi wayfarers to be our understanding, is that the beginner must recollect God until the heart is speaking God's name. He must continue recollecting God until it is superseded by an abode of inspirations (*ilhamat*) and disclosures of God (*tajalliyat*). The wayfarer arrives at the station of annihilation in God, the first step of intimacy with God (*walayat*). Sufis say that annihilation in God is beyond anything the wayfarer sees and knows. What they call the "other" becomes extinguished. Nothing remains in the vision and knowledge of the wayfarer except God almighty. They say that this experience is contemplative witnessing (*shuhud wa-mushahada*), something beyond what is [normally] seen. In their opinion, the goal is to see God almighty. They do not see that which they call the "other." Those who see duality are called "polytheists of the path" (sing. *mushrik-i tariqat*).

You have written that you have this experiential inner knowledge and have been upset by knowledge like this. If the goal of sufis is to see God with physical and/or inner eyes and this witnessing and vision results in an intuitive awareness (*shu'ur*), then they too are polytheists of the path. If they do not mean having intuitive awareness then on what basis and to whom can they report anything? You wrote that what they saw in all its aspects, whether an outward disclosure (*tajalli-yi suri*), an essential disclosure, a disclosure of light, or something else that they saw, was the Essence of God. God be exalted. That which they call the "other" they consider as God's appearance.[45]

---

44. See Hutaki, *Sharh-i Maktubat*, 659-660. He attributes this phrase to Rumi but it is not in any concordance of the *Mathnawi* in this form.

45. This means that they consider God's creation to be the appearance of God. For Sirhindi this is a major error of perception, which he associates with those who assert the ontological unity of being (*wahdat-i wujud*).

For you, these considerations are without benefit and irrelevant to the matter at hand. [Indeed] these are against the noble text. The Qur'anic verses, "There is nothing like Him." [Q. 42:11] and "The perceptions do not comprehend Him" [Q. 6:103] provide evidence for the [correct] meaning. So what does this sufi group see and what do they know because they say that they do not see anything other than God, exalted and sublime. They do not know. This situation involves contemplative witnessing. But all of this is just thoughts that the person, his family, and peers have concocted, whether they do not see anything other than God or not.

You should know and be aware that all this long discussion and inappropriate criticism of the shaykhs of the path that you have done is because you do not understand the goal of these notables. God sanctify their innermost beings. The assertion of the unity of contemplative witnessing (*tawhid-i shuhudi*), literally meaning "seeing one," is known to be associated with forgetting all other than God. One imperative of these notables' path is that if one does not [perceive oneness and forget all other than God], then one cannot escape the entanglement of what is other than God. You scorn this good fortune along with others that have had this good fortune. The witnessing and inner vision (*ru'yat*) communicated by notable shaykhs who have experienced the ineffable presence of God almighty pertains to the level of transcendence (*tanzih*). [This experience] is beyond the confines of awareness stemming from the tangible world. The good fortune of experiencing the presence of God (*hudur*) in the world is the special domain of shaykhs' inner being. The outer world is inevitably [experienced as] duality all of the time. Therefore, it is said that if in the macrocosm there is a polytheist and someone who asserts the unity of God (*muwahhid*), then in the microcosm of the human being there is also a combination of a polytheist and someone who asserts the unity of God.

The [person with a] completed interior (*batin-i kamil*) is always someone who asserts the unity of God and whose outer manifestation is a polytheist. Therefore, the person with a completed interior is with God, exalted and sublime. His exterior is involved with what his family and peers have concocted. One should not consider this to be unlawful. It is criticism based on a lack of understanding. By all means, you should not talk like this. You should fear God's jealousy. Exalt God's sovereignty.

Apparently present-day charlatans are able to confuse you. You should pay attention to respected sufis. It would be worthwhile for you to talk to them about the novelties and inventions that these charlatans [have introduced to sufi practice]. Experienced sufis have established these matters and this path is certainly the way. Mere talk is inappropriate in these circumstances. You have seen in my letters and epistles how much has been written on asserting the unity of contemplative witnessing and how I have established the requisites of the path.

You should have politely asked me to explain these manners. This is a rose that has blossomed since the death of the late Mawlana Ahmad [Baraki] (who was his previous teacher). God have mercy on him. During his lifetime, this kind of talk would have never come out of you. It is good that you happened to write and you were reprimanded. From now on whatever happens to you, write! Do not remark on your health or lack thereof. If you are well it is because of happiness and if you are not feeling well, it is a result of your waking up. In any case, do not be lazy in writing. After a year, your letter came with a caravan. Once a year crucial advice is necessary. When you do not write or inquire about things you close the channel of communication.

You had asked whether the heart was an exterior aggregate (*jumla-yi zahir*) or an interior aggregate. I have written about the interior and exterior of a person of inner realization (*'arif*) in a detailed letter to Mulla 'Abdulhayy.[46] I will ask him to send it to you. From there you can comment. You had also asked about a path that was without disclosures and divine unveilings (*kashifiyat*), and in what ways one could become acquainted with the intermediate and advanced stages of this path. Know that it is sufficient for a wayfarer who does not know about his own states to be in the service of a completed and completion-bestowing shaykh who sees the path, knows the path, and who knows the state of that wayfarer. With the shaykh's advice he will get to know the intermediate and advanced stages of the path. If that shaykh gives a disciple some kind of permission to teach (there are restricted and unrestricted permissions), the states of the disciple's students will become the mirror of the disciple. Then the deficiencies and perfections of the disciple will become evident. Another indication concerning the inner experiential knowledge of an advanced seeker is that there is no need for anything other than God almighty. In his purified heart there is no need for anything other than God. The end of the path (where an advanced seeker is) has many levels, one above the other. The first step in the advanced stage is when one recollects God and God almighty approves.

You had written that the kind of knowledge that is consoling for a confused person is knowledge of the shariat. That is, each legal judgment is a small doorway to God that delivers one to the city of the goal. It is a sign from that King of no signs, that very place which is in full view [facing the eye of the heart]. We are traveling but whom will we see? We go to God so that the whole world will be behind us. Your knowledge is very essential, sublime, and gives hope. Reading this inner knowledge has made me very happy. There is no discordance like in the first letter. God almighty has

46. It may have been an unpublished letter. The letters written to 'Abdulhayy are 1.277, 1.291, 1.304, 2.7, 2.37. Letter 1.291 is in this book.

delivered you to the goal by this very path.

You had asked about some men and women who had come wanting you to initiate them, but who had purchased food and clothing with illicit funds.[47] Instead of avoiding [the charging of interest] they said that they were able to find a legal loophole (*hila-yi shari'i*). You asked whether or not to initiate them.

Initiate them and encourage them to avoid what is forbidden. Perhaps the blessing of the lineage (*tariqat*) will get them out of this mistake. You asked another question about those two white flags in the direction of the east following one another in the sky and have asked for an explanation. I have already explained this in a letter written to other companions. I will ask Mulla 'Abdulhayy to also send you this if God almighty wills.[48] You had also asked about finishing the recitation of the Qur'an, performing supererogatory prayers (*namaz-i nafl*), saying "Praise the Lord," saying "There is no god but God" and whether the reward in doing those things with one's parents, teacher, brothers is greater than doing them alone. You should know that doing them with others is better because it benefits others and oneself. Doing them alone only benefits oneself. Perhaps doing those actions by means of others is accepted [by God]. Peace.

Introduction to types of seekers on the path: Letter 1.292

This letter is addressed to 'Abdulhamid Bangali (d. 1050/1640 in Mangalkot, Bengal), otherwise known as Hamid Bengali, a jurist who spent a year with Ahmad Sirhindi before receiving permission to teach others.[49] Here the discussion is on the types of seekers on the path and the appropriate guidance for them. Sirhindi begins by noting those desiring God (*murid*) and those desired by God (*murad*) corresponding respectively to a wayfarer ecstatically attracted to God (*salik-i majdhub*) of a non-Muhammadan disposition and an ecstatic one wayfaring (*majdhub-i salik*) of a Muhammadan disposition. Both of these kinds of seekers arrive closer to God through the four-fold Naqshbandi practices of recollection of God, spiritual companionship with the guide (*suhbat*), the intimate bond between the shaykh and disciple (*rabita*), and contemplative exercises (*riyadat*). The completed and completion-bestowing shaykh facilitates all these four practices so the seeker can arrive at the goal. Spiritual companionship with the shaykh is not only a prerequisite but also a matter of following the sunnat since the Companions are defined as those whose spiritual companionship was with

47. The footnotes explain that the money came from charging of interest on loans, which is forbidden in Islamic law.

48. See letter 2.68 in *Collected Letters*.

49. Five letters were addressed to him in Sirhindi's *Collected Letters*, including 2.46, which is included in this translation.

the Prophet in person.[50]

For the disciple to receive any benefit from this spiritual companionship, he or she must behave in an appropriately respectful and beautiful manner. This is the domain of what is called "*adab*" in Islamic cultures, but as Sirhindi explains, there are many more rules and considerations for beautiful behavior in the context of the master-disciple relationship, just like there are when in the presence of a worldly king. It appears that some of the rules for properly beautiful behavior come from the Persian court.[51] The goal of beautiful behavior is to improve one's morals, to assist the student control his or her ego-self, and to facilitate sufi wayfaring. A proper spiritual and psychological bearing is critical to receive the subtle energies of the sufi mentor.

Although it is standard practice for the aspirant to defer totally to the shaykh and to give him his total attention, this is only because of the unruly ego-self. Once one's ego-self has been tamed and other qualities cultivated, the student is in a position to trust his own intuitions, and *should* disagree with the shaykh if these intuitions do not coincide with those of his shaykh. In the contemporary Western world, there is often an assumption that each person can be his own spiritual guide. Some even suggest that a group of people can progress spiritually by reading Ibn al-'Arabi's arcane *Meccan Revelations*.[52] There is no apparent awareness of the wily nature of the ego-self that requires taming *before* one can access one's inner guide. Instead of seeking authentic guidance, there is a tendency for egoic individuality in the modern world, where there are less and less cultural resources to recognize authentic spiritual authority (even though this has always been a challenging task under the best of circumstances). Sirhindi ends the letter reminding the reader that the purpose of the shaykh is to kill and enliven, that is, to kill the dominance of the disciples' ego-self so they can truly come alive after their egos become tranquil.

Letter 1.292

In the name of God, the most compassionate and merciful. Praise God for educating us in the prophetic way of conducting ourselves and for guiding

50. Cf. Uways al-Qarani who never physically saw the Prophet.

51. See Buehler, *Sufi Heirs*, 149.

52. See James Morris, "Ibn 'Arabi's Rhetoric of Realisation: Keys in Reading and "Translating" the *Meccan Illuminations* Parts 1-2 in *Journal of the Muhyiddin Ibn 'Arabi Society* 33 (2003), 54–99, and 34 (2004), 103–45. Note fn 6 on page 57. Ibn al-'Arabi wrote that one could progress on the path by reading eight pages of his *Meccan Illuminations* per day (communication with Mahmud Erol Kiliç, Istanbul, Bayram, 2010). This is another way of saying that *very* advanced seekers can progress by reading.

us in Muhammadan character. God give perfect blessings and peace to him and his family.

Know that there are two kinds of wayfarers on this path: 1) those desiring God (*murid*) and 2) those desired by God (*murad*). The path of love and attraction to God blesses those desired by God as they are strongly attracted and carried along, arriving at the highest goal. They will learn the requisite behavioral conduct with or without mediation [with God]. If they make a mistake, they will become aware of it immediately and take corrective action. If they need to have a living shaykh it will not be necessary to run around looking for him. All in all, the favor of the Eternal is the guarantor of these notables. Exalt God's sovereignty. With or without [apparent] cause, [by God's grace] whatever they do will suffice. "God chooses those he desires." [Q. 42:13]

For those who desire God, their task is difficult without the mediation of a completed and completion-bestowing shaykh who is blessed with attraction to God and can teach contemplative practices required for wayfaring. He will have experienced annihilation and abiding in God in addition to having complete realizations of traveling to and in God (*sayr ila Allah wa-sayr fi 'llah*), traveling through God by God (*sayr 'an Allah billah*), and traveling in the material world with God (*sayr fi 'l-ashya'*). If his attraction to God precedes his wayfaring (*suluk*) and he has trained those desired by God, then he is a very rare and special guide (*kibrit-i ahmar*). His words are curative; his gaze is healing; he brings dead hearts to life. This is all connected to his exalted spiritual power (*tawajjuh*). With this subtle [focus of] attention he revives stagnant souls (sing. *jan*). If someone is not fortunate enough to find such a master, an attracted wayfarer (*salik-i majdhub*) will do since he can also train those in need. Through his mediation they can reach annihilation and abiding in God.

> Although the sky is much lower than the Throne,
> It is still high above the earth.

If by God's favor a seeker finds a completed and completion-bestowing shaykh, then it is incumbent that the seeker considers the shaykh's noble existence like a noble treasure, fully supporting him. The seeker's own happiness or unhappiness is recognized in what pleases or displeases the shaykh. In short, the seeker's desires conform to what pleases the teacher. There is a prophetic hadith that says, "No one will become a believer until his desires conform to what I have brought, (that is, the Qur'an and sunnat)."[53] God give the most complete and perfect blessings to him and his family.

---

53. A hadith mentioned once in *Collected Letters,* and found in al-Bagawi, *Sharh al-sunna*, #104; al-Daylami, *al-Fardaus*, #7791; Ibn Abu 'Asim, *al-Sunna*, #15 [MR].

Know that the requirements of this path include behaving in a beautiful manner (*adab*) in spiritual companionship [with the shaykh] and following certain conditions so that the seeker can benefit from the shaykh. Without this, there are no results from spiritual companionship or fruitful outcomes from the gathering. For this reason, I will write some necessary conditions and rules of acting in a beautiful manner. You should listen very carefully!

Know that the seeker must focus the face of his heart [on the shaykh] and be in his service, not being distracted by anything else. One should not perform supererogatory acts of worship (*nawafil*) or remembrance exercises without his permission. One should not look at anyone but the shaykh, but sit totally focused on him in his presence. Unless he says so, one should not do any recollection exercises. In the shaykh's presence one should only perform the prescribed ritual prayers and the additional sunnat prayers.

It has been related that Jahangir's minister was standing in front of him when, by accident, the minister's attention fell upon his clothing as he grasped his belt. While this was happening, the Sultan noticed that the minister's gaze was no longer focused on him. He angrily shouted, "I cannot tolerate that you are my minister and are distracted by your belt in my presence." One should understand that the world has its situations [like that of the Sultan], making it necessary to behave in a subtle manner.

[Likewise], the means (that is, the shaykh) to arrive at God will necessarily involve behaving in an assiduously beautiful manner. Whenever possible, one should never stand where one's shadow will fall on the shaykh's clothing or his shadow. Nor should one step on the shaykh's prayer rug, do ablutions in his special place of ablution, or use any of his special [ablution] jars. Nor should the seeker drink, eat, talk with anyone, or look at anyone but the shaykh in his presence. In the shaykh's absence one should not extend one's feet toward where he usually sits nor spit in that direction.

Whatever the shaykh says is perceived as correct, even though it may appear otherwise. Whatever he does is inspired by God (*az ilham*) and is done with God's permission. Given this, there is no reason to find fault with the shaykh. It is possible that some aspects of his inspiration are unintentionally in error. A mistake from inspiration is like an error in striving for a correct legal decision (*khata-yi ijtihadi*). Blame and refutation are not permissible. Likewise, a love for the shaykh is created. From the viewpoint of the lover, whatever the Beloved (the shaykh) says or does is loved also. Therefore, there is no place for criticizing the shaykh. One should obey the shaykh in large or small matters, whether in eating, wearing clothing, or sleeping. In ritual prayer one should pray in the manner the shaykh prays; in jurisprudence one should do as the shaykh does.

One who is with the Beloved has everything
And does not need to look at anything else.

There is also no need to find fault with the shaykh's behavior, even over a trifling matter, because criticizing, except that which is clearly prohibited, keeps one from receiving benefits. In this exalted group, the worst thing anyone can do is look for faults. God save us from that great affliction. Do not request miracles from your shaykh, whether that request comes from your heart or from evil temptations. There are no reports that any believer has ever asked a prophet for a miracle. Those who ask for miracles are unbelievers and deniers. (Rumi says),

Miracles are for the sake of conquering enemies.
Scent is for attracting the heart.
Faith is not based on miracles.
A sweet scent attracts honeybees.[54]

If there is any doubt in one's heart, then one should be in the continuous company of the shaykh. If this does not solve it then one should consider that it is one's own shortcoming and not associate any deficiency with the shaykh. Anything that happens [to the seeker] is not hidden from the shaykh, and the seeker should ask the shaykh to interpret these events. Any interpretation that comes to the seeker himself should also be checked with the shaykh to ascertain its validity. Any inspirations (*kashuf*) that come to the seeker should not be trusted, because in this world truth is mixed with falsehood as right is mixed with wrong. Without necessity and permission one should not be apart from the shaykh because to prefer otherwise is negating one's purpose. One should not raise one's voice higher than the shaykh's nor talk to him in a loud voice because this is bad manners. The divine effulgence and insight that one experiences should be imagined as coming by means of the shaykh. If it happens that some divine effulgence [appears to be] coming from other shaykhs, one should attribute this effulgence as coming via one's own shaykh.

Know that the shaykh is the totality of perfections and divine energy (*fuyud*). The special divine energy from the shaykh is suitable only for a seeker with special awareness. A completed shaykh whose overflowing presence manifests outwardly can deliver this special divine energy to the seeker. There is a subtle center of the shaykh corresponding to this divine energy that manifests in the shaykh's appearance. In order to test [the shaykh], a

---

54. See Balkhi/Rumi, *Mathnawi*, 3:341 (In the six-volume *Mathnawi*, Vol. 6 verses 1176-1177 because the couplets are out of order). The miracles here are prophetic miracles, *mu'jizat*, not the out-of-ordinary events that happen around non-prophets.

seeker may imagine that the divine energy of this subtle center is from another shaykh. This is a huge error. God keep us from slipping like this, while maintaining confidence and love of the shaykh in deference to the Prince of the Messengers. God bless him and his family and give them peace.

"Behaving in a beautiful manner (*adab*) is everything on the path," is a very famous saying.[55] No one without beautiful behavior will realize God. If a seeker has some manners and has deficient knowledge, he is bound to fall short in his behavior or another weakness will cause him to fail when trying [to do something]. This is forgiven, but he must recognize his shortcomings. God forbid if one does not follow the rules of behaving in a beautiful manner and does not know his deficiencies. Then he is blocked from the blessings of these noble ones.

> Whoever did not have good fortune
> Did not benefit from looking at the Prophet's face.

Indeed, a seeker who receives the blessing of spiritual energy (*tawajjuh*) from a shaykh and who experiences annihilation and abiding in God, has inspirations, and exhibits intuition (*firasat*) will have [other] shaykhs testifying to his perfection and completeness. This seeker has arrived at the place where he can disagree with his shaykh on some matters of inspiration and act on the requirements of his own inspirations. It has been verified that those near the shaykh can refute him because these particular seekers at this time have left the circle of conformity (*taqlid*). For the seeker to conform would be to go against his own truth. Can't you see that the companions of the Prophet refuted him in matters of independent judgment and non-Qur'anic legal decisions? Sometimes the Companions were correct. Hence there is the saying, "It is not hidden from those who know." God bless and give peace to him and them.

Clearly it is permissible for a seeker, having realized the level of completion, to disagree with the shaykh. This seeker is also far removed from bad manners because [in acting according to his own inspirations] there is still beautiful behavior. The companions of the Prophet acted with completely beautiful behavior. They conformed assiduously [to the Prophetic example]. It was wrong for Abu Yusuf, [the most important student of Abu Hanifa, the founder-figure of the Hanafi school of jurisprudence], after achieving the level of independent legal reasoning, to conform to [the decisions of] Abu Hanifa. God almighty bless both of them. The correct thing to do was to follow his own opinion, not that of Abu Hanifa. A famous saying of Imam Abu Yusuf is, "For six months, I disputed with Abu Hanifa over the question of who created the Qur'an."

---

55. This phrase, *at-tariq kulluhu adab*, is attributed to Abu Hafs 'Amr ibn Salama al-Haddad al-Naysaburi (d. 260/874). See Buehler, *Sufi Heirs*, 148 fn 3.

You may have heard that the perfection of a skill is the result of joining together many thoughts. If [an area of knowledge or skill] rests on one thought then nothing can be added to it. What used to be the science of Arabic grammar in the time of Sibawayh (d. ca. 180/796) has today been perfected with a thousand-fold increase of differences of opinions and perspectives. Since Sibawayh laid the foundation [of Arabic grammar] the greatness is his. Predecessors have preference but the succeeding ones have perfection and completion. This is like the hadith, "My community is like the rain. I do not know who is better, the first ones or the last ones."[56]

Conclusion

This is to relieve the doubts of some seekers. Know that it is said, "The shaykh enlivens or kills." The station of being a shaykh requires enlivening or putting to death. The meaning of enlivening is enlivening the spirit (*ruh*), not the body, and likewise the meaning of putting to death means killing the ego-self not physically killing. The meaning of life and death is annihilation and abiding in God, which seekers realize at the station of intimacy with God (*walayat*) and perfection respectively. An exemplary shaykh (*shaykh-i muqtada'*) is required to guarantee these two stations (annihilation and abiding in God). Therefore, a shaykh has to deal with [spiritually] enlivening or putting to death.[57] Physically enlivening or killing is not the work of a person with the rank of shaykh. Like a magnet, an exemplary shaykh attracts those who are in resonance with him. They run after him like a cat chasing a mouse and receive what they demand from him. Performing miracles is not for attracting seekers. They are attracted because of their essential connection [with the shaykh]. Anyone who does not have such a connection with these notables is cut off from benefiting from their perfections, even if he or she saw a thousand miracles. The situation of Abu Jahil and Abu Lahab is proof of this.[58] You must get this. Concerning the truth of the unbelievers, God almighty said, "If they saw every verse they would still not believe it; so that when they come to argue with you the unbelievers say, "This is just old fairy tales."" [Q. 6:25] Peace.

---

56. A hadith found in al-Tirmidhi's *Sunan al-Tirmidhi*, #2869; Ahmad b. Hanbal, *al-Musnad*, 3:130, 143, 4:119; Ibn Hibban, *al-Sahih*, #7226 [MR], mentioned once in *Collected Letters*. Note Samuela Pagani's analysis of predecessors and successors, [T]he existence of "renewers" proves that successors (*khalaf*s) can be on a par with precursors (*salaf*s) in her "Renewal before Reformism: 'Abd al-Ghani al-Nabulusi's Reading on Ahmad Sirhindi's Ideas on *Tajdid*," in *Journal of the History of Sufism* 5 (2007), 310.

57. Here a repetitive sentence is omitted.

58. Abu Jahil and Abu Lahab were archenemies of Muhammad.

Introduction to the End is Included in the Beginning Letter 1.200

This letter is addressed to Mulla Shakibi Isfahani (d. 1022/1613),[59] a poet in the company of 'Abdurrahman Khan-i Khanan (d. 1037/1627), a noted poet himself and Akbar's deputy (*wakil*) to whom Ahmad Sirhindi wrote thirteen letters. This letter outlines the basics of the Naqshbandi path, differentiating it from other sufi paths. Working on the subtle centers, beginning with the purification of the heart subtle center, Naqshbandis proceed toward God in intoxication. Others begin with cleansing the ego-self and end with purification of the heart subtle center, hence the Naqshbandi adage, "the end (of other paths) is included in the beginning (of the Naqshbandi path)."

This letter has Sirhindi doing an extended, and very creative, interpretation of a story in Jami's *Fragrances of Intimacy*. The interpretation allows him to communicate some intricacies of the Naqshbandi path to Mulla Shakibi, who was apparently beyond the elementary stages of wayfaring. Sirhindi underlines the Naqshbandi path, represented by two Turkmen, and an ordinary sufi wayfarer, Husayn Qussab. If there is a moral to the story, it is to appreciate the untrodden nature of the Naqshbandi path and the crucial role of Naqshbandi shaykhs in helping seekers negotiate their way in this trackless and dangerous wilderness to reach the goal.

Letter 1.200

Thanks to God, Lord of the worlds, who blesses and gives peace to the Master of the Messengers (Muhammad) and his entire pure family. You have written concerning some expressions in the *Fragrances of Intimacy* that are generally difficult to understand. These should be explained because some words are shocking. O master! 'Aynulqudat Hamadani (mart. 526/1132) used to say in explaining words from the *Fragrances of Intimacy* that those without the guidance of a shaykh are proceeding along an untrodden path. "Some of them sheltered themselves in an overpowering state, their intoxication protecting them (lit. providing shade for their heads). Whoever was sensible and prudent was destroyed (lit. their heads were cut off)."

The purpose of a trodden path (*rah-i masluk*) is [to provide] a way of proceeding, for example, traversing the ten well-known stations (from repentance to satisfaction) in an orderly and methodical manner.[60] God almighty knows best. In this method (*tariq*), cleansing the ego-self comes before purifying the heart. This gift is conditional upon repentance. The untrodden path is characterized by attraction to God and love (*mahabbat*),

59. Two letters were written to Mulla Shakibi Isfahani in *Collected Letters*.

60. The ten stations are: repentance, trusting in God, poverty, patience, gratitude, fear, hope, love, inner knowledge, and satisfaction. In this system one cannot go beyond the last station of satisfaction.

where one purifies the heart before cleansing the ego-self. It is a path for a chosen few and not dependent on repentance. Such is the way of beloveds (*mahbuban*) and those desired by God (*muradan*). In contrast, the trodden path is the way of lovers (*muhibbin*) and those desiring God (*muridin*).

Some had an intensity of attraction to God and overflowing love characterized by an overwhelming intoxication that protected them from the evil of inner and outer demons (*shayatin*) and from getting lost, even though they did not have a guide. Due to the grace of God, they received guidance and arrived at the true goal. Exalt God's sovereignty. It was different for those who were sober, that is, those who did not have an intense attraction to God and an overpowering love in their inner reality. Enemies of religion cut them off from the path and destroyed them as they became entangled in eternal death because they did not have a guide.

Husayn Qassab uses two Turkmen as an allusion and symbol of those in overpowered states.[61] He relates (from *Fragrances of Intimacy*), "We were traveling on the road in a large caravan when all of a sudden two Turkmen left the caravan and set out on an untraveled path . . ." until the end of the story.[62] The path on which the large caravan was traveling is the well-traveled path (*rah-i suluk*). This is the path that traverses the ten well-known stations in an orderly and methodical manner that most sufi shaykhs, especially the early ones, traveled to reach their destinations.

The untrodden path taken by the two Turkmen, and by Husayn Qassab who followed them, is the path of attraction to God and love, which is a more direct way to arrive at the goal (*wusul*) than the attested well-trodden path. The beginning of the untrodden path is tasting and tranquility, which is the reason for absence (*ghaybat*) from one's senses and for being distracted from one's perceptions.[63] The metaphor for this state is nightfall. This is because this absence involves forgetting creation while including the presence and feeling of the Creator. The moon alludes to that presence and feeling [of the Creator]. Bless God almighty.

This station requires elucidation so listen carefully. The organizing principle of the physical body (*jasad*) is the spirit subtle center (*ruh*) and the heart subtle center is responsible for the strength of the physical frame

---

61. The Turkmen are Mahmud Ma'shuq Tusi and Amir 'Ali 'Abu, each of whom has an entry in Jami, *Nafahat*, 314-316. Both are mentioned in 'Aynulqudat's letters, Ibid., 808.

62. There is no biographical information concerning Husayn Qassab other than his mention in Jami, *Nafahat*, 315.

63. According to the late Shaykh Ma'sum Naqshbandi (d. 2007), in letter 1.290 *ghaybat* is the experience of "everything perishes except the face of God" referring to Q. 28:88. In this letter the experience of *ghaybat* is the result of love and ecstatic attraction to God (*jadhba*).

(*qalab*). Physical strength comes from the strength of the spirit, and physical sensations utilize the light of the heart. It is inevitable when one focuses the attention of the heart and spirit toward God that laziness finds a way to control and monitor one's physical body/frame. Being attracted to God in the beginning when one is inexperienced is a necessary part of the process. This is the reason for not being aware of one's senses (the absence mentioned above), becoming distracted from one's perceptions, and a strong sluggishness in the limbs of the body such that one throws oneself on the ground involuntarily.[64] It is this state that the esteemed Shaykh Muhyiddin Ibn al-'Arabi (d. 638/1240 Damascus) mentioned in his *Meccan Revelations* [defining it] as listening to music with the spirit (*sama'-i ruhi*). God bless his inner heart. Another kind of listening to music is that which involves dance and whirling, which he labeled as "naturally listening to music" (*sama'-i tabi'i*). He forbade the latter, which involved exaggerated, physical movements. It has been verified that this outer, physical absence (*ghaybat-i suri*) contains an inner, essential presence (*hudur-i ma'nawi*) just as a physical lack of awareness includes a spirit awareness, which can be rightly interpreted [metaphorically] as the moon.

Returning to the original topic (the story told by Husayn Qassab), one should know that black clouds concealing the moon is a metaphor for the appearance of human attributes, which obscures a beginner's consciousness and awareness of God's presence. This concealing [of awareness and presence] continues until the intermediate stage. Intermediates do not experience concealing, even though there is still some covering up. It could be that this is what is meant (in the story), "In the middle of the night, the moon came out again from the clouds and I resumed following the footprints of those two brave men" (the aforementioned Turkmen). This is because the state of expansion (*bast*) is the time of presence and awareness. It becomes the path of light and one travels more quickly. When morning comes, that is, when absence from one's senses and being distracted from one's perceptions disappears, then presence and awareness gain strength along with a focusing of attention on creation. The metaphor for this presence is the sunrise.

The mountain coming into view (that they are climbing in the story) is human existence. In this path, cleansing of the ego-self comes after purifying the heart. Since the two Turkmen had a strong attraction to God and overflowing love, undoubtedly they set out valiantly climbing the mountain of humanness (*bashariyat*) and in an instant were at the top, honored by a kind of annihilation in God. Husayn Qassab, because he did not have that

64. This phenomenon is discussed in Buehler, *Sufi Heirs* and is a characteristic of those overcome by attraction to God and those in the "field" of a shaykh's *tawajjuh*.

strength of attraction to God, had a lot of difficulty climbing the mountain. By the blessing of following the two Turkmen, he made it. Otherwise, he would have been destroyed.

The army camp (in the story) means the level of the fixed entities (*a'yan-i thabita*), which unites the entifications of realities of possibility (*jami'-i ta'ayyunat-i haqa'iq-i imkani*) and the entification of necessary knowledge. These [former] entifications represent the countless tents (in the story), in the middle of which is the great tent, an allusion to the entification of Necessary knowledge, which is said to be the Sultan's tent. When Husayn Qassab heard that this was the Sultan's tent, he imagined that he had arrived at the place he had desired. He wanted to get out of the vehicle of intoxication, which is necessary to traverse the path, and arrive at the goal in contentment.

The right foot signifies the spirit subtle center because on the untrodden path one proceeds with the foot of the heart and spirit subtle centers, not on the foot of acquired knowledge and deeds associated with the trodden path. Descending from intoxication one encounters the spirit subtle center first and then the heart subtle center, which is interpreted as the left foot.[65] So (continuing the story) when he took his foot out of the stirrup he heard a divinely inspired message telling him that the Sultan was not in the tent, which was the truth. Since Husayn Qassab did not have the strength of attraction to God, he came out a bit from intoxication after [hearing] just a bit of the good tidings. The two Turkmen, however, because they had a strong attraction to God and were overcome with love, were not deceived by this same good news and valiantly continued up.[66] Even if Husayn Qassab had waited a thousand years, he would have never found the Sultan in the tent because Almighty God is beyond the beyond.

The words in the story, "Going out hunting on horseback," mean sitting in a majestic place manifesting splendor and hunting lovers' hearts. This voice and meaning were in accordance with the understanding of Husayn Qassab in the way it was communicated to him in words. Otherwise it is meaningless to say that God almighty is sitting or hunting. God's good fortune overflows from that place, but they return empty handed without the Beloved. Another meaning of "Going out hunting on horseback" has occurred to my feeble mind, which is appropriate to the station of singularity (*tafarrud*) and magnificence. Even though this meaning is not worthy of the Holy Presence, it is superior and more fitting than other interpreta-

---

65. Note that the heart subtle center is below the left nipple by roughly two finger widths and the spirit subtle center is below the right nipple by the same distance.

66. These were good tidings because of the Divine message, not because the King was or was not in the tent.

tions. Exalt God's majesty. So here it is. Unity (*wahdat*), the first entification (*ta'ayyun-i awwal*), "sits" above the level of "the all-inclusive unity (*wahidiyat*).[67] Because one aspect of unity is the annihilation of cognitive/epistemological and "corporeally" entified entifications (*ta'ayyunat-i 'ilmi wa-'ayni*) which is understood in this station to correspond to hunting, i. e., the killing of wild animals and birds.

Shaykh Muhammad Ma'shuq Tusi and Amir 'Ali 'Abu (the two Turkmen) arrived at the Sultan's hunting ground and became God's prey, though Ma'shuq Tusi was farther ahead and closer. Husayn Qassab, hoping to find the Sultan, remained in the tent of all-inclusive unity. God almighty knows best concerning the reality of what is desired and what is to be gained or lost in it.

O Master! The notables of the Naqshbandi path have chosen this very untrodden path. God almighty bless their inner hearts. It was an unknown path that has become established by the methods of these notables. From this path, countless people have realized the goal through the spiritual energy and concentration (*bi-tawajjuh wa-tasarruf*) [of the Naqshbandi shaykhs]. If one follows the behavioral guidelines of the beautiful behavior of an exemplary shaykh (*pir-i muqtada*), one necessarily has to arrive using this method. Old, young, women, and men are equal. Even the dead can be hopeful in receiving this bounty. Baha'uddin Naqshband (d. 791/1389 Bukhara) said that he had petitioned God almighty for a path that would guarantee arriving at the goal. God sanctify his inner heart. The primary successor of Baha'uddin, Khwaja 'Ala'uddin 'Attar (d. 803/1400 Hissar, Tajikistan) read this poetry to bring out this meaning: "If it would not have broken the heart of the gatekeeper of the secret, I would have broken all of the locks in the world." God sanctify his inner heart. God almighty make us firm in the path of these notables. Peace.

Introduction to evaluating spiritual rank: Letter 1.293

This letter is written to Shaykh Muhammad Chattari, who was authorized to teach by his shaykh Ahmad Sirhindi.[68] This letter seeks to give the reader ways in which to evaluate spiritual rank. It begins with 'Abdulqadir Jilani (d. 561/1166) asserting his superiority over "every protégé of God." Sirhindi first interprets the words themselves to be "conceited and full of pride," which is how an ordinary person would presumably interpret them. Sirhindi then evaluates this statement as being true for the protégés of God who lived in 'Abdulqadir's time, whether it stemmed from a possible remnant of intoxication and/or it was commanded by God. He

67. See William C. Chittick, "The Five Divine Presences: From al-Qunawi to al-Qaysari" in *Muslim World* 72/2 (April 1982), 107-128.

68. Shaykh Muhammad Chattari had five letters addressed to him in *Collected Letters*.

carefully explains why it could not be true for those living before or after 'Abdulqadir on the basis of what 'Abdulqadir's contemporaries said and on the basis of people who are 'Abdulqadir's spiritual superiors, namely the Companions and the Mahdi. From another perspective, 'Abdulqadir heads the circle of Muhammadan intimacy (*walayat-i Muhammadi*), the highest prophetic intimacy relative to other prophets. It cannot compare with prophetic perfections because the perfections of prophethood are ontologically superior to the perfections of intimacy with God (*kamalat-i walaya*).[69] Sirhindi then expands the context to show the reader that excessive love of a sufi or a Companion, in this case 'Ali b. Abi Talib (assas. 40/661), especially on the basis of miracles, is not the basis on which to ascertain spiritual rank. Indeed, the outward show of miracles connected to this world (*istidraj*) is one way to deceive the common people, who do not even perceive the *real* miracles associated with a person who experiences God. It is about discernment.

Letter 1.293

Praise God. God give peace to God's chosen servants filled with the joyful arrival of the Noble Book (the Qur'an). It is a blessing that the protégés of God remind those who have failed to understand. You write that the Prophet Muhammad said "I have time with God" and that Abu Dharr Ghiffari (d. 32/652) also said this.[70] Also, [you ask about] 'Abdulqadir Jilani's (d. 561/1166) statement, "My foot is on the neck of every protégé of God (*wali*)." Another person also said this. Sometimes a debate ensues over these two sentences. It is more fruitful to ask the meaning of these two sentences and what the difference is between them. Once this is addressed, everything will be clearly explained so that what may seem strange will be understood.

O Master! This poor one (Ahmad Sirhindi) has written in his letters that the Prophet, with his continuous awareness, had a heightened awareness when he performed ritual prayers, according to the sayings, "Ritual prayer is the heavenly ascension of the believer." and "O Bilal, give me some rest."[71] To prove this interpretation there is a bona-fide witness. Abu

69. Ibn al-'Arabi also claimed to be the Seal of Muhammadan Intimacy until Jesus comes on the Last Day.

70. A hadith found in al-Qushayri's *al-Risala al-Qushayriyya* (Tehran: Intisharat-i Bidar, 1998), 155. It is also found in al-Munawi, *Fayd al-qadir*, 4:6; al-Ajluni, *Kashf al-khafa'*, #2159; 'Ali al-Qari, *al-Mathnu'* (*Mawdu'at al-Sughra*), 151 [MR].

71. The former is found in al-Munawi, *Fayd al-qadir*, 1:497; al-Suyuti, *Sharh Sunan Ibn Majah*, 1:313; al-Zurkani, *Sharh al-Muwatta*, 1:111 [MR], mentioned three times in *Collected Letters*. The second is a hadith found in Abu Da'ud, #4985;

Dharr Ghiffari, with the inheritance and following [of the Prophet], was also blessed with this favor. This is because those completely following the Prophet have received all of his perfections and complete good fortune by means of his inheritance and following him. God bless him and his family and give them peace.

Then there is 'Abdulqadir Jilani who said, "My foot is on the neck of every protégé of God (*wali*)." God sanctify his innermost being. [Abu Hafs 'Umar Suhrawardi d. 632/1234] wrote these words, which are conceited and full of pride, in his *The Bounties of Divine Knowledge* (*'Awarif al-ma'arif*). [Abu Hafs] was a disciple of Shaykh Abu Najib Suhrawardi (d. 563/1168), who was a confidant of 'Abdulqadir. These expressions come from shaykhs who have remnants of intoxication as they begin [to experience altered] states. In the *Fragrances of Intimacy*, Shaykh Hammad Dabbas (d. 525/1131), one of 'Abulqadir's shaykhs, said that he had intuited that 'Abdulqadir had such a blessed foot that now his foot is on the necks of all God's protégés and when 'Abdulqadir said, "My foot is on the neck of every protégé of God," it would happen. In any case, what 'Abdulqadir said was true, whether it was attributed to his remnants of intoxication or whether it was commanded by God. With the evidence of Shaykh Hammad, 'Abdulqadir's foot was on the necks of the protégés of God at that time and they were under his foot. But one should know that this injunction applies only to the protégés of God at that time. Those who are before or after ['Abdulqadir's time] are exempt.

From Shaykh Hammad, it is known that 'Abdulqadir's foot was on all the protégés of God at that time. In Baghdad, Shaykh 'Abdulqadir, and Ibn Saqa' 'Abdullah went to visit 'Abdullah Ghawth who intuited the truth about 'Abdulqadir saying, "I see you standing at a pulpit in Baghdad saying, 'My foot is on the neck of every protégé of God' and because of your honor and greatness I see the contemporary protégés of God laying their necks down to you." From the words of this great scholar, one can understand that this injunction [of 'Abdulqadir's] only applies to the protégés of God during 'Abdulqadir's time. If God almighty had wanted another contemporary of 'Abdulqadir's to intuit ['Abdulqadir's spiritual sovereignty] like 'Abdullah Ghawth had done (for a time before or after 'Abdulqadir's time), then someone else would have said, "The necks of the protégés of God of that time are under 'Abdulqadir's foot."

Having made this injunction binding for ['Abdulqadir's] contemporary protégés of God, it did not apply to protégés of God of any other time. For the protégés of God [living] before this injunction, it would have to include

---

Ahmad b. Hanbal, *al-Musnad*, 5:364; al-Tabarani, *al-Kabir*, 6:276-277 [MR], and is mentioned three times in *Collected Letters*. Bilal is the muezzin (the person calling people to prayer).

the noble Companions, who surely are more favored than ‘Abdulqadir. It is not possible for those living after [the injunction] because that would include the arrival of the Mahdi whom the Prophet had already announced. The community rejoices in the Mahdi’s presence, whom the Prophet said is the regent of God. In the same way, the followers of Jesus, who is one of the great prophets (*anbiya’-i ulu al-‘azmi*), are among the predecessors. God bless and give peace to our prophet and him. [After the Mahdi comes], by following the [Islamic] shariat connected with those who follow Muhammad (lit. the Seal of the Messengers), the followers of Jesus are among the latter members of the [Muslim] community. This may be expressed by what the Prophet said, “[My community is like the rain.] I do not know who is better, the first ones or the last ones.”[72]

In short, Shaykh ‘Abdulqadir has a high degree of great intimacy with God, a special Muhammadan intimacy (*walayat*). God bless and give peace to those with this intimacy. [He has achieved this] by means of the mystery subtle center, realizing the last center dot and becoming the head of the group in that circle. Given this, a person should not imagine that just because ‘Abdulqadir is the head of the group in the circle of Muhammadan intimacy that he is the most excellent of all the protégés of God just on the basis of Muhammadan intimacy being the highest of all prophetic intimacies. This is because when we say “the head of the group of Muhammadan intimacy” it [means that this intimacy] has been realized by virtue of the aforementioned mystery subtle center, not that he has absolute Muhammadan intimacy. There is no inherent superiority because it is possible that another person could have precedence through Muhammadan prophetic perfections by means of following [the sunnat] and [the prophetic] inheritance. Preference is demonstrated on the basis of these perfections.

A group of ‘Abdulqadir’s disciples had excessive reactions to him and in their love for him they went beyond acceptable limits. This is like the exaggerated lovers of ‘Ali [b. Abi Talib (assas. 40/661)]. God almighty bless his face. From the words of this group [of ‘Abdulqadir’s exaggerating disciples], it is clear that they consider ‘Abdulqadir to be more excellent than any other protégés of God, before or after his time. Other than the prophets it seems as if they give the greatest preference to ‘Abdulqadir. This is from excessive love. What if it is said that ‘Abdulqadir performed more miracles than anyone else, and therefore he should be given preference? We say that the number of miracles is no proof of preference. It can be said that a person who has performed no miracles is more preferable than one who has manifested miracles. The shaykh of shaykhs (Abu Hafs as-Suhrawardi)

72. A hadith found in al-Tirmidhi, #2869; Ahmad b. Hanbal, *al-Musnad*, 3:130, 143, 4:119; Ibn Hibban, *al-Sahih*, #7226 [MR], and mentioned three times in *Collected Letters*.

in his *The Bounties of Divine Knowledge*, after mentioning the miracles of shaykhs, says,

> All miracles are a gift of God almighty which manifest to some people through unveilings. They share these and [appear to be] superior to others [who do not have the same experiences.] They receive nothing [in terms of spiritual growth] from performing these miracles, which are for strengthening a person's certainty. One who is given certainty does not need miracles. Other than remembrance in the heart and in the Essence, there is no need for miracles.[73]

Performing many miracles to demonstrate one's excellence is like trying to show the preference of 'Ali over Abu Bakr (d. 13/634) by mentioning 'Ali's many excellences and virtues. God almighty be pleased with both of them. 'Ali just did not have that many excellences and virtues.

O brother listen! There are two kinds of out-of-the-ordinary events (*khawariq*). The first is knowledge and experience of God, which are connected with the Necessary Essence, attributes, and deeds of God. These are beyond the purview of the rational mind and run against everyday reality. [Therefore, God] chooses his special servants for these out-of-the-ordinary events. The second kind [of out-of-the-ordinary event] is disclosing what is in peoples' hearts and revealing the secrets [therein] that are connected to the world. The first kind is specific to people of Truth (*ahl-i haqq*) and those possessing experiential knowledge of God. The second kind includes both those speaking the truth and liars. It includes those who deceive people [by giving them a false sense of security] (*ahl-i istidraj*). The first kind is close to God in eminence and perspective and specially pertains to the protégés of God. The enemies [of God] do not have any part in this. The second kind is close to the common people who esteem these out-of-the-ordinary events to the point that when deceivers manifest such events, ignorant people worship them. Whatever the deceivers order them to do they obey. Common people do not know about the first kind of out-of-the-ordinary events, and do not recognize them as miracles because they are limited by the second kind of out-of-the-ordinary events happening around them. Miracles, in these ignorant people's view, are connected with the disclosure of appearances and advice concerning personal secrets. O ignorant ones! This knowledge, whether manifest or hidden, is connected to people's states. What kind of glory and dignity can be found in this? On the contrary, this knowledge is contingent upon turning from ignorance until one forgets people and their states. Experiential knowledge of God is necessary. [Only] God almighty is worthy of glory, dignity, honor, and respect.

---

73. Translated from the Arabic.

The beautiful one is hiding her face
The Devil is parading beauty like a beauty queen.
Burning the mind with bewilderment,
How strange this is.[74]

Pertaining to what has been said above, we mention Shaykh al-Islam ['Abdullah] Harawi Ansari (d. 481/1089), author of *Stations of the Wayfarers* (*Manazil al-sa'irin*), a commentator on that book (Kamaluddin 'Abdurrazzaq al-Kashani d. 736/1336),[75] and that which I have proved by experience. Those with experience of God almighty have an intuition that enables them to discriminate between what holds true in the presence of God and what does not. Those capable of working in the way of God and arriving in the encompassing presence of God *know*. Such is the intuition of those having experience of God. Ascetics (*ahl-i riyada*) perform fasts in solitude and purify their inner selves without arriving near God almighty [or achieving real intuition]. Their intuition reveals appearances and people's inner secrets. They can only inform others what concerns created beings because they themselves are veiled from God almighty.

As for those having the experience of God, their work concerns their experiences of God almighty. They are only aware of that which involves God almighty. Most of those in the world are cut off from God almighty and work for the world. Their hearts are inclined towards those who disclose the appearances of things and hidden aspects of people's states (like telling them of past events in their lives that few people know). [People] glorify them and believe that they are people of God and God's elite. They renounce the disclosures of the truthful ones and suspect what people of the Truth inform them about God almighty. The people of the world say, "If those people were really people of Truth as they claim, then they would tell us about our inner states and the states of [other] people. If they are not able to disclose the inner states of people then how can they disclose matters higher than those affairs?" The people of the world, deceiving themselves with this unsound analogy, are unaware of authentic reports. They do not know that God almighty has already protected the people of Truth from seeing [the plight of] created beings. God favors them and diverts the people of Truth from anything other than God by caring for them and protecting them.

---

74. The rest of this letter is translated from Arabic.

75. See 'Abdullah ibn Muhammad Ansari al-Harawi, *Kitab Manazil al-sa'irin*, eds. Ahmad 'Abdurrahim Sayih and Tawfiq 'Ali Wahbah (Cairo: Maktabat al-Thaqafah al-Diniyah, 2007); 'Abdurrazzaq al-Kashani, *Kitab sharh Manazil al-sa'irin* (Beirut: Dar al-Mujtaba, 1995). Kashani also wrote a commentary on Ibn al-'Arabi's *Fusus al-hikam*.

If there were a person of Truth who turned his attention to people's states it would not be worthy of God almighty. We have already seen that when people of the Truth turn their slightest attention to revealing appearances, they realize what is happening as no one else can with an intuition proven by those having experience of God. This intuition is connected with God almighty and what is close to God. The intuition of the "folk of purity" (*ahl al-safa'*),[76] who are devoid of a true desire for God, is connected to creation instead of God almighty or anything close to God. Muslims, Christians, Jews, and all other groups participate in this [intuition of the folk of purity] because they do not have a respectable place with God almighty, a place solely dedicated to the people of Truth who have experienced God.

Introduction to Those Who Think They Are Further Along Than They Are: Letter 1.220

Sirhindi wrote this letter to Shaykh Hamid Bengali (d. 1050/1641) in Mangalkot, Bengal),[77] a jurist, who spent a year with Ahmad Sirhindi before receiving permission to teach others. Of the four extant teaching certificates that Ahmad Sirhindi wrote, one of them is to Hamid Bengali. It reads,

> And now, give thanks to God. God bless Muhammad. [This is] the poor one whom God the Sovereign has blessed, Ahmad, son of the Shaykh 'Abdulahad, al-Faruqi al-Naqshbandi. God bless him amply. He (Ahmad Sirhindi) declares that Shaykh Hamid al-Bengali is a righteous brother and veracious scholar who has comprehended knowledge of the shariat, sufi path, and Reality. God has given him success, loving him and finding satisfaction with him when he traversed the way stations of the path in attracted ascension. He has arrived at the level of intimacy with God (*walayat*). There Shaykh Hamid al-Bengali realized that the end is included in the beginning. I allow him to teach the methods of the path [trodden] by the Naqshbandi shaykhs—God almighty bless their inner hearts—to seekers requesting guidance and to sincere aspirants after requesting permission from God (*istikhara*) and receiving it. He is accountable to God who safeguards him in his actions, which must adhere to those of the

76. This could be a reference to the Brethren of Purity (*ikhwan al-safa'*). They use the term "folk of purity." See Aaron W. Hughes, *The Texture of the Divine: Imagination in Medieval Islamic and Jewish Thought* (Bloomington, IN: Indiana University Press, 2003), 26; and Khaliq Ahmad Nizami, *Akbar and Religion* (Delhi, Jayyed Press, 1989), 70-71.

77. Hamid Bengali had five letters addressed to him in Sirhindi's *Collected Letters*, including 1.292 and 2.46 in this translation.

Lord of the Messengers (Muhammad). God bless them.[78]

This letter addresses seekers who think that they are further along the path than they actually are. One reason for this inflated self-perception is that seekers conflate the experience of their own comprehensiveness, the lesser comprehensiveness of the human being, with the encompassing comprehensiveness of the name of God that sustains them. In other words, the eight essential attributes of God all contain each other in each other.[79] Human attributes only work one at a time, for example, sight involves only what is seen, and hearing is not involved in what is being seen. Sometimes seekers fail to clearly discern their experiences of the attributes. A second reason that a person can have an inflated self-perception is that those who are lovers (*muhibbin*) and those who desire God (*muridin*) confuse their fleeting experiences in the shadows of the attributes with the experiences of wayfaring in the attributes. The origin of divine effulgence for prophets, beloveds (*mahbuban*), and those desired by God (*muradan*) is God's attributes. Their wayfaring is in the attribute itself and its comprehensive nature. Lovers and those desiring God (*muridin*), in contrast, do their wayfaring in the shadows of the attributes and in the partial details. There is a major qualitative difference between wayfaring in the attributes and the shadows of the attributes!

Often a seeker traveling in the shadows can have disclosures along the way, but these are the result of following a prophet and the shariat of that prophet, not the result of one's own realizations. The seeker is still in the shadows and any perfections the seeker acquires will be in the shadows. The prophet who the seeker is following has perfections in the Essence. Another scenario is that of a seeker of the Jesus disposition who is wayfaring in the attribute of power thinking that he is in a more comprehensive place [than he actually is]. He mistakenly thinks that because Adam was only in the attribute of origination, and Moses was only in the attribute of speech, and he is wayfaring in origination, speech *and* power. Not only is the seeker traveling in the *shadow* of the attribute of power, but also he is *not* traveling in any of the other attributes.

This is one reason why Sirhindi has written this letter. It is because so many seekers think they are in a higher place than they actually are. It is easy to see the mistake since the shadows of the name that sustains each seeker *is* comprehensive (mirroring the Essence's comprehensiveness). However, there is a big difference between the attribute and the shadow

78. See Ahmad Sirhindi, *Mukashafat-i 'ayniya*, ed. and Urdu translation by Ghulam Mustafa Khan (Karachi: Educational Press, 1965), 12-13.

79. These eight essential attributes are: knowledge, life, power, will, speech, hearing, sight, and origination. See Buehler, *Sufi Heirs*, 115.

of an attribute, even though both are comprehensive. The prophets have greater intimacy with God (*walayat-i kubra*), while protégés of God have a fundamental intimacy with God (*walayat-i asli*). The beloveds of God with the Muhammadan disposition mentioned above experience the disclosure of the Essence (*tajalli-yi dhat*).[80] By the time Sirhindi had written this letter, it appears that Sirhindi too had publicly announced that he had found himself in a higher place than he actually was. One example is letter 1.11 where he says that he had reached a higher place than Abu Bakr. This letter functions as a public apology for his misperceptions.

Letter 1.220

Praise God, Sustainer of the two worlds. God bless and give peace to Muhammad, the Master of Messengers, and all of his family and companions. The states and situations of the sufis (*fuqara'*) here is the reason for increasing thanks each day. One hopes that the same [holds true] for far-flung friends.

O dear one! In this strangest of paths, there are many places for wayfarers to slip and fall. So, in articles of faith and actions, hold the rope of the shariat firmly. Life passes quickly. This is my advice whether you are in presence or in absence—just in case you experience heedlessness. I am going to write about some of the errors of this path and specify the origins of these blunders. You should observe these from a perspective of comparison and, with this in mind, act in a way that is beyond the details.

Know that some of the errors are as follows. Sometimes a wayfarer ascends in the stations and perceives himself to be higher than others. The error is that the others are really in a higher station. This discrepancy has been supported by a consensus of jurists. Certainly [the mistaken] wayfarer's station is below the stations of those notables. Sometimes it happens that people even think they are superior to the prophets, who are certainly superior to all other created beings. God give them peace. God almighty save us from that! The origin of their collective mistake is [that they are unaware] that each of the prophets and protégés of God (*awliya*) first ascends to God's names, which is the origin (*mabda'*) of the entifications of their existence (*ta'ayyunat-i wujud-i ishan*). With this ascent they verify their closeness to God (*walayat*). Secondly, there is an ascent in these names of God and from there to where God almighty wishes.[81] But in spite of this ascent, their abode and way station is in the same name of God, which is the origin of its entification of existence. Therefore, in the stations of ascent anyone who looks for the notables will find most of them in these very names (in the origins of the entifications) because the natural place of these

80. Additional commentary is given in Hutaki, *Sharh-i Maktubat*, 288-291.

81. For prophets and some protégés of God this would mean traveling back to the physical world.

notables is to be in the levels of ascent of these same names. Ascent and descent from these names happens by accident and external events.

So the wayfarer with a high degree of innate capacity (*salik-i buland fitrat*) undoubtedly will go higher than the names [which are the natural place of notables]. From this, the wayfarer will experience a delusion [of being more advanced than the friends of God]. God almighty save us from that and dispel the aforementioned delusion of certainty and [affirm] the consensus that prophets are superior and more preferred than the protégés of God. God bless them. This is where wayfarers backslide. Seekers do not know that these notables have made countless ascensions beyond these names of God, arriving way above. Nor do they know that the names of God, which are the natural places of these notables' ascent, are higher than where they are. For the wayfarer, there is a natural place also, but it is lower in the names of God and lower than where the notables are. This is because the superiority of each person is in accordance with the precedence (*aqdamiya*) of his name, which is the origin of his entification.

It is in this manner that some shaykhs have said that sometimes a person of inner experience (*'arif*), in ascending the stations, does not experience the obstacle of [crossing] the major interface (*barzakhiyat-i kubra'i*). The wayfarer thereby progresses without its intermediary [benefits]. Baqibillah, my master shaykh, used to say that Rabi'a (d. 185/801 Basra) was among a similar group (those who did not experience the obstacle of crossing a major interface). When this group was ascending from one of God's names, which is the origin of the entification of the major interface, they thought that the interface was not an intervening impediment. From the major interface they desired the Muhammadan reality. God bless and give peace to him and his family.

The truth of the matter has been discussed above. For others, the source of the error happens (thinking that they are in a higher station than the notables) when a wayfarer travels in one of God's names that is the origin of his entification and the comprehensive totality of God's names. This is because the comprehensiveness of a human being is by means of the comprehensiveness of that same name of God. So inevitably, in the meantime, there are also God's names that are the origins of other shaykhs' entifications. The aforementioned gifted wayfarer will also proceed on the same path of comprehensiveness (*ijmal*) and, passing each station, will arrive at the end of the name. He will experience the same delusion of superiority mentioned above. He does not know that what he has seen is from the shaykhs' stations. He has only experienced a sample of their stations, not the reality of those stations. This is because in this station he experiences himself as being comprehensive and imagines others as parts of himself. Undoubtedly he finds himself in a delusion of superiority. In such a station Bayazid

Bistami (d. 261/875) in a fit of being overcome by intoxication said, "My banner is higher than Muhammad's." He did not know that his banner was not higher than Muhammad's but was only a small swath of Muhammad's banner, contemplatively witnessed and contained in the reality of Muhammad's name. God bless and give peace to him and his family.

Likewise, Bayazid said concerning the expanse of his own heart, "If the Throne and its contents were in the corner of the heart of one of inner knowledge (*'arif*), he would not notice." This is also mistaking a sample of something for the entire truth of it. Otherwise how could the Throne, which God almighty said was great, have any credibility or scope compared to the heart of one who has inner knowledge? A hundredth of the Throne's manifestation is not within the heart, even if it were the heart of a person of inner knowledge. Seeing God (*ru'yat*) in the next world with the appearance of the Throne has been verified (in the hadith). In saying this, although it will annoy some sufis now, it will be reasonable for them later.[82]

An example will clarify what I am saying. A human being, with respect to the elements and heavens, is a comprehensive whole. Whenever he glances at his comprehensiveness he sees the elements and heavens as part of himself. When this way of perceiving overcomes him [in intoxication], it is just a small step for him to say that he is larger than the Earth and greater than the heavens. Meanwhile, those of sound mind know that the greatness and vastness (*kalani*) of a human being are parts of himself, and that the Earth and heavens in reality are not part of him. The parts of a human being are made out of small amounts of the elements and heavens. His greatness comes from these small amounts that are parts of him, not from the earthly and heavenly reality. This is the same as mistaking the sample of something for the total reality of that thing. Muhyiddin Ibn al-'Arabi (d. 638/1240) said that the Muhammadan comprehensiveness was more comprehensive (*ajma'*) than God because the Muhammadan comprehensiveness includes the worldly and divine realities. He did not know that the Muhammadan comprehensiveness is but a shadow among the shadows of a divine level, a fragment of that divine level and in reality not that holy level itself. Compared to that holy level, which is necessarily great and majestic, Muhammadan comprehensiveness is incommensurate. What does dust have to do with the Sustainer of sustainers?

Likewise, in this station the wayfarer's journey occurs in one of God's names that govern the wayfarer. Sometimes the wayfarer imagines that some protégés of God and prophets, who are surely superior to him, have

82. Cf. Letter 1.287 Inner Knowledge 4 in this book where Sirhindi discusses the heart beyond a space-time context. The context of the heart discussed here in Letter 1.220 is a heart that has entered the space-time realm. This might have something to do with Bayazid's intoxicated heart at the time of his utterance.

progressed through his mediation and have reached some higher degree of attainment. Here is where wayfarers backslide. God almighty save us from the thought that we are superior and save us from the prospect of eternal calamity. It is as if a king of great splendor and complete power were to go to a landlord's property in his kingdom and, through that landlord's intervention, the King eventually arrives somewhere and gets some villages. How strange and what superiority [can one attribute to the landlord]?

In short, there is probably benefit in some things here beyond the inquiry itself. This is because weavers and barbers have specialized creative skills just like chameleon-like philosophers (*bu qalamun*) that give them a kind of superiority.[83] But this superiority is relative to externals. That which is authentic is a universal superiority confirmed by a jurist (*'alim*) or a sage (*hakim*). This poor one (Ahmad Sirhindi) also made a lot of these mistakes. So much proceeded from this kind of thinking that I had this state for a long time. Besides, God was protecting me in this state so that I did not deviate at all from my previous certainty nor was there any slackening of the articles of faith associated with this certainty. Exalt God's sovereignty! Thanks to God almighty for that exalted favor, and all of God's blessings. I did not consider anything that went against those articles of faith, interpreting everything in a way as to reconcile well with them.

Generally, I came to know this much, which is that when considering the authenticity of this unveiling (*kashf*), its plenitude ends up in a partial superiority. No matter how much this suspicion (*waswasa*) is prevented, the scope of superiority is in closeness to God. Any plenitude is in this closeness. So why is it a partial superiority? Exalt God's sovereignty. [It is partial because] compared to the previous certainty, this suspicion is like scattered dust and worthless. However, with repentance and asking for forgiveness one can return to God. With supplication and humility, one can entreat God so that these kinds of unveilings (*kushuf*) do not appear, and absolutely nothing gets revealed that is against the articles of faith of the rightly guided Sunni mainstream.

One day this fear overcame me. God forbid that I might be held to account for these unveilings or for thinking of these questions. I became overwhelmed by fear, making me restless and uneasy. Humbly turning toward God, I became weak and this state continued for a time. Exalt God's sovereignty. Suddenly, at that time it happened that I passed by the tomb of a notable (*'azizi*) and I asked for his help. Meanwhile, God's favor manifested and confirmed the reality of what was going on. This is as it should be. The spirit (*ruhaniyat*) of the Presence of the Messenger (Muhammad), who is the mercy of heaven and earth, appeared at that time and consoled my sad

83. Coming from one of the *ashraf* (see Introduction) this is a major put-down of philosophers.

heart. God bless him and his family and give them peace. Then I knew that intimacy with God is required for absolute preference (*fadl-i kulli*). But this closeness that you have realized is a nearness of one of the shadows of the divine level specific for one of God's names that governs you. Therefore, there is no necessity for absolute preference. How the imaginal form of this station became revealed to you leaves no room for doubt and completely removes any suspicions.

Some of what I have written in books and letters had mistakes and the potential for interpretation and reading between the lines. These have been circulated. I want the source of errors in this knowledge to be clear, written, and distributed by means of God's grace. Exalt God's affair. For a sin that has been committed in public, it is appropriate that the repentance also be public so that people do not understand anything to be against the shariat from this knowledge. Nor will they fall into error by choosing ignorance and error by following [my words]. Nor will they fall into error through fanaticism or acting in an unnatural manner. With this utmost-hidden path, flowers will blossom. One group receives guidance and another falls into error. I heard my father advising me. God bless his inner heart. He said that most of the seventy-two groups had fallen into error and had lost the right path.[84] The reason for this was their entering the sufi path and not realizing the goal. They committed mistakes and proceeded in error. Peace.

Introduction to Naqshbandi Cosmology: Letter 1.257

This letter is addressed to Mir Muhammad Nu'man Badakhshi (d. 1058/1648),[85] who was directed by his shaykh, 'Abdullah 'Ishqi in Balkh, to go to India where he became a disciple of Baqibillah. In 1016/1609 Shaykh Sirhindi authorized Mir Nu'man to teach, making him one of the first of Sirhindi's successors. In this letter, the Naqshbandi path is outlined cosmologically. After one purifies one's subtle centers, the journey necessarily continues in the origins of these centers located above the Throne to travel in the shadows of God's names and attributes. The shadows are the interface between the world of necessity and the world of possibility. Then the wayfarer experiences God's names and attributes, the qualities (*shuyunat*), and aspects (*i'tibarat*) in turn. At this point, the seeker has completed the work with the subtle centers. The next stage involves transforming an unruly ego-self (*nafs-i ammara*) to a tranquil ego-self (*nafs-i mutma'inna*), reaching the end of the ten stations, the station of contentment and satisfaction.

Another way of describing the Naqshbandi path is that one starts in

---

84. See footnote 36 in letter 2.67 in this volume.

85. Thirty-three letters are addressed to Mir Muhammad Nu'man in *Collected Letters* (the most popular recipient of Sirhindi's extant letters), including 2.92, which is in this selected translation.

the world of command before proceeding to the inner name (*ism-i batin*). While wayfaring in the shadows of the names, one is experiencing lesser intimacy with God (*walayat-i sughra*). Experiencing the names themselves is greater intimacy with God (*walayat-i kubra*). The cleansing of the ego-self is finished by the time one has reached the disclosures of the Essence (*tajalliyat-i dhatiya*) via the aspects of the Essence and the bow. The journey in the Essence itself is still yet to begin.

LETTER 1.257

After delivering praise, blessings, and good wishes, the esteemed letter that you sent via Shaykh Ahmad Farmali has arrived and it gave me great pleasure. You had requested a letter explaining the sufi path. All I have is rough drafts. If I find divine favor, I will send you a properly written version. Presently I will briefly write some sentences elucidating the method. So listen attentively.

It is a glorious path we have chosen! In the beginning, wayfaring is from the heart subtle center located in the world of command. After passing through the heart, wayfaring is in the levels of the spirit subtle center (*ruh*), which is above the heart. Passing the spirit one proceeds to the mystery subtle center above the spirit. The same process applies for the arcane and super-arcane subtle centers.[86] After passing the way stations of these five subtle centers, realizing the inner and outer knowledge associated with each discrete subtle center, and after verification of the states and ecstasies (*muwajid*) experienced separately in each of the five subtle centers, one travels in the origins (sing. *asl*) of the subtle centers located in the macrocosm. This is because whatever is in the microcosm has its origin in the macrocosm. Microcosm means the human being while macrocosm means all of creation.

The glorious Throne,[87] the origin of the human heart subtle center, is the beginning of the wayfaring in the origins of the five subtle centers. The origin of the human spirit subtle center is above that, and the origin of the human mystery subtle center is above that followed by the origin of the arcane and the origin of the superarcane subtle centers. When one has traversed in detail these five aspects of the macrocosm, one arrives at the final

86. Here Sirhindi is not talking about the location in the body but in the microcosmic path in Figure 2.

87. The "Throne of God" is said to encompass both Heaven and Earth. Some commentators have designated the furthest two of the seven heavens as the Throne. Sirhindi designates the Throne as something that is beyond the heavens and earth, *Collected Letters*, 2.76.73; the most honored thing in the macrocosm, ibid., 3.11.21; the interface between the world of command and the physical world, ibid., 2.10.30; and beyond time and space, ibid., 1.14.30.

dot of the macrocosm, having completed all wayfaring in the circle of possibility.[88] One has stepped in the first way station of annihilation in God.

After this, with further progress, one enters the shadows of the necessary names and attributes of God. These shadows are like interfaces (*barazikh*) between the necessary and the possible, and are the origins of the five levels of the macrocosm. Wayfaring in these shadows is done in the same order as (in the microcosm and macrocosm) discussed above. If one has the grace of God, one can also traverse numerous way stations in these shadows, arriving at the final dot. Exalt God's sovereignty. Then one begins wayfaring in the necessary names and attributes of God, traveling in the disclosures of the names and attributes. One experiences the splendors of appearances of the qualities and aspects. At this time, the five-fold aspect of the world of command has been completed and one has fulfilled the truth of the subtle centers.

With God's favor one can progress beyond this station and experience tranquility of the ego-self, easily realizing the station of satisfaction, which is the end of the wayfaring stations. Exalt God's affair. In this station, one experiences the expanded chest (*sharh-i sadr*) and is honored with real submission to God (*islam-i haqiqi*). Comparing the perfections that are achieved in this station to the perfections associated with the world of command is like comparing a drop of water to an ocean. All of these aforementioned perfections are associated with the outer name.[89] There are other perfections associated with the inner name, which pertain to the inner and hidden.

When the perfections of these two blessed names are completely realized, they act like two wings. This makes it easy for the wayfarer who utilizes the strength of these two wings to travel in the holy world (*'alam-i quds*) and make great advances. The details of this are already in some rough drafts, which my dear son is diligently compiling.[90] Secondly, you should come here if it is convenient for you, provided that you are still in this station and do not interfere with it. Come alone. Choose a qualified person from your companions whom you think can lead the group [while you are away] and then come. God knows best whether there will another opportunity. Bless God. Peace.

---

88. The bottom half of the circle of possibility involves outer wayfaring (*sayr-i afaqi*), and the upper half involves inner wayfaring (*sayr-i anfusi*).

89. That is, the perfections of the subtle centers and the world of command including their origins, the perfections of the shadows of the necessary names and attributes, and the perfections of the station of tranquility and satisfaction.

90. This is probably letter 1.260 in this volume.

Introduction to Sirhindi interpreting verses of Sharafuddin Maneri: Letter 3.33

This letter is written to Mulla Shams (d. 1067/1657), who was in Shah Jahan's (r. 1037/1628 – 1068/1658) service of with a rank (*mansab*) of three thousand.[91] This is a fairly high rank since there were only seventy amirs with a rank above 2500 (the highest rank being 7000) around this time. Mulla Shams has sent two very enigmatic and transgressive quotes to Sirhindi from the writing of Sharafuddin Yahya Maneri (d. 782/1381). Sirhindi begins with a discussion of two kinds of submission to God (*islam*) and two kinds of covering up the truth of God (*kufr*, commonly known as infidelity).[92] Outer submission to God is the domain of the superficial jurists who perform shariat practices without having confirmed the reality of the shariat through experience. Real submission to God involves contemplatively witnessing the reality of the articles of faith (see letter 2.67 in this book) and the shariat injunctions. One is tentatively protected from the shadowy aspects of reality but not conclusively protected like the prophets.[93]

Likewise, there is the appearance of covering up the truth of God and the reality of it. "Infidelity of *islam*" (*kufr-i islam*) is the experience of union (*jam'*) where the Necessary and contingent appear to be the same. As Sirhindi has experienced himself and has explained in earlier letters in his first volume of *Collected Letters* (some of which are in this book), this state is the result of overpowering love and characterizes the sufis whom Sirhindi calls "*wujudi*s." It is not an article of faith for sufis, just a state. Sirhindi continually urges those on the sufi path to go beyond this state to realize that the experience of unity is one of contemplative witnessing, not the reality of the objective world. It is only after this experience of union that one experiences the reality of *islam*.[94] The problem with this experience of union, according to Sirhindi, is that people think they have arrived at oneness with God and are therefore at the end of the path. Sirhindi's experience tells him that anyone who really gets close to God is quite humble and does not dare to utter any kind of ecstatic utterance or to talk about union or oneness.[95]

Sirhindi then interjects another transgressive saying of Maneri's, using it to explain the relationship of one's ego-self (*nafs*) to Satan. In one sense, the external enemy is Satan and the internal enemy is one's own ego-self.

---

91. There are two letters addressed to Mulla Shams in *Collected Letters*.

92. Later in the letter I use "infidelity" for *kufr* because the English phrase becomes unduly cumbersome.

93. See Hutaki, *Sharh-i Maktubat*, 708.

94. See ibid., 709.

95. See ibid., 710.

The reason why even people of insight and intuition are not often aware of Satan is that the ego-self does Satan's work. As Sirhindi poignantly remarks, "our afflictions are from our egos, the enemy we love so much."

In answering the last question, Sirhindi responds in a way to discuss the five necessary entifications pioneered by Ibn al-'Arabi's spiritual insights and called the five emanations (*tanazzulat-i khamsa*) or the five divine presences (*hadarat-i khamsa*). In this context, he discusses fixed entities (sing. *'ayn-i thabita*). According to Sirhindi, *wujudi*s perceive the fixed entities as rays of the attributes in cognitive form (*surat-i 'ilmi*). For Sirhindi, the fixed entities are the rays of disclosure of the fixed attributes. In short, Maneri's phrase, "Until one has sex with his own mother (mother meaning fixed essence) he is not a *muslim*." means that one cannot completely submit to God (be a *muslim*) until one arrives at the level of the fixed entities.

LETTER 3.33

May Mulla Shams be acting with integrity. He had asked what the Shaykh of Shaykhs, Shaykh Sharafuddin Yahya Maneri (d. 782/1381) had written in his epistle, *Guidance for the Wayfarers* (*Irshad al-salikin*): "Until one becomes an infidel (*kafir*) one is not a *muslim*." "Until one reveals the secret of one's brother one is not a *muslim*." "Until one has sex with his own mother he is not a *muslim*."[96] What is the meaning of these words?

(Sirhindi's reply) The meaning of infidelity is "infidelity of the path" (*kufr-i tariqat*) which involves the level of union (*jam'*) in a hidden realm. It is a station in which the wayfarer cannot discriminate between the beauty of Islam and the ugliness of infidelity. Since surrendering to God is known to be praiseworthy, infidelity in the station of union is also experienced as good. Both are experienced as manifestations (sing. *mazhar*) of God's names, "Guide" and "Deceiver," and both bring good fortune and joy. This is the infidelity described by Mansur al-Hallaj (mart. 309/922), lived by him, and through which he died. Hallaj said, "I became an infidel to the religion of God and infidelity is obligatory." In the presence of Muslims [this statement] is detestable. These are ecstatic utterances (*shathiyat*) like "I am the Truth" (by al-Hallaj); "Glory be to me" (by Bayazid Bistami d. 261/875); and "In my robe there is nothing but God" (by Junayd d. 297/910). All of these are fruits of the tree of unity, the source of overflowing love and overpowering of love for the true Beloved. From the perspective of those speaking ecstatic utterances, everything other than the Beloved is hidden. Nothing remains except seeing the Beloved. This station is one of igno-

96. Sharafuddin Maneri's "Irshad al-salikin wa-burhan al-'arifin" is still in manuscript form. See Ahmad Munzawi, *Fihrist-i mushtarak-i nuska-ha-yi khatti-yi farsi-yi Pakistan*, 12 Vols. (Islamabad: Markaz-i tahqiqat-i Iran wa-Pakistan, 1984), 3:1237.

rance and bewilderment. But this ignorance is blessed and this bewilderment is praised.

With the divine favor of God almighty, there is wayfaring higher than this level of union. Knowledge (*'ilm*) joins with ignorance and inner knowledge (*ma'rifat*) becomes a companion to bewilderment. Difference and discrimination are experienced, and sobriety overshadows intoxication. True submission to God appears, and the truth of faith (*iman*) comes easily. This submission and faith are protected from vanishing and from backsliding into infidelity. In a supplication passed down from Muhammad it says, "Oh God I ask you for a faith that is not after infidelity."[97] This is a faith that is protected from vanishing! The Qur'anic phrase, "Surely God's friends will not fear nor have sorrow." [Q. 10:62] points to the state of those with this kind of faith because closeness to God without this kind of faith cannot be imagined. Although intimacy with God (*walayat*) is not associated with the level of union, there is still closeness to God. However, this intimacy is deficient and limited, always attaching itself tenuously to that level. This is because completion is in faith and experiential inner knowledge (*ma'rifat*), not in infidelity and ignorance, no matter what kind of infidelity or ignorance. So some have said that it is true that Shaykh Maneri had said, "Until one verifies infidelity of the path one is not honored by a true submission to God." He also said, "Until you kill your own brother you are not a Muslim." The meaning of one's own brother here is that Satan, who is one's companion and who always points one to wickedness and mischief.

In a hadith it says that no prophet is a human being unless he has a jinn (a disembodied spirit, in this case Satan) as a companion. God bless Muhammad and give him peace. His companions asked the Prophet if he had a jinn as a companion and he said yes but that God almighty had given him power over the jinn to protect him from the jinn's evil. This is on the supposition that the words "I submit to God" (*fa-aslamu*) in the hadith were communicated in the first person singular. If it was spoken in the past tense (*fa-islamu*) then the meaning would be "my companion became a Muslim." This latter meaning is famous.[98] "Killing that companion" [in Maneri's phrase] means that there is no way for Muhammad to be obedient to Satan. He holds Satan in contempt.

Question: Why does a human being, with a mind and intuition, become

97. A prayer attributed to Muhammad. According to 3.32.82 fn 4b, it is found in *The Inaccessible Stronghold* by Ibn al-Jazari. See his *al-Hisn al-hasin min kalam Sayyid al-Mursalin*, ed. ʻAbdurra'uf ibn Muhammad ibn Ahmad Kamali (Kuwait: Ghiras lil-Nashr wa'l-Tawziʻ wa'l-Diʻayah wa'l-Iʻlan, 2008).

98. In the original Arabic the orthography is identical hence the two possibilities of interpretation. A paraphrase of the commonly understood meaning is "Satan became a Muslim at my hands."

overwhelmed by Satan when Satan makes haste with his evil indications and he engages in things not pleasing to God? Exalt God's affair.

Answer: Satan is a temptation and affliction whom God almighty has appointed for trials and tribulations of God's servants. Satan is hidden from their view. They are not aware of Satan's affairs, though he clearly sees their affairs.[99] Satan circulates in their veins and skin, having the color of blood. It is cheering to know that God protects one from the deceptions of such afflictions. Therefore, God almighty has reminded us of the weakness of Satan's evil in the Qur'an. God has made the happy ones fearless. Indeed, with the help of God, Satan is decreed to being a fox with God's authority. Without the help of God's favor, Satan is a rapacious lion.

When you give me the heart and see my fearlessness.
Call me your fox and I will be a lion [in front of Satan].

Answer: Satan comes to a person by means of human passions. A person's greed leads him inevitably to getting tied up with the ego-self. [This occurs] with the help of the ego-self inciting to evil (*nafs-i ammara*), which is his internal enemy. Satan's deceit, within the limits of a person's essence (*dhat*), is weak because the internal enemy does Satan's work. In truth, our afflictions are from our egos, the enemy we love so much.
At the same time, Satan is not one's internal enemy but that contemptible outside enemy who operates with the assistance of the ego-self. So first one must cut the head of the ego-self (I-ness) and extricate oneself from obedience to the ego. He must hold Satan in contempt. The brother's head meanwhile will get cut off. In this effort (*jihad*) Satan will become contemptible. A person's ego-self veils the way. Satan (the brother) is outside of the investigation because he wickedly invites people from afar, taking them from the straight path to crooked, devious paths. After taming the ego-self, it becomes easy to avert the external enemy (Satan) with the help of God. Exalt God's sovereignty. "You have no authority over my servants. Your Lord suffices as a guardian." [Q. 17:65] This is good news. Servants who have extricated themselves from the bondage of the ego-self have ended up worshiping the true God. God almighty is successful.

As for the quote, "Until one has sex with his own mother he is not a Muslim," it is possible that "his mother" means his fixed entity (*'ayn-i thabita*) because his fixed entity is the cause of his existence in the objective (outside) world. In sufi technical vocabulary "fixed entity" is considered to be equivalent in meaning to "mother." A notable said, "My mother gave birth to her father. That surely is strange."[100] The meaning of mother

99. There is a break in the text here.

100. In Kabir's (d. 923/1518 Varanasi) *Bijak*, there are almost identical expressions. The fifth Sikh guru, Guru Arjan Dev, collected a lot of Kabir's poetry and put

is fixed entity and the father of that mother is the name of God. Exalt God's authority. It means that the fixed entity is the shadow, reflection, and ray of God's name. Because the appearance of that name is in the objective world, by means of that name it becomes a fixed entity. That appearance is interpreted as a birth.

Generally sufis say mother when they mean fixed entity. They also call it "necessary entification" (*ta'ayyun-i wujubi*) because according to this exalted group of sufis there are five such necessary entifications called the five emanations or the five divine presences. They have confirmed two entifications at the level of necessity (*wujub*), the entifications of exclusive unity (*ahadiyat*) and unity (*wahdat*).[101] Both of these are at the level of knowledge depending on whether it is comprehensive or detailed. There are three entifications at the level of possibility (*imkan*), the spirit entification (*ta'ayyun-i ruhi*), the imaginal entification (*ta'ayyun-i mithali*), and the corporeal entification (*ta'ayyun-i jasadi*). Since the second entification is at the level of unity its entification is necessary. The truth of a person is possibly the same fixed entity because it is a necessary entification. It is like the person rests in the shadow of the entity. So the mother of this person is from the necessary world because he has manifested in the world of possibility.

Having sex with his mother means that this person's entification of possibility becomes united with the necessary entification, which is the person's truth. When one comes out of possibility then nothing remains except the Necessary. This means that his entification of possibility becomes hidden from his view and his individuality separates from the necessary entification. It does not mean that the entification of possibility has essentially united with the necessary entification because that is impossible. That would necessitate apostasy and heresy because the matter here is one of contemplative witnessing (*shuhud*). Whether there is a vanishing of the entification or unification, it is connected to contemplative witnessing. Neither that changes into this nor does this become that. Difficulties will become easy for you.

When that person experiences this entification itself uniting with that entification it is hoped that he escapes from any possible contamination and becomes honored with the good fortune of Islam and obedience to the level of Necessity. One should know that the five emanations that sufis speak of are separate aspects in existence and connected to being revealed

---

it in what became the principal Sikh scripture, the *Guru Granth Sahib*.

101. Sadruddin Qunawi (d. 673/1274), Ibn al-'Arabi's chief disciple, coined these two terms. Exclusive unity is the total negation of corporeal manifestation. Unity is the level of knowledge. In the six-fold ontological schema there is another level between exclusive unity and unity, inclusive unity (*wahidiyat*), which is the level of comprehensive knowledge. See footnote 34 p. 128.

(*kashf*) and to contemplative witnessing. They are not truly emanations. They change and transform. Praise that which never changes in essence with the occurrence of events, neither in its attributes nor in its names.

Sufis can say many things from their own visions that outwardly should not be tolerated when they are experiencing intoxication and overpowering states. One must employ interpretation and explanation. The speech of intoxicated ones takes one to worthwhile places, but one should avoid its outward aspects. God almighty knows best the entire truth of these matters. Since these anxiety-causing words came from Sharafuddin Maneri, by necessity you wrote in the way that you did. Otherwise, this poor one [Sirhindi], would not have considered these sensory words by writing an opposing letter nor would he have touched upon refuting and accepting these ideas. May our Sustainer forgive our sins and what we squander in our affairs. Help us step firmly, and let us triumph over those who cover up the truth of God. Praise the God of the two worlds from the beginning to the end. God bless God's messenger eternally, his noble family, and great companions until the Day of Resurrection and give them peace.

Chapter Four
Sufi Treatise 1: Letter 1.260

Introduction to Letter 1.260

This letter describing the Naqshbandi path in great detail was written to Muhammad Sadiq (d. 1025/1616), the eldest son of Ahmad Sirhindi,[1] and may be the treatise being prepared by his son mentioned in letter 1.257. In any case, this letter outlines the Naqshbandi path, starting with the world of command and ending in the material world—which counter-intuitively is the furthest point on the path and the realm of the prophets. Looking at the Naqshbandi path from another perspective, the first section of the path, the ascent, is defined as lesser intimacy with God (*walayat-i sughra*), traveling in the shadows of God's attributes, which is followed by a continuing ascent called "wayfaring in God" (*sayr fi 'llah*). Descent involves a greater intimacy with God (*walayat-i kubra*), associated with the prophets. If one follows a prophet assiduously a non-prophet can also experience greater intimacy with God, which is wayfaring in the names and attributes of God.

Throughout his writings, Sirhindi points out that many sufis who think they are close or intimate with God are still only in the realm of lesser intimacy with God and are only experiencing outer (*suri*) annihilation and subsistence in God in their journey to God (*sayr ila Allah*). Once the seeker crosses from the world of contingent existence (*'alam-i mumkinat*) to the shadows of God's names and attributes (a transitional realm), the seeker experiences real (*haqiqi*) annihilation and subsistence in God. Likewise, according to Sirhindi, many sufis are in the shadows of God's attributes and names and are far from the attributes of God, much less the Essence itself. Given this context, the discussion in this letter is necessarily quite detailed. Sirhindi explains the differences between the shadows of the origins (sing. *mabda'*) and the origins themselves, both of which are ineffable, and the entifications (*ta'ayyunat*), which are the first manifestations of form.

The disclosures (sing. *tajalli*) of God's names and attributes as such do not blend with other levels of being. As one goes downward, another level of being is created, ending up in the world of contingent existence, the top point of which is the world of command, specifically the circle of the superarcane subtle center. In cosmological terms, it is like there are three circular cones stacked on top of each other vertically and the vertex point of one touching the center of the circular base of the one below. The Origin

1. There are five letters addressed to Muhammad Sadiq in *Collected Letters*.

of Origins is at the top with the cone of Origin with the names attributes, qualities, and aspects in the middle cone. The lowest cone is the world of command (a simplified way of showing the world of contingent existence) with its uppermost point being the superarcane subtle center (See Figure 4). The diagram shows a very rough model of someone beginning at the heart subtle center, as Naqshbandi-Mujaddidis do, and the progression to utmost ascent in the Origin of Origins and the resulting descent and completion of the element of earth.

Another reason for such great detail in this letter is to clarify the difference between God's friends (*awliya'*) and prophets. Ontologically, according to Sunni creed, protégés of God—and everyone else—are different than prophets. Sirhindi explains these differences in minute detail. The friends of God receive their divine energy (*fayd*) from the shadows of the attributes while the prophets receive their divine energy from God's attributes directly. In the Sunni hierarchy where Abu Bakr has the highest spiritual rank of all non-prophets, his divine energy comes from the highest point in the circle of the shadows of God's names and attributes. This situation does not prevent individuals from ascending far beyond the shadows of the attributes or even the attributes themselves. Many people can participate in one attribute but in different ways. For example, Abraham, Muhammad, and a sufi can all participate in the attribute of knowledge. The sufi is governed by the shadow of knowledge of the attribute; Abraham has the experience of the details or particularities of that attribute; and Muhammad experiences a comprehensive knowledge of the attribute.

In a more detailed view of the "middle cone" of God's attributes (not shown in Figure 4), it is described as two bows. The one facing downwards contains the names and attributes that are shared in the lower worlds and the one facing upwards contains the qualities (*shuyunat*) and aspects (*i'tibarat*).[2] The attributes, qualities, and aspects do not have objective existence in the material world. Their perfections can only be realized with a tranquil ego. When the seeker traverses the inner name, then the seeker has knowledge of God's being. After traversing both the inner and outer names, the seeker contemplatively witnesses God. Wayfaring in the outer name is in the attributes but without contemplatively observing the Essence of the attributes. In contrast, wayfaring in the inner name is wayfaring in the attributes while including the contemplative witnessing of the Essence.

The origin of the divine energy associated with the existence of creation comes from the great angels who are associated with the greatest intimacy (*walayat-i 'ulya*). Although this intimacy is "higher" than the greater intimacy with God associated with prophets, the latter have greater rank

2. The shared attributes are: hearing, sight, speech, will, power, knowledge, life, and creation.

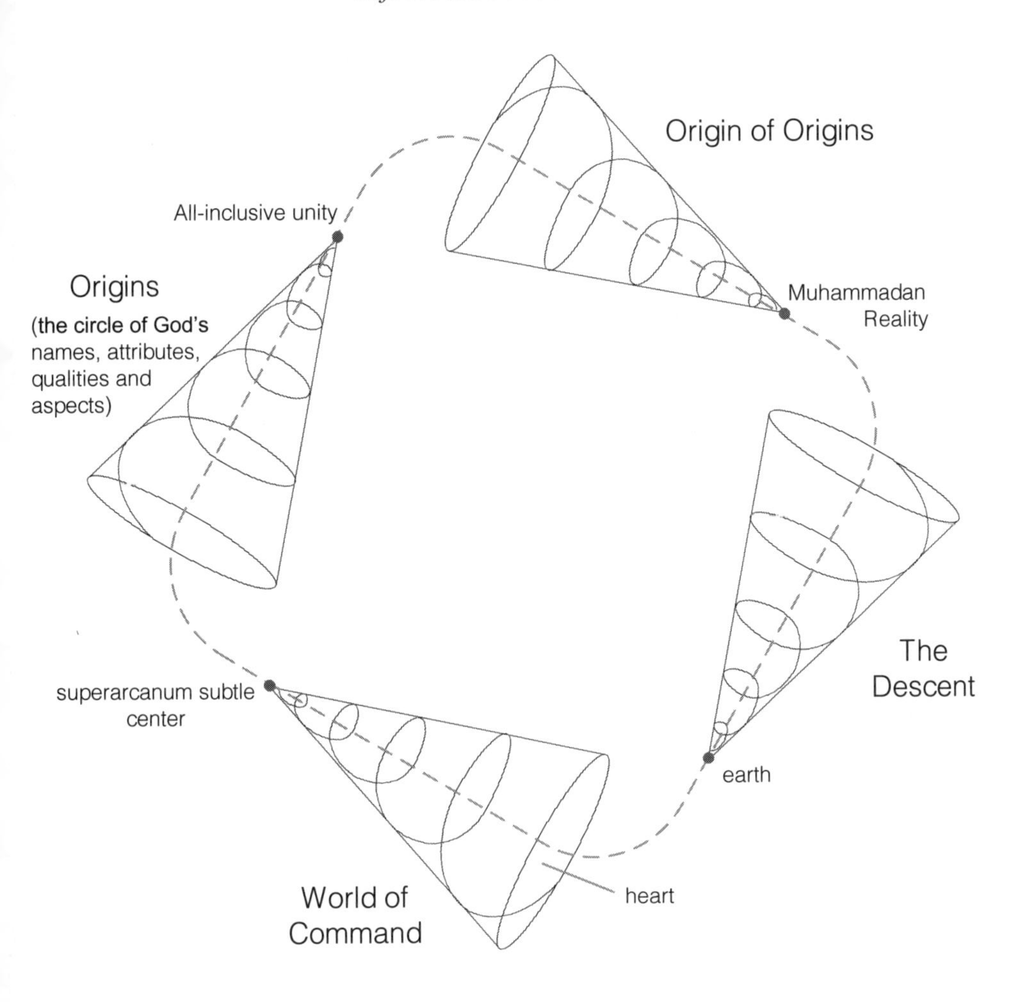

Figure 4. The Mujaddidi Path: The end included in the beginning

because of their perfections of prophethood (and the preference of the element earth which will be discussed below). The station of prophethood is connected with the manifestations of the Essence. The origin of divine energy for protégés of God is the shadows of the attributes, for prophets it is the attributes themselves, and for great angels it is the qualities.

Then comes the discussion of the relative ranking of prophets. Jesus' closeness to God in the world of command is higher than that of Moses.

This is obvious by comparing what Jesus was able to manifest in the physical world via his stature in the world of command, the world that "rules" the material world. In terms of prophetic perfections, Moses is more preferable to Jesus. When one compares the two as prophets qua prophets this too is clear. For example, the closeness of both Moses and Jesus is greater than that of Abraham in their perfections in the world of command. Yet Abraham is far beyond them in terms of his being in the outer reality of the Ka'ba in the first entification. But his mastery over the particularities of the Ka'ba does not compare to Muhammad's comprehensive awareness of the Ka'ba. The origin of divine energy for Abraham is the attribute of knowledge, while that of Muhammad is the quality of knowledge. It is this correspondence with respect to the Ka'ba and the attribute of knowledge that has the Muslim community praying toward the Ka'ba of Abraham. In this letter, Sirhindi also clarifies the ontological status of the Reality of the Ka'ba—being superior to the Reality of Muhammad, the quality of knowledge, and to the perfections of prophethood.[3]

Closeness to God among friends of God while traveling in the shadows is a function of the subtle center in which the seeker is wayfaring. In the shadows themselves there is a clear demarcation from low to high: heart, spirit, mystery, arcane, and superarcane. After that, it is a function of descending to the material world—the realm of the prophets. As Sirhindi states in the letter, the essential message here is the superiority of the created world over the world of command. This makes sense for Naqshbandis who start wayfaring in the world of command purifying the subtle centers and "finish" wayfaring in the created world cleansing the ego-self. Seeing God (*ru'yat*) and contemplatively witnessing the Source is associated with the station of prophethood, which is in the realm of the created world, as is the vision of heaven. It is implied that the Prophet did have a physical vision of God in his heavenly ascent (though the hadiths attributed to 'Aisha and others deny this), but the word *ru'yat* (not to be confused with *ru'yā*, a vision in a dream) is still vague in this letter.[4]

After one calms the ego-self, then one has to deal with the elements (earth, air, water, and fire) associated with the physical frame (*qalab*), where the element earth is the last to be cleansed. It is this element of earth

---

3. Sirhindi received much opposition from his asserting that the Reality of the Ka'ba was closer to God than the Reality of Muhammad. This opposition continued through the nineteenth century. See Buehler, *Sufi Heirs*, 246-247.

4. In *Collected Letters*, 3.122.140 Sirhindi states that Muhammad was blessed with a vision in this world that is particular to Muhammad only. In ibid., 3.68.152 he states that the station of *ru'yat* is higher than the Seal of the Prophets. For everyone else, all visions of God occur in the heart (ibid., 3.90.40) or in the world of imaginal forms (*'alam-i mithal*). See ibid., 3.44.103.

that is the highest of all. Returning transformed to this apparently "inferior" world is the goal for Sirhindi. Human completion is manifested in the material world.[5] This is the prophetic path, not the path that stops halfway in ascent.

In this letter there are allusions to Sirhindi's place in the spiritual hierarchy. Though Sirhindi never explicitly states his exact position, it is very strongly implied. Sirhindi writes about a person who is "the leader of the time and successor of the age." He mentions that the entire letter was written in harmony with the station of the axial guide (*qutb-i irshad*), who has the total perfections of uniqueness (*fardiyat*), but yet is under the (undescribed) "imam." In his other writings, Sirhindi had declared himself to be the unique one (*fard*), having absolute authority from the empyrean to earth.[6] Subsequently he came to have the title, "the renewer of the second millennium" (*mujaddid-i alf-i thani*).[7] Throughout *Collected Letters* Sirhindi is very conscious of the spiritual hierarchy, his perceived mis-interpretations of it (like Ibn al-'Arabi's in this letter), and his own place in its schema.

Letter 1.260

In the name of God, the compassionate and merciful. Give thanks to God, the Lord of heaven and earth. God bless and give peace to the lord of the messengers [Muhammad], all of the [other] messengers, his family, and his pure companions.

O son! May God, the almighty and glorious, assist you. Know that the five-fold world of command has the aspects of heart, spirit, mystery, arcane, and superarcane. Originating in the macrocosm (*'alam-i kabir*), these aspects correspond respectively to parts of the human microcosm (*'alam-i saghir*). Humans also consist of four elements (earth, fire, water, air) that originate in the macrocosm. The sources (*usul*) of the aforementioned five aspects appear above the Throne,[8] and are described as being beyond physical space. From here, it is said that the world of command is beyond space-time. The circle of contingent existence (*da'irah-i imkan*) encompasses the material world, the world of command, the microcosm, and the macrocosm to the end of these sources. The circle of contingent ex-

5. See Buehler, *Sufi Heirs*, 100.

6. See Sirhindi, *Mabda' wa-ma'ad*, 9-11.

7. See Hashim Kishmi's narrative in the Introduction. Muhammad Hashim Kishmi, *Zubdat al-maqamat* (Istanbul: Işık Kitabevi, 1997), 176.

8. According to Sirhindi, the Throne is separate from the traces of the heavens and earth and one of the noblest "parts" of the macrocosm, acting as an interface between the world of creation and the world of command. See *Collected Letters,* 2.21.49-50, 1.44.95. The heart subtle center is the Throne of the human microcosm. See *Collected Letters,* 2.11.34.

istence consists of non-being mixed with being. It is the source of all that is contingent upon the Necessary Essence. In this domain, one becomes realized (*muntahi gardad*). When the wayfarer of Muhammadan disposition is guided, he/she first traverses the five-fold world of command before going to its sources located in the macrocosm. This great boon, that is, arriving at the final center after systematically traversing the attributes of God, results from the absolute grace of the sublime Eternal.

By traveling through each aspect of the circle of contingent existence, one completes the stage of "wayfaring to God" (*sayr ila Allah*). Being released from the [shadow of the] name, one then realizes annihilation of I-ness (*fana'-i khud*). Then one begins to proceed in the stage called "lesser intimacy with God" (*walayat-i sughra*), the closeness to God almighty attained by God's protégés. After this, if one travels in the shadows of God's necessary names, which actually are the sources of the five aspects of the macrocosm mixed with non-being, no path is found. It only happens with God's grace. Exalt God's majesty. Proceeding along the path of "wayfaring in God" (*sayr fi 'llah*), one arrives at the end of the circle of shadows of the necessary names. Continuing, one arrives at the level of God's necessary names and attributes. Up to here is the end of ascent in the "lesser intimacy of God." In this realm, one begins to realize the reality of ego annihilation [in God]. One step further leads one to the beginning of "greater intimacy with God" (*walayat-i kubra*), the closeness of prophets.

One should know that the circle of shadows includes the principles underlying the entifications (*ta'ayyunat*) of creatures, with the exception of the noble prophets and the great angels. God bless them and give them peace. The shadow of each name of God is the origin (*mabda'*) of a specific person, until one reaches the specific origin of the exalted presence of Abu Bakr as-Siddiq (Muhammad's successor d. 13/634), which is a dot above this circle of shadows. He is the most favored human after the prophets. The Masters of the path say that when a wayfarer arrives at one of God's names that is the origin of a personal attribute of Abu Bakr's, then the stage of "wayfaring to God" is completed. The goal of arriving at one of these names is to arrive at the shadow of God's name.

One should also know that this is only a part of the shadow of God's name, not the origin of it. This circle of shadows actually only comprises the details of the names and attributes [not their comprehensive nature]. For example, knowledge is an attribute having many aspects. The details of knowledge are the shadows of knowledge and have a relationship to the whole. Each aspect of that attribute is the reality of a person, except for the noble prophets and great angels. The origins of the entifications of the prophets and angels are the origins of these shadows. In other words, these origins totally encompass the variegated aspects of any given attribute such as knowledge, power, will, and so on. Many people can share an attribute that is the origin of a common entification. Each person participates in a different aspect of the attribute. For example, the origin of the entification of the Seal of the Prophets (Muhammad) is in the domain of knowledge. This attribute of knowledge has a special relationship with the origin of the entification of the exalted presence of Abraham. God bless and give peace to our prophet and him. Also this attribute with [another special] aspect is the origin of the entification of the exalted presence of Noah. Specifics concerning these aspects are mentioned in a letter addressed to Khwaja Muhammad Ashraf.[9]

Some shaykhs have said that the Muhammadan Reality is the first entification, the comprehensive presence, which they call "absolute unity" (*wahdat*). From what this poor one (Ahmad Sirhindi) understands of their meaning, they think that this circle of shadows is the first entification. God knows best about this affair. The center of this circle is called "absolute unity," which these shaykhs understand to be comprehensive in nature. They call the details of this center surrounding the circle "the all-inclusive unity" (*wahidiyat*). They imagine that the station above the circle of shadows, which is the circle of names and attributes, is undifferentiated Essence, far removed from any entification. They also say that any attribute is the origin of the Essence and they cannot conceive of anything beyond that.

It is not like this. We say that the center of this circle is the shadow of the shadow of the center of the circle above it. This upper circle is the origin of the lower circle and named "the circle of God's names, attributes, qualities, and aspects." In truth, the Muhammadan Reality is the center of this circle of origin, encompassing the names and attributes. The details of God's names and attributes in this circle are at the level of all-inclusive unity.[10] To put absolute unity and all-inclusive unity on the level of the shadows of God's names is the result of mistaking the shadows for the origins. Likewise, their reference to "wayfaring in God" is in truth just "wayfaring to God." That is the way it is.

If there is any ascent after this, it will be in the circle of names and attributes, the origin of the prior circle of shadows. To proceed along the path of "wayfaring in God," one begins in the perfections of "greater intimacy with God," which is special for prophets. By assiduously following the [practice of] prophets, the noble Companions share in this bounty. The bottom half of this circle contains the names and attributes of God and the upper half includes the necessary qualities and aspects. The end of the five-fold ascent

---

9. See *Collected Letters*, 1.251.53-54

10. See Chittick, "The Five Divine Presences," 107-128. See also the discussion at the end of letter 3.33. Perhaps exclusive unity (*ahadiyat*) is meant here instead of absolute unity (*wahdat*).

from the world of command is at the end of this circle of names and qualities. After that, with God's encompassing grace, one proceeds beyond attributes and qualities going past the circle of origins to the circle of origins of origins. After traversing these circles, a bow appears from the circle above. Beyond this, nothing came into my view other than the bow.[11]

In all of this, there is a secret from the unseen that has not yet been divulged. The aforementioned three-fold origins of the names and attributes are separate aspects in God almighty's presence that are the foundations of the previous attributes and qualities.[12] A tranquil ego (*nafs-i mutma'inna*) is necessary to achieve a complete realization of these three-fold origins. For one desired by God (*murad*), tranquility will come easily. In this station, one realizes the expanded chest (*sharh-i sadr*) as the wayfarer becomes honored by authentic submission to God.[13] It is in this domain that one sits tranquilly on the throne of the chest as one ascends to the station of satisfaction. This is the realm at the end of greater intimacy with God, the intimacy of prophets. God bless them and give them peace.

As soon as I arrived at this point and imagined that the work was completed, a voice from the unseen world informed me that all of this traveling was in the multiplicity of the outer name, which is only one wing. To fly in the divine world [one needs] the second wing, the inner name, which was yet to come. After traveling through the realm of particulars, the two wings are able to fly. Through God's favor, one finishes wayfaring in the inner name and it actually becomes easy to fly. Praise God, who brings us to this point. We would not have been guided without God showing us the way and unless the messengers of our Lord had come with the truth.

O son! From wayfaring in the inner name, what can be written to correspond with that state? That wayfaring is hidden. This much from that station can be revealed, namely that wayfaring in the outer name is in the attributes without the almighty and holy Essence being perceived inside the attributes. One is able to perceive the almighty Essence while wayfaring in the inner name, although it is still in the names. These names function like veils of the almighty and blessed, exalted presence of the Essence. For example, in the attribute of knowledge, the almighty Essence is not perceived. In the name of the All Knowing One (*'alīm*), the almighty Es-

11. The bow is associated with the highest of God's qualities, the quality of knowledge. See Buehler, *Sufi Heirs*, 245. This bow is associated with the Qur'anic verse [53:8] referring to Muhammad's ascension where Muhammad came "two bows length or closer."

12. The three-fold origins are: the circle of the attributes and qualities, the circle of the origins of the origins, and the circle above this where only a bow is seen. See Figure 1.

13. See Buehler, *Sufi Heirs,* 244 and *Collected Letters*, 1.257.68 and 3.15.25.

sence is perceived behind the veil of the attribute. This is because the All Knowing One is one Essence whose attribute is knowledge. So wayfaring in knowledge is traveling in the outer name and traveling in the All Knowing One is traveling in the inner name. The same principle applies to other attributes and names. The names associated with the inner name are the origins of the entifications of the great angels. God bless and give blessings to our prophet and them.

Initiating wayfaring in God's names is to proceed toward the greatest intimacy with God (*walayat-i 'ulya*), the closeness associated with the great angels. There is a difference between knowledge and the All Knowing One corresponding to the [qualitative] difference between the outer and the inner names as explained above. Do not say or even think that the difference between knowledge and the All Knowing One is minor. Absolutely to the contrary, it is like the difference between a speck of earth and the highest firmament of heavens or like the difference between a drop and the ocean. It is easy to say that something is near but to attain it is an entirely different story. It is just like this.

[Let me] mention the stations that manifest on the comprehensive path to God. It has been said that after traversing the five aspects of the world of command, one commences to travel in their origins until the end of the circle of contingent existence. This wayfaring to God discussed in detail above would take [a person] fifty thousand years [to achieve]. The Qur'anic verse, "The angels and the Spirit ascend to God in a day that is equivalent to fifty thousand years" alludes to this meaning. [Q. 70:4] In short, the attraction of God's favor is near. A task that would take a long period [to accomplish] can be facilitated in the blink of an eye. There is no difficulty for those distinguished by God's favor.

Likewise, it has been said that after traversing the circle of the names, attributes, qualities, and aspects, one begins wayfaring in the origins. Traversing all of the names, attributes, qualities, and aspects is easy to say but extremely difficult to do. The Masters of the path have declared that the stages leading to God are endless and it is impossible to reach the end.

God has infinite beauty of perfection.
Words cannot express this.
It is a thirst that cannot be quenched.
While the sea remains unchanged.

Do not think that the continuous, non-ending path [leading to God] has anything to do with what [the shaykhs] have said about disclosures (*tajalliyat*) of the Essence or disclosures of the attributes. When shaykhs talk about completion, it is completion of the Essence, not of the attributes. I say that the disclosures of the Essence are perceived with the qualities and aspects.

This complete divine beauty is veiled by the merciful attributes No one could say anything without these veils. Whoever knows God is silent. The disclosure [that they discuss] is like a shadow [rather than the Essence]. One cannot help but notice the qualities in that station. Those stages of arriving and the degrees of complete beauty are inside the circle of names and qualities. According to the Masters, it is difficult to separate these stages and degrees from the circle of names and qualities.

Something from the unseen world was revealed to this dervish (Ahmad Sirhindi) concerning what is behind disclosures and manifestations (*zuhur*) in general, whether it is a disclosure of the Essence or it is a disclosure of the attributes. This is also behind divine beauty, whether beauty of the Essence or beauty of the attributes. The lofty purposes all have been arranged comprehensively in a series of short explanations. It is like trying to put the limitless seas into some water jugs. Do not be among those who fall short of the goal.

Now we return to the prior subject of discussion (Ahmad Sirhindi's experiences on the preceding page). After realizing the two wings of the inner and outer name, this poor one (Ahmad Sirhindi) flew higher and higher with greater ease. I discovered that these developments originated in the elements of fire, air, and water. The noble angels also share these three elements. It also happens that some of the angels are created from fire and ice and they praise God by saying, "Praise be to the one who joined fire and ice." While wayfaring, I had a vision where they showed me a path on which to proceed. After going a long way, I started to feel totally exhausted and desired a walking staff to make the going easier. But it did not work. I reached out, grasping sticks and thorns, to allow me to continue on the path. I had no choice but to go forward. So I continued going along like this until the outskirts of a city appeared. After awhile, I entered the city and realized that this city was the primary entification (*ta'ayyun-i awwal*) of the Essence that encompasses all levels of the names, attributes, qualities, and aspects. It also encompasses the origins of these levels, the origins of their origins, and the utmost limits of the essential aspects. These all can be distinguished by acquired knowledge (*'ilm-i husuli*). Any wayfaring after that is the domain of knowledge-by-identity (*'ilm-i huduri*).

O son, The expression of acquired knowledge and knowledge-by-identity in that holy Presence is by means of allegory and simile (not in reality) because these attributes are outside (*za'id*) the being of the almighty and holy Essence. So acquired knowledge is the suitable way of knowing [them] (since one can know by appearance). Essential aspects, which are never outside the Essence, cannot be imagined and must be known by identity. There is no relationship between knowledge and what is known unless the knower has acquired something of what is known (hence knowledge by presence/identity). Understand this subtle point!

The consolidation of the intimacy of the noble prophets and great angels and the utmost limit of the greatest intimacy, the domain of the highest angels, is from the first entification of the Essence (the city mentioned above is the encompassing metaphor for this first entification). When one is first in this station, one wonders whether the first entification is the Muhammadan Reality or not. From what has been mentioned above, [one can see that] it obviously is [the Muhammadan Reality]. What is said to be the first entification is such that the center mentioned above (four pages before) is the shadow of the first entification and comprehensively includes the names, attributes, qualities, and aspects. Any wayfaring above this place begins in the perfections of prophethood. These perfections are associated with the prophets and proceed from the station of prophethood. The perfected followers of the prophets partake of this bounty. God bless them and give them peace.

In the midst of the human subtle centers, abundance from these perfections comes originally from the element of earth. All aspects of the human, whether from the world of command or the material world, all conform to this pure element [earth] in this station. By means of this, they are blessed with this favor. Since this element of earth is associated with human beings, distinguished humans become preferable to distinguished angels. All humans are benefited by this element to some extent, [whether they have purified the element of earth or not]. After coming close [to God], the reality of nearness appears in this domain. The secret of the Qur'anic verse, "It was at the distance of two bows' length or nearer." becomes revealed. [Q. 53:9]

As one proceeds beyond the aforementioned city, one realizes that one has arrived at the perfections of all types of intimacy with God. Whether involving lesser, greater, or greatest intimacy with God, all these are in the shadows of the perfections of the station of prophethood. The perfections of intimacy with God remotely resemble the realities of the splendid perfections of prophethood. Just traversing a dot [in the perfections of prophethood involves] much more than traversing all the perfections of the station of intimacy with God. When it dawns on someone that the dot is related to this wayfaring, then one asks about the relationship between the perfections of [lesser] intimacy and the perfections of prophethood. By analogy, [it is like comparing] a drop of water to the ocean. In both these cases, the relationship is [ultimately] nonexistent. We say that that the relationship between the station of prophethood and the station of [lesser] intimacy with God is like [the difference between something] infinite and finite. Praise be to God!

Someone ignorant of prophethood said that intimacy with God is preferable to prophethood, while another unaware individual stated that the Prophet's closeness to God is preferable to his prophethood. Their words are distressing. By favor of God the most glorious, God's dear friend (Muhammad) arrived at the end of the path.[14] He saw that if he had taken one more step along the path, it would have ended up disappearing into absolute nonbeing. There is nothing beyond this point except absolute nonbeing.

O son, from this experience do not think that the 'Anqa can be hunted or that the Simurg has fallen into a trap.[15]

> The 'Anqa can never be captured in a trap designed for a Chinese falcon.
> It is like trying to catch the wind in one's hand.
> God the most glorious is after the beyond of the beyond, then beyond the beyond, and then beyond the beyond.
> You high up in the tower of the palace.[16]
> Beware of the desire to arrive.

This discovery does not involve veils because the veils have been completely lifted. Instead, there is a proof of sublimity and grandeur that blocks comprehension and negates ecstasy. He, the most glorious, is closest to existence and the farthest from ecstasy. Indeed, some of the most accomplished travelers (*muradan*) are given sublime tents of majesty by means of the prophets.[17] The prophets give these wayfarers a place of refuge by building them a sacred court. What happens there cannot be described in words.[18]

O son! This affair involves the consolidated subtle centers of the human being (literally the unitary form *qalab*) resulting from the confluence of the material world and the world of command. Therefore, in this domain the ruling element is earth.[19] Let us return to the quote mentioned above, namely, "there is nothing behind a certain point except absolute nonbeing." After traversing all the levels of objective being, (that is, independent of one's individual consciousness *wujud-i kharij*) and subjective being (*wu-*

---

14. In other places Sirhindi states that there is no end to the path (cf. letter 1.13 in this translation and earlier in this very letter 1.260).

15. The '*anqā'* (Arabic) is the name of the "phoenix" while *simurgh* (Persian meaning literally "thirty birds") has been used as an allegory for the relationship between God and humans. Often sufis use these two words interchangeably as Sirhindi does here.

16. Reading *ista'ala* from al-Manzalawi's Arabic translation instead of *istaghana* from Nur Ahmad's edition. See al-Manzalawi al-Qazani's translation of Sirhindi's *Maktubat: al-durar al-maknunat*, 1:244.

17. Nur Ahmad's edition lacks a phrase found in the Arabic translation. See ibid.

18. Nur Ahmad refers to Q. 20:78 where the waters "overwhelm and cover up." See *Collected Letters*, 1.260.80, fn 3.

19. From this point to the end of the next paragraph, there is a partial translation in Ansari, *Sufism and Sharī'ah,* 287-288.

jud-i 'ilmi) one realizes that nonbeing is the antithesis of objective being. The Essence of God the most glorious is beyond both being and nonbeing. Just as nonbeing has no path [to God], neither does being. This is because any being having nonbeing as its opposite is in the realm of duality and not the Absolute. How amazing is that great Presence! Exalt that Presence. If I put the absoluteness of being on that level [of duality] the narrowness of my interpretation would be such that nonbeing would not have the possibility of being the opposite of being.

In some prior letters, this poor one (Ahmad Sirhindi) had written that the reality of the divine Presence is absolute being.[20] One who had not yet arrived [at the truth] wrote these ideas. Really, the affair is like this. Some, who are aware of the unity of all being (*tawhid-i wujudi*), have written that the secret of the unity of being is unknowable at the beginning of the path. Actually, they have realized aspects of the truth of the matter for beginners or intermediates on the path. Later, they repented for what they had written. I ask God for forgiveness and repentance from all that displeases God almighty.

In this regard, it is evident that the perfections of prophethood are in the upper levels and that one faces God almighty in the prophetic ascents. Most people believe to the contrary, namely that one witnesses God in contemplation at the level of [lesser] intimacy with God. In prophethood, one is oriented toward creation. This involves levels of descent. [They believe that] God's intimacy only involves levels of ascent. From this, one can [mistakenly] imagine that [lesser] intimacy with God is preferable to prophethood. Indeed, both [lesser] intimacy with God and prophethood involve ascent and descent. In ascent, both are oriented toward God almighty. In descent, both are oriented toward creation.

Briefly, in descent, prophethood is completely oriented toward creation. [Lesser] intimacy with God is not completely oriented toward creation,[21] since one's inner self is with God and the outer is oriented toward creation. The secret of this is that one who is wayfaring in God's [lesser] intimacy embarks on descent before having completed all the stages of ascent. Necessarily, the expectation is to be in the ascendant phase all the time. One feels safe. A total orientation toward creation would be counterproductive. On the other hand, the wayfarer in prophethood descends only after having completed the ascent, and therefore can focus his entire being on inviting people to God. Understand that no one has ever discussed this exalted, inner experiential knowledge or anything like it.

---

20. See ter Haar, *Follower and Heir of the Prophet*, 119-122 for a discussion of Sirhindi's thought on the ontological unity of being. For references to the actual letters see ibid., 33, note 20 and 34, note 21. See also, Yohanan Friedmann, *Shaykh Ahmad Sirhindi*, 59-60.

21. Note the discussion of ascent and descent in *Collected Letters*, 1.95.

One should know that as one goes through the various levels of ascent, the element of earth is the most privileged element. In the stations of descent, it becomes the lowest of all. So why is the element of earth privileged at all when it is naturally the lowest element? In its fall to the lowest of low, calling people to God becomes completed. [Under these circumstances] there is utmost benefit to those hearing the message.[22]

O son! The Naqshbandi path starts with wayfaring in the heart subtle center located in the world of command. All other lineages (in India these are generally considered to be the Qadiriyya, Chishtiyya, and Suhrawardiyya) begin by purifying the ego-self and the physical body, after which they proceed to the world of command if God almighty desires it. From there they ascend. Hence, the ending stage of other lineages is included in the starting point for Naqshbandis, greatly shortening the distance to the goal for those on the Naqshbandi path. This is the shortest path enabling one to most effectively achieve purification of the ego-self (*nafs*) and body through wayfaring in the heart. Naqshbandi shaykhs explicitly consider traveling in the material world to be a useless waste, because it is harmful and a hindrance to arriving at the goal.

Those of other sufi lineages purify their ego-self and perform strenuous exercises, traversing the beginnings of the appearance of the material world,[23] saying that this is the beginning of the world of command. They experience attraction in the heart and satisfaction of the spirit (*ruh*). It is enough that they are content with this attraction and satisfaction. They become attached to thinking that their experience in the world of attraction and satisfaction is beyond physical space. To conflate the incommensurability of that world with true incommensurability is, however, a hindrance [to realization]. A traveler once said that he spent thirty years at the level of the spirit subtle center worshipping God in this station. Another remarked that the secret of completion and manifestation of transcendence (*tanzih*) above the Throne is from hidden knowledge. From the previous discussion, it is known that transcendence also is within the circle of contingent existence. It appears to be transcendence, but in truth it is immanence.

On the other hand, the notables of the lofty Naqshbandi path begin in the station of attraction to God and advance by means of these delightful [attractions]. This [Naqshbandi] attraction to God and the pleasures thereof contrast with the ascetic exercises of non-Naqshbandi sufis, who are prevented from arriving at the ultimate goal. Naqshbandis, assisted by the non-

22. Here we are reminded of the Zen ox-herding pictures. See Figure 3 in the Introduction for the nine donkey-herding pictures.

23. Here the contrast is between the appearance of the material world and the reality of the material world. Traversing the latter is difficult without having first traversed the world of command.

spatiality [*la makaniyat*] of the world of command, are able to conceive of the origin of spatiality, which they regard as genuine non-spatiality. The ineffable (*be chuni*) nature of the world of command is the origin of the manifest world. Naqshbandis ascend to the true unmanifest realms and are not fascinated with others' preoccupation with intoxicated states. They proceed along the path to God sparing no effort. Unlike useless sufis, Naqshbandis do not engage in frivolous festivities (*mubahat*). Nor do they glorify the ecstatic utterances (*shatihat*) of sufi masters. Instead, Naqshbandis focus on absolute exclusive unity (*ahadiyat-i sirf*) and do not desire partial aspects of the holy Essence such as the names and attributes.

One should know that this aforementioned ascent of ours is a distinguishing mark of the Muhammadan disposition (*mashrab*). It is the good fortune of complete attainment resulting from the perfections of the five subtle centers located in the world of command. Whether from the microcosm, the macrocosm, or even from the origins of the five-fold world (the shadows of the necessary names), there is great benefit from completing the five subtle centers. Likewise, it is from the origins of those shadows where the names and attributes are located. There is a complete attainment because there is also divine favor in the outward aspect of the Muhammadan disposition. This results from the perfections of the superarcanum subtle center at the end of the world of command.

However, one cannot arrive at the end of the superarcanum subtle center. Nor is the last center dot [in the superarcanum realm] its utmost end, even though it remains in the beginning and the intermediate stages of the journey. To the extent that one finishes the superarcanum, one will finish in the origins [of the superarcanum], reaching the goal. The same relationship exists with the other four subtle centers of the world of command such that complete attainment at each level is dependent upon arriving at the final goal. One is only partially aware of the last center dot of the superarcanum in the beginning and middle of the journey, even though one is only a hair's width from the end.

Even half a hair's width of separation from the friend is too much.

This gap separating one from the goal penetrates both the origins and the origins of the origins. It prevents one from arriving at the goal. As I said before, this explanation is relevant for the Muhammadan disposition,[24] since those still having other dispositions are limited.

For example, in the first degree of intimacy with God, one is at the level of the heart. In the second degree, one is at the station of the spirit. Another person could be at the pinnacle of a complete ascent to the third or fourth degree, that is, the station of the mystery or arcane subtle center respectively. The first degree correlates with the disclosure of the active

24. That is, for travel in the superarcanum subtle center, the "fifth degree."

attributes, the second with the disclosure of the fixed essential attributes (*sifat-i dhatiya*),[25] the third with the essential qualities and aspects, and the fourth with the negative attributes,[26] a transcendent and holy station. Each of these degrees of intimacy with God is governed by (lit. under the foot of) a great prophet (pl. *ulu al-'azmi*). The first degree of intimacy with God is supervised by the exalted presence of Adam. His authority is the attribute of physical formation (*takwin*), the origin where actions arise. The second degree is supervised by the exalted presences of Abraham and Noah. Their authority is the attribute of knowledge, the sum of all the essential attributes. The third degree is supervised by the exalted presence of Moses whose authority is speech, derived from the station of his qualities. The fourth degree is supervised by the exalted presence of Jesus. His authority is from the negative attributes, which are not fixed attributes (these latter attributes are the domain of divinity and transcendence). Most of the noble angels share this domain with the exalted presence of Jesus. Angels attain a magnificent realization in this station. God bless and give peace to our prophet and them.

The fifth degree is supervised by the Seal of the prophets [Muhammad].[27] His authority is the authority of all authority encompassing the divine attributes, qualities, and transcendences. God bless him and give him peace. It is the center of the circle of all these perfections. At the level of the attributes and qualities, the nature of that encompassing authority corresponds to the quality of knowledge (*sha'n-i 'ilm*).[28] This is a glorious affair, involving a synthesis of all perfections. The same correspondence exists between Muhammad's community and the community of the exalted presence of Abraham whose direction to prayer is the same as Muhammad's.

One should know that preference is on the basis of intimacy with God, not on the basis of being ahead or behind in degrees. Just because a person is in the superarcanum does not mean that there is an automatic precedence over someone in the previous degrees (that is, the subtle centers of the

---

25. These are the attributes of hearing, sight, speech, will, power, knowledge, life and creation.

26. These negative attributes include God not having substance, a form, a body, or limitation.

27. This is the level of the superarcanum subtle center and associated with manifestations from the Essence, which are blessed by the almighty Eternal.

28. The quality of knowledge is related to all of the attributes, qualities, and aspects. Collectively all the attributes, qualities, and aspects are known as "the comprehensive synthesis" (*sha'n-i jami'*) or the universal quality (*sha'n-i kulli*). The quality of knowledge is of particularities, each of which is the origin of divine energy for a protégé of God having a Muhammadan disposition. See Hutaki, *Sharh-i Maktubat*, 352-353.

heart, spirit, mystery, or arcanum). It is about nearness and distance from the Origin and the extent to which one has traversed the levels of shadows. Therefore, the person who is traveling in the heart close to the Origin is more preferred than one who is in the superarcanum without that degree of closeness. So the [incomparable] intimacy of the Prophet, which is in the first degree (that is, the heart) is absolutely more favored than anyone who is in the last degree, that is, the superarcanum, and only at the first degree of intimacy with God.

Wayfaring in the subtle centers proceeds in the aforementioned order: from heart to spirit, to mystery, to arcanum, and to superarcanum. The latter is the special domain of the Muhammadan disposition. Everything is built upon this five-fold arrangement of the world of command. Then one proceeds to the origins of these subtle centers and then to the origins of the origins until arriving at the goal. The way described above is a wide path, but upon arrival a quite narrow one (*sirat-i mustaqim*). On the other hand, travelers in exclusive unity (*ahadiyat*) have another kind of intimacy with God, described as penetrating through each stage until they arrive. For example, from the station of the heart they spirally penetrate [like a drill] to the active attributes that are the origin of the origin of the heart. After arriving there, they are said to bore through from the station of the spirit to arrive at the essential attributes and so on through the rest of the subtle centers. There is no doubt that the actions and attributes of God almighty are not separate from God's Essence. If they appear to be so, it is in the shadows. In that domain, those arriving at the active attributes,[29] by means of a spiral penetration process will realize the disclosures of the holy and almighty Essence. In the same manner, one who has completed the work in the domain of the superarcane subtle center, [that is, a person having a Muhammadan disposition], will easily achieve the aforementioned experiences of the disclosures of the Essence. The distinction between high and low still remains.

One should not equate a person traveling in the heart center with one in the superarcane. However, do not mistakenly think that the distinctions mentioned above (between a person wayfaring in the heart subtle center versus one in the superarcane subtle center or between high and low) apply to different protégés of God. Someone having intimacy with God originating in the heart subtle center is not necessarily lower than one whose intimacy arises through the superarcane subtle center. After arriving at the goal, both achieve a certain degree of completion. However, such a distinction does not apply when comparing protégés of God (*awliya'*) to prophets.

29. This refers to those who do not have a Muhammadan disposition and the limit of their perfections is at the arcanum subtle center, pertaining to the negative attributes. See Nur Ahmad's comment, *Collected Letters*, 1.260.84, fn 4.

God bless them and give them peace. A prophet's intimacy originating from the station of the heart is superior to the intimacy of a protégé of God whose intimacy arises from the superarcane subtle center. Although the protégé of God possessing the perfections of the superarcane has arrived at the goal, the prophet associated with the respective subtle center always supervises that person's wayfaring.[30] God, glorious and almighty, said, "Our word has already been communicated to the servants we sent in order to assist them in making God's truth manifest." [Q. 37:171-173]

Indeed, distinction between the relative highness and lowness of prophets is [ultimately] imaginary. Until the end of the circle of perfections located in the world of command, distinctions between prophets still exist. After that, preference does not depend on highness or lowness. It is possible that one at a lower level in a given station beyond the world of command is more complete than another at a higher level in the same domain.[31]

This is like the differences we have seen before between Moses and Jesus beyond the world of command. Jesus (who was gifted in awareness of the unseen) did not have the great stature and consequence of Moses. We know the distinction between Moses and Jesus in the world of command. The last point, however, is entirely another matter since it is beyond highness and lowness. Look! If God wills, I will clarify this subject later in detail with the perfection of God's grace, fortune, and almighty blessings (see below). In this way, we find that Abraham, the friend of God, and Muhammad, the Seal of the messengers, are distinguished from the rest of the prophets.[32] Abraham and Muhammad are blessed in the perfections associated with the reality of the divine Ka'ba, a reality above all human and angelic realities. God bless all the prophets and give them peace. Abraham has great significance and high status. No one can match him in importance or rank.

(and moving on to another subject) The elegant station (*maqam-i shigarf*) is a station where great, vast pavilions appear.[33] The perfections of this station's center, that is, the station of comprehensiveness (*ijmal*), belong to Muhammad, the Seal of the prophets. The rest of the details (*mufassal*) are

30. As stated earlier in this letter, the prophet associated with the superarcane is Muhammad.

31. The following paragraph is translated from the Arabic.

32. According to Sunni hadith, there have been 124,000 prophets sent to humankind. Of these, a small number are messengers, those prophets who have brought a "book." Thus, Moses (Torah), David (Psalms), Jesus (Bible), and Muhammad (Qur'an) are considered messengers in the Islamic tradition.

33. For an extended discussion of *maqam-i shigarf*, see Muhammad Ma'sum, *Maktubat-i Ma'sumiyya*, 3 vols., ed. by Ghulam Mustafa Khan (Karachi: Walend Military Press, n.d.), 3.94.

entrusted to the exalted presence of God's friend, Abraham. Everyone else, all the other prophets and the completed protégés of God, is an uninvited guest (*tufayli*) of Abraham and Muhammad.[34] Undoubtedly our messenger (Muhammad) summoned the details of that comprehensiveness. Just compare the blessings that are requested for Muhammad [in the ritual prayer] and the blessings requested for Abraham.[35]

It became evident to this poor one (Ahmad Sirhindi) that after the passage of one thousand years the particularities of Muhammad are also readily available, since the blessings requested for Muhammad have been granted.[36] Praise God for that and for all of God's favors. The perfections of the reality of the Ka'ba are above the perfections of intimacy with God, the perfections of prophethood, and the perfections of messengership. Why shouldn't the reality of the Ka'ba be higher than the noble prophets and great angels who prostrate to it? In the treatise, *Return to the Source*, written by this poor one (Ahmad Sirhindi),[37] it is discussed how I ascended from my station to the Reality of Muhammad and from there to the Station of the Reality of the Ka'ba. Arriving above the Reality of the Ka'ba everything became one [in unitary awareness]. The Reality of Muhammad became designated "the Reality of Ahmad" as I realized that the Reality of the Ka'ba was a shadow of the Reality of Ahmad. When the Reality of Ahmad disappeared, there was nothing but the Reality of the Ka'ba. This mistake occurred often when the shadow (Reality of the Ka'ba) became confused with the origin (Reality of Ahmad) and taken for reality every time that the origin disappeared. It is clear that one station has many levels of appearances mixed with both origins and shadows. It is for this reason

---

34. In a culture of hospitality, being an uninvited guest is generally not an issue. One is blessed to be there under any circumstances.

35. *Allahuma salli 'ala sayyidina Muhammadin wa-'ala ali Muhammadin kama sallayta 'ala Ibrahim wa-'ala ali Ibrahim.* Oh God bless our lord Muhammad and his family like you blessed Abraham and his family. This is said in the last part of the ritual prayer.

36. In the interlinear notes on *Collected Letters*, 1.260.85 Nur Ahmad says that the comprehensive essence has already been facilitated, a logical conclusion based upon the particle *niz*. Yohanan Friedmann in his *Shaykh Ahmad Sirhindi* discusses in detail Sirhindi's self-perception in terms of renewing Islam in the second millennium.

37. See Sirhindi, *Mabda' wa-ma'ad*, 78-79. See also a partial English translation of this treatise in Arthur Buehler, "Ahmad Sirhindi's Indian Mujaddidi Sufism,"*Journal of the History of Sufism* 4 (2005), 209-228. There is also a complete translation in Giordani Demetrio, "Le 'mabda' o ma' ad" [sic] un cahier de notes de Shaykh Ahmad Sirhindi, soufi indien du XVIIe siècle," Ph.D dissertation (Paris: École des Hautes Études en Sciences Sociales (EHESS), 1999).

that the appearances of the Reality of the Ka'ba are from the viewpoint of the shadows of that station. (The reality of the Ka'ba appears the way it does because one is viewing it from the shadows.) In truth, the station of the Reality of the Ka'ba is one and the same, appearing as such in the last level.

One may ask how to ascertain which appearance of the station is the last level, so that its reality can be understood. My answer is that the acquisition of knowledge concerning the darkness of appearances comes prior to reliable evidence. (In other words, at the time of acquiring a certain level, investigation is impossible.) Because this knowledge of appearances is not acquired until one already knows the reality of each appearance, one cannot imagine that one is viewing shadows (that is, instead of an origin, it is just a shadow). One still does not know from where the differences of these realities arise. So understand!

O son! From the preceding discussion, it is known that the perfections associated with the world of command are preliminary, like stairs leading to the perfections connected to the material world. The former perfections connected to the world of command contain darkness and are attributed to stations of intimacy with God. When the latter perfections connected to the material world emerge beyond the darkness corresponding to the appearances of worldly existence, then these perfections can partake in the stations of Prophethood.

The path and the reality (*tariqat wa-haqiqat*) are servants of the shariat, which emerges from the level of prophethood. Intimacy with God is a step. From this exposition, it is known that the Naqshbandi notables have chosen the way of prophetic ascent. God sanctify their innermost beings. They begin in the world of command, the lowest and most appropriate starting point, and progress to the highest, the material world. One must not go from highest to the lowest. What can be done? Not everyone has figured out this difficult matter. Gazing only at appearances, others see the material world as low and ascend from seeming lowness to apparent height. They do not know the truth of the matter, that is, that apparent lowness is actual height and vice-versa. Indeed! The last point is the material world, located near the first point, the origin of the origin.[38] This is the closest point in the circle. For each one deserving of a miracle, there are many sinners.

This knowledge comes from the lamp of prophethood. Those who privilege [lesser] intimacy with God are not aware of this wisdom. The prophets began their wayfaring from the world of command and arrived at the shariat (the material world) from reality (the world of command). In short, the

38. The principle here, partially elucidated in *Collected Letters*, 1.260.86, fn 4, is the spiraling movement from the outer circumference of a circle to the center. Then one proceeds from this center to the outer circumference of the next circle.

wayfaring of the completed friends of God conforms to that of the prophets. In the beginning, there is the appearance of the shariat. In the intermediate stages there is the path, the reality of intimacy with God, and the world of command. In the last stage, there is the reality of the shariat, which is the fruit of prophethood.

It is established that going along the path and realizing the reality of God are basic preliminaries to achieving the reality of the shariat. The beginning of completed protégés of God and prophets sent to humanity is realizing the reality of God, while the end for both groups is the shariat. This is *not* the meaning of the phrase "The beginning of the [non-completed] friends of God is the end for the prophets," where the intent is the shariat being the beginning for the protégés of God and the end for prophets Indeed! When that miserable one (Ahmad Sirhindi) was unaware of the reality of God, it was necessary to utter an ecstatic utterance.[39] No one has ever spoken this wisdom [concerning the reality of the shariat] because it is far from anyone's understanding. Actually most have said the opposite. Recognizing the greatness of the prophets and the shariat allows the righteous one to triumph. It is possible that by accepting these hidden secrets, their acceptance will be a means to increase faith (*iman*).

O son! Listen! The prophets are restricted to inviting people to God (*da'wat*) in the material world. God bless them and give them peace. Islam is based on the five pillars.[40] Inviting to God is also suitable when the heart has been verified as being more in accordance with the material world [than the world of command]. Those who call people to God do not discuss anything beyond the heart (that is, they do not discuss the spirit, mystery, arcane, or superarcane subtle centers) because that would be a waste of time and counterproductive. Indeed, the enjoyments of paradise, the misfortunes of hell, the boon of seeing God on the Day of Judgment, and the misfortune of doing something unlawful are all connected to the material world. The world of command has no connection to that. Other actions associated with the physical body, for example, necessary religious duties (sing. *fard-i wajib*) and the sunnat, are closely related to the material world. Voluntary actions (technically called supererogatory actions or *nawafil*) affect the world of command. The resulting nearness [to God] will be commensurate with

39. This utterance, found in *Collected Letters*, 1.31, is discussed in detail by ter Haar, *Follower and Heir*, 34-37.

40. The five pillars of Islam are the attestation of faith in one God and God's messenger, ritual prayer, fasting during Ramadan, alms, and pilgrimage to Mecca. This is a hadith found in al-Bukhari, #8; al-Muslim, *Iman*, 19-22 (#16); al-Tirmidhi, *Iman*, 3 (#2609); al-Nasa'i, *Iman*, 13 (8:107); Ahmad b. Hanbal, *al-Musnad*, 2:26, 93, 120, 143 [MR].

these deeds.[41]

By necessity, the nearness from performing obligatory religious duties (*fara'id*) will manifest in the material world in the same manner as voluntary acts affect the world of command. Without any doubt, the performance of religious duties or the sunnat, compared with voluntary acts, is like the difference between the ocean and a drop of water, even though the difference between performing religious duties and the sunnat is equally vast. One should realize the [qualitative difference] in degrees of closeness to God by comparing the superiority of the material world to the world of command.

When people do not understand this [qualitative difference], the performance of obligatory religious duties usually deteriorates as people emphasize voluntary actions. Ignorant sufis (*sufi-yi kham*) stress the utmost necessity of remembrance and meditation (*dhikr wa-fikr*) while neglecting obligatory and sunnat prayers. By performing austerities and solitary forty-day retreats, they abandon the Friday prayer and the larger Muslim community. They do not know that performing one's religious duty with other Muslims is thousands of times better than their solitary retreats. Indeed, observing the rituals of the shariat enhances remembrance and meditation.

Heedless jurists also give priority to voluntary acts. They neglect required ritual prayers, which they consider worthless. For example, the [special supplementary] prayer on the tenth of Muharram is not authentically linked to the Prophet. But this prayer is still performed in congregation by the Muslim community even though they know that the [Sunni] juristic consensus clearly disapproves of performing voluntary prayer in congregation. They are lax in performing the required prayers. It is rare that ritual prayer is performed at the preferred time but they even make it permissible to pray at other than the principal times [designated for prayer].[42] They do not care about [the proper way to perform] congregational prayer and are content to pray in [many groups of] one or two persons. So many perform their obliga-

---

41. The following discussion assumes a familiarity with three kinds of religious actions, which Sirhindi puts into the context of prayer. In the Hanafi school of jurisprudence, each prayer has a required number of ritual prayer cycles (sing. *raka'*). In addition, there are sunnat prayers associated with each of the five prayers (though most who pray the sunnat prayers omit sunnat prayers before the afternoon prayer), adding an additional seventeen (or twenty-one) prayer cycles to the required seventeen. Voluntary or supererogatory prayers are any other ritual prayer cycles in addition to sunnat ritual prayer or required ritual prayer.

42. The principal time is between the preferred time, right after the call to prayer, and the disapproved time, which depends on the prayer and the school of jurisprudence. For example, Hanafis disapprove of praying the evening prayer after midnight.

tory prayers individually! If Muslims behave like this everywhere, what does this say about the common people?[43] It is from the misfortune of such behavior that weakness in Islam begins. From the darkness of this conduct, the passions of the ego-self and innovations are evident.

After sharing a bit of sadness with you,
If you have not heard a weary heart,
I fear that you might have been hurt.

Also, performance of voluntary prayers facilitates a closeness [with God] that is in the shadows. Praying the obligatory prayers facilitates a nearness to the source (*qurb-i asl*), not resembling shadows even though voluntary prayers are done to perfect the obligatory prayers, bringing one closer to the source. In addition, obligatory prayers are associated with the material world, oriented toward the source, while voluntary prayers are oriented toward the world of command. Their surface is covered in the darkness of shadows. All of the obligatory prayers give nearness to the source and are the most preferable and praised of all prayers. As you may have heard, "Ritual prayer is the heavenly ascension of the believer." and "God's servant is closest to his Lord when in ritual prayer."[44] The Prophet had a special time during prayer as explained by [the expression] "The time I spend with God."[45] This happened once to this poor one (Ahmad Sirhindi) in prayer. Ritual prayer is the covering of one's sins and the prohibiting of what is reprehensible. The Prophet used to search for comfort in prayer, saying, "Soothe me O Bilal."[46] Prayer is one of the pillars of the religion and the distinguishing characteristic between Islam and other religions.[47]

---

43. This is an indication that Sirhindi is talking about the nobles (*ashraf*), the common people being the *ajlaf.*

44. The former is a hadith found in al-Munawi, *Fayd al-qadir*, 1:497; as-Suyuti, *Sharh Sunan Ibn Majah*, 1:313; al-Zurkani, *Sharh al-Muwatta*, 1:111 [MR], and is mentioned three times in *Collected Letters*. The second is a hadith authenticated by al-Muslim, *Salat*, 42 (#482); Abu Da'ud, #875; al-Tirmidhi, #3579; Nasa'i, 2:226 [MR], and mentioned four times in *Collected Letters*.

45. A hadith mentioned seven times in *Collected Letters*, and found in al-Munawi, *Fayd al-qadir*, 4:6; al-Ajluni, *Kashf al-khafa'*, #2159; 'Ali al-Qari, *al-Mathnu'* (*Mawdu'at al-Sughra*), 151 [MR].

46. Bilal is the muezzin who called people to prayer. This hadith is found in Abu Da'ud, #4985; Ahmad b. Hanbal, *al-Musnad*, 5:364; al-Tabarani, *al-Kabir*, 6:276-277 [MR], and is mentioned three times in *Collected Letters.*

47. This sentence combines two hadiths, "Ritual prayer is a pillar of religion and whoever prays supports the religion and whoever does not destroys the religion"; and "The difference between the servant of God and covering up the truth of God (*kufr*) is performing ritual prayer." The former hadith is found in al-Dayla-

Now we have come to the essential part of the discourse. With respect to the excellence of the material world over the world of command, I say that the world of command receives abundance and acquires visions (sing. *mushahada*) from the material world. The ineffable (*bi-la kayf*) sight of God (*ru'yat*) comes easily in the material world on the Day of Judgment. A visionary experience of God [in contemplation] involves the shadow of the Necessary. Seeing God in the next world is unavoidable. There is [an equivalent] qualitative difference between a visionary experience of God [in contemplation] and [physically] seeing God [ineffably] as there is between shadowness and the origin, and between the world of command and the material world. Know, without a shade of a doubt, that contemplatively witnessing God is the result of intimacy with God, while seeing God [with the senses] is associated with prophethood.[48] Ordinary followers of the prophets can facilitate the fruits of prophethood [for themselves] by imitating the prophets. God bless them and give them peace. Understand the difference between intimacy with God and prophethood.

Warning! Anyone with inner experiential knowledge (*'arif*), who is largely connected to the world of command, will be mostly in the perfections of intimacy (*kamalat-i walayat*) with God. Whoever tends to be connected to the material world is in the perfections of prophethood, which is more excellent [than perfections of intimacy with God]. The presence of Jesus predominated in his intimacy with God, while Moses tended to be more in prophethood. God bless and give peace to our prophet and the two of them. Thus, Moses prevails over Jesus [in the material world]. Since Jesus is attracted more to spirits [*ruhaniyan*], he prevails over Moses in the world of command. This is why Moses was not content with just witnessing God [with non-physical senses], but requested to see him with his [physical] eyes. This clarifies the reasons behind distinguishing the prophets in the perfections of prophethood, which I promised to explain previously. The issue is not the highness or lowness of subtle centers when considering the contrast between the perfections of intimacy with God [and the perfections of prophethood].

O son! The prophetic sciences of Islamic law and its legal judgments

mi, *al-Firdaws*, #3795; al-Bayhaqi, *Sawab al-iman*, #2799, 2807; and the latter is found in al-Muslim, *Iman*, 134 (#82); al-Tirmidhi, #2618-2621; al-Nasa'i, 1:231-232; Abu Da'ud, #4678; Ibn Majah, #1078-1080 [MR].

48. In Hutaki, *Sharh-i Maktubat*, 357, it explains that the visionary experience of the Source in contemplation involves the world of command and is for protégés of God who see shadowy disclosures. Seeing the Source physically involves the world of creation and is associated with the station of prophethood. A realized knower (*'arif*) sees the Source with the heart/spirit while Muhammad sees the Source with his eyes. This is why *ru'yat* is generally an ineffable experience.

overwhelmingly are concerned with the physical body, just as the prophets have a general affinity with the material world. God bless them and give them peace. Given this, it is supposed that prophethood involves an ascent through the stations of closeness to God (the lesser intimacy with God) followed by a descent in order to call people to God. What is not realized [in this supposition] is that the end of ascent and the goal of closeness are [merely] in the domain of intimacy with God. [Such a closeness] is but a shadow of the closeness of prophethood, although the appearance of closeness of prophethood is imagined to be more distant.[49] The first ascent on the path is intimacy with God, itself only a reflection of the ascent associated with closeness of prophethood, but appearing to be a descent.

The center of the circle that appears to be the furthest point in relation to the circumference of the circle [is the closest]. Actually, there is no point closer to the circumference than the center because [in reality] the center dot comprehensively encompasses the circumference of particularities. No other dot shares this attribute of the center. (See Figure 4) People only looking at outward appearances cannot comprehend the closeness of the center. Instead, they attribute farness to the center and consider anyone who thinks otherwise to be an ignorant fool. "We ask for God's help against those who portray things like that."[50] [Q. 12:18]

One should know that the realization of tranquility in the ego-self occurs after achieving the expanded chest, which is one of the requirements associated with "greater intimacy with God." The ascent begins from there and proceeds to the throne of the chest where an experience of contentment is established, overcoming the dominions of nearness. In reality, this throne of the chest is above all the stations of ascent and the levels associated with greater intimacy with God. Coming to this throne, one sees the passing of the innermost of the inner and penetrates into the innermost secrets (origin of the origins). Yes! The person who reaches the highest place has the penetrating vision to see the most remotely distant object. After becoming firmly established in this tranquility of mind, one ascends from that station. The wayfarer becomes tranquil as the ego-self and rational mind harmonize

---

49. To connect this discussion of circles/centers and ascent/descent, with the prior discussion, I have added "closeness of the protégés of God" or "closeness of Prophethood." The basic issue, commonly occurring in these kinds of discussions, is that appearances are not reality. So the center of the circle appears to be the farthest, while in reality it is the nearest. In reality, the center of the circle is the origin for the effect of the circumference surrounding it.

50. If one conceives of a circle and center as a circular cone, Sirhindi's discussion makes more sense. From the circular base of the cone, the tip of the cone (the apparent center) appears far away. When at the tip of the cone, the center is the closest and the circular base of the cone (the apparent circumference) is far away.

in a unitary consciousness (*ittihad*). This is called "the rational mind (*'aql*) returning to the source."

O son! This tranquility totally precludes any difference or capacity to resist. All that remains is entirely involved in the goal of God's satisfaction. Exalt God's sovereignty! The purpose, other than obedience and worship of the almighty and most glorious, is [to train] the unruly base ego-self (*nafs-i ammara*), which is [our] worst trait. After realizing tranquility and the satisfaction of the praiseworthy presence of the Leader of the subtle centers (God), the traveler passes through the world of command and becomes the leader of one's own peers. Indeed! The reliable messenger (Muhammad) said, "If you understand, the outstanding among you in pre-Islamic times are the same people during the time of Islam." God bless him and his family and give them peace.[51]

If there is the appearance of discord and rebellion after realizing tranquility, it stems from the nature of the four elements (earth, air, fire, water) that make up the physical human body. This is where the power of anger, lust, greed, desire, avarice, and meanness arise. Don't you see that animals, although lacking rebellious ego-selves, have perfected these base animal qualities? It could be that there is a different meaning of "greater jihad" when the exalted presence of Muhammad said, "We returned from the lesser jihad to the greater jihad."[52] God bless him and his family and give them peace. Instead of the [normative sufi interpretation], where greater jihad is [linked with taming] the ego-self, greater jihad concerns the physical body. [It is mistakenly said] that when the tranquil ego-self has completed its task in contentment [when God is satisfied with the servant and vice-versa], then one always behaves correctly. [This way of thinking] assumes that the goal of [the lesser jihad] is to eliminate outward discordant and rebellious behavior resulting from the physical body. Then one does only what is permitted and avoids what is forbidden. The intention is not to do what is forbidden and to abandon required religious practices, which the person considers detrimental. (This is one extreme, transcendental escape)

O son! The perfections of the four elements are above the perfections of tranquility of the ego-self. Tranquility, because of its connection to the station of intimacy with God and the world of command, is associated with those who are spiritually intoxicated. In their station of being overwhelmed in God, they do not have the strength to remain rebellious to God. The four elements have a greater affinity to the station of prophethood, where so-

51. A hadith found in al-Muslim, *Fada'il*, 168 (#2378); al-Bukhari, *Anbiya'*, 171; *al-Adab al-mufrad*, #129 [MR], and mentioned twice in *Collected Letters*.

52. This hadith, found in as-Suyuti, *al-Jami' al-saghir*, #6107; and in al-Bayhaqi, *al-Zuhd*, #373 [MR], is found three times in *Collected Letters*. See the note explaining this hadith in *Collected Letters*, 1.41.4.

briety is the rule. By necessity, the appearance of rebellion still exists [for those in the station of prophethood] as an instrument for receiving some benefits.[53] So understand!

One should know that the highest rank of prophethood is with the Seal of the prophets. God bless him and his family and give them peace.[54] It is a perfect gift to follow the path of those imitating him, those who have received the perfections of that office. These perfections predominated during the generation of the Companions. During the succeeding two generations this felicity did not penetrate the hearts of wayfarers as much. After that, the way became hidden as the lesser intimacy with God [instead of the intimacy of the prophets] manifested. It is hoped that [the perfections of prophethood] will be renewed afresh and generally practiced after a thousand years have passed [from the time of Muhammad's hijra to Medina]. May the original perfections appear [in the light] as the shadowy perfections become hidden. God be contented as the presence of the Mahdi outwardly and inwardly communicates this exalted process.[55]

O son! A person who perfectly imitates the Prophet becomes complete when that imitation is based upon the perfections of the station of prophethood. God bless him and give him peace. If that person is among the dignitaries [in imitating the Prophet], he (the Prophet's successor to be) will be elevated to leadership in that station. After completing the perfections of greater intimacy with God (that is, the intimacy of prophethood) and becoming worthy of high office, he will be honored with being the Prophet's successor.[56] The person presiding over the stations of shadowy perfections under the imam has the office of axial guide (*qutb-i irshad*),[57] while the office under the successor, is called the central axial authority (*qutb-i madar*).

---

53. Nur Ahmad explains that when a person's *nafs* is totally blocked from the attributes of God (that is, only concentrating on the Essence), it is blocked from further development.

54. This statement reflects conventional reality. What was said earlier about there being no difference between prophets is from the perspective of ultimate reality.

55. The Mahdi (lit. the rightly guided one) initiates the last days preceding the Day of Judgment.

56. The dignitaries and "those worthy of high office" probably refer to jurists. The successor and actual person who achieves this position after one thousand years is almost certainly Ahmad Sirhindi himself. Yohanan Friedman discusses this latter point in his *Shaykh Ahmad Sirhindi*.

57. The imam probably refers to Muhammad. Note below in this letter where Sirhindi alludes to his being the central figure (*madar-i bina'*) of a special path. For Sirhindi's experience developing from axial guide (*qutb-i irshad*) to the unique one. See Sirhindi, *Mabda' wa-ma'ad*, 9-11.

They say that these two lower stations (the axial guide and the station of shadowy perfections) are the shadows of the upper two stations (the central axial authority and successor to Muhammad).

According to Shaykh Muhyiddin Ibn al-'Arabi (d. 638/1240), the position of supreme helper (*ghawth*) is the same as that of the central axial authority. Thus, the office of supreme helper is not separate. This poor one (Ahmad Sirhindi) asserts, to the contrary, that the axial authority asks the supreme helper for assistance in some affairs and is involved in establishing the order of the substitutes (*abdal*). "God gives that favor to whomever God desires and is the master of all grace." [Q. 62:4]

Postscript

The inner and outer way of knowing for those in the station of prophethood is [through] the revealed laws of the prophets. God bless them and give them peace. Because there are distinctions of ranks of prophethood, accordingly there are differing distinctions in the revealed laws of the prophets. Shaykhs' ecstatic utterances pertain to a type of inner knowledge of those in the station of [lesser] intimacy with God. They experience union with God (*tawhid*) and a unity (*ittihad*) that penetrates and encompasses everything. They provide examples of nearness [to God] and togetherness with God (*ma'iyat*) as they make known the mirror and darkness, affirming visions they have witnessed [in contemplation]. Just as prophets' experience and knowledge generally center on the Qur'an and sunnat, that of the protégés of God concerns [Ibn al-'Arabi's] *Meccan Revelations* and *Bezels of Wisdom*.[58]

My view of springtime is from my rose garden.

The intimacy of friends of God, verified by visions, results from nearness to God. The intimacy of prophets, confirmed by an ineffable affinity, is a sign of utmost closeness to God (*aqrabiyat*). Protégés of God do not have the faintest idea about the nature of this utmost closeness. Prophets' intimacy with God, in spite of its closeness, is a proximity known from afar, as contemplative witnessing is understood from a hidden eye.[59]

Explaining this could go on forever.

---

58. This is purposely putting down those who selectively read Ibn al-'Arabi's writings and end up not living in accord with the sunnat. Sirhindi acknowledges Ibn al-'Arabi's writings to be deeply intertwined with the Qur'an and Hadith, The *Meccan Revelations* have not been translated into English. See Muhyiddin Ibn al-'Arabi, *al-Futuhat al-Makkiyya*, 14 vols., ed., Osman Yahya (Cairo: al-Hayah al-Misriyah al-`Ammah lil-Kitab, 1972-1989); Muhyiddin Ibn al-'Arabi, *al-Futuhat al-Makkiyya*, 4 vols. (Cairo: Bulaq, 1911); and *Fusus al-hikam*, trans. R.W.J. Austin, *The Bezels of Wisdom* (Marwah, NJ: Paulist Press, 1980).

59. Note that there is no *union* with God here. Cf. Sirhindi's remarks about *wujudi* sufis throughout the letters.

O son! This lengthy discussion has clarified the preference of the perfections of prophethood over intimacy with God, the three kinds of intimacy (lesser, greater, and greatest), and the appropriate inner knowledge concerning the relationship of each of these and the places associated with them. The sections [of this letter] have been laid out to explain the meaning in such a way that it will be accessible to people's understanding in an irrefutable manner, despite the extremely strange and unfamiliar nature of the topic. This knowledge is revealed and self-evident, not theoretical and requiring rational proof. [The intent of this letter] is not to mention some preliminaries that increase awareness for those of ordinary understanding. Instead, it is for those of special perception. It explains and clarifies the distinguished path to God, almighty and glorious, that God bestowed on this poor one (Ahmad Sirhindi).

From the beginning to the end, the foundation of this [path] is linked with the Naqshbandi lineage and includes the principle of "The end is included in the beginning." Many buildings and palaces have been built upon this foundation. The entire enterprise up to now would not have prospered if this foundation had not existed. A seed, originally from the earth of Medina and Mecca, coming via Bukhara and Samarqand, was planted in the ground of India. This seed flourished for years, was raised with an education in beneficence (*ihsan*), until it finally reached maturity.[60] The inner and outer knowledge [in this letter] are the result. "Praise God who guided us to this. Had God not guided us, surely we would have never been guided. Indeed, our Lord's messengers came with the truth." [Q. 7:43]

You should know that wayfaring in this exalted path is connected with a firm heart connection (*rabita-yi mahabbat*) with the shaykh, enabling one to go along this path to the goal. Through the power of attraction, one becomes imbued with the shaykh's perfections. His glance heals afflictions of the heart and his focused spiritual energy (*tawajjuh*) wards off spiritual defects. A person with these perfections is the leader of the time and successor of the age, with the axial leaders (*aqtab*) and substitutes (*abdal*) contented in the shadows of his stations, as the pillars (*awtad*) and nobles (*nujaba'*) are satisfied with a drop from the oceans of his perfections.[61] The

---

60. The place names are allusions to the history of the Naqshbandi lineage whose founder-figure, Baha'uddin Naqshband (791/1389), came from the Bukhara-Samarqand area and whose teachings followed that of the Prophet, born in Mecca and later residing in Medina. The fruition alludes to Baqibillah, Ahmad Sirhindi, and what was to become the Naqshbandi-Mujaddidi lineage.

61. The spiritual hierarchy is traditionally conceived as headed by an axial leader (*qutb*) with three nobles (*nujaba'*), four pillars (*awtad*), seven pious ones (*abrar*), and forty substitutes (*abdal*). See the introduction to letter 1.287 for more background information on this spiritual hierarchy.

light of his guidance, without his intention or desire, spontaneously radiates to everyone like sunlight. How could this happen by his own desire when such a wish is not within his sphere of authority? How many times has he requested something when that wish did not originate from him? It is not necessary that the people who receive guidance from his light or from his intercession (*tawassul*) understand this meaning.

In addition, there is a lot in the essence (*ma'na*) of the guidance itself (its comprehensive nature) that those on the path do not need to know.[62] Nonetheless, they will become convinced of the completeness of an exemplary shaykh. This is because, instead of teaching the entire world, the shaykh does not guide or share his inner knowledge concerning the details of wayfaring along the stations with just anyone. Indeed! A shaykh like this is the central figure (*madar-i bina'*) of a special path to realize God based upon his own venerable being. Of course he has religious knowledge, including the awareness of the details of others' wayfaring. By means of this knowledge, others not only reach the level of completion, as they are honored in their experience of annihilation of the ego-self and abiding in God consciousness (*fana' wa-baqa'*), but they can bestow this completion on others. Human beings! You were specially created to help others!

The master-disciple relationship (lit. benefiting and being benefited) is a reflective process that can be described as colors blending into each other. For example, the disciple having a firm bonding of the heart with an exemplary shaykh is continually being imbued with the qualities of the shaykh. Through a process of reflection, the shaykh's light illuminates the disciple. Apparently, rational knowledge is not necessary [in this process] for either the master or the disciple. [Let's use an example of] a watermelon ripening day after day in the warmth of the sun until, with the passage of time, it becomes completely ripe. Of what use is the watermelon being aware of its own ripening or the sun knowing that the watermelon was ripening? Indeed! For other sufi lineages, knowledge is necessary to make decisions about wayfaring. Our lineage, that of the noble Companions, is one in which knowledge of wayfaring is not essential. God be content with them. However, there is no doubt that the exemplary shaykh who founded this path had complete inner and outer religious knowledge. In this exalted path, all people, whether living, dead, young, middle-aged, or old, are equal in terms of the reality of arriving to God. By having a firm heart connection with the shaykh and by receiving spiritual energy from him, they realize their ultimate goals. "God gives favor to whomever God desires and is the master of all grace." [Q. 62:4]

One should know that there are fully realized persons (sing. *muntahi*) who are not [religiously] learned and who have no control over the mani-

62. See the second note after this one.

festation of miracles (lit. out-of-the-ordinary events).[63] Sometimes these unusual events happen involuntarily. Even if there are many occurrences, they can happen without his knowledge. [Thus, it can happen that other] people observe these apparent miracles while he is unaware of them. So it is said that a fully realized person has no knowledge (*'ilm*). But this lack of knowledge is that which concerns the specific details of altered states. It does not mean that a fully realized person does not have any knowledge at all. Rather it means that he does not understand anything about his own states. This [situation] has been alluded to before.[64]

The light of the realized shaykh's guidance shines on his disciples, with and without intermediaries. This continues unless changes contaminate his special path and the resultant innovations eventually destroy it. "God does not change a people unless they transform themselves first." [Q. 13:11] It is strange that a group of innovators believe that these modifications perfect the path. They even imagine that they [themselves] have arrived at the end of the path. They do not know that perfection and completion is not the end of the work for any aspirant. Making up stories about reaching [the goal] is not proper for those who are helpless.

> There are too many delicate meanings, finer than a hair.
> Not everyone who shaves his head knows how to be a Qalandar.[65]

With the darkness of innovations they have covered the light of the sunnat. God bless its master [Muhammad] and give him peace. With the darkness of unfortunate deeds they have extinguished the Muhammadan light of the Muslim community. It is even stranger that these same people consider these destructive modifications to be praiseworthy. They seek the completion of religion and the fulfillment of the Muslim community by committing so-called praiseworthy actions, which promote [yet more] temptations. God, the most glorious, guided them in everything else except the straight path. They do not know that long before these innovations, the religion had been completed in complete blessings and approval by the presence of Truth, glorious and almighty. As God almighty said, "Today I completed your religion and perfected my grace for you, sanctioning the submission to God as a way of living (*din*)." [Q. 5:3] Thus, to search for the completion of religion from these destructive changes is, in truth, denying what this

63. According to Islamic dogma, there are two kinds of miracles, prophetic (*mu'jizat*) and those performed by Muslims who are not prophets (*karamat* or *khawariq*).

64. Alludes to the sentence marked by two footnotes before this one.

65. Qalandars typically shaved all their facial hair. They are often represented in Persian literature as those who own taverns, drink wine, and generally live transgressive lifestyles, presumably as a way of training their ego-self.

Qur'anic verse says.

> After sharing a bit of sadness with you,
> If you have not heard a weary heart,
> I fear that you might have been hurt.

Jurists striving for greater clarification in religious practice have formulated legal judgments in conformity with prophetic guidance. So [unprecedented] legal decisions stemming from the legitimate application of the Qur'an and sunnat (*ahkam-i ijtihadiya*) have nothing to do with unprecedented innovations. This is because the use of analogy [to formulate legal decisions] is the fourth source of authority [in Sunni jurisprudence].[66]

O son! The inner knowledge contained in *Return to the Source* and the preceding section on the master-disciple relationship relating to the axial guide (*qutb-i irshad*) was written when it harmonized with this station, and it was useful. The inner knowledge in this letter was also written in harmony with that station. Consider how extraordinary the axial guide really is. He has the total perfections of uniqueness (*fardiyat*).[67] After many centuries and the innumerable passage of time, this kind of jewel appears! The dark world becomes filled with light from the light of his appearance. His light of guidance encompasses the whole world from the ocean of the Throne to the center of the earth. Any guidance, faith, and inner knowledge that a person receives and benefits from comes from his path. No one can get these benefits except by his mediation.[68]

For example, the light of his guidance fills the entire world like an

---

66. Striving to find the correct legal judgment, that is, independent legal reasoning (*ijtihad*), involves the educated use of the Qur'an, hadith, and juristic consensus. If one cannot make a decision with these three sources alone then the Sunni jurist uses analogy based on these sources.

67. Note that Sirhindi declared himself to be the unique one (*fard*), having absolute authority from the empyrean to earth. For Sirhindi's experience developing from axial guide (*qutb-i irshad*) to the unique one. See Sirhindi, *Mabda' wa-ma'ad*, 9-11.

68. Cf. two centuries later, a prominent Naqshbandi-Mujaddidi shaykh in Delhi, Ghulam 'Ali Shah (d. 1240/1824), said that for any person intimate with God in the second millennium, that is, one thousand lunar years after 622 CE, the way is not open without the intercession of Ahmad Sirhindi. In another passage, 'Abdulqadir Jilani tells Ghulam 'Ali Shah that Ahmad Sirhindi is 'Abdulqadir Jilani's foremost deputy and before Ahmad Sirhindi no one had reached intimacy with God without 'Abdulqadir Jilani's mediation. Now in the second millennium, the mediation of both Ahmad Sirhindi and 'Abdulqadir Jilani is necessary. See Arthur Buehler, "Mawlana Khalid and Shah Ghulam 'Ali," in *The Journal of the History of Sufism* 5 (2007), 210.

encompassing ocean. It is said that this ocean is frozen because it never moves. When a seeker sincerely turns his attention toward this noble guide, then he directs his attention to the seeker's condition. During this interaction, what could be called a small orifice opens up in the aspirant's heart. In that way, depending on the sincerity [of the seeker] and attention [focused by the guide], the aspirant's thirst is quenched from the ocean.

In the same way, there are those focused on recollecting God the sublime and never concern themselves with that exceptional teacher. Although they cannot deny him because they do not [even] recognize who he is, they still receive the same benefit. This situation is much better than the next one. The second group of people either denies the [qualifications of the] aforementioned guide or the guide himself is displeased with and weary of them. Although they busy themselves with recollecting almighty and holy God, they are shut off from the truth of his guidance. This very denial and tormenting cuts them off from the path of his focusing divine effulgence. Without divine effulgence there cannot be any benefit from him nor can they harm him. The essence (*ma'na*) of guidance is blocked from them because the appearance of guidance has little benefit. Sincere people who love that extraordinary person but do not turn their attention toward him or recollect God still receive the light of guidance by means of pure love. This inner knowledge is the last part of the letter. (Rumi says),

> I stop myself here
> This is enough for the ear
> I called out.
> Can anyone hear?[69]

Praise be to God, Lord of the worlds, the compassionate and merciful, from the beginning to the end. God bless and give peace to God's messenger Muhammad and his family forever and ever.

69. See Jalaluddin Balkhi/Rumi, *Mathnawi-yi ma'nawi*, 2:441 (In the six-volume *Mathnawi*, Vol. 4 verse 2770).

Chapter Five
Sufi Treatise 2: Letter 1.287

Introduction to Letter 1.287

This letter is addressed to Miyan Ghulam Muhammad,[1] Ahmad Sirhindi's younger brother. It starts off seeking to correct the mistaken ideas that common people and superficial jurists have about sufism. Sirhindi's observation is that even though they have the proper creed and faith in the formless Real, they are not arriving at the goal because they lack knowledge of the goal and mistake the shadow of the divine disclosure (*tajalli-yi zilli*) for the ineffable Essence (*dhat-i bi-chun*). This is what the story about the two pilgrims to the Ka'ba illustrates. Jurists are better off than the mistaken sufis discussed here because juristic knowledge is based on the reliable sources of the Qur'an and sunnat. However, the states of beginning sufis are better than those of the superficial jurists (*ulama'-i zawahir*) because at least the beginners have started on the path to God. The superficial jurists only are aware of the outer form (*surat*) of the shariat and have no idea of the reality of the shariat.

As for sufi masters—and spiritual teachers generally—there has been very little quality control of *who* is qualified to teach and to what level one is qualified to teach. One of Sirhindi's goals, and a common theme in his letters, is providing tools for discernment. He starts with ecstatics because many in the Indo-Pakistan Subcontinent have associated (and continue to associate) these ecstatic states with spiritual attainment.[2] As the reader already knows by now, Sirhindi is quite direct in his criticisms. He is also, in my opinion, scientific in that he provides experiential data to support his claims. So he begins by explaining why this misperception of ecstatics exists. It is because those who have very little experience in the suprarational contemplative realms can only rely on external data of their outer senses and therefore cannot discern the difference between ecstatic wayfarers (lit. attracted ones who are wayfaring *majdhuban-i suluk*) and wayfarers who are ecstatic (*salikan bi-majdhub*). To the inexperienced they look identical. Making matters more difficult, ecstatic wayfarers have no idea that what

1. There are two letters addressed to Miyan Ghulam Muhammad in *Collected Letters*.

2. The most exhaustive "study" of *majdhubs* is an account of Meher Baba's lengthy tours around India over a period of seven years, 1939-1946, and his interactions with them. See William Donkin, *The Wayfarers: An account of the work of Meher Baba with the God-intoxicated* (Ahmednagar, India: Adi K. Irani, 1948).

they *think* is the Essence is just the shadow. So if you ask them about their experiences they describe them in the same terms as the wayfarers who are ecstatic.

The reason ecstatic wayfarers end up in this situation is because of the way they are taught. According to Sirhindi, the overflowing love of God, associated with a state of ecstatic attraction to God, should come after the cleansing and taming of the ego-self (*nafs*). This latter process is associated with "wayfaring in God" (*sayr fi'llah*). Until the ego-self is cleansed, any love is contingent, weakened, and deficient.[3] Wayfaring in God is a result of extensive contemplative witnessing (*shuhud*) to the point of it becoming an ineffable experience outside the awareness of those in consensus reality. That is a litmus test for being close to God. What the others experience is a cognitive closeness (*qurb-i 'ilmi*).[4]

For Sirhindi, the ecstasy of beginners is associated with asserting the unity of being (*tawhid-i wujudi*), which causes ecstatics to mistake the contingent for the Real. Part of the difficulty, as the letter explains, is that they have not gone beyond the station of the heart to differentiate the spirit from the ego-self. The touchstone of knowing that one is realizing a greater affinity to God is a corresponding decreasing affinity for the world. Sirhindi exhorts them to realize the necessity for cultivating an inner attraction to God, without which they will never achieve their goal. At first this is a superficial attraction (*jadhba-yi suri*) before the heart, spirit, and ego-self are separated. Then it becomes a real attraction to God (*jadhba-yi haqiqi*) involving just the spirit.[5] The Naqshbandi path and its practices are designed to cultivate this inner attraction to God right at the beginning. Again, outwardly both these ecstasies appear to be the same.

Then Sirhindi details types of sufi shaykhs. An exemplary shaykh has ascended and returned to the world keeping his reality with God and only a superficial connection to the world. This is the kind of shaykh best suited for advanced seekers because he can transmit more divine effulgence to his disciples, who are able to receive it. An exemplary shaykh can focus on the spirit while *not* focusing on the ego-self when transmitting divine effulgence, which makes him suitable for advanced seekers. The ecstatic shaykh has just started to come back from the peak of ascent. He is ideal for beginning students because his connection to the world is still real. A realized shaykh who has not yet returned to the world is still totally with God and cannot guide others because a shaykh is a bridge between two worlds.

Sufis who think that ecstatic states are the final realization, whom I

---

3. See Hutaki, *Sharh-i Maktubat*, 422.
4. See ibid.
5. See ibid., 423.

have called *wujudis* (*sufiyah-i wujudiya*),[6] believe (according to Sirhindi) that the shaykh bridges the world of immanence (*tashbih*), associated with the world of possibility and the ego-self and the world of transcendence (*tanzih*), associated with the necessary level of reality (*martaba-yi wujub*), which is the upper half of the second entification.[7] According to Sirhindi, it is impossible for them to be bridges as they claim because they clearly exhibit intoxicated, ecstatic states that result from the mixing of the spirit and ego-self. These shaykhs cannot be bridges between the two worlds until they themselves have separated their own spirits and ego-selves. This means that they must have already ascended and returned to the world. Here Sirhindi is attempting to clear up what he perceives as basic conceptual/experiential misunderstandings. Ecstatic shaykhs have their important roles; they just need to let their students know that their guidance is conditional.

Aspirants with an inclination for ascent experience two types of attraction. The first is an inclination by attraction (*tawajjuh-i jadhabati*) and the second is an inclination by wayfaring (*tawajjuh-i suluki*).[8] The first kind is superficial, because it involves outside factors, that is, it involves the shaykh's spiritual energy (*tawajjuh*) or the wayfarer's following the sunnat. The second involves inner transformation of the wayfarer, cleansing the ego-self and purifying the subtle centers. It is the Naqshbandi way. There are a series of annihilations and abidings. The annihilations come by virtue of the name that governs one's wayfaring (*ism-i murabbi*) and forgetting everything other than God. Abiding involves going from the reflections and becoming refined to the perfections of the governing name. This results in an absolute annihilation and a tranquil abiding in God.

There are two types of annihilation: 1) one is annihilated in one's authoritative name (*ism-i murabbi*); this is also called absolute annihilation, not annihilation in God; and 2) the seeker goes from his authoritative name via the qualities to the Essence, beyond absolute annihilation and annihilation in God. The first type of annihilation cannot go to annihilation in God because there has not been annihilation in the Essence. These annihilations correspond to kinds of sanctity or intimacy with God, a lesser intimacy with God (*walayat-i sughra*) where one is in the active and secondary (*idafi*) attributes or a greater intimacy with God (*walayat-i kubra*) where one is in the essential attributes.

The two kinds of divine effulgence come from either the attributes, the divine effulgence that underlies peoples' births, or from the qualities. One of the major points of this letter is the necessity to distinguish between the attributes and the qualities. Those of a Muhammadan disposition contem-

6. See ibid., 425.

7. See Buehler, *Sufi Heirs*, 107, and Dhawqi, *Sirr-i dilbaran*, 353.

8. See Hutaki, *Sharh-i Maktubat*, 427.

platively witness the qualities. Since others of a non-Muhammadan disposition have no experience of the qualities, they cannot discern between the attributes and the qualities. Sirhindi gives an example of this difficulty of discernment through the tendency of water to flow downhill. It is like thinking that water goes downhill because it has a will of its own. Therefore, the derivation of will from water flowing downward is on the basis of a quality (will) that has no objective existence. Will has a separate existence from the water flowing downhill. Likewise one cannot say that water has desire, life, or knowledge. Thus, the attribute of water flowing downward, verifiable in the objective world, is not on the same existential level as the quality of will just as the attributes are not on the same existential level as the qualities. The *wujudi* sufis (*sufiyah-i wujudi*) have not realized that the attributes are in the objective world and do not even know that the qualities, which are not in the objective world, even exist.

There is an underlying creedal issue at stake here also. Apparently many sufis in India at the time believed, along with many philosophers and the Mu'tazilites before them, that the attributes were identical with the Essence.[9] Sirhindi is taking the Maturidi doctrinal position that the attributes are neither the Essence nor other than the Essence (*wa-hiya la huwa wa-la ghayrahu*).[10] In this letter, which focuses on sufi experience rather than on correct articles of faith, he does not express the relationship between the attributes and Essence in theological terms. Instead Sirhindi details the bridging interface between the qualities (which are Essence) and

9. Sirhindi apparently encountered many who equated God's attributes with the origin of God's essence. In *Collected Letters*, 1.266.110 he has them saying, "The attributes are separate [from God] in thought but in reality are in God's Essence." In Fadlullah Shihabuddin Turpushti's *al-Mu'tamad fi'l-mu'taqad*, Turpushti accuses the philosophers and Mu'tazilites of asserting "*sifatuhu 'ayn dhatuhu,*" (the attributes are the same as the Essence) and immediately curses them for it. Sirhindi highly recommends this book and its methodology for those who need to correct their creedal beliefs. See *Collected Letters*, 1.193.80. Ter Haar includes Ibn al-'Arabi among those who equated God's attributes with the origin of God's essence. Given the nuances of Ibn al-'Arabi's treatment of this vast subject, a statement such as this probably does not do justice to Ibn al-'Arabi's thoughts on the subject. See ter Haar, *Follower and Heir*, 63.

10. Sa'duddin 'Umar al-Taftazani, *Sharh al-'aqa'id al-Nasafi fi usul al-din wa-'ilm al-kalam*, ed. Claude Salamé (Damascus: Manshurat Wazarat al-Thaqafa wa'l-Irshad al-Qummi, 1974), 46. In a discussion of the four "rightly guided" Sunni caliphs, Sirhindi mentions how he highly regards this author but disagrees with some of his commentary. See *Collected Letters*, 1.266.131.

the attributes that are not in the Essence.[11] In the exposition of ontological realities, Sirhindi is relying on his own subjective experiences of traveling in these realms. At the same time, he is very keen to have everything conform to the creedal dictates of Maturidi-Hanafi jurisprudence, or as he often says the "folk who follow the sunnat" (*ahl-i sunnat*). Accordingly, God has eight fixed attributes that exist separately (*za'id*) from God and from each other. They also exist in the objective/outside world (*dar kharij*).[12] Given this framework, the *wujudi* sufis' conflation of the Essence and attributes is for Sirhindi a denial of the attributes. The Maturidi creed, which affirms not only their separateness but their actual existence, acts as a safeguard to their denial.[13] Continually throughout the letters Sirhindi seeks to correct what he considers creedal errors, that is, anything differing from the Maturidi-Hanafi school of jurisprudence. He also articulates what he considers to be misinterpretations of sufi experience, that is, anything differing from his own verified experience in a larger context.[14] Generally throughout *Collected Letters* his focus and discussion is from the viewpoint of his own sufi traveling experience, which is explained using sufi vocabulary.[15]

In the next part of the letter, Sirhindi details the superiority of Muhammad and those of the Muhammadan disposition in terms of divine effulgence. Muhammad is distinguished by being ruled by a name of God, the shadow of which is knowledge (*'ilm*). The origin of his divine effulgence is the quality of knowledge (*sha'n-i 'ilm*).[16] The quality of knowledge presides over the other qualities and knows all the attributes. Those of a Muhammadan disposition develop through this quality of knowledge by sharing parts of it (while Muhammad shares in it comprehensively). In this connection to God, Muhammad receives divine effulgence via the qualities,

---

11. See Letter 2.67 (translated in this book) where Sirhindi explicitly defines nineteen doctrinal points, including those concerning God and his attributes (points 3 +4).

12. See *Collected Letters*, 1.266.110. Because of the paradox of the essential or fixed attributes being both of the Essence and not of the Essence note, "There is no doubt that the actions and attributes of God almighty are not separate from God's Essence. If they appear to be so, it is in the shadows." See letter 1.260 in this book, page 249.

13. See ibid., 1.266.110-111.

14. When discussing subjective experience, Sirhindi usually notes carefully that he has already experienced what the other person has experienced, but having gone "higher on the mountain" his view encompasses more.

15. See chapter 1 for a selection of letters that are more shariat oriented.

16. The bow is associated with the highest of God's qualities, the quality of knowledge. See Buehler, *Sufi Heirs*, 245. This bow is associated with the Qur'anic verse [53:8] referring to Muhammad's ascension where Muhammad came "two bows length or closer."

which by virtue of not having objective existence are not a barrier for the transmission of divine effulgence.

Those following other prophets only get divine effulgence from one attribute. Because the attributes have objective existence, the divine effulgence is blocked to a certain extent. Of the two kinds of divine effulgence, the first is that which gives human birth (*fayd-i takhliqi*). Muhammad receives that divine effulgence from the Essence comprehensively. Other prophets receive divine effulgence from the Essence through only one attribute. When the first and second types of divine effulgence manifest through the prophet Moses, there is the capability or potentiality of the Essence along with the attribute of speech. With Adam there is also the capability of the Essence along with the attribute of physical formation (*takwin*). Jesus had the capability of the Essence along with the attribute of power. These various capabilities (speech, physical formation, and power) are only parts of the comprehensive capability of God. This latter capability of the Essence expressed in its comprehensive nature is the domain of Muhammad.[17] Since those of a non-Muhammadan disposition are in the attributes, they cannot experience annihilation in God or abiding in God because their annihilation and abiding occurs only in the attributes, not in the Essence.

Sirhindi also differentiates certain experiences as being contemplative (*shuhudi*) instead of actual physical experiences (*wujudi*). Any annihilation and abiding occur contemplatively. It is obvious to anyone that annihilation is not of the physical body but of the ego-self. Perhaps Sirhindi is directing his comments toward the large numbers of Mahdawis who believed in Muhammad Ghauth's reporting a bodily ascension experience (where it is implied that his physical body was absent during the ascension).[18] In any case, a person of inner experience can experience annihilation as he ascends from the world of possibility to the level of necessary Being. This is another case of Sirhindi differentiating between the contemplative realm and the objective world "out there" when considering knowledge and experience.

What is generally known as wayfaring or contemplative practice (*suluk*) involves one arriving at the governing name (*ism-i murabbi*) and then going through higher and higher stations. An uncustomary way of wayfaring is for someone not in contact with the governing name to ascend through the stations. The annihilation in the governing name is for beginners, while

17. See Hutaki, *Sharh-i Maktubat*, 430-431. In ibid., 433 the rationale for Muhammad's comprehensiveness is that the Islamic shariat and the Qur'an encompass all the "heavenly religions."

18. Doctrinally any type of existential disappearance (into God) would be the inverse of God incarnating into the finite (*hulul*), which just is not possible according to Sunni Muslim creed. It would be like putting the entire ocean into a cup or pouring a cup and getting the ocean.

one who also has annihilation in the qualities and the Essence experiences absolute annihilation.[19]

Sirhindi outlines four kinds of wayfaring, which can be simplified into two kinds including the previous categories already discussed: 1) that of beginners/intermediates who are lovers and 2) that of realized wayfarers who are beloveds. Naqshbandis are the latter and their attraction to God involves following the sunnat and purifying their subtle centers. To arrive at the goal one has to arrive at the governing name, which involves the separation of the spirit and the ego-self. The separated spirit guides the ascent and the tamed ego-self guides the descent. Before arriving at the governing name all the subtle centers are conglomerated together. After arrival, each subtle center is connected to its source of divine effulgence and the governing name. Beginners/intermediates, whose experiential knowledge is associated with asserting the unity of being, has them seeing the ineffableness of the spirit as a designation of the Essence because of their overflowing love.[20] Wayfaring without attraction to God is a characteristic of these beginners. In contrast, realized wayfarers discern the difference between the ineffableness of the world of command and the ineffableness of the Essence. To arrive at the goal one needs sufficient attraction to proceed in wayfaring. To simply have attraction toward God without wayfaring or without following the shariat and sunnat leaves a person in the hapless situation of being an "attracted one."[21]

A person of inner knowledge (*'arif*) experiences the disclosure of the Essence on the inside and the disclosure of the attributes on the outside. Beginners experience the world of divine command on the inside and the world of creation on the outside. As Sirhindi often reminds his readers, the outward appearance and the inner reality of the realized ones is not like that of the common people.

The masters of the heart and those who have not yet arrived at the qualities, even if they are realized (*muntahi*), can still return to human attributes. Someone who is a Naqshbandi of Muhammadan disposition, experiencing the divine effulgence from the origin, will experience essential belovedness (*mahbubiyat-i dhati*).

In *Collected Letters*, Sirhindi often clarifies how the world's spiritual hierarchy is organized, apparently from his own experiences in the more subtle realms.[22] Since the ninth century, there have been numerous elaborations of this hierarchy, stemming from the *hadith al-ghibta*, which states

19. See Hutaki, *Sharh-i Maktubat*, 436.

20. Ibid., 437.

21. See Donkin's study of *majdhub*s cited above.

22. Sometimes Sirhindi has his own formulations, for example, the *qayyum*, the living person having the highest spiritual rank of all sufis on earth. According

that there are people whom prophets and martyrs will admire (the word used here, *ghibta*, usually means envy) on the Day of Judgment because of their rank.[23] One typical formulation is that of one axial leader (*qutb*) surrounded by three nobles (*nujaba'*), four pillars (*awtad*), seven pious ones (*abrar*), and forty substitutes (*abdal*). Sirhindi is saying in this letter that the unique axial leader (*qutb-i fard*) rules over the central axial authority (*qutb-i madar*) and the axial guide (*qutb-i irshad*).[24] There are various axial leaders involved in Sirhindi's version of the spiritual hierarchy, and one of these axial leaders rules over the substitutes and is associated with the archangel Raphael.[25]

Sirhindi emphasizes the differences between intoxication and sobriety. His assertions of the essential non-existence of the world are to counter intoxicated sufis' thinking that there is one continuum between the world and God whereby God's encompassing embrace and God's essential togetherness (*ma'iyat*) is in the world. As Sirhindi keeps saying in various ways throughout *Collected Letters*, the physical world is incommensurate with the Essence and only exists by virtue of the rays of God's names and attributes.[26] God's omnipresence (*ma'iyat wa-ihata*) manifests in the world as omnipresence but it is on the basis of God's attribute of knowledge not Essence. The protégés of God are in the shadows of the attributes and see the disclosure of the Essence from afar while the prophets are in the attri-

---

to Sirhindi, he had realized all the attributes of being the *qayyum*. See Sirhindi, *Mabda' wa-ma'ad*, 9.

23. See Louis Massignon, *Essay on the Origins of the Technical Language of Islamic Mysticism*, trans. Benjamin Clark (Notre Dame, IN: University of Notre Dame Press, 1997), 92.

24. Note that Sirhindi declared himself to be the unique one (*fard*), having absolute authority from the empyrean to earth. For Sirhindi's experience developing from axial guide (*qutb-i irshad*) to the unique one, see Sirhindi, *Mabda' wa-ma'ad*, 9-11. Sirhindi alludes to his being the central figure (*madar-i bina'*) of a special path in letter 1.260 in this book, page 262. The substitutes had a strong connection with ascetics and some early sources say the substitutes were divided between Syria and Iraq. See Ofer Livne-Kafri, "Early Muslim Ascetics and the World of Christian Monasticism," *Jerusalem Studies in Arabic and Islam* 20 (1996), 122-124 [105-129].

25. A hadith transmitted by 'Abdullah b. Ma'sud discusses three hundred friends of God, one of whom (of unspecified rank) has a heart like that of Raphael (*Israfil*). Ruzbihan Baqli (d. 606/1209) was apparently the first to formally associate the axial leader with Raphael. According to him, the axial leader's heart was equal to that of the archangel Raphael's. See Henry Corbin, *The Man of Light in Iranian Sufism*, trans. by Nancy Pearson (Boston: Shambhala, 1978), 55.

26. See Hutaki, *Sharh-i Maktubat*, 445.

butes and see the disclosure of the Essence close by.

Letter 1.287

In the name of God, the compassionate and merciful, let us give thanks to God who has guided us. If God had not given us guidance, we would not have been rightly guided. Messengers of our Lord truly did come. Muhammad, who came with the utmost sincerity, is the last messenger and the best and most completed and perfected of them. May God's grace, the most glorious, bless him, his family, the prophets, and all those who follow them until the Day of Judgment. Amen.

[The number of] seekers [has dwindled] because of their low aspirations, their baseness of character, and their not being able to find the spiritual companionship (*suhbat*) of a completed and completion-bestowing shaykh. The long path with a lofty goal has been debased to a shortcut leading nowhere. Proceeding along on the way, they are satisfied with very little and have a limited understanding of where they are going. [Nonetheless], they think that they have reached the end of the path in completeness, declaring that they have achieved the states of accomplished wayfarers who have reached the final goal. This lowly group, overcome by their own imagined power, has covered up perfected states with their own deficient ones. That is the story. In sleep a mouse becomes a camel.

[It is one thing to go] from the deep ocean to a drop, another to go from the surface of a drop from the sea of Oman to a dewdrop, but they have become contented with the surface of a dewdrop. They imagine the effable to be ineffable and take comfort [in reducing] the infinite to the finite and in trivializing the incomparable. The condition of people who unquestioningly believe in an ineffable God is many degrees better than the situation of those seekers who have not completed wayfaring on the path or those seeking comfort in illusion (lit. quenching one's thirst at a mirage). There is as large a difference between a speaker of truth and a speaker of lies as there is between a person who behaves in a proper manner and a person who exhibits criminal behavior. Woe on non-realized seekers who think that innovations are well-established practices and who confuse the effable and the ineffable. If they are not excused from incorrect interpretations of personal inspiration (*kashf*), then they are called to account for that mistake. "Our Lord, do not hold us accountable if we forget or make a mistake." [Q. 2:286]

For example, there was a person who desired to go to the Ka'ba. From intense longing, he set off in the direction of the Ka'ba. All of a sudden, while proceeding along, a house, appearing like the Ka'ba, came into view in front of him. Although the house only appeared like the Ka'ba in a vision, the person imagined that it was the real Ka'ba, and secluded himself there. Another person had learned about the special features of the Ka'ba from those who had already been there. [From their reports] he confirmed [the existence of] the Ka'ba. Without taking one step on the way to the Ka'ba, he did not mistake the Ka'ba for something else, even though [he thought] he knew for certain what the Ka'ba was on the basis of his own confirmations. His situation is better than that of the [first] mistaken seeker mentioned previously. Indeed! [There is a third] person, who has [set out toward the Ka'ba but] has not reached the goal. He does not [even] know the goal. He is better off than the second person who thinks he knows [the goal] on the basis of following others' information and who has not taken a step toward the goal. [The third person], in spite of not having confirmed the goal, is moving toward the goal. His overall preference is verified.

There is a group who imagine themselves to be completed and supposedly realized. They attract people because of their old age and popularity. The deficiencies of these shaykhs cause them to ruin the potential of many of those who are capable of developing perfections. By the unfortunate coldness of their companionship, they dampen the enthusiasm of seekers. It is the case of the blind leading the blind.

Those who have not realized the goal and [claim] imaginary perfections and a supposed attainment of the goal are more prevalent among ecstatic wayfarers (lit. attracted ones who are wayfaring *majdhuban-i suluk*) than wayfarers who are ecstatic (*salikan bi-majdhub*). This is because both beginners and realized seekers outwardly share the same appearance of ecstasy as they express love. In truth, these two [developmental phases] are incommensurate and their states are completely distinct.

What relationship is there between earth and the Lord of lords?

In the beginning [of the path], one is completely deficient and is too full [of ego-self] to receive. At the end of the path, all is with Truth and for Truth. If God wills, the details of this discussion, including the flights of imagination [justifying] this apparent resemblance and outer connection, will be mentioned below [in the first section].

In the exalted Naqshbandi path, ecstatic attraction to God occurs prior to wayfaring. The reason why a deluded imagination completely predominates over those who are ecstatically attracted to God is because their [sufi] lineage does not benefit from [experienced knowledge of] wayfaring. Others, overwhelmed by ecstatic attraction to God, [mistakenly] think that their oscillation between states is an indication that they are traversing the way stations along the path to God (*sayr ila Allah*). When their weak minds reach some kind of stability, they perceive themselves as ecstatic wayfarers. The sections below explain the truth of attraction to God, the truth of wayfaring, and the difference between both of these stations. [The letter will] mention the special characteristics distinguishing one from the other as well as the difference between the attraction of a beginner and that of an accomplished wayfarer. It will also discuss the truth of the completion-bestowing station, in addition to the knowledge and guidance pertaining to this station. "That God may confirm the truth and foil what is false in spite of evildoers' opposition." [Q. 8:8] Now, with the beauty of God's most glorious good fortune, I begin this explanation. He is the most glorious guide of the path, the perfect master and protector.

This letter has two sections (sing. *maqsad*) and an epilogue [and some more]. The first section explains knowledge related to the station of attraction to God. The second section pertains to wayfaring/contemplative practice (*suluk*). The epilogue clarifies miscellaneous [aspects of] inner and outer knowledge, which will greatly benefit seekers.

Part One

Know that ecstatic wayfarers who are not yet fully realized, although they experience strong attraction to God, are in the circle of the heart. No matter what path they choose, they experience [the same kind of] attraction. Without [guided] wayfaring and purification of the ego-self, they cannot go beyond the station of the heart and arrive at the Invigorator of the heart (lit. He who makes hearts fluctuate, *muqallib al-qulub*, that is, God). Their attraction is attraction of the heart. Their love is contingent (*'ardi*), not genuinely and intentionally of the Essence. Also [in this station], the ego-self is mixed with the spirit (*ruh*) like darkness and light.[27] One has to totally emerge from the constraints of the heart station in order to be [intimately] connected with the Invigorator of the heart. Until the spirit escapes from the ego-self, the spirit will not be able to focus on the goal. Likewise, until the ego-self becomes separated from the spirit, it is not possible for the ego-self to descend into the station of servanthood. As long as the ego-self and spirit are entwined together, the heart synthesis (*jami'a-yi qalbiya*) is firmly established and pure attraction of the spirit is not possible. Nor is it possible to purify the spirit from the ego-self until one traverses the stages of wayfaring, which include wayfaring to God (*sayr ila Allah*) and wayfaring in God (*sayr fi'llah*). It is only after attaining the station of separation after synthesis (*maqam al-farq ba'd al-jami'*),[28] which is connected to returning

---

27. In this letter, heart (*qalb*) and spirit (*ruh*) are not explicitly specified as subtle centers (sing. *latifa*), though in a context of contemplative practice they would be. In any case, the reader is reminded that subtle centers are most probably layers of increasingly subtle sheaths/bodies that interpenetrate each other, and the physical body. Unless otherwise stated, the terms heart and spirit will refer to these sheaths. There is a subtle center called the ego-self (*nafs*), which is apparently the same as the ego-self.

28. There is a discussion of this station in *Collected Letters*, 1.285.45-46 explaining how the attributes and qualities are in the world of command and how

to the world of creation for God and by means of God (*sayr 'an Allah bil-lah*), that anything is possible. A beggar is not a warrior, nor can a gnat ever become Solomon.

So see the difference between the attraction of the realized person and that of a beginner! The experience of these intoxicated heart-centered ones is of the veil of multiplicity, whether or not they make known their inner condition. In this multiplicity, they only experience the world of spirits (*'alam-i arwah*). Its subtle, encompassing, and penetrating nature [has them feeling like] they are experiencing a form resembling God. "God created Adam in God's image."[29] With this as their frame of reference, they interpret their experience in the spirit as experience of the almighty and holy Truth. Likewise, they experience the encompassing and penetrating nature, closeness, and togetherness (*ma'iyat*) of the spirit as that of God. This is because the wayfarer's vision can only see as far as the station above his present station (here referring to the station of the heart), which is the station of the spirit, not the station three levels above. Seeing above the station of the spirit will be blocked until one actually arrives at the station of the spirit. [In an analogous way, the feelings of] love and attraction to God (interpreted as such in the station of the heart) are also like the experience of the most glorious Truth in the station of the heart. The difference, however, is that love and attraction to God in the station of the heart are related to realizing annihilation in God, which happens after the end of wayfaring to God.

> As long as no one is there,
> One can be annihilated in God.
> God's court is not a place.
> So no road goes there.

Expressing the contemplative experiences (*shuhud*) of this station [of the heart] is constrained by [the limitations of] interpretation. And except for that, [Naqshbandi] notables operate beyond the beyond of everyday consensus reality (*shuhud-i muta'rafat*). In the same manner, their goal is the eternal and the ineffable. Their being united with God, the most glorious, is also eternal and ineffable. There is no path from the finite to the infinite. Only the King's camel can carry the King's gifts. The connection between God and human souls is indescribable and incomparable.

According to the investigations of experienced wayfarers (*arbab-i suluk*), that is, those who have arrived at the end of the path (lit. work *kar*), the encompassing and penetrating nature, closeness, and togetherness of the

---

the spirit (*ruh*) is an interface between two aspects, form (*chun*) and formlessness (*be-chun*).

29. A hadith found in both al-Bukhari, *Istidhan*, 1 (#6227) and al-Muslim, *Jannat*, 12 (#2612, 2841) [MR], and mentioned eight times in *Collected Letters*.

Truth, most glorious, is a branch of knowledge. Such knowledge is harmonious with [the understanding of] authentic jurists (*'ulama'-i ahl-i haqq*). God thank them for their efforts. According to these jurists, determining closeness to God and other related topics can only be done from afar by those who have not achieved the goal. Those who are close to God are not in a position to determine it. A notable once said, "Whoever says he is close [to God] is far and whoever is far [from his ego-self] is close [to God]. This is sufism." A branch of knowledge that pertains to experiencing the unity of being (*tawhid-i wujud*) has attraction to God and love [overflowing] from the heart as its source. Those who are centered on the heart, who have not first cultivated an attraction to God, but who still set out wayfaring and traversing the way stations of the path, have no affinity for this branch of knowledge.

It is exactly the same situation for those ecstatics who begin wayfaring from the heart focused on the Invigorator of the heart and who are indifferent to this knowledge. May they ask God's forgiveness. Some of those ecstatically attracted to God, even though they set out wayfaring through the stages, do not progress because their vision never goes beyond the station of the familiar to develop higher aspirations. They do not recognize that this kind of knowledge even exists, and cannot get out of their predicament. Thus, they are unable to ascend through the various degrees of closeness to God. "Please God, take us away from this oppressive town. Appoint a protector and defender for us." [Q. 4:75] The sign of arriving at the end of the goal is having gone beyond this knowledge. To the extent that one develops a greater affinity to transcendence, one experiences less affinity with the Creator and the world. During this time he thinks that the world is the same as the Creator or considers the Creator to be an ocean with the Essence encompassing the world. This makes no sense at all. What relationship is there between earth and the Lord of lords?

Inner meaning 1 (*ma'rifat*)

Baha'uddin Naqshband (lit. the exalted presence of the master Naqshband) said that his group [followed the principle of] "including the end in the beginning."[30] God almighty bless his most holy secret. This means that the attraction and love realized by accomplished seekers [in other lineages] at the end of the path are gradually introduced at the beginning of the path for those in the Naqshbandi lineage. This is because, for realized seekers, attraction to God stems from the spirit, while attraction for beginners is from the heart. The heart is an interface between the spirit and the ego-self. So attraction to God associated with the heart becomes mixed with that

30. This is Baha'uddin Naqshband (d. 791/1389 Bukhara), the founder-figure of the Naqshbandiyya.

of the spirit. Naqshbandis stress the [principle] of including the end in the beginning although the concept [of arriving to God] is found in all types of attraction to God. It is because of this that the great Naqshbandi shaykhs have established a method to actually [arrive at God] and have specified a path to arrive at this goal.

Those of other lineages [only] randomly experience this concept [of arriving at God] as they go along the path but they cannot deliberately actualize it. Naqshbandi notables in the station of attraction have a special kind of attraction to God that others do not, or if they do, it is rare. Therefore, some of these non-Naqshbandis are in the station of attraction without traversing the stages of the path. Their annihilation and abiding in God resembles those who have already traversed the stations along the path. [Included in their station of attraction] there is a portion of the completion-bestowing (*takmil*) station that resembles the station of returning to the world of creation for God and by means of God. Along with this, they train those who are prepared. Further substantiation of this topic will be found below if God almighty wills. This is only an introduction.

One must know that the spirit develops a kind of attentive inclination (*tawajjuh*) toward the goal before its attachment to the [physical] body. After the spirit becomes attached to the body, this tendency [to turn toward the goal] lessens. The notables of this exalted lineage have established a method in order to cultivate the aforementioned inclination. But when the spirit is attached to the body, an attentive inclination develops toward the heart, which combines the inclinations of the spirit and the ego-self. Without a doubt, the inclination of spirit is contained in the inclination of the heart. For realized wayfarers, however, the inclination of their spirit manifests after the annihilation of the spirit and residing in it with pure being, which leads to abiding in God.

There is an inclination (*tawajjuh*) of the spirit included in the inclination of the heart. However, the inclination of the spirit, which is prior in its connection with the body, is an inclination *with* the spirit's existence because there is no way for the spirit to become annihilated [at that point]. There is a lot of difference between the spirit's inclination when the spirit's being is existent and when the spirit is annihilated. To say that inclination toward the spirit is included at the end [is only valid] from the viewpoint of the [pure nature of the] spirit's inclination because at the end this is all that remains. "The end is included in the beginning" means the outer appearance (*surat*) of the end, not the reality (*haqiqat*) of the end. It is impossible for the reality of the end to be included in the beginning. It is possible that the word "outer appearance" was omitted [in the phrase "the end is included in the beginning"] to allure seekers to this lineage. Truth is what I have figured out with the help of God almighty.

Wayfarers who make quick progress and appear to be ahead of others have an attraction to God that does not produce results, even though they have come with focus and presence. They still have an attraction stemming from the heart, a sign that the inclination of the spirit is not entirely disassociated from the physical body. There is another group, which has achieved some results because of the manifestation of a spirit inclination. They have forgotten about this inclination because of its connection to the body. These so-called gains are a result of a warning to focus on the spirit and to remember what they have lost. Those who have forgotten the inclination of the spirit have a more subtle ability to progress on the path than those quickly progressing wayfarers. This is because their being totally focused on the body, and becoming lost alerts them to their having completely forgotten the inclination of the spirit. Not forgetting the inclination of the spirit is something else altogether.

In short, quickly progressing wayfarers [should] cultivate an overall inclination permeating everything such that their spirit takes control over the physical body just like [the situation of] beloveds that God desires (sing. *murad*). When beloveds go wayfaring it is like the reality of something, and for quickly progressing wayfarers it is like the outer form. Those who can recognize the essence are aware of its appearance. Indeed! Lovers who arrive and seekers who are completed verify this kind of [reality-tasting] wayfaring. Like a lightning bolt, this experience is not constant. Constant wayfaring is a special situation for beloveds.

Inner meaning 2

When divinely attracted ecstatics, masters of hearts (*arbab-i qulub*), become established in the station of the heart, a sobriety and knowledge appropriate to that station is also facilitated for them. It is possible for these intoxicated ones to be of benefit to seekers who, in spiritual companionship, can realize more love and attraction to God through the heart. Yet, ecstatics cannot bring others to completion because they themselves are not yet completed.

It is well known that completion cannot come from deficiency. [Paradoxically], the benefit of ecstatic shaykhs for others, no matter how much it may be, is more than that of the wayfaring masters (*arbab-i suluk*), even if the latter have finished all their wayfaring and have realized the kind of attraction to God associated with accomplished wayfarers. In the station of the heart, wayfarers are not on the path returning to the world of creation for God and by means of God. Anyone at the end of the path who has not returned to help humanity has not reached the level of completion bestowing (*takmil*). This is because the person has no inclination and affinity for the world, without which he cannot help others.

An exemplary shaykh (*shaykh-i muqtada'*) is called an interface (*barzakh*) from the standpoint of his being in the station of being an interface (*barzakhiyat*), after having come down from the station of the heart.[31] He encompasses both sides, the spirit and the ego-self. From the reference point of the spirit, the exemplary shaykh is favored by [divine emanations from] above and relative to the ego-self, he is favored from below because he unites a focus (*tawajjuh*) toward God with a focus toward humanity without any veils whatsoever. Thus, the exemplary shaykh realizes the union of the benefited and the benefiter.

Some shaykhs say that bridging is between God and humans instead of the bridging of an exemplary shaykh. They say that a shaykh who functions as an interface unites the transcendent and the immanent. Being an interface based upon ecstatic attraction is not appropriate for the station of a shaykh, which instead should be based on sobriety. Intoxication (*sukr*) is not proper for the station of a shaykh because the lights of the spirit that are included in this station [of being a shaykh] overpower the ego-self and [themselves] are the source of intoxication. In the station of being an interface of the heart (*maqam-i barzakhiyat-i qalb*), the spirit and the ego-self are separate. There is no possibility for intoxication to take over. All is sobriety, which is the station of inviting others to God. Keep this in mind.

When a completed shaykh (*shaykh-i kamil*) is able to return (lit. go down) from ascent in the station of the heart, he develops an affinity (*munasabat*) with the world and enables qualified seekers to acquire perfections through his being an interface. One who is firmly established in ecstatic attraction to God (hereafter established ecstatic shaykh) is in the station of the heart.[32] He also has an affinity with the world. He does not withhold love, intoxication, or supernatural power (*tawajjuh*) [to help others]. Even though these are of the heart, one benefits. Undoubtedly, the established ecstatic shaykh is open to help others. I assert that the established ecstatic shaykh provides more benefit [in some ways] than the realized shaykh (*shaykh-i muntahi*) who has returned to the world (also called the completed shaykh in this discussion). The *quality* of the realized shaykh's state, however, benefits others more than that of the ecstatic shaykh. This

31. The discussion here concerns two categories of shaykhs. There are three kinds in the first category: an exemplary shaykh (*shaykh-i muqtada*), a completed shaykh (*shaykh-i kamil*), and a realized shaykh (*shaykh-i muntahi*), who all contrast with an ecstatic shaykh (*shaykh-i majdhub*), the second category. The realized shaykh has many advantages over the ecstatic shaykh. First, there is the quality and ability to transmit spiritual energy of the realized shaykh compared to the "quantity" and lack of spiritual energy transmission of the ecstatic shaykh. Second, there are no conditions as explained in the text. See *Collected Letters*, 1.287.59, fn 1.

32. They are established in the station of the heart subtle center.

is because the realized shaykh only has an outward affinity with the world. In reality, he is separate from the world and imbued with the origin (*asl*), where he remains. The ecstatic shaykh has a real affinity to the world and remains with all aspects of the world. The world abides in this remaining.

Seekers definitely get more benefit from ecstatic shaykhs than with realized shaykhs because of real affinity [with the world]. However, the realized shaykh specializes in benefiting others in the levels of perfections associated with intimacy with God (*walayat*). Without a doubt the benefits of a realized shaykh prevail, even though in reality he does not have supernatural power (*tawajjuh* or *himmat*) to further [the development of] the seeker like the ecstatic shaykh can. With the ecstatic shaykh, however, a seeker cannot reach the limits of completion. In addition, seekers receive considerable supernatural power from ecstatic shaykhs, associated with the spirit subtle center. Although they have forgotten [this connection with the spirit], in spiritual companionship with the ecstatic shaykh, seekers are reminded [of it], since it is included in the supernatural power associated with the heart.

On the other hand, the supernatural power found in the spiritual companionship of a realized shaykh is new [for the seekers]. While they have not experienced it before in the state of annihilation of the spirit, they experience it in the divine presence as the state of remaining in the spirit. The supernatural power [from an ecstatic shaykh] is easy to receive and assimilate, while that [of a realized shaykh] is hard to feel and correspondingly much less is received. What is easier is more common and what is harder is more rare. They say that an exemplary shaykh (one who is an interface) is not the way to realize attraction to God since the seeker already has that type of connection [with an ecstatic shaykh]. When correction and learning are necessary because the student has forgotten, a teaching shaykh (*shaykh-i ta'lim*) is necessary, not a directing shaykh (*shaykh-i tarbiya*).[33] For traversing the stages of the path, an exemplary shaykh is effective and the direction [given by such a shaykh] becomes necessary.[34] It is not appropriate for an exemplary shaykh to give an established ecstatic shaykh unconditional permission to teach others or to appoint him to the station of bestowing completion. To be in spiritual companionship with an ecstatic shaykh would probably cause some seekers to lose their great aptitude and their ability to become completed and completion bestowing. For example, if a good wheat seed is planted in land that has the total ability to grow

33. It appears that a teaching shaykh could be either an exemplary shaykh or an ecstatic shaykh. There is an extended discussion of teaching and directing shaykhs in Buehler, *Sufi Heirs*.

34. Here there is an indication that a directing shaykh (*shaykh-i tarbiya*) is an exemplary shaykh.

wheat, it will grow according to its potential. If a bad seed is planted, the place where it would have sprouted has lost its potential to grow wheat.

If we assume an exemplary shaykh finds it advisable to give an ecstatic shaykh permission to teach in order that some essential benefit will result, then his teaching must be restricted by certain stipulations. These include an apparent affinity of the seeker and the ecstatic shaykh's method of teaching, maintaining the aptitude of the seeker during spiritual companionship with the ecstatic shaykh, and making sure that there is no flaring up of his ego-self while supervising seekers. In the latter case, the seeker's capricious impulses from the ego-self will not decrease because there has been no purification of the ego-self. When the ecstatic shaykh knows that the seeker has reached the end of his teaching and still has ability and potential to develop, the ecstatic shaykh must make this known to the seeker and give him permission to work with another shaykh in order that he can finish his training. [In this way], the ecstatic shaykh will not consider himself to be fully realized and wayfarers will be saved from highway robbery along the path [because this admission of limitation is made public]. The ecstatic shaykh gives the seeker permission along the same lines as he himself was given permission by the exemplary shaykh, that is, with stipulations (like those mentioned above) suitable for the specific situation and with a specific mandate to fulfill.

An exemplary shaykh does not need these restrictions to teach or to bestow completion on others. He has a special connection [with God] by virtue of [his embodying] the universality of all sufi lineages and their dispositions. Each person can benefit [from his presence] to the extent of his or her aptitude. Although there are distinctions of how quickly one can progress [with one exemplary shaykh or another] because of a [relatively] strong or weak connection with God, in the context of spiritual companionship with shaykhs or exemplary shaykhs, [these distinctions] are also imaginary. Essentially, all shaykhs' teachings involve the same steps. The exemplary shaykh, while teaching a student, must take refuge in the majesty of the most glorious Truth and cling tightly to God's strong rope (tangibly interpreted to be the Qur'an, sunnat, and the shariat) inside God's omnipresence in order to be safe from fearing the most glorious of God's ruses. Taking refuge in God is not just for this situation, but for all situations. The most holy and glorious Truth always provides favors, and is not separated from any deed or moment. "God gives favor to whomever God desires and is the Master of all grace." [Q. 62:4]

Part Two

This discussion is associated with wayfaring. Know that if a seeker is proceeding on a path going upwards and he realizes a name [of God] such that it manifests through him (lit. he becomes a master of a name) to such an extent that the annihilation of ego-self occurs, it is correct for him to abandon this annihilation. After abiding in this name, abandoning this abiding is, for him, preserving it. With this annihilation and abiding, one becomes honored with the first level of intimacy with God. Here is a detail that must be discussed at length.

Introduction

There are two kinds of divine effulgence (*fayd*) that emanate from the almighty and holy Essence. The first kind is associated with creation, preservation, nourishing, giving life, causing to die, and other attributes like these. The second kind relates to faith (*iman*), and experiential suprarational knowledge, and all the rest of the perfections of the levels of intimacy with God and prophethood.[35] The first kind of divine effulgence is only associated with the divine attributes, while the second kind emanates partially through the attributes and partially through the qualities (*shuyunat*). The difference between attributes and qualities is very subtle. It does not appear to anyone except to the intimates of God having a Muhammadan disposition. No one else has spoken about it.[36]

In short, attributes of God exist in the objective, physical world (*dar kharij*) separate from the almighty and holy Essence while the qualities are only aspects (*i'tibarat*) in the Essence. Glorify God's sovereignty. An example will shed some light on this discussion. Water flows downhill naturally. This natural event has us imagine that water has life, knowledge, will, and power. For example, those with knowledge, by means of their heaviness and according to the demands of their knowledge, will go from top to bottom and will not be able to go upwards. Knowledge is predicated on life; will is predicated on knowledge; and power is also affirmed since will specifies one of two possibilities (either knowledge or will). These aspects [which are thought to be] in the essence of water are at the stage of the qualities.[37]

Even without these aspects, attributes outside the Essence confirmed in

35. According to Nur Ahmad, the first kind of divine effulgence is the domain of the axial leader of the substitutes (*qutb-i abdal*) and the second is the domain of the axial guide (*qutb-i irshad*). See *Collected Letters,* 1.287.61, fn. 4 and 5.

36. Mulla Sadra Shirazi (d. 1050/1641), a contemporary of Sirhindi, has mentioned *sifat, shuyunat,* and *i'tibarat.* See Hossein Nasr, "The Qur'anic Commentaries of Mulla Sadra," in Jalal al-Din Ashtiyani et. al., eds., *Consciousness and Reality: Studies in Memory of Toshihiko Izutsu* (Leiden: Brill, 2000), 54.

37. Since qualities and aspects are usually differentiated, they are at the same stage if "stage" is considered to be the stage of Essence. Drs. Mehmet Toprak and Necdet Tosun of Marmara University in Istanbul helped me clarify this paragraph.

the essence of water still are co-existent with attributes outside the Essence. It cannot be said that water has the primary aspects of being alive, knowing, having power, and desiring. One must separate these names from the confirmed attributes outside the Essence. Thus, according to the explanation of some shaykhs, [the phenomenon of] water is separate from these aforementioned names because [they say that] there is no difference between qualities and attributes. They also negate the existence of attributes [in the created world] on the basis of this lack of difference.[38] Another difference between qualities and attributes is that the station of qualities is directly facing the Essence. For attributes it is not.

(Returning to the discussion of God's effulgence)

God's messenger, Muhammad, receives the second kind of divine effulgence through the qualities. God almighty bless him, his family, and the intimates of God (*awliya'*) who are under his supervision. God almighty be satisfied with all of them. The rest of the prophets and those who follow them receive the first kind of divine effulgence from the attributes. I declare that the shadow of the quality of knowledge is the name that rules over Muhammad (lit. that Pleasure) and is the means for the second type of divine effulgence to arrive.[39] The quality of knowledge is the comprehensive synthesis of all the comprehensive and particular qualities. The shadow of the quality of knowledge is a potentiality (the ability to receive *qabiliyat,* also

38. Sirhindi is seeking to show that attributes cannot be conflated with qualities or aspects. To conflate these hierarchical levels is to conflate an attribute of water observable in the physical world, for example, water flowing downhill, with a quality (of knowledge, will, and power, for example) and/or an aspect (knowing, desiring, having power). It follows that the attribute of flowing downhill is associated with a quality/aspect that does not tangibly exist in the physical realm, such as will or desiring. This is like a person observing running water who thinks that the flowing water has a will of its own and that will is just another attribute of water. This is impossible since the quality of will does not have any objective existence in the material world, separate from the water itself. Instead will is a quality that exists beyond the physical world. See Hutaki, *Sharh-i Maktubat*, 428-429. Nur Ahmad refers to Sirhindi's *Divine Knowledge* (*Ma'arif-i laduniya*) in *Collected Letters,* 1.287.62 fn 1, explaining that anyone who equates the qualities and attributes thereby also equates the attributes and the Essence, along with equating the qualities with the objective/physical world. See Ahmad Sirhindi, *Ma'arif-i laduniya*, ed. with Urdu translation by Zawwar Husayn Shah (Karachi: Ahmad Brothers Printers, 1986), 12-14; 36-37; 42. This means denying the attributes and goes against the consensus of those who know the truth (*ahl-i haqq*), that is, those who follow the Maturidi creed.

39. This quality of knowledge is considered the highest of God's qualities. See Buehler, *Sufi Heirs*, 245.

translated as capability) of the Essence and the potentiality of all the comprehensive and particular qualities including the quality of knowledge.

One must know that the potentiality of God acts as an interface between the exalted Essence and the quality of knowledge. When the Essence aspect of the interface loses all color so does the interface, and the interface takes on the color of the other side, that is, the color of the quality of knowledge. Therefore, it is imperative to discuss the shadow of this quality [because it functions as an interface]. The shadow of a thing consists of the appearance of the thing itself, although it is only a resemblance [of the original] at the second level.[40] The realization of the interface comes after realizing both aspects. When a person has an unveiling (*mukashafa*), [the quality of knowledge side of] the interface becomes visible [at a level] below the quality [of knowledge]. With respect to this manifestation (*zuhur*), until it ends, it is appropriate to stay out of the shadow.

There is a group of God's protégés under the supervision of Muhammad. God bless them and give them peace. They have realized (lit. are masters of) the names where the second kind of divine effulgence arrives. They comprehend and encompass the shadows of potentiality. For the shadow of totality, the shadows of potentiality are like the details. Those who follow the rest of the prophets receive the first and second types of divine effulgence by means of the power and potentialities of the sovereign Essence, which is characterized by attributes with existence outside the Essence (*sifat-i mawjuda-yi za'ida*).[41] There is also a group following these prophets that is characterized by attributes (that is, the potential of the attributes in detail *qabiliyat-i sifat*), not potential or capability characterized by Essence (*qabiliyat-i dhat*), through which they receive the first and second types of divine effulgence. The means of transmitting the first type of divine effulgence to Muhammad is the divine potentiality characterized by the almighty and holy Essence along with all the divine attributes. Thus, the potentials [of the attributes] are the means of transmitting divine effulgence to the rest of the prophets. God bless our prophet and them. The potentials of the attributes are the shadows of the comprehensive potentiality [of God] and are like the details of the overall whole.[42]

---

40. The second level here is the next level down toward the physical world or the second level of manifestation, that of the names and attributes.

41. These include: God being alive, speaking, omnipotent, willing, hearing, and seeing. Mustafa Ceric, *Roots of Synthetic Theology in Islam: A Study of the Theology of Abu Mansur al-Maturidi* (Kuala Lumpur: International Institute of Islamic Thought and Civilization, 1995), 159. Notice that the capabilities/potentialities function as an interface.

42. Some specific examples are in order here. When the first and second types of divine effulgence manifested through the prophet Moses, there was the capabil-

There is a group under the authority of Muhammad. They receive the first type of divine effulgence, associated with the attributes, separately [from the second type]. This is because those of a Muhammadan disposition receive the first type of divine effulgence separate from the mode of the second type of divine effulgence.[43] On the other hand, those that follow other prophets receive only one mode of divine effulgence. Some shaykhs limit Muhammad's potential. For these shaykhs, there is no difference between the qualities and the attributes. This indicates a lack of knowledge about the station of the qualities. God manifests the truth and guides us to the straight path.

It has been verified that the origin of Muhammad (lit. that presence) is the Lord of lords, whether in the station of qualities or whether in the place of the attributes, and is the means for both types of divine effulgence. God bless him and give him peace. It also has become well known that divine effulgence comes from the Essence via the levels of the perfections of intimacy (*kamalat-i walayat*) of Muhammad (lit. that presence). This occurs without the mediation of anything outside of the Essence (*amr-i za'id*). A quality the same as the Essence or an additional aspect is [just] a mental construct [as opposed to being in the Essence]. Therefore, the disclosure of the Essence (*tajalli-yi dhati*) is special to Muhammad and his completed followers because they receive divine effulgence from his path and become favored with a part of this station. Others receive divine effulgence by means of the attributes, which exist outside the Essence (*wujud-i za'id*), and they are caught in the middle. This causes a major impediment to come [between them and the goal] and they become destined for the [mere] disclosure of attributes (*tajalli-yi sifati*).[44]

---

ity/potentiality of the Essence along with the attribute of speech. With Adam there was also the capability of the Essence along with the attribute of physical formation (*takwin*). Jesus had the capability of the Essence along with the attribute of power. These various capabilities (speech, physical formation, and power) are only parts of the comprehensive capability of God. This latter capability of the Essence expressed in its comprehensive nature is the domain of Muhammad. See Hutaki, *Sharh-i Maktubat*, 430-431.

43. This is largely because the darkness in the shadow of the quality of knowledge is a transitional interface to the divine capability. See *Collected Letters,* 1.287.63 fn 3.

44. The principle here is that the attributes outside the Essence are considered to have objective existence (*wujud-i khariji*) and are not a part of the Essence. Thus the attributes, since they are derived from the Essence, are an obstacle between divine capability of the Essence (*qabiliyat-i dhat*) and humans, unlike the qualities (*shuyunat*) whose divine effulgence is mediated by Muhammad. The divine effulgence that comes from other prophets originates in the attributes (*fayd-i wujudi*).

One should know that the capability or potential to characterize an attribute, to the extent that it is an aspect, has no existence outside the Essence because attributes are existent (*mawjud*), while the [inherent] capabilities of the attributes are not. Capabilities act as interfaces between the attributes and the Essence. Between the qualities and attributes is an interface, which itself takes on the characteristics of both aspects. As the interface takes on the characteristics of the attributes, obstacles and impediments are created. Even half a hair's width of separation from the friend is too much.

From this discussion, it is clear that the unveiled appearance of the almighty and holy Essence is in accordance with the disclosure of contemplative witnessing (*tajalli-yi shuhudi*), while the disclosure of being (*tajalli-yi wujudi*) is not.[45] Therefore, Muhammad received a contemplatively witnessed divine effulgence (*fayd-i shuhudi*—the second type via the qualities) in the multi-faceted perfections of intimacy with God without any veils coming between [him and the Source]. God bless him and give him peace. On the other hand, veils between him and the source of existential divine effulgence (*fayd-i wujudi*—the first type via the attributes) did come from the "capability/potential characterized by Essence" discussed above. It should not be said that just because qualities and their respective capabilities are from aspects of the mind (see discussion above), that mental existence is proved. For this reason, the veil of knowledge must come [into being].

Briefly, the veils of the attributes are objective in the physical world (*khariji*) and the veils of the qualities are cognitive (*'ilmi*).[46] I say that mental existence cannot be a veil between two objective existences (sing. *mawjud*).[47] However, objective existence is its own veil. If one gives up [certain perspectives], then through attainment of [a certain kind of] knowledge, the cognitive veils of knowledge can be lifted. On the contrary, it is not possible that the veils of the objective world will disappear.

When these preliminaries are known, then for those of a Muhammadan disposition, their last [stage of] wayfaring (in the heart) is named "wayfaring to God" until the shadow of the quality that is its name.[48] After annihilation in that name, they become honored by annihilation in God. If they remain in that name, abiding in God also becomes easy. With that an-

See Hutaki, *Sharh-i Maktubat*, 432. The context of Sirhindi's discussion here is practical advice in contemplative practice. Theologically the attributes are neither of the Essence nor not of the Essence.

45. According to Maturidi-Hanafi dogma only Muhammad can see God with physical eyes.

46. Any knowledge presupposes the duality of a knower and a known.

47. Two examples given in the margin of *Collected Letters,* 1.287.64 are between the Creator and the created or between Muhammad's words and God.

48. There are further stages. This is the last one while traveling in the heart.

nihilation and abiding, they enter the first level of a special Muhammadan intimacy with God. God bless and give peace to those who achieve this. For those who are not of a Muhammadan disposition, they arrive at the capability or potential of the attribute or the attribute itself, which is its governing principle (lit. its lord). If they become annihilated in this name, then they cannot be annihilated in God. Likewise, if one remains in that name, there is no abiding in God.

The name of God means the level at which the totality of all the qualities and attributes exist. From the standpoint of the qualities, most attributes are relative, [that is, mental, not objectively existing]. The qualities are identical to the Essence and to each other. This is because annihilation in one aspect (the discussion has now shifted from qualities to aspects but both are beyond attributes) is annihilation in all the aspects and annihilation in the almighty and holy Essence. Likewise, abiding in one aspect is abiding in all the aspects. Therefore, to say annihilation and abiding in God is correct in this case. On the contrary, from the viewpoint of attributes outside the Essence, these aspects and qualities are interchangeable with the Essence. This is a real relationship, not a relative one. So annihilation in one attribute does not imply or require that there will be annihilation in all the attributes. Such is the case with abiding also.

One must not say that this annihilation is annihilation in God or that this abiding is remaining in God. One can talk about absolute annihilation or absolute abiding or qualify a specific attribute,[49] for example, annihilation in the attribute of knowledge or remaining in that attribute. Thus, the annihilation of Muhammadans (those with a Muhammadan disposition) is more complete and their abiding is more perfected. [In a similar manner], the Muhammadan ascent is superior because it goes to the qualities, which are incommensurate with the material world, a world that is the shadow of the attributes, not the shadow of the qualities. The annihilation of a wayfarer in a quality means that he or she must have achieved an absolute annihilation such that the wayfarer has no trace of existence remaining. Similarly, abiding completely with that quality, one becomes utterly abiding.

In contrast, when annihilated in an attribute one never emerges entirely from oneself. Its trace (*athar*) does not go away because the existence of the wayfarer is a trace (*athar*) of that very attribute and its shadow. The appearance of the source (*asl*) does not completely wipe away the existence of the shadow, which makes the abiding as incomplete as the annihilation. A Muhammadan is protected against ever returning to human attributes because he has completely transcended himself, abiding in God the most

49. Sirhindi does not appear to ever specify traveling in a specific attribute though his shaykh mentioned travel in the attributes of *qahr* and *jamal* (wrath and mercy respectively). See Baqibillah, *Kulliyat-i Baqibillah*, 96.

glorious. In this situation, return is not possible. On the other hand, an appearance of annihilation in the attributes makes return possible because of the remaining trace stemming from the wayfarer's existence.

It is at this point that disagreements occur among shaykhs concerning the possibility of returning or not returning [to human attributes]. God sanctify their innermost beings. The truth is that if a person is a Muhammadan, then he or she is protected from return. Otherwise one has a risk [of returning].[50] There also exists a difference of opinion concerning the disappearance of the traces of existence for wayfarers after their annihilation. Some say they disappear in the Essence with a residual trace of existence in the attributes. Others say that traces of existence cannot possibly disappear. The truth is that for a Muhammadan, the entity (*'ayn,* glossed as *dhat*, Essence) and trace (glossed as attribute) are both lost [because a person is at the level of the qualities]. For others not of Muhammadan disposition, the trace of existence does not go away because the attribute, which is its origin (*asl*), still remains [in the physical world]. [From the standpoint of the Essence and trace], the disappearance of the shadow [of existence] is totally impossible. Here is a subtle point.

One must know that the disappearance of the entity and any trace of the entity is a contemplative perception (*shuhudi*),[51] not an existential reality (*wujudi*), because to declare existential disappearance (*zawal-i wujudi*) is paramount to apostasy and heresy.[52] There are some in this group who have imagined existential disappearance, yet deny the possibility that traces of existence can disappear. They know that their ideas are those of apostates and heretics. The truth is what I have confirmed with signs of the most Glorious. It is strange that they have spoken about existential disappearance [of the traces of existence, that is, creation] while asserting the existential disappearance of the entity. To think that the disappearance of the entity is like the disappearance of the trace [of the entity] is paramount to apostasy and heresy. In short, existential disappearance of both entity and trace is impossible, although from a contemplative experience (*shuhudi*) both the entity and trace can and do disappear. This only happens, however, for those of a

---

50. This is because a Muhammadan is in the realm of the qualities, which do not have any connection to the physical world.

51. According to the glosses in the text and the context, entity (*'ayn*) has a meaning of Essence when contrasted with attributes. "The entity is the very thing itself and fixed in God's knowledge." See William C. Chittick, *The Self-Disclosure of God: Principles of Ibn al-'Arabi's Cosmology* (Albany: State University of New York Press, 1998), 389 note 9.

52. Cf. Muhammad Ghawth Gwaliori who claimed to have a bodily ascension experience and was declared by many as a heretic on this basis. Note the following footnote.

Muhammadan disposition.[53]

When the Muhammadans completely finish with the heart, and join with God [lit. the Invigorator of the heart], they are completely free [in their perfection] of fluctuating states and servitude to anything other than God. Others have no escape from the station of the heart because of their attachment to traces of existence and because of the continual fluctuating states in their lives, (which Sirhindi calls being "a son of time" (*ibn-i waqt*)). This is because the existence of traces and fluctuating states is from a branch of illuminated truth in the heart synthesis. The visionary experience (*shuhud*) of others (non-Muhammadans) is always obscured by a veil because to the extent that the remaining part of the wayfarer's existence is confirmed, the goal is veiled. When the trace of existence remains, to that extent the trace is veiled.

Inner Meaning 1

If a wayfarer on the path arrives unexpectedly and without vision on a level above the name that governs his wayfaring, without reaching this name, he will become annihilated on this level. It is correct to say that [he is experiencing] annihilation in God or that [he is experiencing] remaining on this level. From the standpoint [of Muhammadans], annihilation in God is at the first level [that is, at the level of Essence, not attributes or other levels].

Inner Meaning 2

There are many kinds of wayfaring: 1) those whose wayfaring precedes being attracted to God, 2) those who have an attraction to God at the beginning of the path, 3) those who experience attraction to God as they proceed along the path, and 4) those who easily traverse the stages along the path but do not experience attraction to God.[54] The beloveds of God (*mahbuban*) have an attraction to God at the beginning of the path, while the other three kinds of wayfaring are for lovers (*muhibban*) of God, whose wayfaring involves the well-known traversing of the ten stations in a careful and diligent way.[55] In the wayfaring of God's beloveds, they realize the essence (*khulasa*) of the ten stations without a great deal of effort. They adhere to

53. There are aspects of this discussion which bring to mind the kinds of issues raised by the ascension of Muhammad Ghawth Gwaliori, particularly whether he ascended spiritually or whether he ascended bodily. See Scott Kugle, *Sufis & Saints' Bodies: Mysticism, Corporeality, & Sacred Power in Islam* (Chapel Hill, NC: University of North Carolina Press, 2007). See the discussion of lesser intimacy in letter 1.260 in this book.

54. These numbers are not in the original text.

55. The ten stations are (in order): repentance, trusting in God, poverty, patience, gratitude, fear, hope, love, inner knowledge, and satisfaction.

[the principle] of the unity of being from their understanding the essential interpenetrating and interconnectedness [of being], which is connected to the attraction associated with beginners and intermediates. Pure wayfaring and the attraction of realized wayfarers (*muntahiyan*) have no connection with [experience informed by] these types of knowledge. This has been explained already.

Realized wayfarers' certitude of truth (*haqq-i yaqin*) also has no relationship with [experience informed by] knowledge associated with experiencing the unity of being. Whenever those in the station of unity of being explain the certitude of truth, that certitude of truth pertains to [the level of awareness of] those ecstatically attracted to God who are either beginners or intermediates [not the certitude of truth of realized wayfarers].[56]

Inner Meaning 3

Some shaykhs have said that when the seeker's efforts have resulted in ecstasy in God, the attraction itself will be his or her guide. And that is that. They mean that there is no need for the mediation of another guide, that is, attraction is sufficient. If they mean an attraction associated with wayfaring in God, then, yes, it is enough [if they want to realize the goal]. But the word "guide" (used above as attraction is the guide) does not make any sense here because after wayfaring in God, there is no "where" to go, and [therefore] no need for a guide. In a similar way, [it makes no sense here to] discuss an attraction that is at the beginning of the path as the outward meaning [of attraction] implies [because this attraction feels good but does not help one along the path]. So they must mean the attraction of intermediate-level wayfarers. It is not certain that this kind of attraction is enough [to arrive at the goal] because most intermediate-level wayfarers, at the time of realizing this attraction, start ascending and think that their type of attraction is the attraction of realized seekers. If their type of attraction were sufficient, then they would not leave the path while wayfaring. Indeed! Because the attraction associated with beloveds is at the beginning of the path, when it is sufficient, it has the potential [to take them to the goal]. Beloveds merely pull the ring of divine favor and do not leave the middle of the path. This sufficiency [that is, not needing a guide], with respect to all types of attraction experienced at the beginning of the path, is forbidden [that is, it is only for attraction of beloveds]. An attraction that pulls one to the goal is

56. *Haqq al-yaqin* is also discussed in letter 1.290 in this book. Shaykh Ma'sum Naqshbandi has explained certain truth (*haqq al-yaqin*) as experiencing truth by being that truth (knowledge-by-identity); *'ayn al-yaqin* is the actual experience of something (knowledge-by-acquaintance); perceiving something from afar and *'ilm al-yaqin* is merely hearing about something from reliable transmitted knowledge (knowledge-about).

sufficient. If an ecstatic does not start wayfaring, then he is worthless and not a beloved of God.

EPILOGUE

Some shaykhs have said that the disclosure of the Essence is without feeling and perceptual awareness. God sanctify their innermost beings. Others, [according to] their own condition, have said that when the disclosure of the Essence occurs, there is no awareness or sensation of anything for a while—as if one were dead. [A third group] insist that no one [even] discuss [the subject] of the disclosure of the Essence. The reality is such that the disclosure of the Essence is veiled by one of the names. This remaining veil is a result of the traces stemming from the existential vestiges of the person experiencing the disclosure. Any lack of sensation or awareness [one experiences] is from the lingering existence of the individual. If one experiences a total annihilation and then is honored [with the experience of] abiding in God then one always is consciously aware of that disclosure of God.

One who puts his hand in the fire is burned
How can one made of fire be burned?

The first one touches the fire, certainly gets burned, and is annihilated. The other is the essence of fire. How can that one get burned? We assert that the disclosure that is veiled is not a disclosure of the Essence but is a disclosure of the attributes. The disclosure of the Essence is especially associated with Muhammad. God bless him and give him peace. It is a disclosure without veils. The sign of veils is the lack of perceptual awareness (*bi-shu'uri*), a result of being far away [from God]. The proof of no veiling is being aware with an aware presence (*shu'uri*). Someone [experiencing] this disclosure is firmly rooted and independent.[57] Like this, he can report what he has said above. May he be forgiven.

Moses fainted after experiencing one ray of the divine attributes.[58]
But you [Muhammad] see the entity of the Essence and smile.

The beloveds [of God] have a continuous experience of this very disclosure of the Essence with no veils. Lovers [only] have an intermittent [experience]. [The beloveds' experience is continuous] because the beloveds' bodies have become imbued with their spirits (lit. taken on the color). That affinity between body and spirit has deeply penetrated [their being], while for lovers it is still in the beginning stages of the process. The Prophetic hadith relates, "The time I spend with God."[59] The meaning of "time" here is

57. The implication is that this notable is Ahmad Sirhindi.

58. This refers to Qur'an 7.143 where Moses faints.

59. See letter 1.260 in this book where Sirhindi writes: "As you may have heard, 'Ritual prayer is the heavenly ascension of the believer.' and 'God's servant

not this intermittent [experience of] disclosure but a continuous disclosure. This is because this disclosure occurs in the reality of Muhammad, who is the king of the beloveds. God bless him and give him peace. Continuous disclosure of God is one [aspect] particular to him, and happens rarely. This phenomenon is not hidden from experienced wayfarers.

Inner Knowledge 1

Shaykhs are divided into two groups over the explanation of the hadith, "The time I spend with God has no place for any special angel, or dispatched prophet." There are those who think that "time" (mentioned in the preceding paragraph) is continuous. The other group say that time has an unusual quality to it. The truth is that along with the existence of the continuity of time, there is also a wondrous experience of time (*waqt-i nadir*). This is just like what has been indicated in the previous section. According to this poor one (Ahmad Sirhindi), that precious time is experienced while engaging in ritual prayer. Perhaps Muhammad has alluded to this in the hadith, "There is no joy like ritual prayer." (*qurratul'ayn fi'l-salawat*).[60] God bless him and give him peace. He also said, "The subservient one (*'abd*) is closest to his Lord in ritual prayer."[61] God, blessed and almighty, [also said], "and prostrate and get close [to God]." [Q. 96:19]

Each time that one gets closer to God the potential for anything else other than God decreases [even] more, as some shaykhs have said on the basis of their own experience. God sanctify their innermost beings. They have also reported the continuity of the experience saying, "My state in ritual prayer is like my state before praying." This contradicts other hadiths and the Qur'anic passage [mentioned in the previous paragraph]. Know that continuity of time has been verified. In spite of continuity, one can either experience an unusual state or not. One group, not having the experience of this wondrous time, denies it. Another group is favored by having the station [of experiencing this unusual time] and they acknowledge it. The truth is that those few who [have ever] reached a deep tranquility in ritual prayer, by means of Muhammad and the favor of closeness [with God], have been given a portion of that abundance. May God, by means of Muhammad, provide a share of that station [of tranquility and closeness] from God's perfect

---

is closest to his Lord when in ritual prayer.' The Prophet had a special time during prayer as explained by [the expression] 'The time I spend with God.' This happened once to this poor one (Ahmad Sirhindi) in prayer."

60. A hadith found in al-Nisa'i's *Sunan al-Nasa'i, Isharat al-nisa'*, 1 (7:61-62); Ahmad b. Hanbal, *al-Musnad*, 3:128, 199, 285; al-Hakim, *al-Mustadrak*, 2:160 [MR], and mentioned three times in *Collected Letters*.

61. A hadith found in Muslim, *Salat* 42 (#482); Abu Da'ud, #875; al-Tirmidhi, #3579; al-Nasa'i, 2:226 [MR], and mentioned five times in *Collected Letters*.

generosity. God bless him and his family and give them peace.

Inner Knowledge 2

Those who have fully realized the attributes of God are similar to ecstatics (sing. *majdhub*) in terms of transmitted and experiential knowledge (*'ulum wa-ma'arif*), and in terms of contemplative witnessing. This is because these two [types of sufis] are masters of the heart (*arbab-i qulub*).[62] But there are differences [between these two groups]. Those who have realized the attributes of God are intermediates on the path (not beginners), having ascended higher, [and therefore] are aware of the particularities/details while the ecstatics are not. Nor have ecstatics begun to ascend. Love (*mahabbat*) of the origin (*asl*) connects them [with God] even though it (love) is a veil. How strange. According to [the hadith], "The lover is with the beloved,"[63] ecstatics are considered to be intimate with the origin. Then [it follows that] in their love ecstatics are associated with the Muhammadans (those who have fully realized the attributes of God). Although [ecstatics'] love of the Essence (*hubb-i dhati*) involves many veils [separating it from God], it is attested and well established by them.

Inner Knowledge 3

Some members of this group have considered axial leaders (sing. *qutb*) to be those who have experiences of the disclosures of the attributes (sing. *tajalli-yi sifati*), while the unique ones (*afrad*) are [supposed to be] those who have had disclosures of the Essence. This talk falls into the scope of this discussion given that the axial leader is of a Muhammadan disposition and that Muhammadans experience disclosures of the Essence. Look! There are still distinctions. The closeness to God of the unique ones is not the closeness of the axial leaders. Both are associated with the disclosure of the Essence [but they do not share equally in that disclosure]. When I say the axial leader, it means the axial leader of the substitutes (*qutb-i abdal*),[64] who is under the authority of (lit. under the foot of) Raphael (*Israfil*) not that of Muhammad.[65]

---

62. This means that the phenomena manifesting through these two "types" manifest through the heart.

63. A hadith found in both Bukhari's and Muslim's *Sahih*, and mentioned twenty times in *Collected Letters*, and quoted more than any other hadith. See the footnote at the beginning of Letter 2.67.

64. The hierarchy of spiritual authority is discussed in the introduction to this letter.

65. Israfil is the archangel who will blow the trumpet on the Day of Judgment. It is said that he was a companion of the Prophet for three years as he initiated Muhammad into the work of a prophet. See Wensinck, A.J. "Isrāfīl." *Encyclopaedia of*

Inner Knowledge 4

"God created Adam in God's image."[66] God almighty is formless and ineffable. Adam's spirit (*ruh*), the essence of Adam, was created in the image of this formlessness (*bi-chuni*) and ineffability (*bi-chigunah*). Likewise, [just as] the Real (*haqq*) is beyond physical location, so is the spirit. The connection of the spirit with the physical body is like God's connection to the physical world, which means God [and the spirit] are neither in the material world, nor outside of it, nor contiguous to it, nor separate from it.

[Other than] self-abiding existence (*qayyumiyat*) there is no other way to conceive of the relationship [either of them have to the material world or the physical body respectively]. The spirit underlies the existence of each atom of the body like God almighty's organizing principle supports the material world. God almighty undergirds the physical body by means of the spirit. The divine effulgence [from God] that manifests does so first through the spirit and it is by means of the spirit that divine effulgence gets conducted to the physical body. Because the spirit has been created in the form of incomparability and ineffability, it has the potential for real inimitable and ineffable being.

[There is a hadith], "The earth and heaven cannot contain Me but the heart of my faithful servant contains me."[67] This is because the earth and sky, in spite of their expanse, are in the space-time realm (lit. the circle of specific place or *da'ira-yi makani*). They are characterized by form (*chuni*) and the quality of having form (*chunagi*) and do not have the capability to exist beyond space-time (*la makani*), free of quantity and quality. [Anything] existing beyond the space-time realm has no capability to be in a [specific] place [just as] something without qualities cannot have any [specific] quality. It has been verified that the capability of the faithful servant's heart can only exist beyond space-time, free of quantity and quality. This is why the heart of a faithful servant is special because a less-than-perfect faithful heart has fallen from the peak of transcending space-time. Having entered the space-time realm by means of this descent and bondage, this heart has

Islam, Second Edition. Online version. Edited by: P. Bearman, Th. Bianquis, C.E. Bosworth, E. van Donzel and W.P. Heinrichs. (Leiden: Brill, 2009), 4:211. According to Sirhindi, the dominion (*walayat*) of Israfil is the same as that of Abraham. The origin of Abraham's entification is the first entification, which is the entification of being (*ta'ayyun-i wujudi*). The center of this entification is the origin of Muhammad's entification. See *Collected Letters,* 3.114.101.

66. A hadith found in both Bukhari's and Muslim's *Sahih* and mentioned eight times in *Collected Letters*. See the footnote in Part 1 of this letter.

67. A hadith found in Ahmad b. Hanbal, *al-Zuhd*, #384; al-Suyuti, *al-Durar al-muntathira*, #362; Ibn Rajab, *Jami' al-'ulum*, 3:67, 164 [MR], and mentioned six times in *Collected Letters*.

taken on quantity and quality and the limitations thereof. When quality is created, that capability [of going beyond space-time] is lost. "They are like cattle—no they are even more astray." [Q. 7:179] Each of the shaykhs who has reported an expansion of his heart has meant [an experience] of the heart beyond space-time. No matter how expansive a place is, it is still narrow [compared to something beyond space-time]. God's Throne, in spite of its greatness and expanse, is still a [specific] place. Comparing it to [something] beyond space-time [such as] the spirit is like [declaring something on] the authority of idle opinion, or even less.[68]

I declare the heart as the place of disclosure of eternal lights, already abiding with the Eternal. If one were to put God's Throne and what is in it [into the heart], [God's Throne] would become effaced and it would be like nothing with no remaining trace [compared to the vastness of the heart]. It is like what Junayd (lit. the Master of the Assembly, *Sayyid al-ta'ifa*) said about this station, "When God speaks through a person who is united with the Eternal, nothing remains of him." This is [like] a single piece of clothing specially sewn length-wise along the spirit. Angels do not have this special distinction [of transcending space-time] either [since], being in the realm of space-time, they are characterized by quality. Undoubtedly human beings are the deputies (sing. *khalifa*) of the most Compassionate. Exalt God's dominion. Yes! The form of a thing is what follows that thing unless the form of that thing is uncreated. [In that case], it is not possible [for anything] to follow that thing. As long as following is not appropriate, following cannot support the trust of its own origin (*imanat-i asl-i khud*). Only the King's camel can carry the King's gifts. God said, "We offered the trust to the heavens, earth, and mountains but they refused to carry it and feared it. Humans accepted it. They [ended up being] oppressive and ignorant."[69] [Q. 33:72]

People oppress themselves to the extent that no [beneficial] trace or wisdom remains in their being (*wujud*) or in the consequences of their reality. There is so much ignorance that the [resulting] lack of awareness (*idrak*) keeps them from achieving the goal. Their lack of knowledge is such that they do not know what is required. Awareness for them in this context is awareness of their inability, just as inner experiential knowledge (*ma'rifat*)

---

68. According to Sirhindi, the Throne is separate from the traces of the heavens and earth and one of the noblest "parts" of the macrocosm, acting as an interface between the world of creation and the world of command. See *Collected Letters,* 2.21.49-50, 1.44.95. The heart subtle center is the Throne of the human microcosm. See *Collected Letters,* 2.11.34. Note that Sirhind's response in Letter 1.220 to Bayazid's comment on the Throne and heart was in the context of Bayazid's intoxicated heart at the time of utterance.

69. The following paragraph is translated from the Arabic.

[in this context] is an acknowledgement of their ignorance. Most of those who have experiential knowledge of God (*ma'rifat billah*) say that the most knowledgeable among them have totally bewildering experiences.

Warning 1

When there is an expression involving interpretation (as Sirhindi has done with the aforementioned hadith of Adam) that elicits elegant thinking of God's affair, then this interpretation should be done in an exacting manner. The desired discourse must be in accordance with the learned scholars of the rightly guided community.

Inner knowledge 5

The world, whether microcosm or macrocosm, is a locus of manifestation (*mazhar*) of the names and attributes of God, a mirror of God's essential qualities and perfections. He was a hidden treasure and a secret that wanted to be revealed.[70] He was able to create the world from the [most] comprehensive to the [smallest] details so God could point to the origin (*asl*) itself and indicate reality itself.

The world is incomparable with and has no attribution to the Creator, other than the world being God's creation. The proof is God's hidden perfections. Beyond this there are [other] dominions in the realm of unity and entity-ness (*'ayniyat*), both in the encompassing nature and togetherness (*ma'iyat*) [experienced by those] in an overpowered and intoxicated state. Notables with upright states drink from the cup of sobriety. [Acquiring] these [religious] sciences, they are absolved and forgiven [if they happen to have an overpowering, ecstatic state]. Although some of them are on the [sufi] path,[71] they will finally complete [their studies of the religious sciences]. In the end, they will pass beyond [these religious sciences] and will show evidence of divine knowledge (*'ulum-i laduni*) in accordance with the sciences of the shariat.

I will explain using an example to substantiate this discussion. An experienced jurist who has perfections wants his hidden perfections and abilities to outwardly manifest [through] the production of words and articulation [of these words]. [In this manner], his perfections will become illuminated through the veil of those words and articulations, manifesting [his] abilities. In this form, the hidden meanings of these words and articulations will make sense. However, no one except that jurist has any connection to these words and articulations. He is their originator and creator and they point to

70. Cf. the hadith qudsi, "I was a hidden treasure and I wanted to be known, so I created the world."

71. The exact wording, *dar ithna'i rah*, could also mean "in the process of learning [these sciences]."

his hidden perfections. It does not make any sense to say that those words and articulations are the same as the jurist or [that they are] the same as their meanings.

In the same manner, to declare this situation to be [all] encompassing or having [utmost] togetherness [with God would be to declare something that] could not actually happen. By their discreetness the meanings are hidden. Indeed! This is because between the meanings, the one [interpreting] the meanings, and the words and articulations [themselves], there is an established relationship between the semantic meaning and the lexical meaning. Some impossible meanings occur in fantasy and imagination. In truth, that jurist and his hidden meanings are free from such extraneous attributions. These words and articulations exist in the objective world, unlike those imagined impossible meanings.

The world that consists of everything other than God exists objectively. It is the shadow reality (*al-wujud al-zilli*) and natural universe, not the world of imagination and fantasy. This [latter] way [of perceiving the world] is called the way of the Sophists (*madhhab-i sufista'i*), who construe the world as fantasy and imagination. They say that the proof of reality is in the world and that the world does not go beyond fantasy and imagination. Thus, reality exists but not the world because they assume that the world is other than reality.

Warning 2

The meaning of the world being both a locus of manifestation (*mazhariyat*) and a mirror of God's names and attributes [means] the forms of the names and attributes not their essences (*a'yan* as entities) because there is no mirror [large enough] for a name or its designation The same goes for attributes and their attributions that can not be limited by any locus of manifestation.

How can the essence (*ma'na*) fit into the narrowness of form?
What business does the King have in a beggar's hut?

Inner knowledge 6

The complete followers of the Prophet become completed by following Muhammad. Their good fortune stems from the disclosure of the Essence and is fundamentally special to Muhammad. The other prophets are associated with the disclosures of the attributes. The disclosure of the Essence is nobler than a disclosure of the attributes. But one must know that these other prophets achieve degrees of closeness to God in the disclosures of the attributes, which the complete followers of this community (that is, those following Muhammad) do not realize in spite of their natural way of realizing from the disclosure of the Essence. God bless and give peace to our prophet and them.

For example, one person moves toward the sun gradually ascending in love with the beauty of the sun. He arrives at the sun without even a thin veil between him and the sun. Another person, in spite of being in love with the essence of the sun in his ascent, does not go as far, and thus has a lesser rank [than the first person]. There is not even a thin veil between him and the sun. Undoubtedly the first person is nearer to the sun and more knowledgeable in perfections and subtleties than the second. So whoever is closer to God and whoever has more experiential knowledge of the divine is more favored. Therefore, there is no protégé of God (*wali*) of this community, the most favored community, [who can rank higher than any prophet] even though this community's prophet (Muhammad) is the most favored prophet with a rank higher than any other prophet. Nonetheless, a protégé of God receives some favor by following the Prophet, who is associated with the most favored station (that is, his direct connection to the disclosure of the Essence). Complete favor is [only] for the prophets. Friends of God are uninvited guests.

This is all I have to say. Praise God for this and for all God's blessings. God bless and give peace to the most favored of God's prophets and to all the prophets, messengers, protégés of God (*muqarribin*), the righteous, martyrs, and the pious ones.

Selected Bibliography

(alphabetical by *nisbat*)

Abu'l-Fadl 'Allami. *Mukatabat-i 'Allami Abu'l-Fadl.* 3 vols. Lucknow: Nawal Kishur, 1911.

———. *Akbar nama.* 3 vols. Translated by H. Beveridge. Delhi: Low Price Publications, 1993.

Ahmad, Imtiaz. "The Ashraf-Ajlaf Dichotomy in Muslim Social Structure in India." *Indian Economic & Social History Review* 3 (1966), 268-278.

Akhtar, Saleem. "Mawlana Muhammad Sadiq Kashmiri and Mawlana Hasan Kashmiri." *Journal of the Pakistan Historical Society* 25 (1977), 197-218.

Alam, Muzaffar. "*Shari'a* and Governance in the Indo-Islamic Context." In *Beyond Turk and Hindu: Rethinking Religious Identities in Islamicate South Asia.* Edited by David Gilmartin and Bruce B. Lawrence. Gainsville, FL: University Press of Florida, 2000, 216-245.

———. "The Mughals, the Sufi Shaikhs, and the Formation of the Akbari Dispensation." *Modern Asian Studies* 43/1 (2009), 135-174.

Algar, Hamid. "A Brief History of the Naqshbandi Order." In *Naqshbandis: cheminements et situation actuelle d'un ordre mystique musulman.* Edited by Marc Gaborieau, Alexandre Popovic, and Thierry Zarcone. Istanbul/Paris: Éditions Isis, 1990, 3-44.

———. "Political Aspects of Islamic History." In *Naqshbandis: cheminements et situation actuelle d'un ordre mystique musulman.* Edited by Marc Gaborieau, Alexandre Popovic, and Thierry Zarcone. Istanbul/Paris: Éditions Isis, 1990, 123-152.

———. "Reflections of Ibn 'Arabi in Early Naqshbandi Tradition." *Journal of the Muhyiddin ibn 'Arabi Society* 10 (1991), 45-66.

———. "Imâm-ı Rabbânî." *Islâm Ansiklopedisi.* 35 vols. Istanbul: Türkiye Diyanet Vakfı, 1988-, 22:194-99.

———. "The Centennial Renewer: Bediüzzaman Said Nursi and the Tradition of *Tajdid.*" *Journal of Islamic Studies* 12/3 (2001), 291-311.

Ali, M. Athar. *Mughal India: Studies in Polity, Ideas, Society, and Culture.* Delhi: Oxford University Press, 2006.

Alusi, Mahmud b. 'Abd Allah al-Husayni al-. *Ruh al-ma'ani.* 15 vols. Multan, Pakistan: Maktaba-yi Imdadiyya, n.d.

Amritsari, Muhammad Musa. "Sarguzasht-i Maktubat." In *Maktubat-i Imam-i Rabbani.* Lahore: Nur Company, 1964-1971, 4-12.

Ansari, Muhammad Abdul Haq. *Sufism and Shari'ah: A Study of Shaykh*

Ahmad Sirhindi's Effort to Reform Sufism. Leicester, UK: The Islamic Foundation, 1986.

Bada'uni, Abdulqadir. *Muntakhab al-tawarikh*, 3 vols. Translated by Wolseley Haig. Calcutta: Baptist Mission Press, 1925.

Balabanlilar, Lisa. "Lords of the Auspicious Conjunction: Turco-Mongol Imperial Identity on the Subcontinent." *Journal of World History* 18/1 (2007), 1-39.

Baqibillah. *Kulliyat-i Baqibillah: majmu'ah-i kalam wa-rasa'il wa-malfuzat wa-maktubat*. Edited by Abu'l-Hasan Zayd Faruqi and Burhan Ahmad Faruqi. Lahore: Din Muhammadi Press, ca. 1967.

Barani, Dia'uddin. *Tarikh-i Firoz Shahi*. Translated by H.M. Eliot. In *The History of India*. Vol. 14, 2nd Edition. Calcutta: Susil Gupta Ltd., 1953.

Buehler, Arthur F. *Sufi Heirs of the Prophet: The Indian Naqshbandiyya and the Rise of the Mediating Shaykh*. Columbia, SC: University of South Carolina Press, 1998.

———. *Fiharis-i tahlili-yi hashtgana-yi maktubat-i Ahmad Sirhindi*. Lahore: Iqbal Academy, 2000.

———. "Ahmad Sirhindi's Indian Mujaddidi Sufism." *Journal of the History of Sufism* 4 (2005), 209-228.

———. "Mawlana Khalid and Shah Ghulam 'Ali." *The Journal of the History of Sufism* 5 (2007), 199-213.

———. "Tales of Renewal: Establishing Ahmad Sirhindi as the Reformer of the Second Millennium." In *Tales of God's Friends: Islamic Hagiography in Translation*. Edited by Jack Renard. Berkeley: University of California Press, 2009, 234-248.

Bukhari, Khurshid Husayn. *Kamal: Sawanih Hadrat Shah Kamal Qadiri Kayt'hli*. Lahore: Al-i Bashir Printers, 1976.

Ceric, Mustafa. *Roots of Synthetic Theology in Islam: A Study of the Theology of Abu Mansur al-Maturidi*. Kuala Lumpur: International Institute of Islamic Thought and Civilization, 1995.

Chittick, William C. "The Five Divine Presences: From al-Qunawi to al-Qaysari." *Muslim World* 72/2 (April 1982), 107-128.

———. *The Sufi path of love: the spiritual teachings of Rumi*. Albany: State University of New York Press, 1983.

———. *Sufi Path of Knowledge*. Albany: State University of New York Press, 1989.

———. "Notes on Ibn al-'Arabi's Influence in the Subcontinent." *The Muslim World* 82/3-4 (1992), 218-241.

———. "Spectrums of Islamic Thought: Sa'id al-Din Farghani on the Implications of Oneness and Manyness." In *The Legacy of Mediaeval Persian Sufism*. Edited by Leonard Lewisohn. New York: Khaniqahi Nimatullahi Publications, 1992, 203-317.

———. "Rumi and *wahdat al-wujud.*" In *Poetry and Mysticism in Islam: The Heritage of Rumi.* Edited by Amin Banani, Richard Hovannisian, and Georges Sabagh. New York: Cambridge University Press, 1994, 70-111.

———. *The Self-disclosure of God: Principles of Ibn al-'Arabi's Cosmology.* Albany: State University of New York Press, 1997.

Chodkiewicz, Michel. *Seal of the Saints: Prophethood and Sainthood in the Doctrine of Ibn 'Arabi.* London: Islamic Texts Society, 1993.

Corbin, Henry. *The Man of Light in Iranian Sufism.* Translated by Nancy Pearson. Boston: Shambhala, 1978.

Culianu, Ioan. "Gnosticism from the Middle Ages to the Present." In Mircea Eliade, ed. *The Encyclopedia of Religion.* 15 vols. New York: MacMillan, 1987, 5:574-578.

———. *Tree of Gnosis*. New York: Harper Collins, 1992.

Dale, Stephen F., and Alam Payind. "The Ahrari Waqf in Kabul in the Year 1546 and the Mughal Naqshbandiyyah." *Journal of the American Oriental Society* 119/2 (April-June 1999), 218-233.

Damrel, David. "The 'Naqshbandî Reaction' Reconsidered." In *Beyond Turk and Hindu: Rethinking Religious Identities in Islamicate South Asia.* Edited by David Gilmartin and Bruce B. Lawrence. Gainsville, FL: University Press of Florida, 2000, 176-198.

Dhawqi, Muhammad. *Sirr-i dilbaran.* Karachi: Mashhur Offset Press, 1985.

Digby, Simon. "Abd al-Quddus Gangohi (1456-1537 A.D.): The Personality and Attitudes of a Medieval Indian Sufi." In *Medieval India*, New York: Asia Publishing House, 1975, 1-65.

Dihlawi, 'Abdulhaqq Muhaddith. *Kitab al-makatib wa-rasa'il ila arbab al-kamal wa'l-fada'il.* Delhi: Matba'-i Mujtaba'i, 1867.

Dihlawi, Ghulam 'Ali. *Malfuzat-i sharifa.* Edited by Ghulam Muhyiddin Qusuri. Translated into Urdu by Iqbal Ahmad Faruqi. Lahore: Maktaba-yi Nabawiyya, 1978.

———. *Maqamat-i mahzari.* Translated into Urdu by Iqbal Mujaddidi. Lahore: Zarin Art Press, 1983.

———. *Sharh-i durr al-ma'arif: minhaj al-raghibayn ila makubat imam al-muttaqin Imam-i Rabbani Mujaddid-i Alf-i Thani.* Edited by Ayyub Ganji. Sanandaj, Iran: Intisharat-i Kurdistan, 1997.

Donkin, William. *The Wayfarers: An account of the work of Meher Baba with the God-intoxicated.* Ahmednagar, India: Adi K. Irani, 1948.

Eaton, Richard M. *Essays on Islam and Indian History*. Delhi: Oxford University Press, 2000.

Ernst, Carl W. *Words of Ecstasy*. Albany: State University of New York Press, 1985.

———. "The Man Without Attributes: Ibn 'Arabi's Interpretation of Abu Yazid al-Bistami." *Journal of the Muhyiddin Ibn 'Arabi Society* 13 (1993), 14-15.

———. "Lives of Sufi Saints." In *Religions of India in Practice.* Edited by Donald S. Lopez. Princeton: Princeton University Press, 1995, 495-512.

———, and Bruce B. Lawrence. *Sufi Martyrs of Love*. New York: Palgrave Macmillan, 2002.

Faruqui, Munis D. "The Forgotten Prince: Mirza Hakim and the Formation of the Mughal Empire in India." *Journal of the Economic and Social History of the Orient* 48/4 (2005), 487-523.

Foltz, Richard C. "The Central Asian Naqshbandi Connections of the Mughal Emperors." *Journal of Islamic Studies* 7/2 (1996), 229-239.

———. *Mughal India and Central Asia*. Karachi: Oxford University Press, 1998.

Friedmann, Yohanan. *Shaykh Ahmad Sirhindi: An Outline of His Thoughts and a Study of His Image in the Eyes of Posterity*. Montreal, London: McGill-Queen's University Press, 1971.

———. *Prophecy Continuous: Aspects of Ahmadi Religious Thought and its Medieval Background.* Berkeley: University of California Press, 1989.

Gaborieau, Marc, Alexandre Popovic, and Thierry Zarcone, eds. *Naqshbandis: cheminements et situation actuelle d'un ordre mystique musulman.* Istanbul/Paris: Éditions Isis, 1990.

Gangohi, 'Abdulquddus. *Lata'if-i quddusi*. Edited by Ruknuddin. Delhi: Matba'-i Mujtaba'i, 1894.

Ghulam Mustafa Khan. *Baqiyat-i baqi*. N.p., 1989.

Giordani, Demetrio. "Le "mabda' o ma' ad" [sic] un cahier de notes de Shaykh Ahmad Sirhindi, soufi indien du XVIIe siècle." Ph.D dissertation. Paris: École des Hautes Études en Sciences Sociales (EHESS), 1999.

Haar, J.G.J ter. "The collected letters of Shaykh Ahmad Sirhindi." *Manuscripts of the Middle East* 3 (1988), 41-43.

———. *Follower and Heir of the Prophet: Shaykh Ahmad Sirhindi (1564-1624) as Mystic*. Leiden: Van Het Oosters Instituut, 1992.

Habib, Irfan M. "The Political Role of Shaykh Ahmad Sirhindi and Shah Waliullah." In *Essays in Indian Art, Religion, and Society*. Edited by Krishna Mohan Shrimali. New Delhi: Munshiram Manoharlal, 1987, 219-235.

Harawi, Husayn 'Ali. *Sharh-i Ghazalha-yi Hafiz*. 4 vols. Tehran: Nashr-i Naw, 1991.

Hasani, Abdulhayy b. Fakruddin. *Nuzhat al-khawatir*. 8 vols. Hyderabad,

Deccan: Da'irat al-Ma'arif al-'Uthmania, 1976.
Hori, Victor Sōgen. *Zen Sand: The Book of Capping Phrases for Kōan Practice*. Honolulu: University of Hawaii Press, 2003.
Hughes, Aaron W. *The Texture of the Divine: Imagination in Medieval Islamic and Jewish Thought*. Bloomington, IN: Indiana University Press, 2003.
Husain, Afzal. *The Nobility under Akbar and Jahangir: A Study of Family Groups*. Delhi: Manohar, 1999.
Hutaki, Nasrullah. *Sharh-i Maktubat-i qudsi ayat*. Peshawar: Taj Mahal Company, ca. 1976.
Ibn al-'Arabi, Muhyiddin. *Futuhat al-Makkiyya*. 4 vols. Cairo: Bulaq, 1911.
Ilahabadi, Muhibbullah. *Manazir akhass al-khawass*. Edited by Muhammad Tahir Ali. Santiniketan: Vishva Bharati Research Publications, 1993.
Islam, Riazul. *Sufism in South Asia: Impact on Fourteenth Century Muslim Society*. Karachi: Oxford University Press, 2002.
Izutsu, Toshihiko. *Creation and the Timeless Order of Things: Essays in Islamic Mystical Philosophy*. Ashland, OR: White Cloud Press, 1994.
Jahangir. *Memoirs of Jahangir* (*Tuzuk-i Jahangiri*). 2 vols. Translated by Alexander Rogers. Edited by Henry Beveridge. Delhi: Munshiram Manoharlal, 1968.
Jami, 'Abdurrahman. *Nafahat al-uns min hadarat al-quds*. Edited by Mahmud 'Abidi. Tehran: Intisharat-i Ittila'at, 1992.
Kaka'i, Qasim. *Wahdat al-wujud bi-riwayat-i Ibn 'Arabi wa-Meister Eckhart*. Tehran: Intisharat-i Hurmus, 2007.
Kashani, 'Abdurrazzaq. *Lata'if al-i'lam fi isharat ahl al-ilham*. Edited by Sa'id 'Abdulfattah. Cairo: National Library Press, 1996.
Kashmiri Hamadani, Muhammad Sadiq. *Kalimat-i sadiqin*. Edited by Muhammad Saleem Akhtar. Lahore: al-Quraysh Publishers, 1988.
Kishmi, Muhammad Hashim. *Zubdat al-maqamat*. Translated into Urdu by Ghulam Mustafa Khan. Sialkot, Pakistan: Maktaba-yi Nu'maniya, 1987.
———. *Nasamat al-quds*. Translated into Urdu by Mahbub Hasan Wasiti. Sialkot: Maktaba-yi Nu'maniya, 1990.
———. *Zubdat al-maqamat*. Istanbul: Işık Kitabevi, 1997.
Kugle, Scott. *Rebel between Spirit and Law: Ahmad Zarruq, Sainthood, and Authority in Islam*. Bloomington, IN: Indiana University Press, 1996.
———. "Abd al-Haqq Dihlawi, an Accidental Revivalist: Knowledge and Power in the Passage from Delhi to Makka." *Journal of Islamic Studies* 19/2 (2008), 196-246.
Landolt, Hermann. "Simnani on Wahdat al-Wujud." In *Collected Papers on*

Islamic Philosophy and Mysticism. Edited by M. Mohaghegh and H. Landolt. Tehran: Institute of Islamic Studies, 1971, 93-111.

———. "Der Briefwechsel zwischen Kashani und Simnani über *Wahdat al-Wujud*." *Der Islam* 50 (1973), 29-81.

———. "Le 'Double Èchelle' d'Ibn 'Arabi chez Simnani." In *Le Voyage Initiatique en Terre d'Islam: Ascensions cèleste et itineraries spirituals*. Edited by Mohammad Ali Amir-Moezzi. Louvain-Paris: Peeters, 1996, 251-264.

Lawrence, Bruce. *Nizam ad-din Awliya: Morals for the Heart*. Mahwah, NY: Paulist Press, 1992.

———. "Problems of Translating Sufi Texts from Indo-Persian to American English." In *Sufism: Evolution and Practice.* Edited by Mohamed Taher. Delhi: Anmol Publications, 1997, 206-229.

Livne-Kafri, Ofer. "Early Muslim Ascetics and the World of Christian Monasticism." *Jerusalem Studies in Arabic and Islam* 20 (1996), 105-129.

Mandawi Ghawthi, Muhammad. *Adhkar-i abrar: Urdu tarjama-yi gulzar al-abrar.* Translated into Urdu by Fadl Ahmad Jewari. Lahore: Islamic Book Foundation, 1975.

Manzalawi al-Qazani, Muhammad Murad al-. *Maktubat: al-durar al-maknunat al-nafisa*. 2 vols. Istanbul: Maktabat al-Mahmudiyya, n.d.

Massignon, Louis. *Essay on the Origins of the Technical Language of Islamic Mysticism*. Translated by Benjamin Clark. Notre Dame, IN: University of Notre Dame Press, 1997.

Muhammad Ikram. "Hadrat-i Mujaddid-i Alf-i Thani Shaykh Ahmad Sirhindi quddus sirrahu." In *Hadrat-i Mujaddid-i Alf-i Thani.* Edited by Muhammad Ikram Chaghatai. Lahore: Sang-e Meel Publications, 2009, 226-303.

Muhammad Mas'ud Ahmad, ed. *Jahan-i Imam-i Rabbani*: *Mujaddid-i Alf-i Thani Shaykh Ahmad Sirhindi*. 11 vols. Karachi: Imam Rabbani Foundation, 2005-2007.

Muhammad Ma'sum. *Maktubat-Ma'sumiyya*. 3 vols. Edited by Ghulam Mustafa Khan. Karachi: Walend Military Press, n.d.

Muhammad Zafaruddin Fadl Bihar. *Chud'dwin sadi ke mujaddid*. Lahore: Maktaba-yi Ridwiyya, n.d.

Mujaddidi, Muhammad Hasan. *Insab al-anjab*. In *Nur al-Islam* 33/1 (Jan./ Feb. 1988), 127-241.

Mujaddidi, Muhammad Iqbal. "Hadarat Mujaddid-i Alf-i Thani ke dafa' men lik'hi jani wali kitaben." *Nur al-Islam* 33/1 (Jan./Feb. 1988), 45-72.

Mujaddidi, Muhammad Sa'id Ahmad. *al-Bayyinat: sharh-i Maktubat*. Lahore: Tanzim al-Islam Publications, 2002.

Munzawi, Ahmad. *Fihrist-i mushtarak-i nuska-ha-yi khatti-yi farsi-yi Pakistan*. 12 Vols. Islamabad: Markaz-i tahqiqat-i Iran wa-Pakistan, 1984.

Nasr, Hossein. "The Quranic Commentaries of Mulla Sadra." In *Consciousness and Reality: Studies in Memory of Toshihiko Izutsu*. Edited by Jalal al-Din Ashtiyani, Hideichi Matsubara, Takashi Iwami, and Akiro Matsumoto. Leiden: Brill, 2000, 45-58.

Ni'mat Allah. *The Tarikh-i Khan-i Jahani of Khwajah Ni'mat Allah*. Edited by S. M. Imam al-Din. Dacca: Asiatic Society of Pakistan, 1960.

Nizami, Khaliq Ahmad. *State and Culture in Medieval India*. Delhi: Adam Publishers & Distributors, 1985.

———. *Akbar and Religion*. Delhi: Jayyed Press, 1989.

Pagani, Samuela. *Il Rinnovamento Mistico Dell'Islam: Un commento di 'Abd al-Ghani al-Nabulusi a Ahmad Sirhindi*. Naples: Universita Degli studi di Napoli "l'Orientali," 2003.

———. "Renewal before Reformism: 'Abd al-Ghani al-Nabulusi's Readings of Ahmad Sirhindi's Ideas on *Tajdid*." *Journal of the History of Sufism* 5 (2007), 291-317.

Qushayri, Abu'l-Qasim al-. *al-Risala al-Qushayriyya*. Tehran: Intisharat-i Bidar, 1998.

Rampuri, Ghiyath al-Din Muhammad. *Ghiyath al-lughat*. Edited by Siraj al-Din 'Ali Khan Arzu. Kanpur: Nawal Kishur, 1878.

Razi, Najmuddin. *The Path of God's bondsmen from origin to return*. Translated by Hamid Algar. Delmar, NY: Caravan Books, 1982.

Rumi, Jalaluddin Balkhi. *Mathnawi-yi ma'nawi*. 4 vols. Edited by Reynold Nicholson and Nasrullah Purjawadi. Tehran: Mu'assasa-yi Intisharat-i Amir Kabir, 1985.

Sabir, Iqbal. "Khwaja Mohammad Hashim Kishmi: A Famous Seventeenth Century Naqshbandi Sufi." In *Sufis, Sultans and Feudal Orders: Professor Nurul Hasan Commemoration Volume*. Edited by Mansura Haidar. New Delhi: Manohar, 2004, 63-70.

Schimmel, Annemarie. *Mystical Dimensions of Islam*. Chapel Hill, NC: University of North Carolina Press, 1975.

Shah Waliullah. *al-Tafimat al-ilahiyya*. 2 vols. Edited by Ghulam Mustafa al-Qasimi. Hyderabad, Sind: al-Matba' al-Haydari, 1967.

Shahjahanpuri, Muhammad 'Abdulhakim Khan Akhtar. *Tajalliyat-i Imam-i Rabbani*. Lahore: Maktaba-yi Nabawiyya, 1978.

Sharif, Ja'far. *Islam in India: The Customs of the Muslamans of India*. Translated by G. A. Herklots. Edited by William Crooke. Delhi: Oriental Books Reprint Corporation, 1972.

Shikarpuri, Faqirullah. *Qutb al-irshad*. Quetta: Maktaba-yi Islamiyya, 1978.

———. *Maktubat-i Faqirullah*. Edited by Mawlwi Karam Bakhsh. Lahore: Islamiyya Steam Press, n.d.

Simnani, 'Ala'uddawla. *Musannifat-i Farsi*. Edited by Najib Mayil Harawi. Tehran: Shirkat-i Intisharat-i 'Ilmi wa-Farhangi, 1991.

Simnani, Sayyid Ashraf Jahangir. *Lata'if-i ashrafi fi bayan-i tawaf-i sufi*. 2 vols. Karachi: Maktabat-i Simnani, 1999.

Sirhindi, 'Abdulahad Wadat. *Sabil al-rashad*. N.p., 1978.

Sirhindi, Ahmad. *Maktubat: al-durar al-maknunat al-nafisa*. 2 vols. Translated by Muhammad Murad al-Manzalawi al-Qazani. Istanbul: Maktabat al-Mahmudiyya, n.d.

———. *Mukashafat-i 'ayniyya*. Edited by and translated into Urdu by Ghulam Mustafa Khan. Karachi: Educational Press, 1965.

———. *Sharh-i ruba'iyat-i Khwaja Baqibillah*. Edited by Thana'l-haqq Siddiqi. Karachi: Educational Press, 1966.

———. *Maktubat-i Imam-i Rabbani*. 3 vols. Edited by Nur Ahmad. Karachi: Educational Press, 1972.

———. *Radd-i madhhab-i Shi'ia* (*Ta'id-i ahl-i sunnat*). Edited and translated into Urdu by Ghulam Mustafa Khan. Karachi: Anjuman Press, 1974.

———. *Risala-yi tahliliyya*. Edited and translated into Urdu by Rashid Ahmad. Karachi: Idarah-i Mujaddidiyya, 1983.

———. *Ithbat al-nubuwat*. Translated into Urdu by Ghulam Mustafa Khan. Karachi: Ahmad Brothers Printers, 1984.

———. *Mabda' wa-ma'ad*. Edited and translated into Urdu by Zawwar Husayn. Karachi: Ahmad Brothers Printers, 1984.

———. *Ma'arif-i ladunya*. Edited and translated into Urdu by Zawwar Husayn. Karachi: Idarah-i Mujaddidiyya, 1986.

———. *Maktubat-i Hadrat-i Mujaddid-i Alf-i Thani*, 4 vols. Translated by Zawwar Husayn. Karachi: Ahmad Brothers Printers, 1991.

———. *Mektubat-ı Rabbani*. 3 vols. Translated into Turkish by Talha Hakan Alp, Ömer Faruk Tokat, and Ahmet Hamdi Yıldırım. Istanbul: Semerkand Yayınları, 2004.

Sirhindi, Badruddin. *Hadarat al-quds*. Edited by Mahbub Ilahi. Lahore: Maqama-yi Awqaf, 1971.

Sirhindi, Muhammad Ihsan Mujaddidi. *Rawdat al-Qayyumiyya*. 4 vols. Translated by Iqbal Ahmad Faruqi. Lahore: Maktaba-yi Nubuwwiyyah, 1989.

Taftazani, Sa'duddin Mas'ud b. 'Umar al-. *Sharh al-'aqa'id al-Nasafi fi usul al-din wa-'ilm al-kalam*. Edited by Claude Salamé. Damascus: Manshurat Wazarat al-Thaqafa wa'l-Irshad al-Qummi, 1974.

Temir, Ahmet. "Doğumunun 130. ve Ölülümün 50. Yılı Dolayısıyla Kazanlı Tarihçi." *Türk Tarih Kurumu Belleten* 50/197 (1986), 495-505.

Tosun, Necdet. *Bahâeddîn Nakşbend: Hayatı, Görüşleri, Tarîkatı*. Istanbul: Insan Yayınları, 2002.

———. *Imâm-i Rabbânî Ahmed Sirhindî: Hayatı, Eserleri, Tasavvufî Görüsleri*. Istanbul: Insan Yayınları, 2005.

Wensinck, A.J. "Isrāfīl." *Encyclopaedia of Islam,* Second Edition. Online version. Edited by: P. Bearman, Th. Bianquis, C.E. Bosworth, E. van Donzel, and W.P. Heinrichs. Leiden: Brill, 2009.

Wilson, C. Roderick. "Seeing They See Not." In David E. Young and Jean-Guy Goulet, eds. *Being Changed: The Anthropology of Extraordinary Experience*. New York: Broadview Press, 1994.

Wink, André. *Akbar*. Oxford: Oneworld, 2009.

Index

C

D

E

N

O

P

Y

Page from the Nur Ahmad Persian lithographed edition
by master calligrapher Ghulam Muhammad Amritsari